SHIROICHI AMAUI &
KONEKONEKO PRESENTS

CHARACTER DESIGN
TAMAGONOKIMI

The HERO LIFE of a (Self-Proclaimed) "Mediocre" DEMON!

1

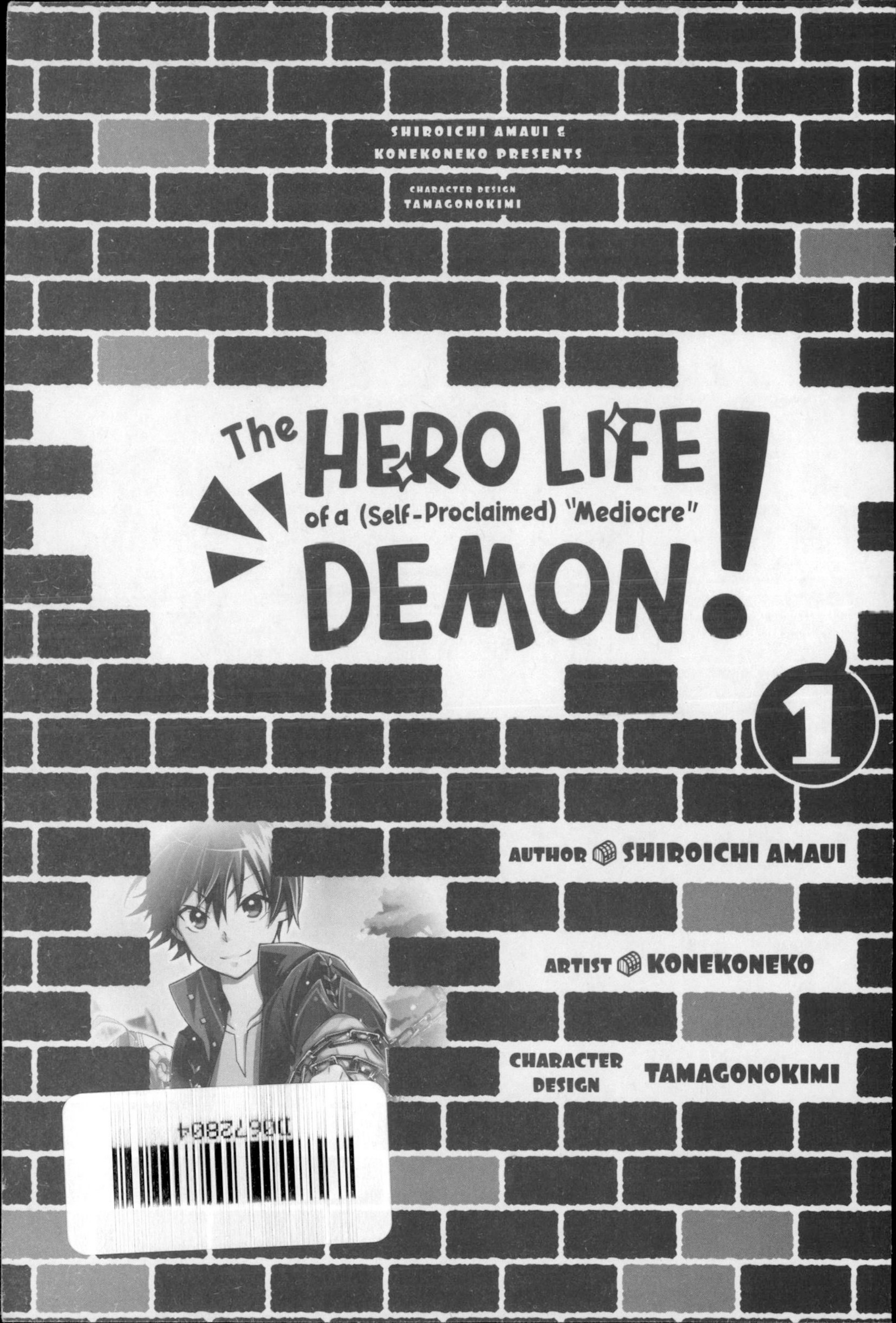

AUTHOR SHIROICHI AMAUI

ARTIST KONEKONEKO

CHARACTER DESIGN TAMAGONOKIMI

CONTENTS

THE HERO LIFE OF A (SELF-PROCLAIMED) "MEDIOCRE" DEMON!

The HERO LIFE of a (Self-Proclaimed) "Mediocre" DEMON!

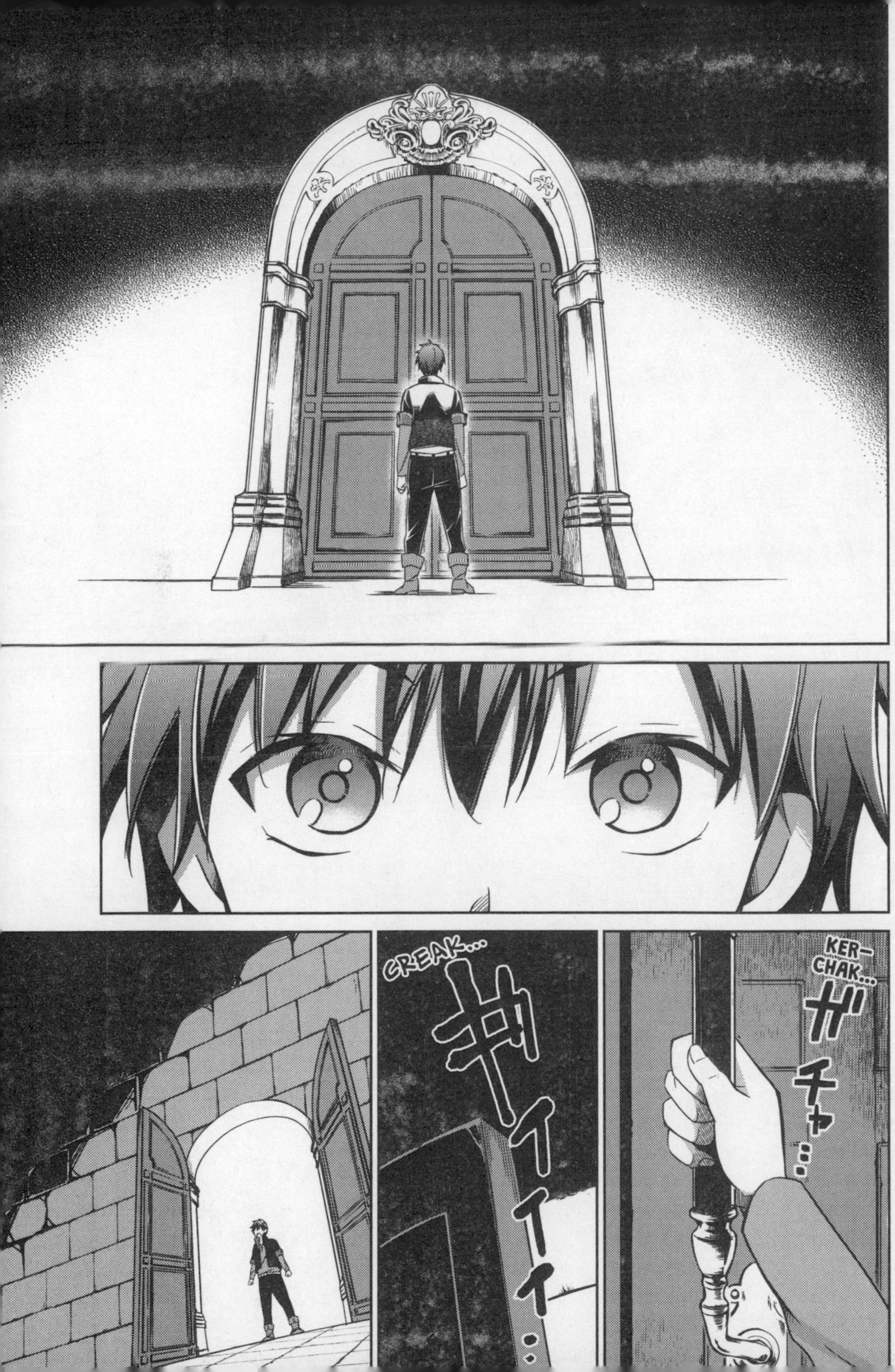
KER-CHAK...
ガチャ…
CREAK...
ギィィィ…

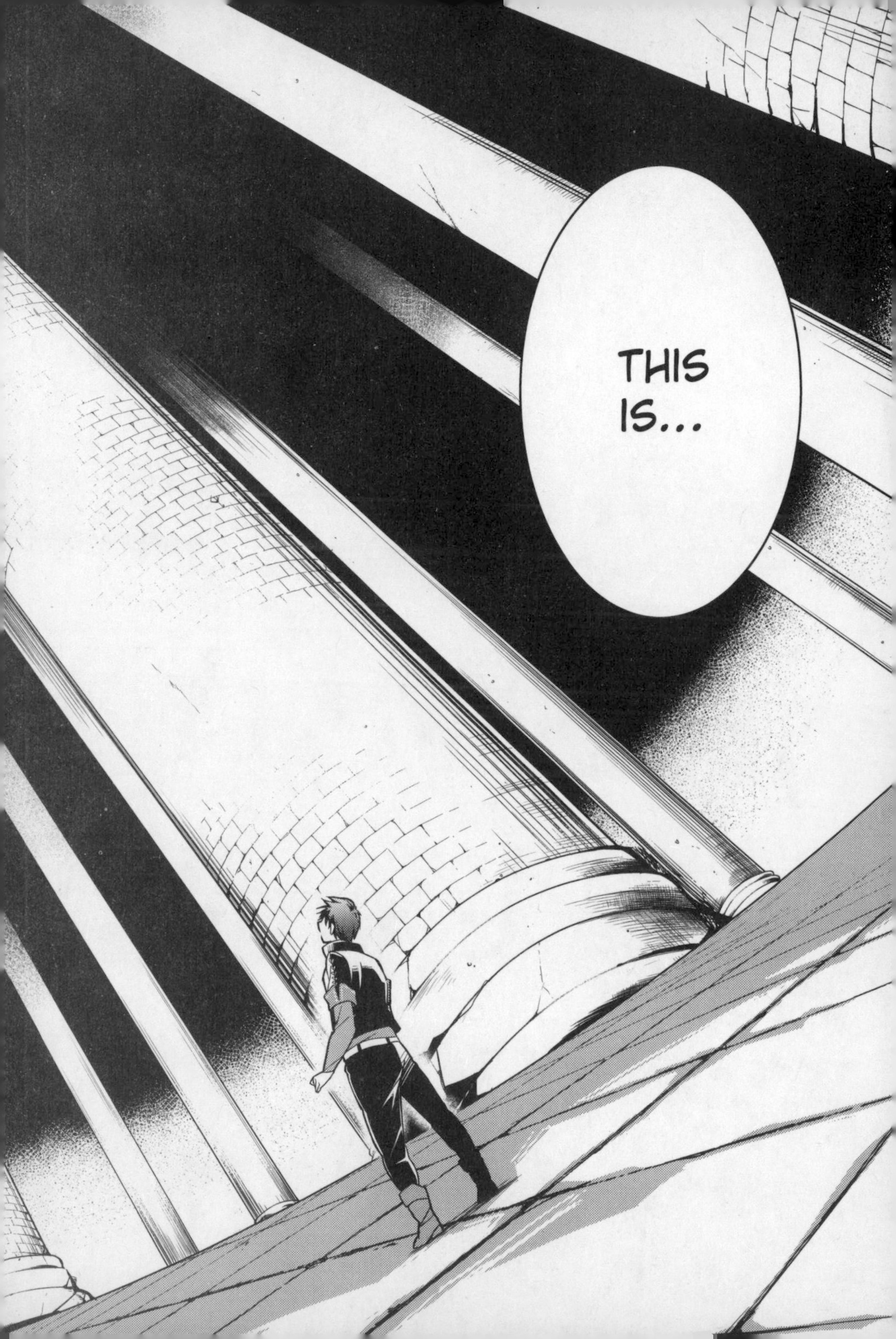
THIS IS...

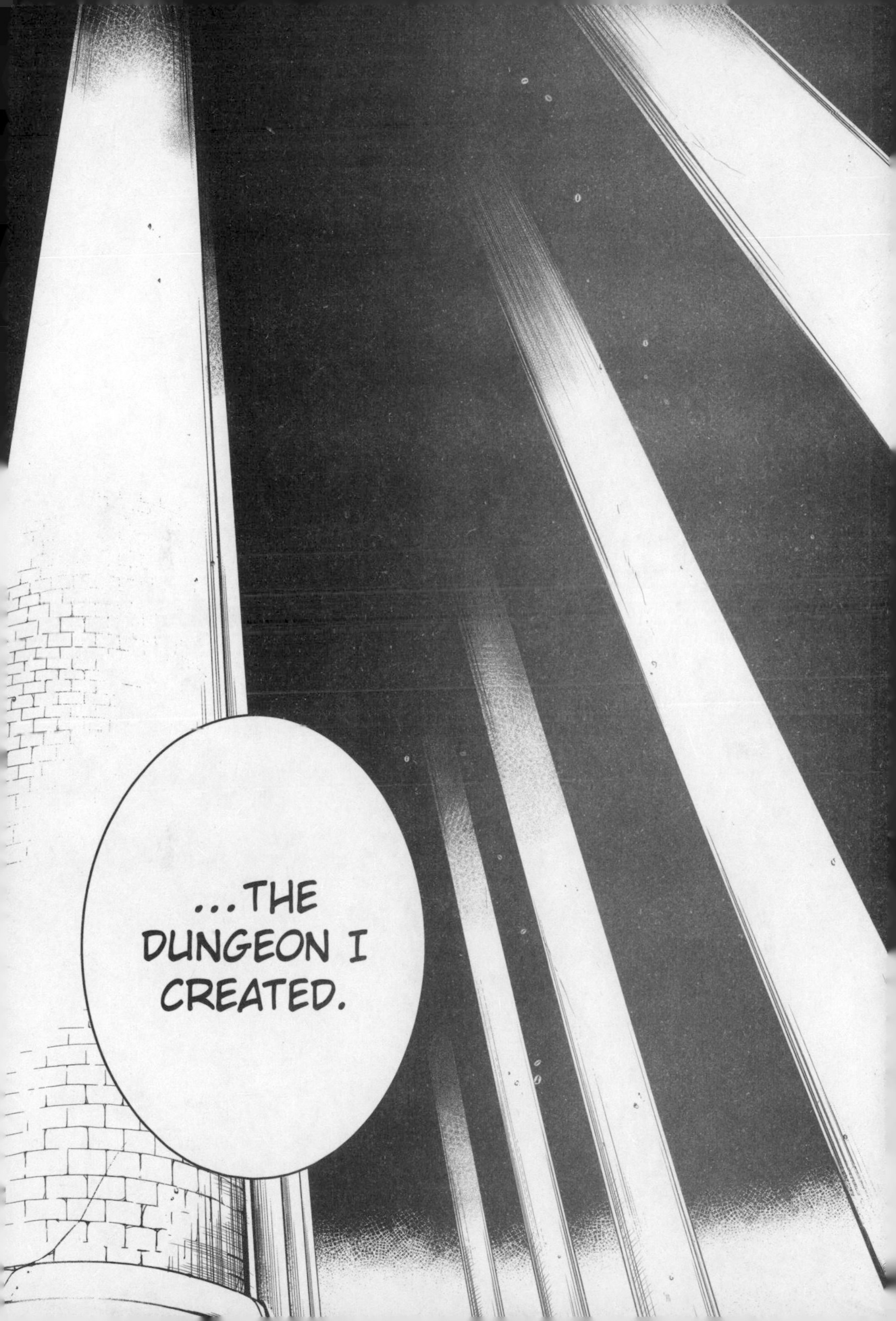
...THE DUNGEON I CREATED.

CHAPTER 1 CHRONO IS IN THE DEMON KING'S CASTLE

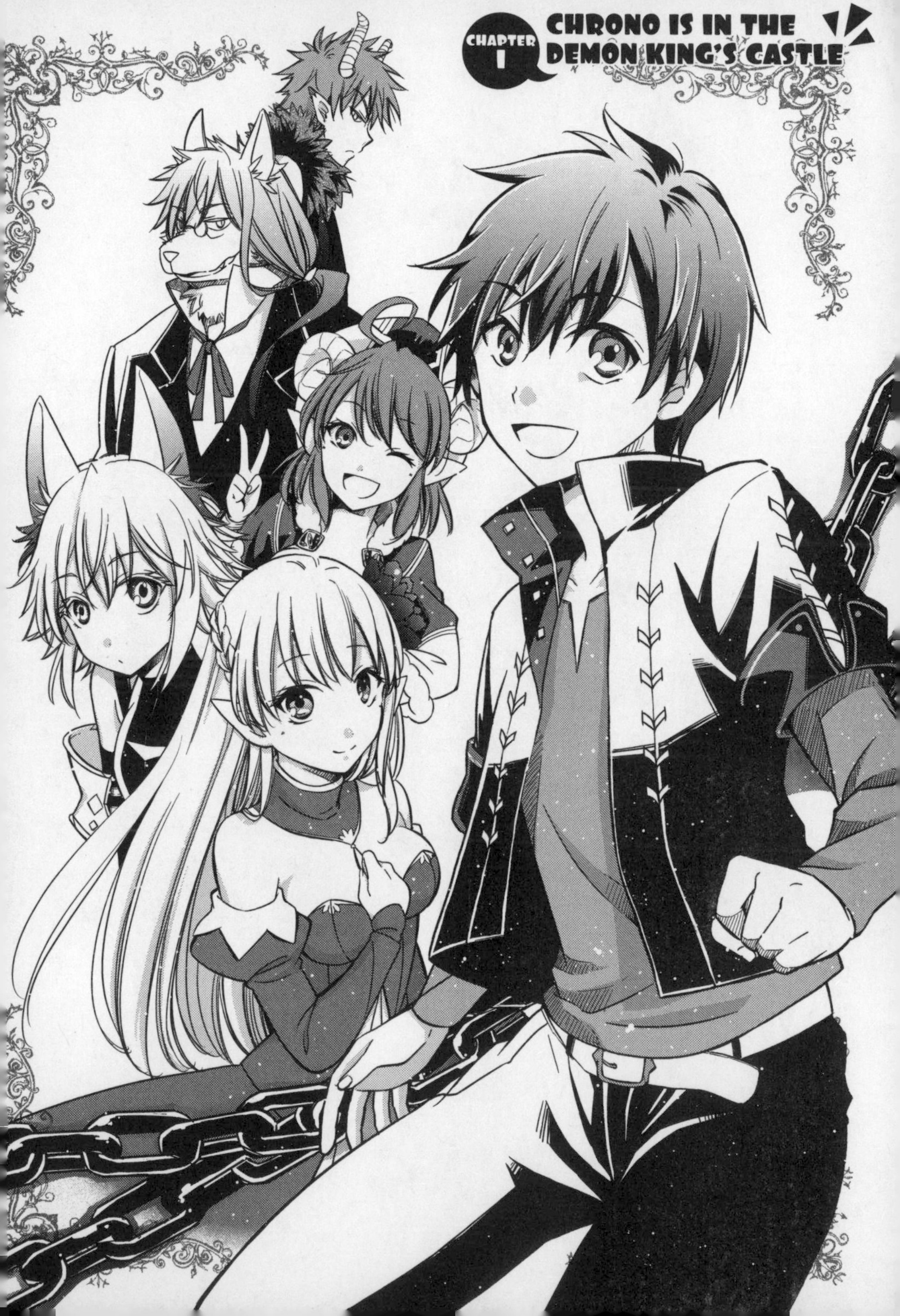

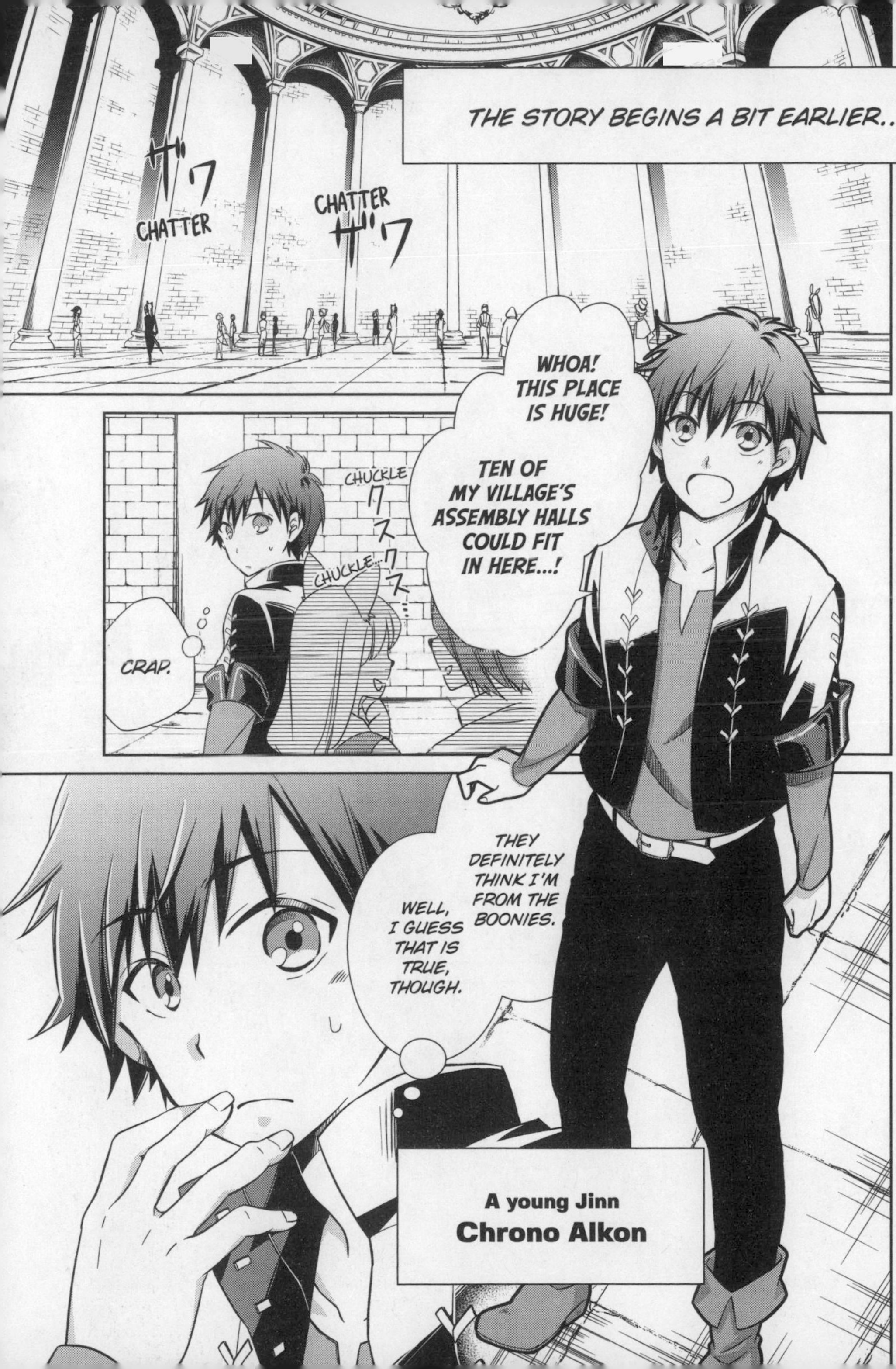
THE STORY BEGINS A BIT EARLIER...
CHATTER
ザワ
ザワ
CHATTER
WHOA! THIS PLACE IS HUGE!
TEN OF MY VILLAGE'S ASSEMBLY HALLS COULD FIT IN HERE...!
CHUCKLE
クス
CHUCKLE...
クス...
CRAP.
THEY DEFINITELY THINK I'M FROM THE BOONIES.
WELL, I GUESS THAT IS TRUE, THOUGH.
A young Jinn
Chrono Alkon

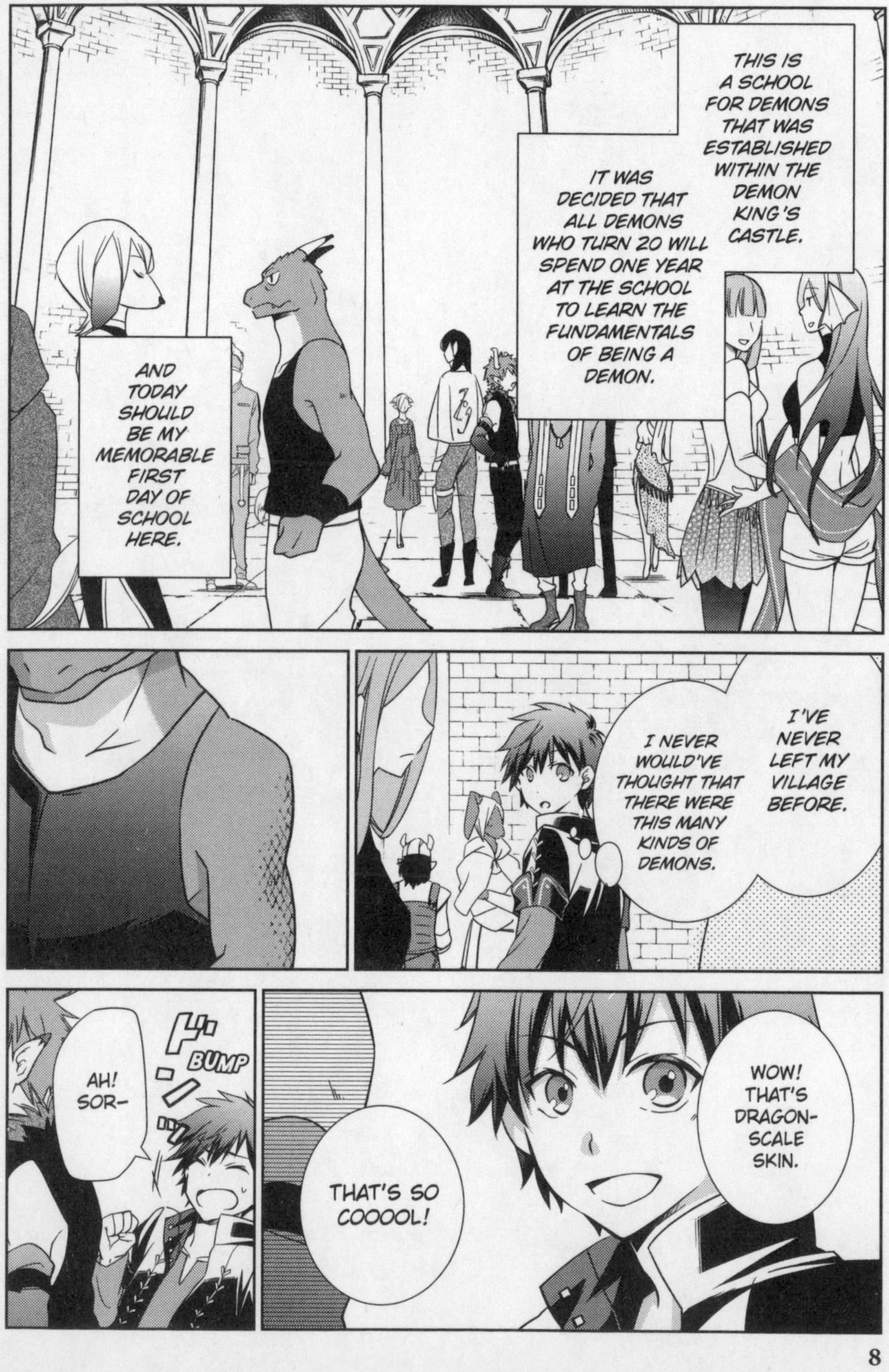
THIS IS A SCHOOL FOR DEMONS THAT WAS ESTABLISHED WITHIN THE DEMON KING'S CASTLE.
IT WAS DECIDED THAT ALL DEMONS WHO TURN 20 WILL SPEND ONE YEAR AT THE SCHOOL TO LEARN THE FUNDAMENTALS OF BEING A DEMON.
AND TODAY SHOULD BE MY MEMORABLE FIRST DAY OF SCHOOL HERE.
I'VE NEVER LEFT MY VILLAGE BEFORE.
I NEVER WOULD'VE THOUGHT THAT THERE WERE THIS MANY KINDS OF DEMONS.
WOW! THAT'S DRAGON-SCALE SKIN.
THAT'S SO COOOOL!
BUMP
AH! SOR-

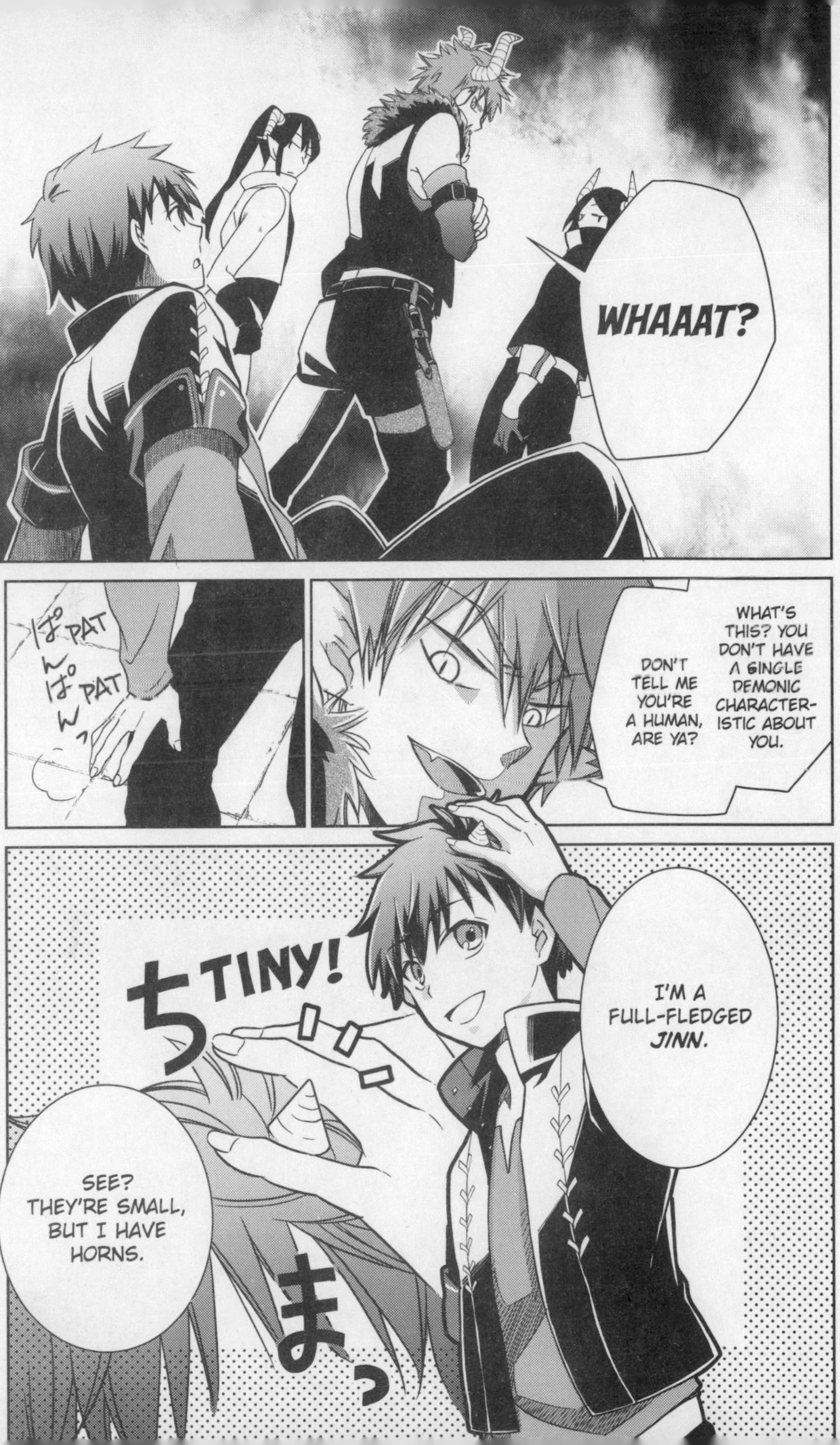
WHAAAT?
WHAT'S THIS? YOU DON'T HAVE A SINGLE DEMONIC CHARACTER-ISTIC ABOUT YOU.
DON'T TELL ME YOU'RE A HUMAN, ARE YA?
ぱんぱんっ PAT PAT
I'M A FULL-FLEDGED JINN.
ち TINY!
SEE? THEY'RE SMALL, BUT I HAVE HORNS.
まっ

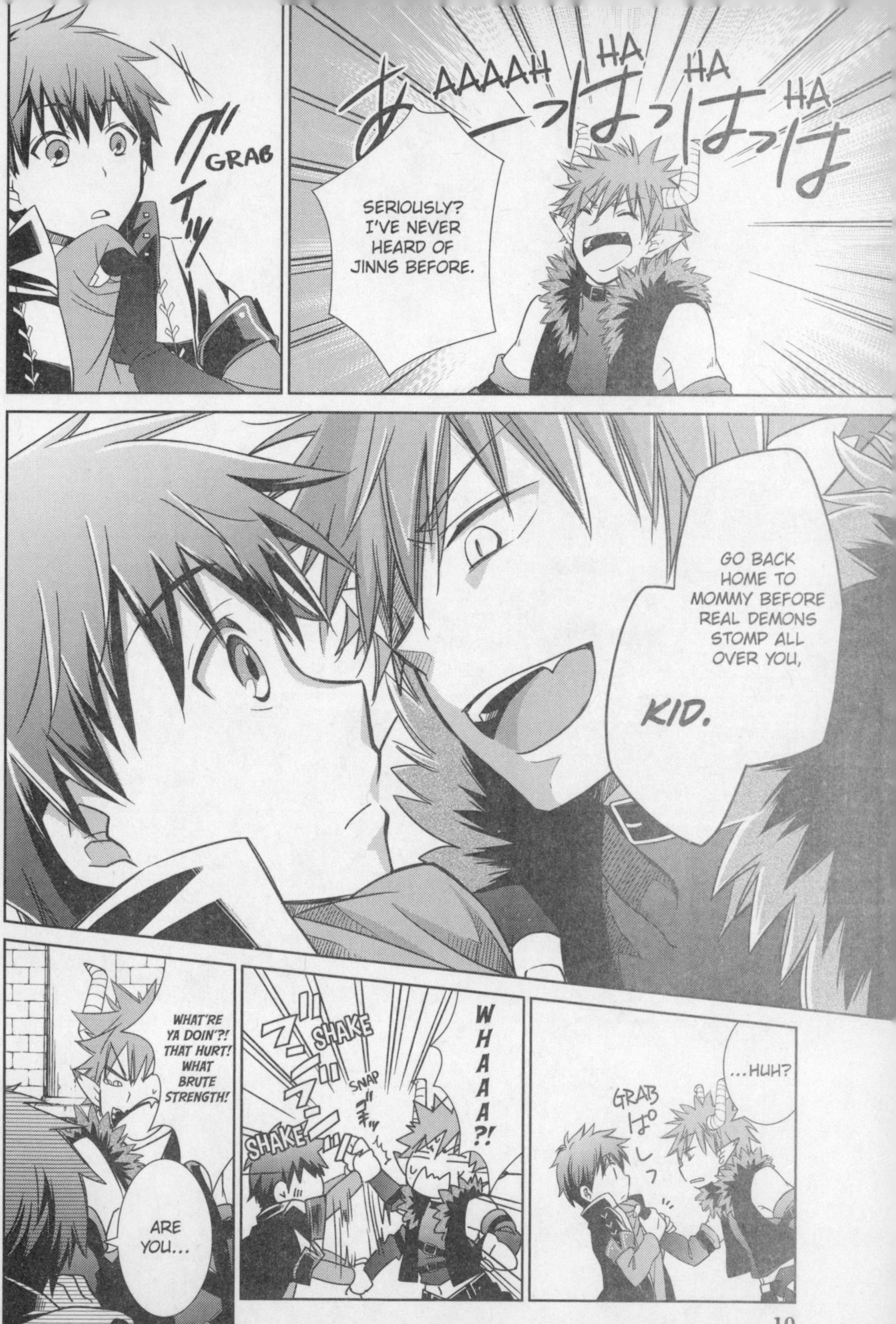
AAAAH HA HA HA
SERIOUSLY? I'VE NEVER HEARD OF JINNS BEFORE.
GRAB
GO BACK HOME TO MOMMY BEFORE REAL DEMONS STOMP ALL OVER YOU,
KID.
...HUH?
GRAB
WHAAAA?!
SHAKE
SNAP
SHAKE
WHAT'RE YA DOIN'?! THAT HURT! WHAT BRUTE STRENGTH!
ARE YOU...

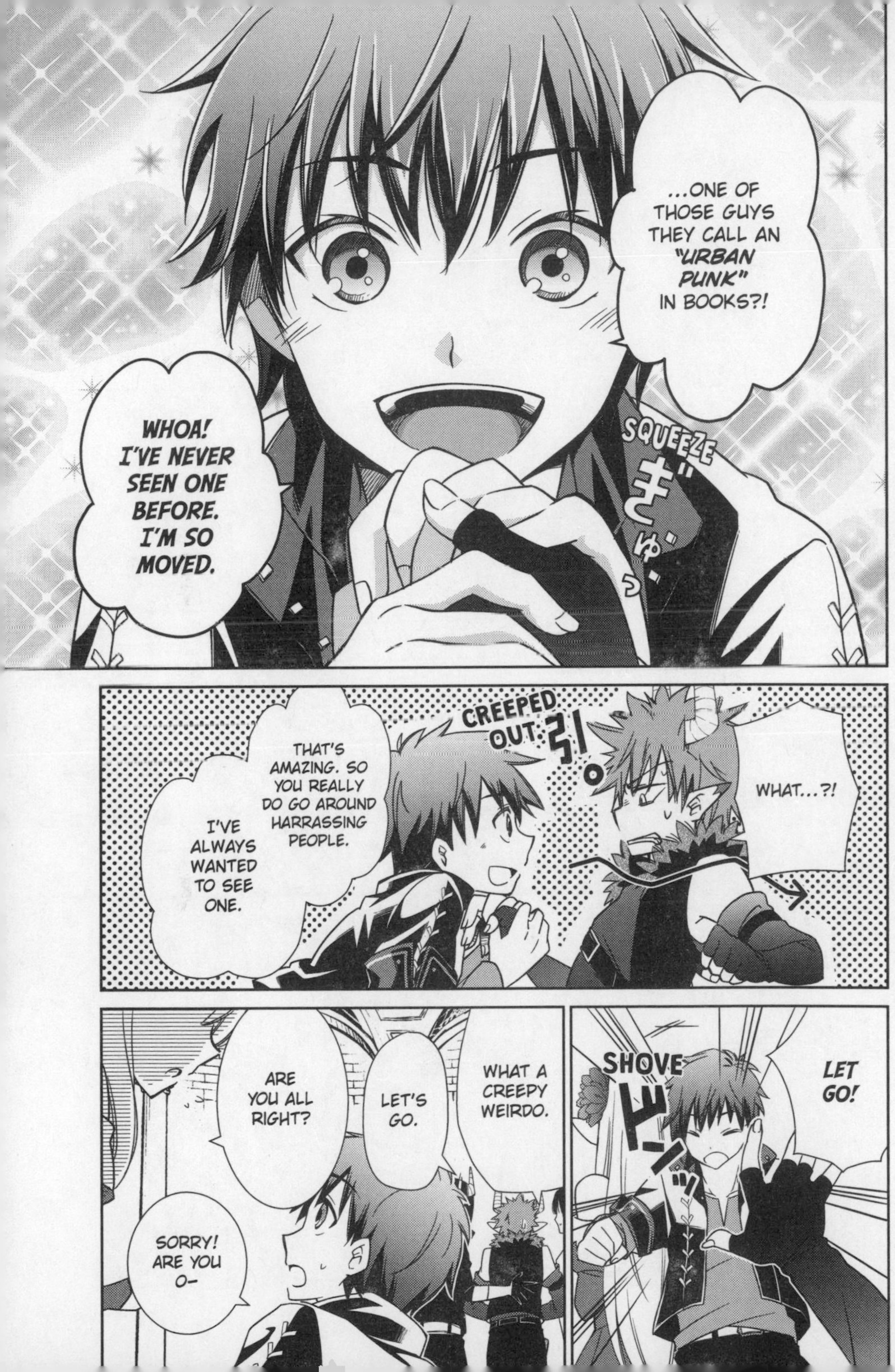
...ONE OF THOSE GUYS THEY CALL AN "URBAN PUNK" IN BOOKS?!
SQUEEZE
WHOA! I'VE NEVER SEEN ONE BEFORE. I'M SO MOVED.
WHAT...?!
CREEPED OUT
THAT'S AMAZING. SO YOU REALLY DO GO AROUND HARRASSING PEOPLE.
I'VE ALWAYS WANTED TO SEE ONE.
LET GO!
SHOVE
WHAT A CREEPY WEIRDO.
LET'S GO.
ARE YOU ALL RIGHT?
SORRY! ARE YOU O–

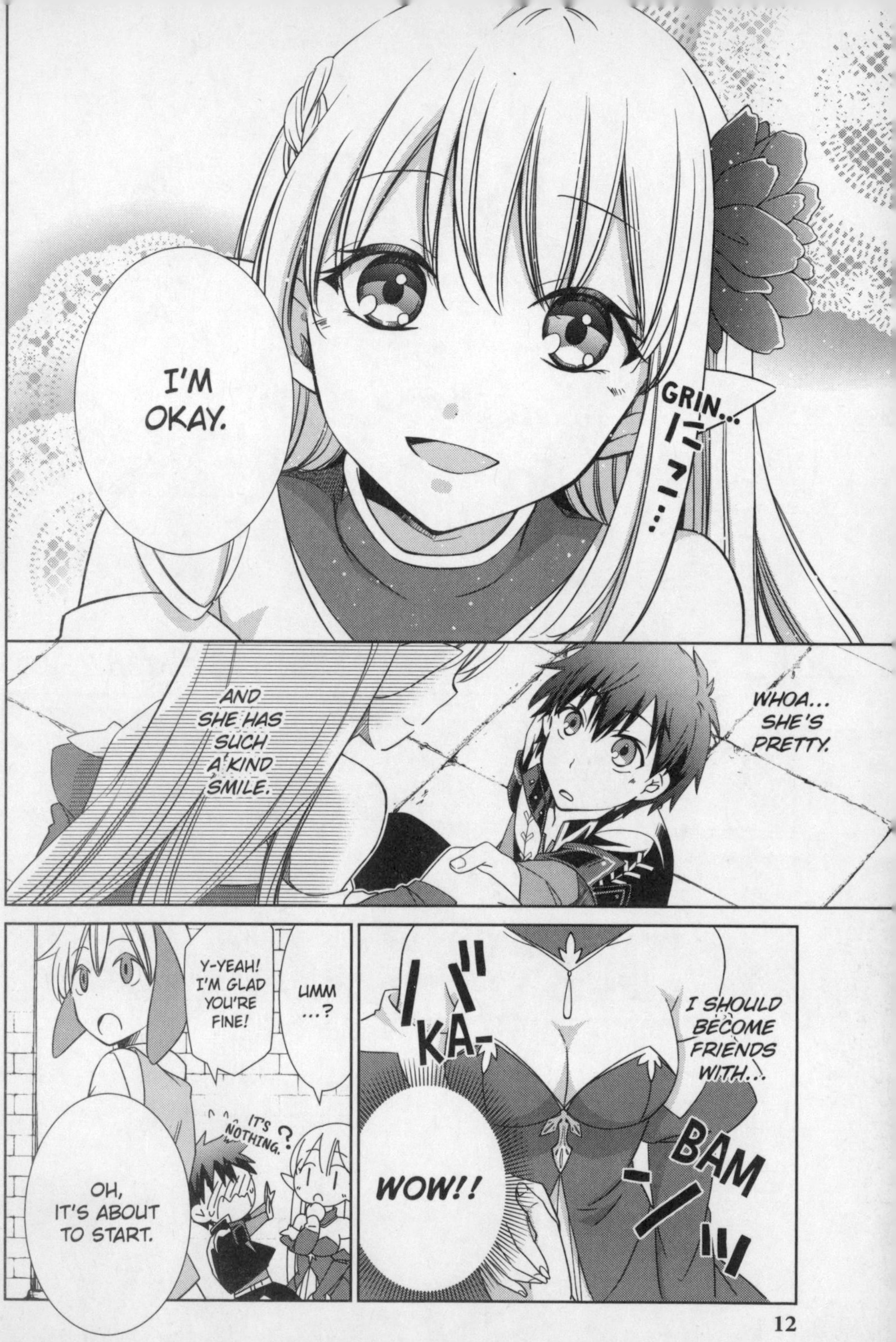
I'M OKAY.
GRIN...
ニコー…
WHOA... SHE'S PRETTY.
AND SHE HAS SUCH A KIND SMILE.
I SHOULD BECOME FRIENDS WITH...
KA-
BAM
WOW!!
UMM ...?
Y-YEAH! I'M GLAD YOU'RE FINE!
IT'S NOTHING.
OH, IT'S ABOUT TO START.

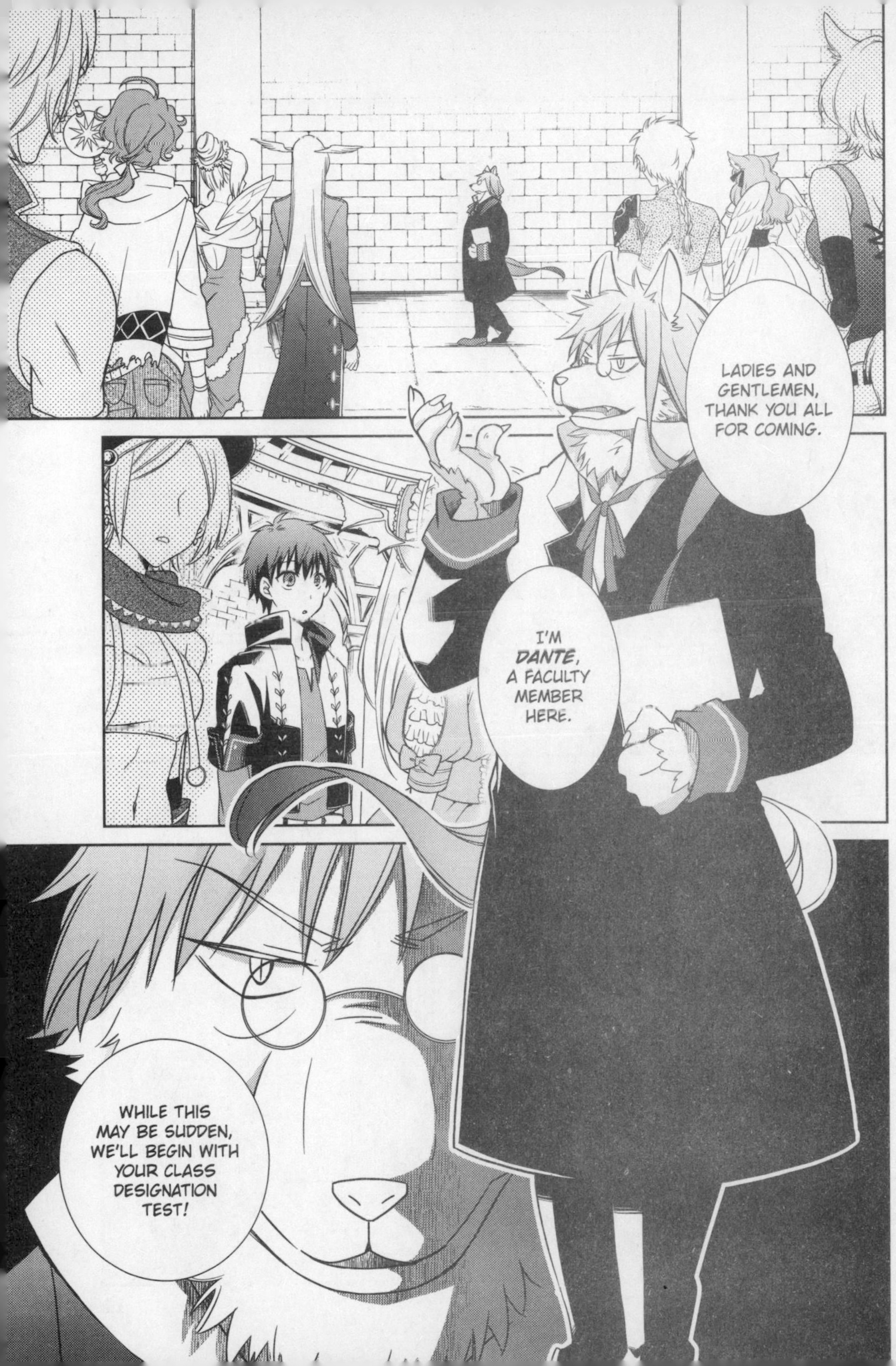
LADIES AND GENTLEMEN, THANK YOU ALL FOR COMING.
I'M *DANTE*, A FACULTY MEMBER HERE.
WHILE THIS MAY BE SUDDEN, WE'LL BEGIN WITH YOUR CLASS DESIGNATION TEST!

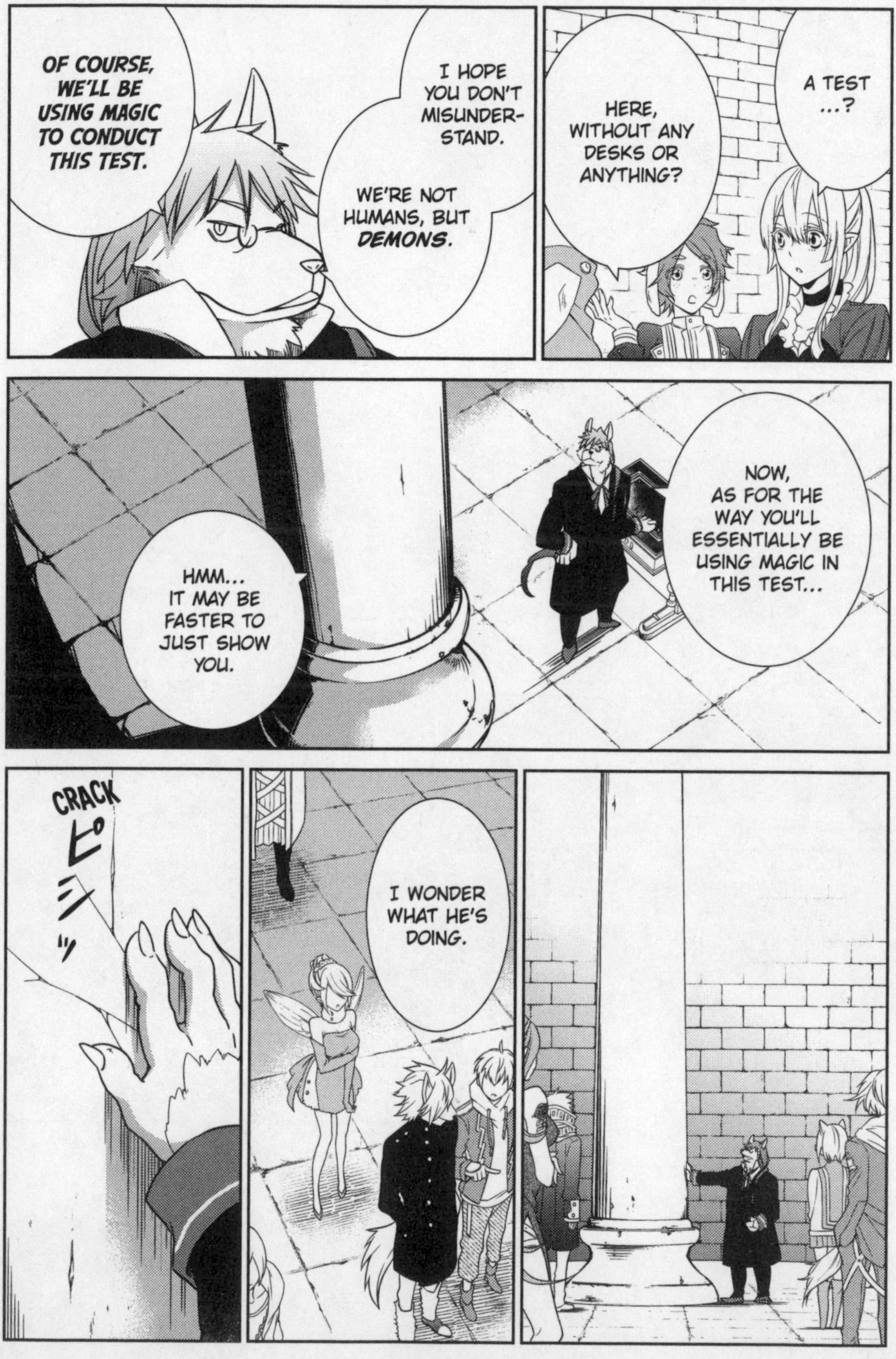
A TEST ...?
HERE, WITHOUT ANY DESKS OR ANYTHING?
I HOPE YOU DON'T MISUNDERSTAND.
WE'RE NOT HUMANS, BUT DEMONS.
OF COURSE, WE'LL BE USING MAGIC TO CONDUCT THIS TEST.
NOW, AS FOR THE WAY YOU'LL ESSENTIALLY BE USING MAGIC IN THIS TEST...
HMM... IT MAY BE FASTER TO JUST SHOW YOU.
I WONDER WHAT HE'S DOING.
CRACK
ピシッ

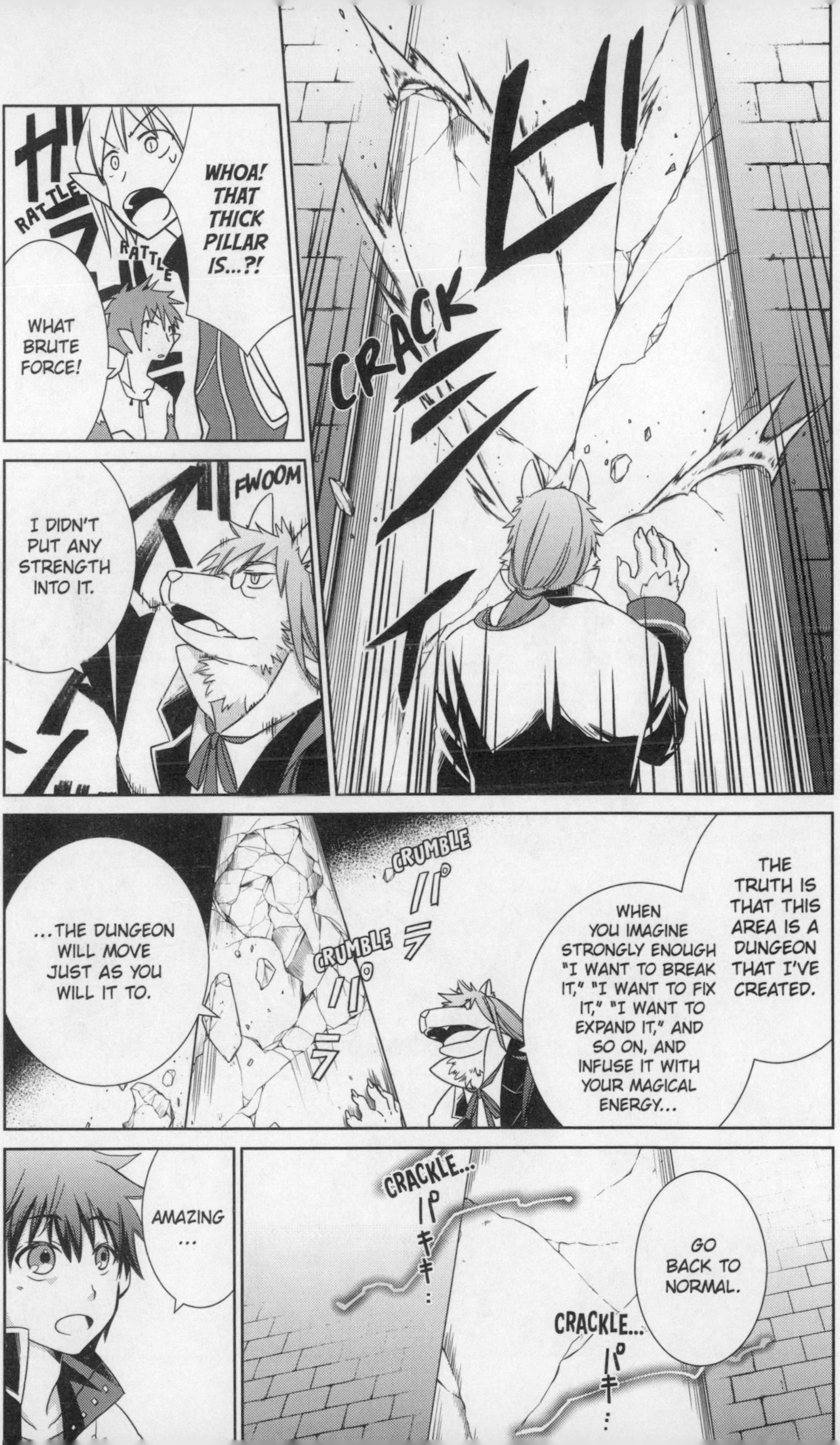
CRACK
RATTLE
RATTLE
WHOA! THAT THICK PILLAR IS...?!
WHAT BRUTE FORCE!
FWOOM
I DIDN'T PUT ANY STRENGTH INTO IT.
THE TRUTH IS THAT THIS AREA IS A DUNGEON THAT I'VE CREATED.
WHEN YOU IMAGINE STRONGLY ENOUGH "I WANT TO BREAK IT," "I WANT TO FIX IT," "I WANT TO EXPAND IT," AND SO ON, AND INFUSE IT WITH YOUR MAGICAL ENERGY...
CRUMBLE
パラ
CRUMBLE
パラ
...THE DUNGEON WILL MOVE JUST AS YOU WILL IT TO.
GO BACK TO NORMAL.
CRACKLE...
パキキ...
CRACKLE...
パキ...
AMAZING ...

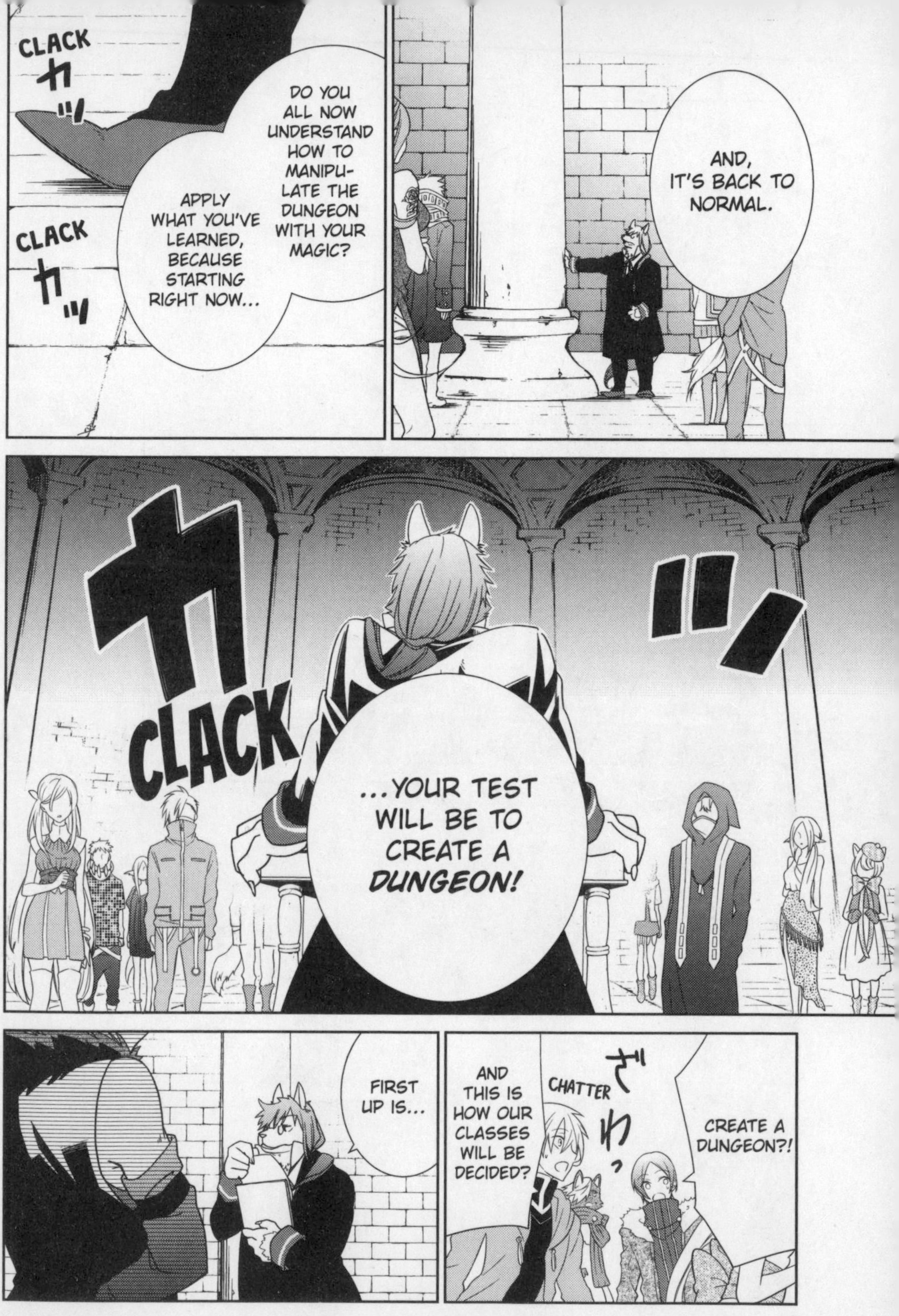
AND, IT'S BACK TO NORMAL.
CLACK
カッ
DO YOU ALL NOW UNDERSTAND HOW TO MANIPU-LATE THE DUNGEON WITH YOUR MAGIC?
APPLY WHAT YOU'VE LEARNED, BECAUSE STARTING RIGHT NOW...
CLACK
カッ
カッ
CLACK
...YOUR TEST WILL BE TO CREATE A DUNGEON!
CREATE A DUNGEON?!
ざわ
CHATTER
AND THIS IS HOW OUR CLASSES WILL BE DECIDED?
FIRST UP IS...

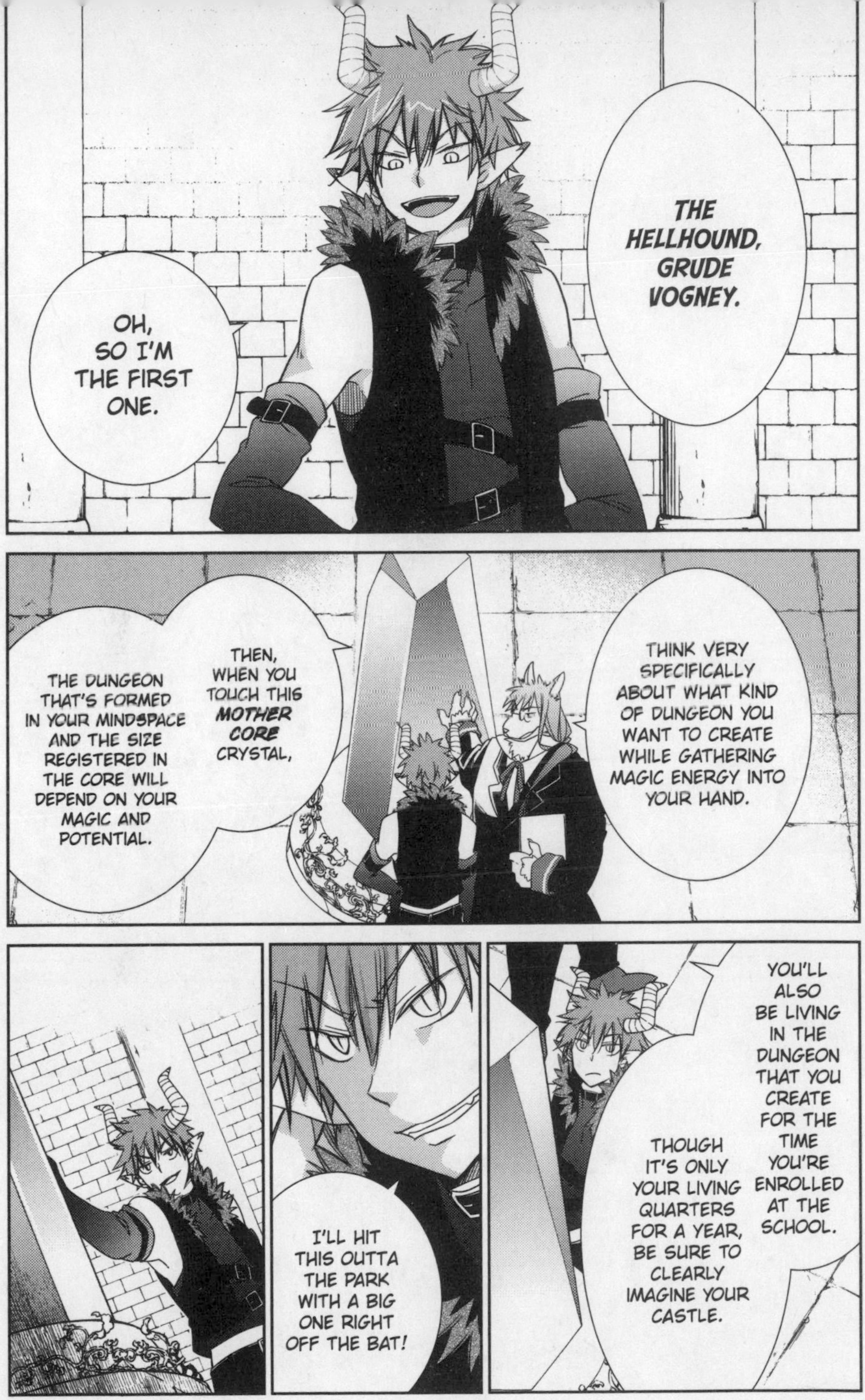
THE HELLHOUND, GRUDE VOGNEY.
OH, SO I'M THE FIRST ONE.
THINK VERY SPECIFICALLY ABOUT WHAT KIND OF DUNGEON YOU WANT TO CREATE WHILE GATHERING MAGIC ENERGY INTO YOUR HAND.
THEN, WHEN YOU TOUCH THIS MOTHER CORE CRYSTAL,
THE DUNGEON THAT'S FORMED IN YOUR MINDSPACE AND THE SIZE REGISTERED IN THE CORE WILL DEPEND ON YOUR MAGIC AND POTENTIAL.
YOU'LL ALSO BE LIVING IN THE DUNGEON THAT YOU CREATE FOR THE TIME YOU'RE ENROLLED AT THE SCHOOL.
THOUGH IT'S ONLY YOUR LIVING QUARTERS FOR A YEAR, BE SURE TO CLEARLY IMAGINE YOUR CASTLE.
I'LL HIT THIS OUTTA THE PARK WITH A BIG ONE RIGHT OFF THE BAT!

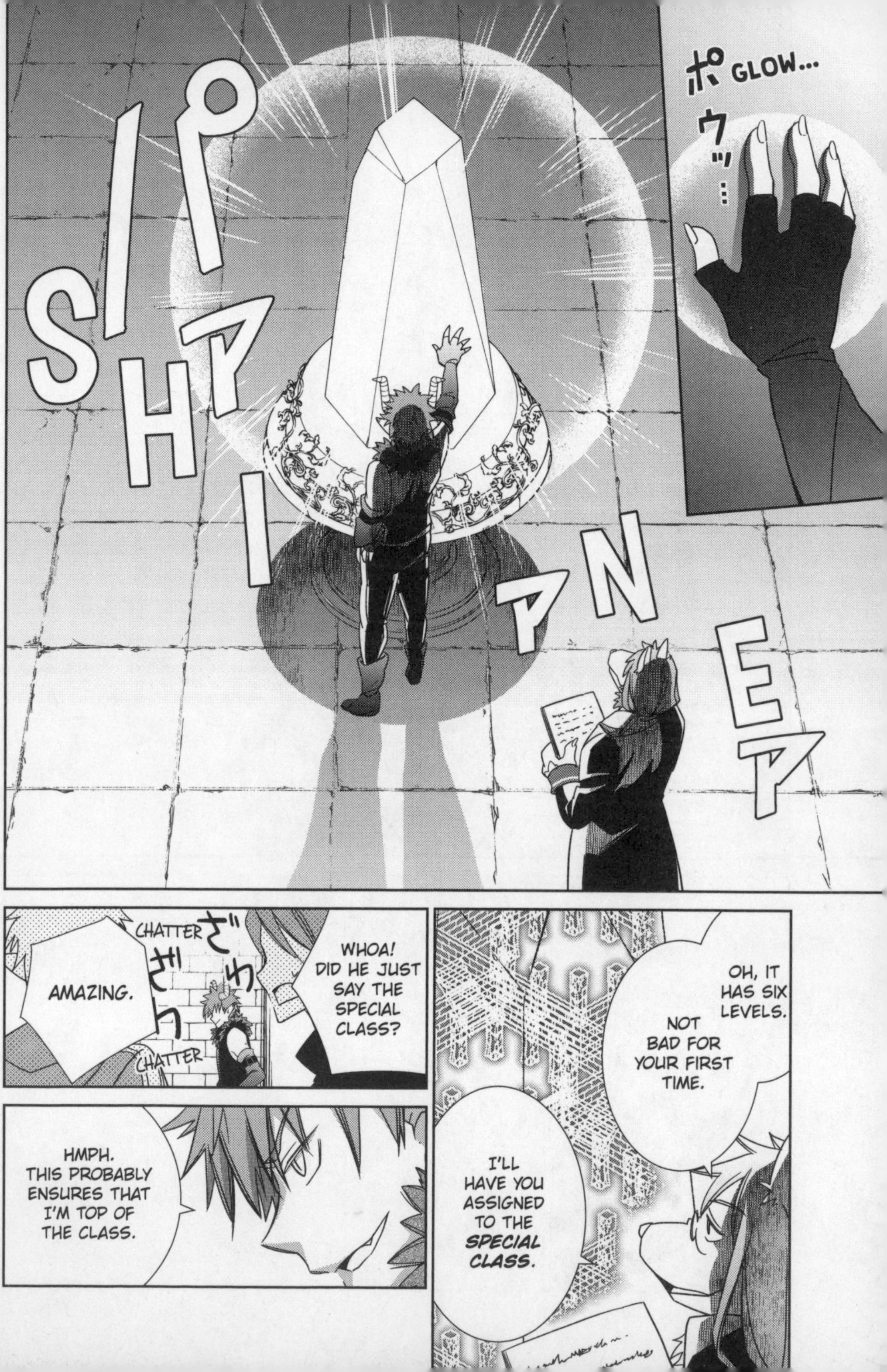
ポウッ…
GLOW...
SHINE
OH, IT HAS SIX LEVELS.
NOT BAD FOR YOUR FIRST TIME.
I'LL HAVE YOU ASSIGNED TO THE **SPECIAL CLASS**.
WHOA! DID HE JUST SAY THE SPECIAL CLASS?
ざわっ
CHATTER
CHATTER
AMAZING.
HMPH. THIS PROBABLY ENSURES THAT I'M TOP OF THE CLASS.

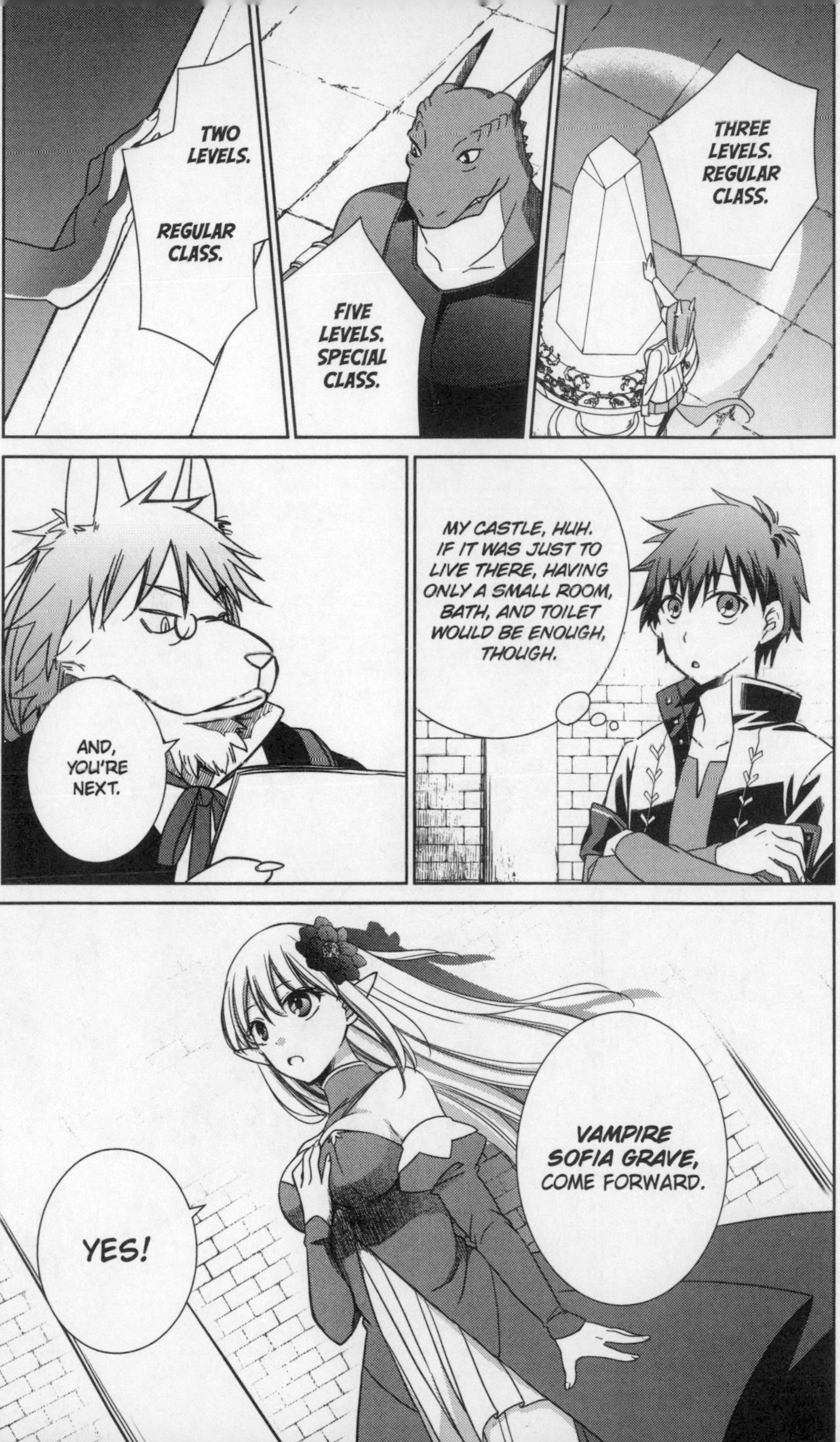
THREE LEVELS. REGULAR CLASS.
FIVE LEVELS. SPECIAL CLASS.
TWO LEVELS.
REGULAR CLASS.
MY CASTLE, HUH. IF IT WAS JUST TO LIVE THERE, HAVING ONLY A SMALL ROOM, BATH, AND TOILET WOULD BE ENOUGH, THOUGH.
AND, YOU'RE NEXT.
VAMPIRE SOFIA GRAVE, COME FORWARD.
YES!

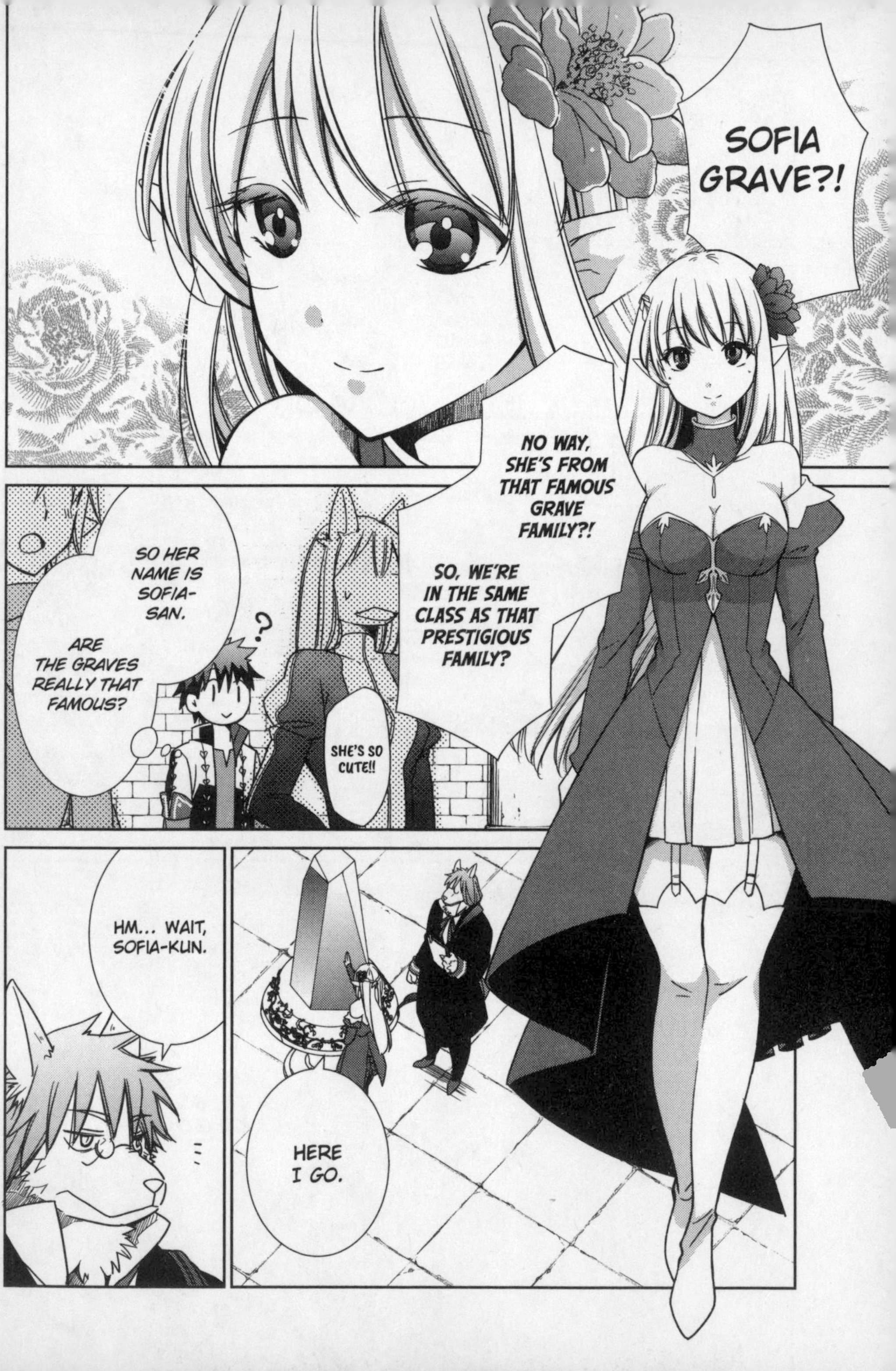
SOFIA GRAVE?!
NO WAY, SHE'S FROM THAT FAMOUS GRAVE FAMILY?!
SO, WE'RE IN THE SAME CLASS AS THAT PRESTIGIOUS FAMILY?
SHE'S SO CUTE!!
SO HER NAME IS SOFIA-SAN.
ARE THE GRAVES REALLY THAT FAMOUS?
HERE I GO.
HM... WAIT, SOFIA-KUN.

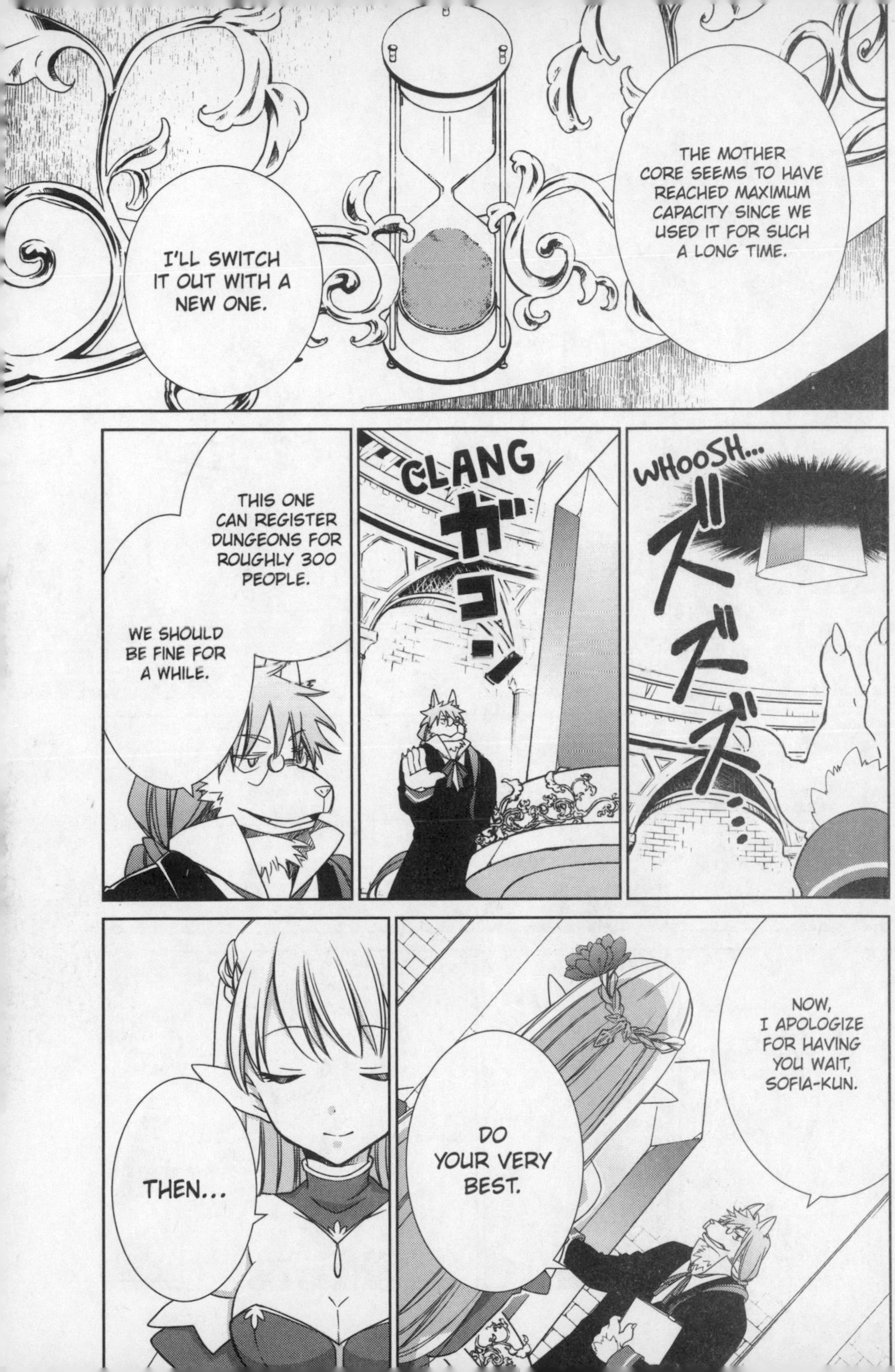
THE MOTHER CORE SEEMS TO HAVE REACHED MAXIMUM CAPACITY SINCE WE USED IT FOR SUCH A LONG TIME.
I'LL SWITCH IT OUT WITH A NEW ONE.
WHOOSH...
ズズズ...
CLANG
ガコッ
THIS ONE CAN REGISTER DUNGEONS FOR ROUGHLY 300 PEOPLE.
WE SHOULD BE FINE FOR A WHILE.
NOW, I APOLOGIZE FOR HAVING YOU WAIT, SOFIA-KUN.
DO YOUR VERY BEST.
THEN...

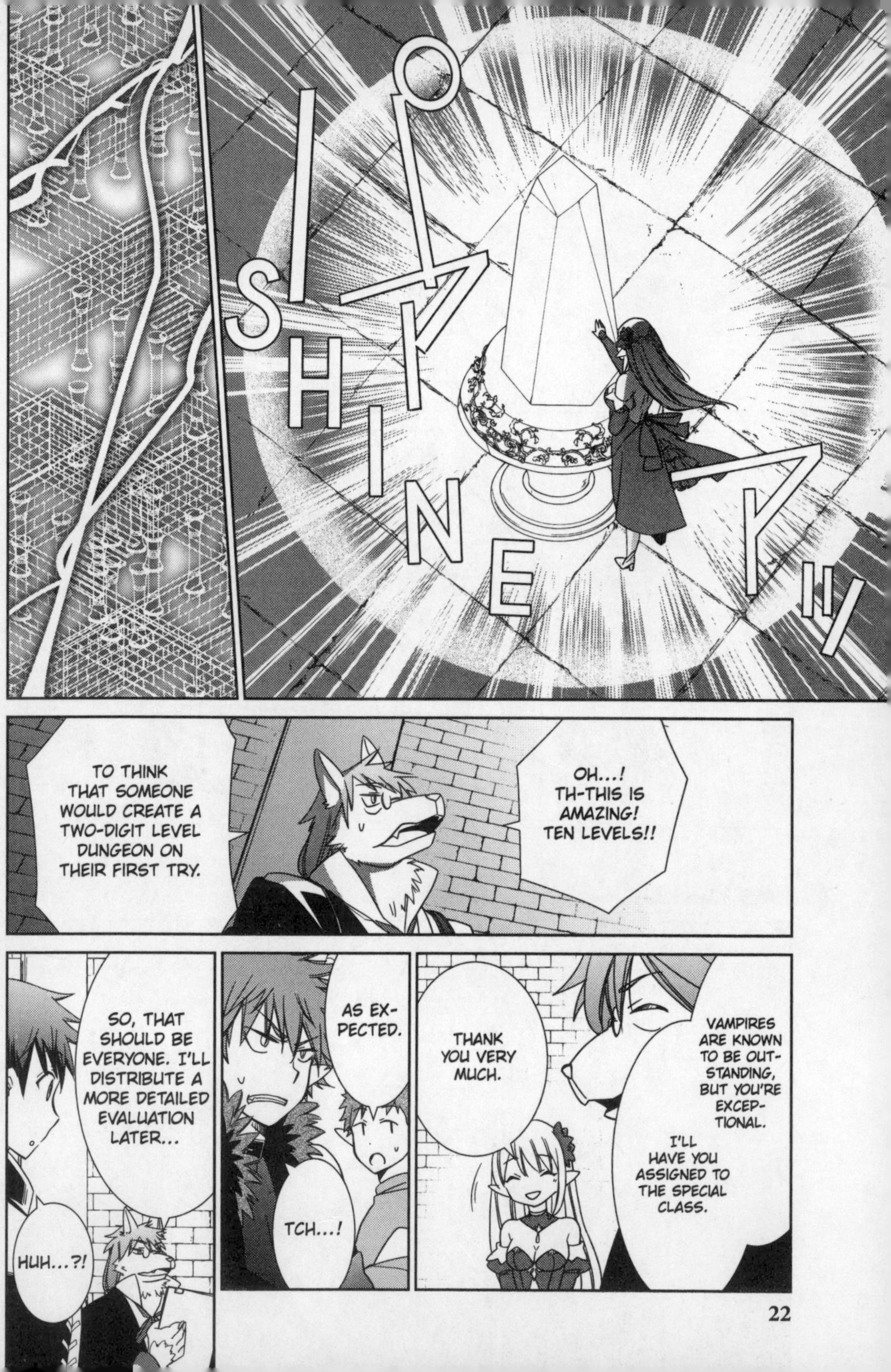
SHINE
OH...! TH-THIS IS AMAZING! TEN LEVELS!!
TO THINK THAT SOMEONE WOULD CREATE A TWO-DIGIT LEVEL DUNGEON ON THEIR FIRST TRY.
VAMPIRES ARE KNOWN TO BE OUT-STANDING, BUT YOU'RE EXCEP-TIONAL.
I'LL HAVE YOU ASSIGNED TO THE SPECIAL CLASS.
THANK YOU VERY MUCH.
AS EX-PECTED.
TCH...!
SO, THAT SHOULD BE EVERYONE. I'LL DISTRIBUTE A MORE DETAILED EVALUATION LATER...
HUH...?!

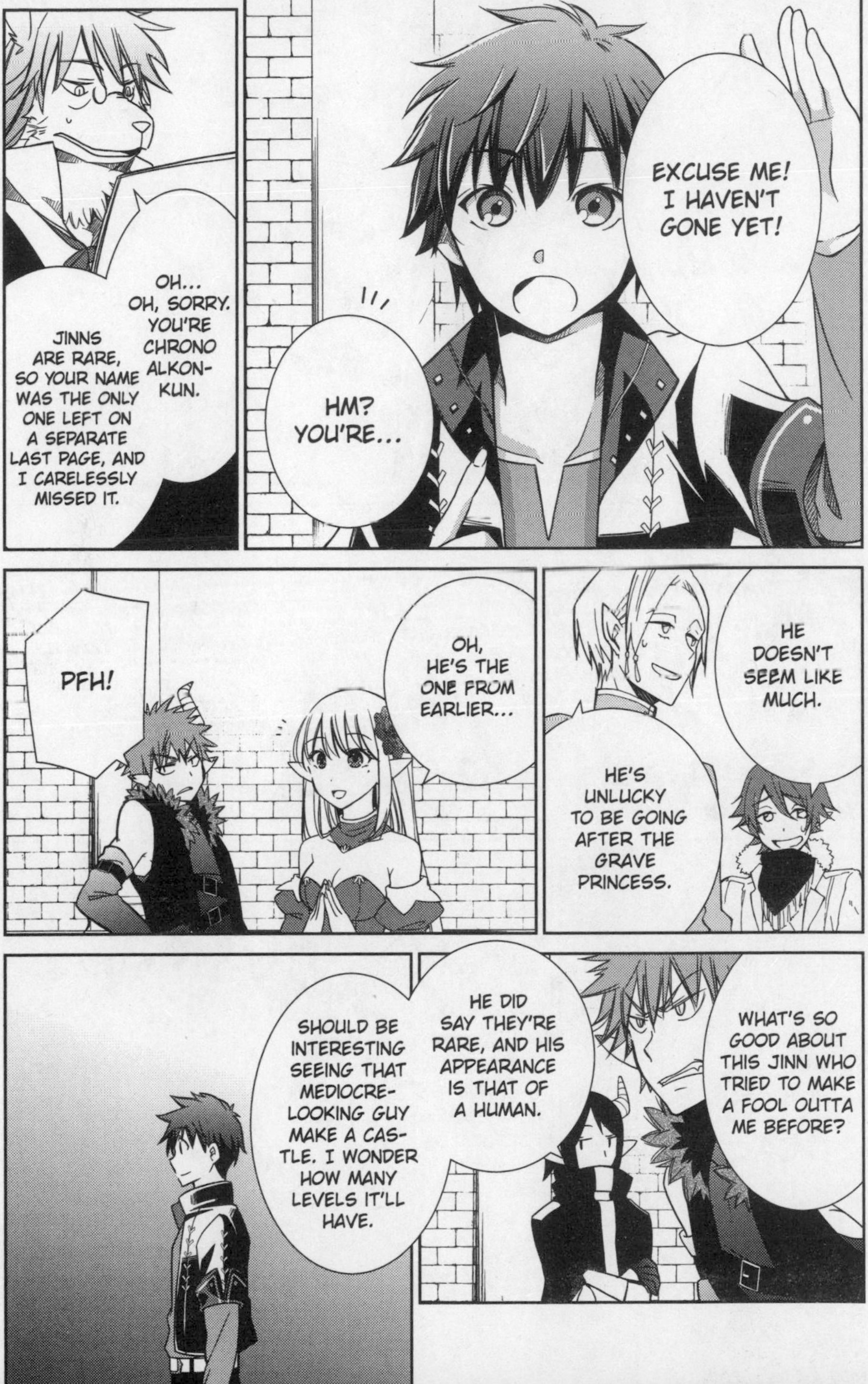
EXCUSE ME! I HAVEN'T GONE YET!
HM? YOU'RE...
OH... OH, SORRY. YOU'RE CHRONO ALKON-KUN.
JINNS ARE RARE, SO YOUR NAME WAS THE ONLY ONE LEFT ON A SEPARATE LAST PAGE, AND I CARELESSLY MISSED IT.
HE DOESN'T SEEM LIKE MUCH.
HE'S UNLUCKY TO BE GOING AFTER THE GRAVE PRINCESS.
OH, HE'S THE ONE FROM EARLIER...
PFH!
WHAT'S SO GOOD ABOUT THIS JINN WHO TRIED TO MAKE A FOOL OUTTA ME BEFORE?
HE DID SAY THEY'RE RARE, AND HIS APPEARANCE IS THAT OF A HUMAN.
SHOULD BE INTERESTING SEEING THAT MEDIOCRE-LOOKING GUY MAKE A CAS-TLE. I WONDER HOW MANY LEVELS IT'LL HAVE.

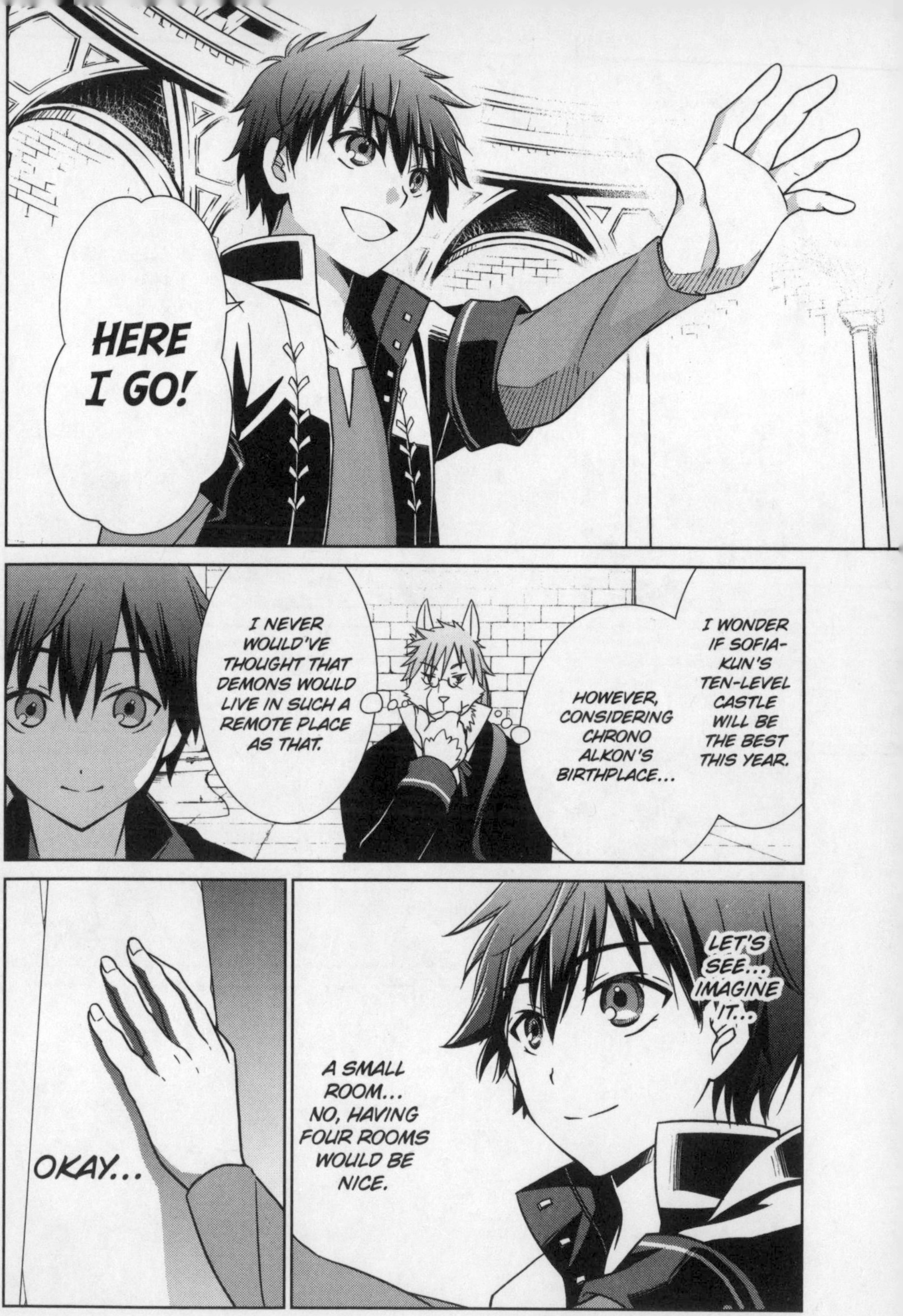
HERE I GO!
I WONDER IF SOFIA-KUN'S TEN-LEVEL CASTLE WILL BE THE BEST THIS YEAR.
HOWEVER, CONSIDERING CHRONO ALKON'S BIRTHPLACE...
I NEVER WOULD'VE THOUGHT THAT DEMONS WOULD LIVE IN SUCH A REMOTE PLACE AS THAT.
LET'S SEE... IMAGINE IT...
A SMALL ROOM... NO, HAVING FOUR ROOMS WOULD BE NICE.
OKAY...

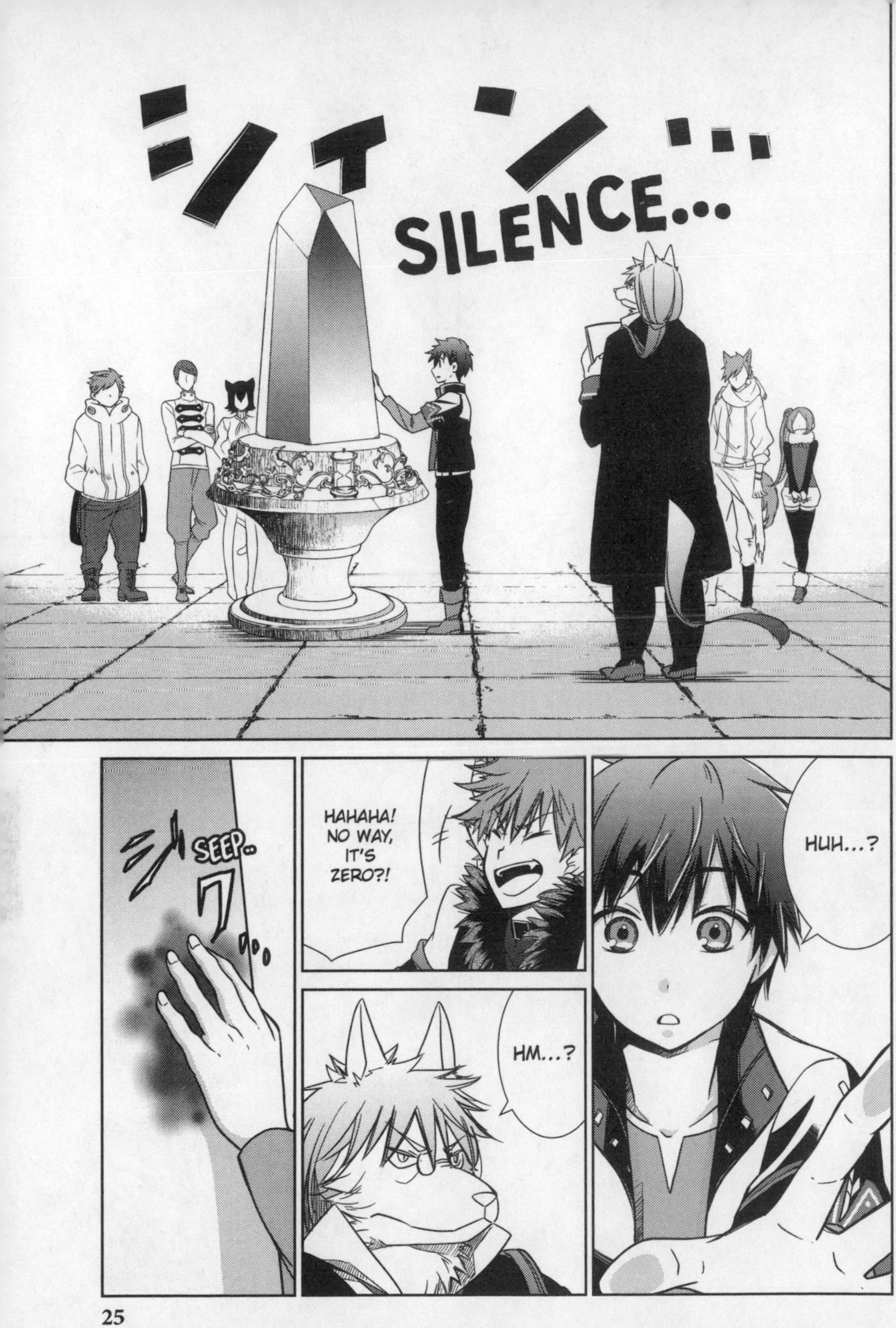
シイーン...
SILENCE...
HUH...?
HAHAHA! NO WAY, IT'S ZERO?!
HM...?
ジワ...
SEEP..

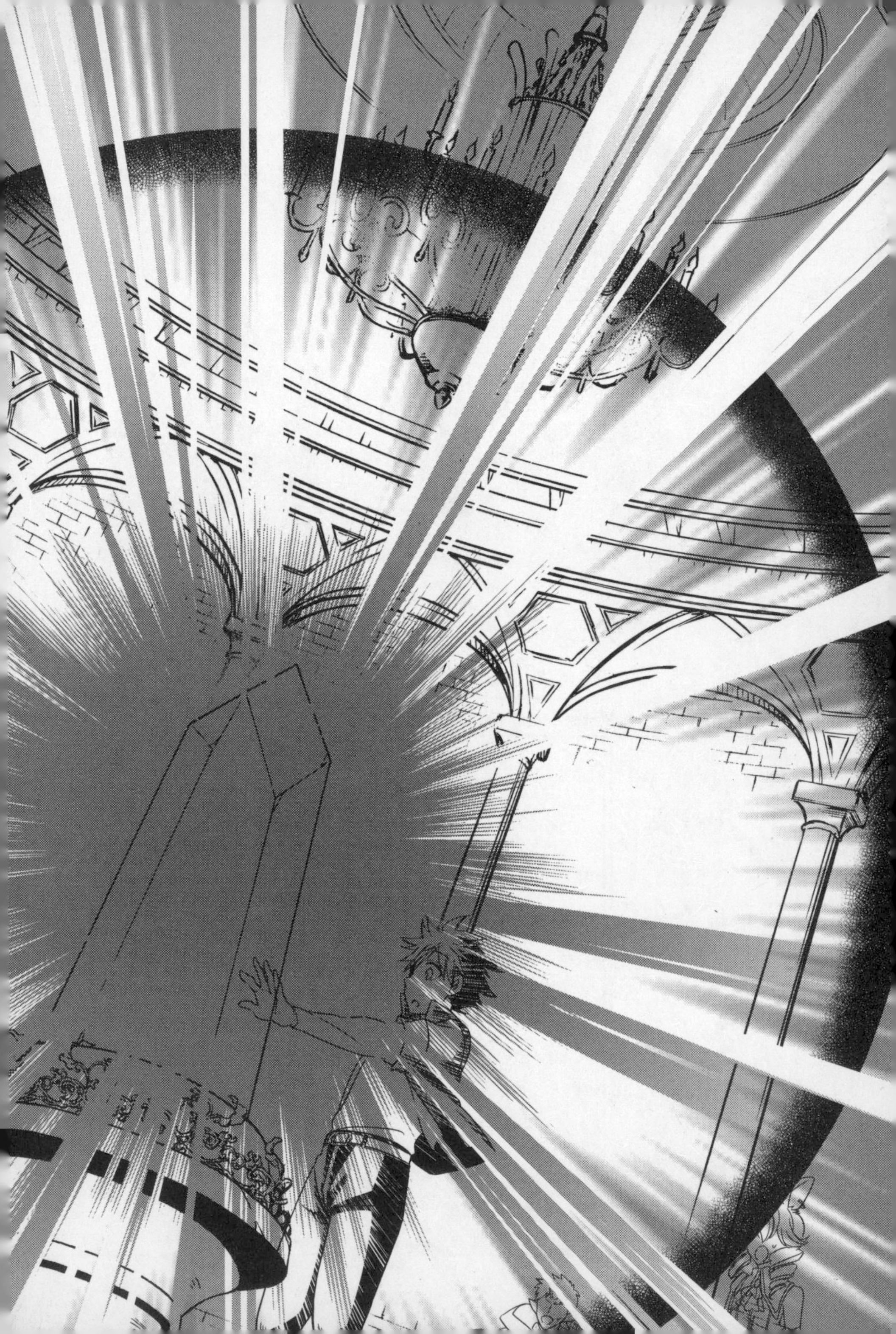

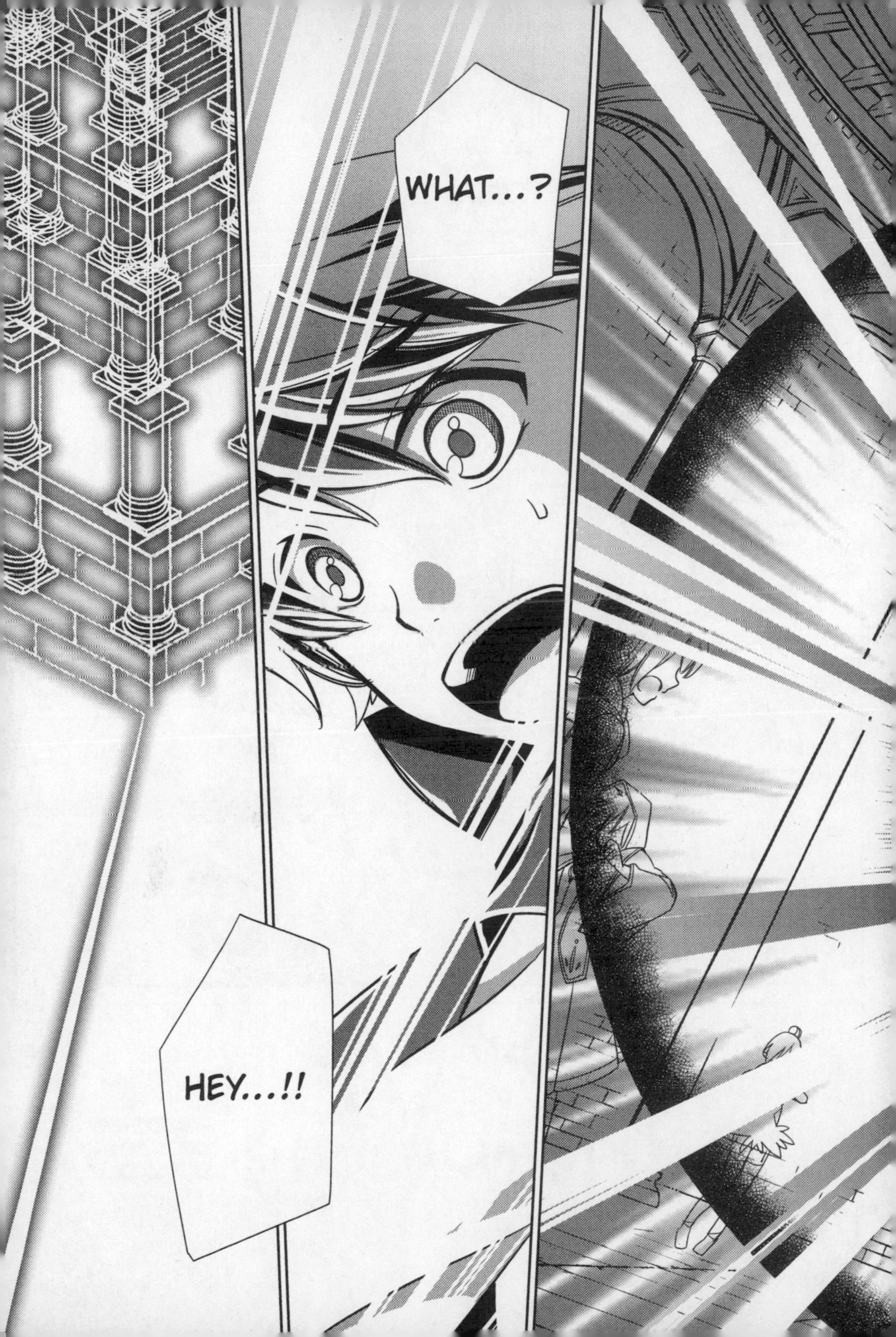
WHAT...?
HEY...!!

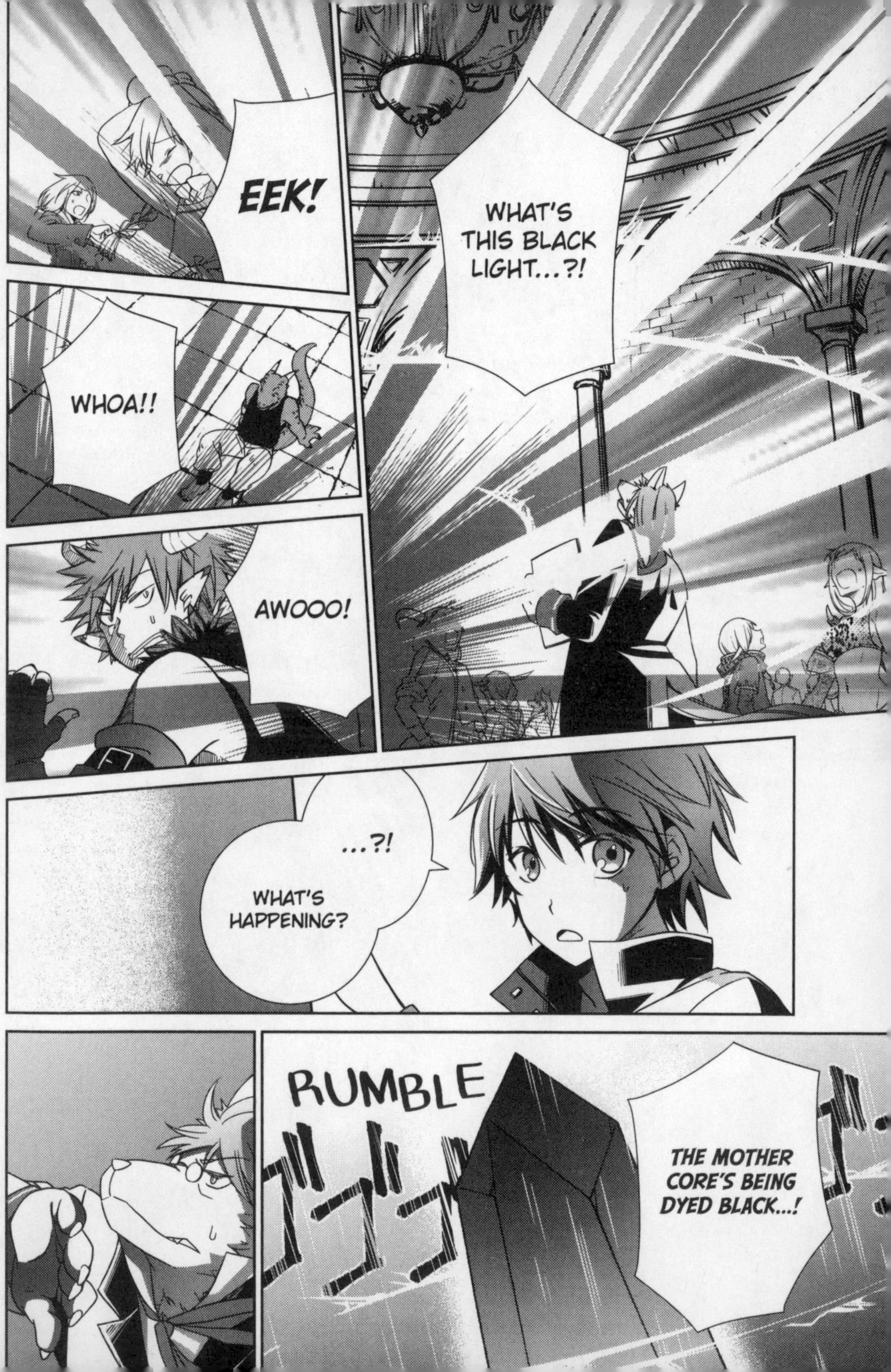
WHAT'S THIS BLACK LIGHT...?!
EEK!
WHOA!!
AWOOO!
...?!
WHAT'S HAPPENING?
RUMBLE
THE MOTHER CORE'S BEING DYED BLACK...!

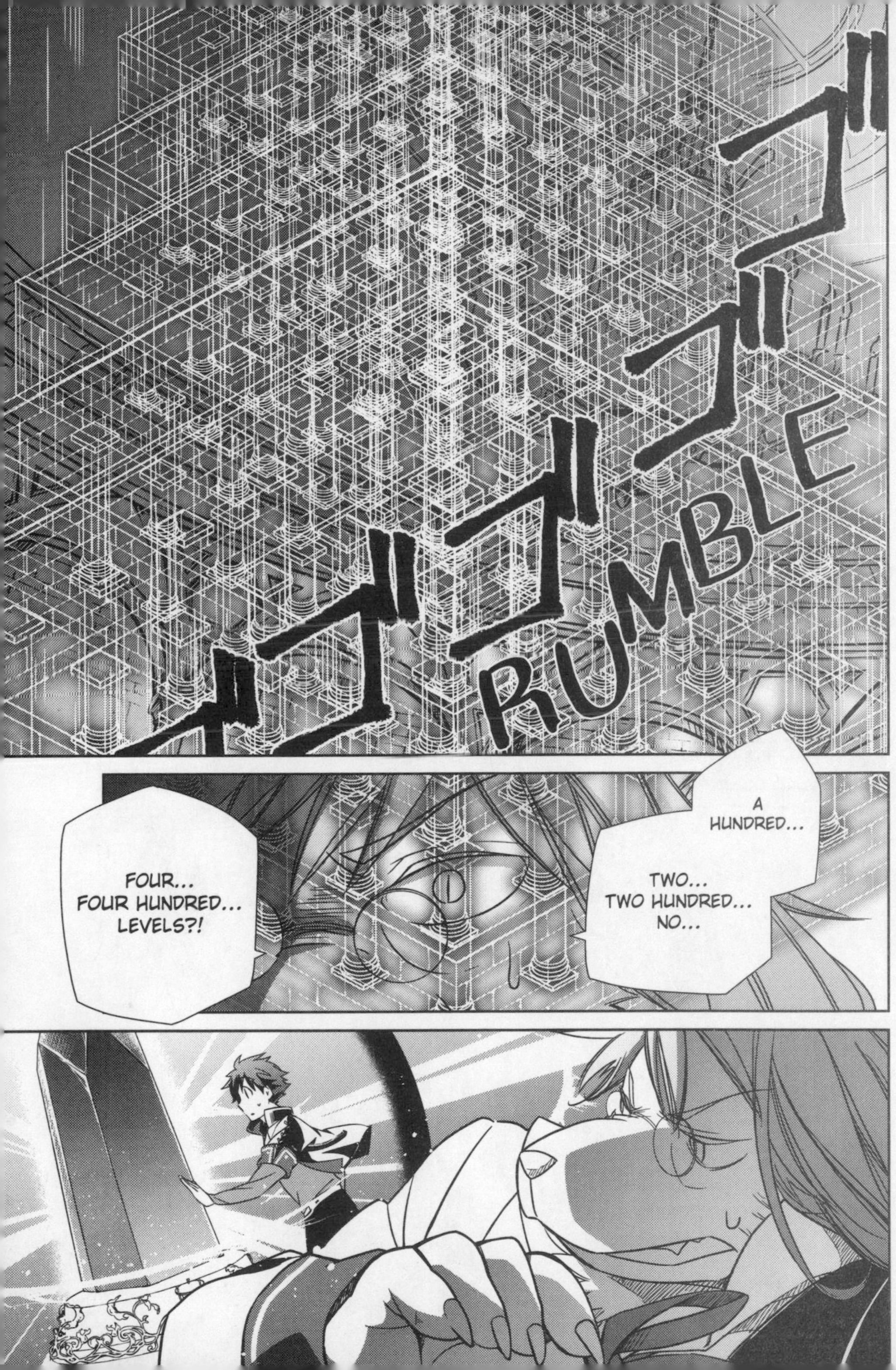
RUMBLE
A HUNDRED...
TWO... TWO HUNDRED... NO...
FOUR... FOUR HUNDRED... LEVELS?!

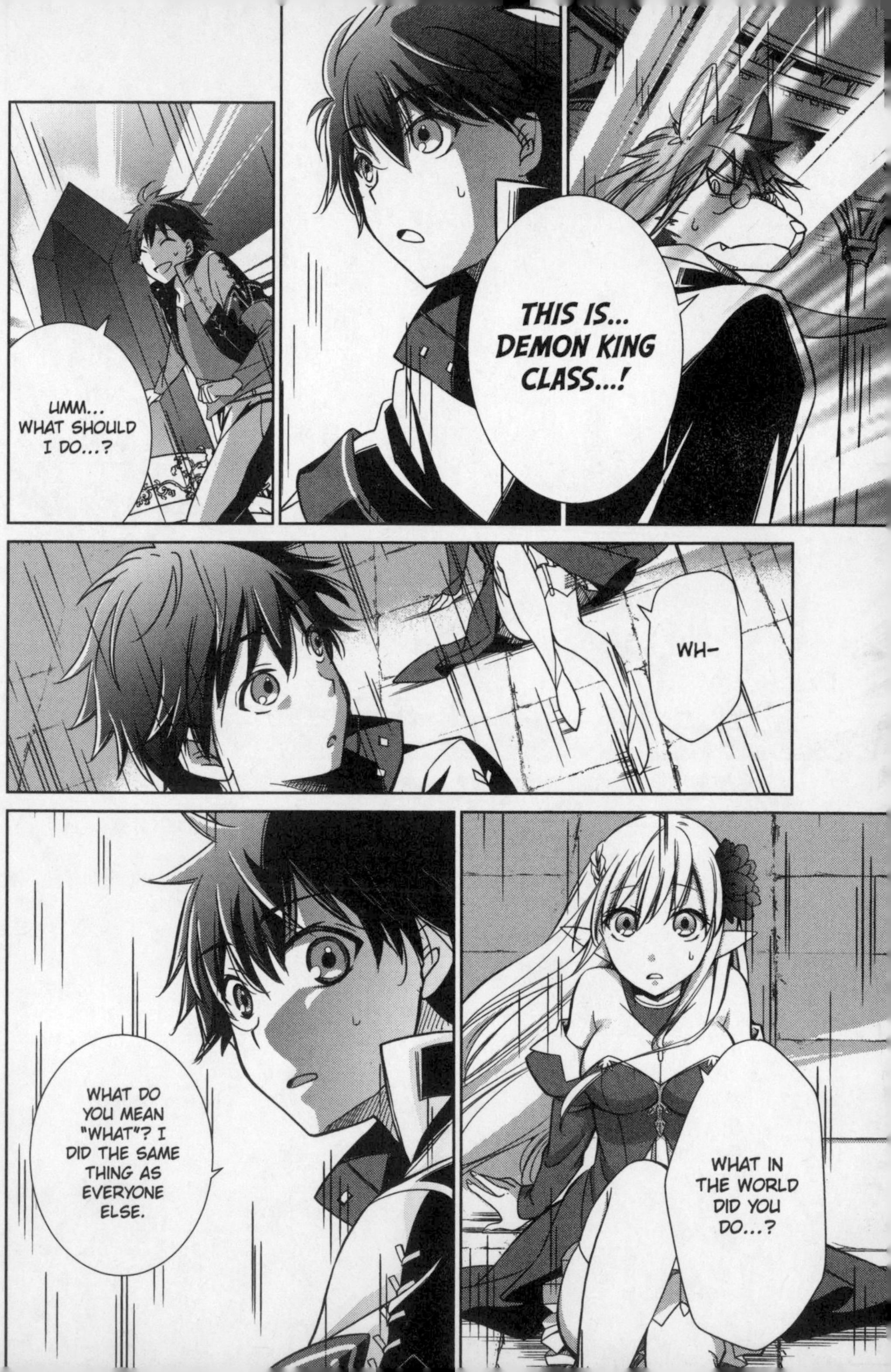
THIS IS... DEMON KING CLASS...!
UMM... WHAT SHOULD I DO...?
WH-
WHAT IN THE WORLD DID YOU DO...?
WHAT DO YOU MEAN "WHAT"? I DID THE SAME THING AS EVERYONE ELSE.

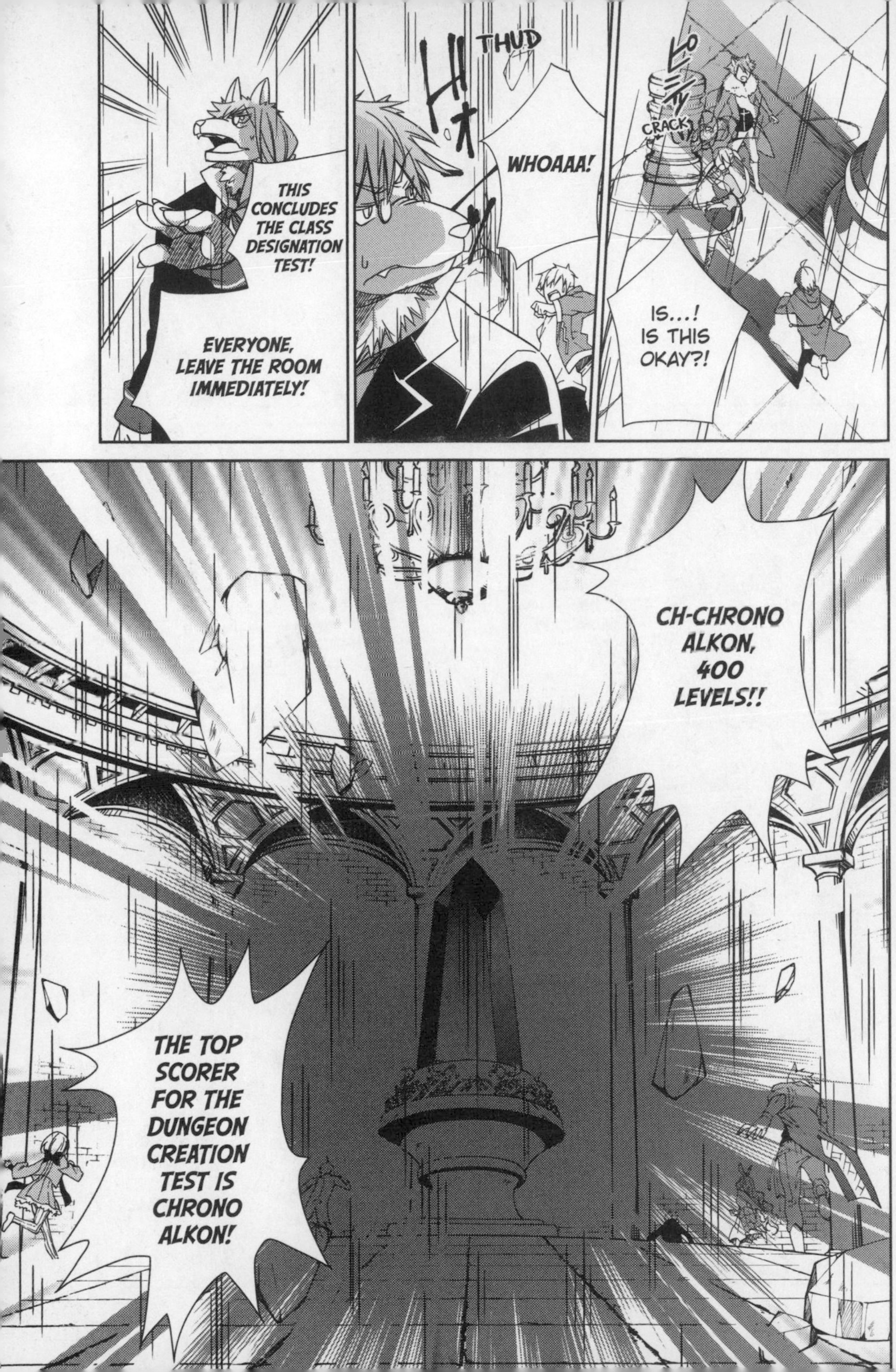
CRACK
IS...! IS THIS OKAY?!
THUD
WHOAAA!
THIS CONCLUDES THE CLASS DESIGNATION TEST!
EVERYONE, LEAVE THE ROOM IMMEDIATELY!
CH-CHRONO ALKON, 400 LEVELS!!
THE TOP SCORER FOR THE DUNGEON CREATION TEST IS CHRONO ALKON!

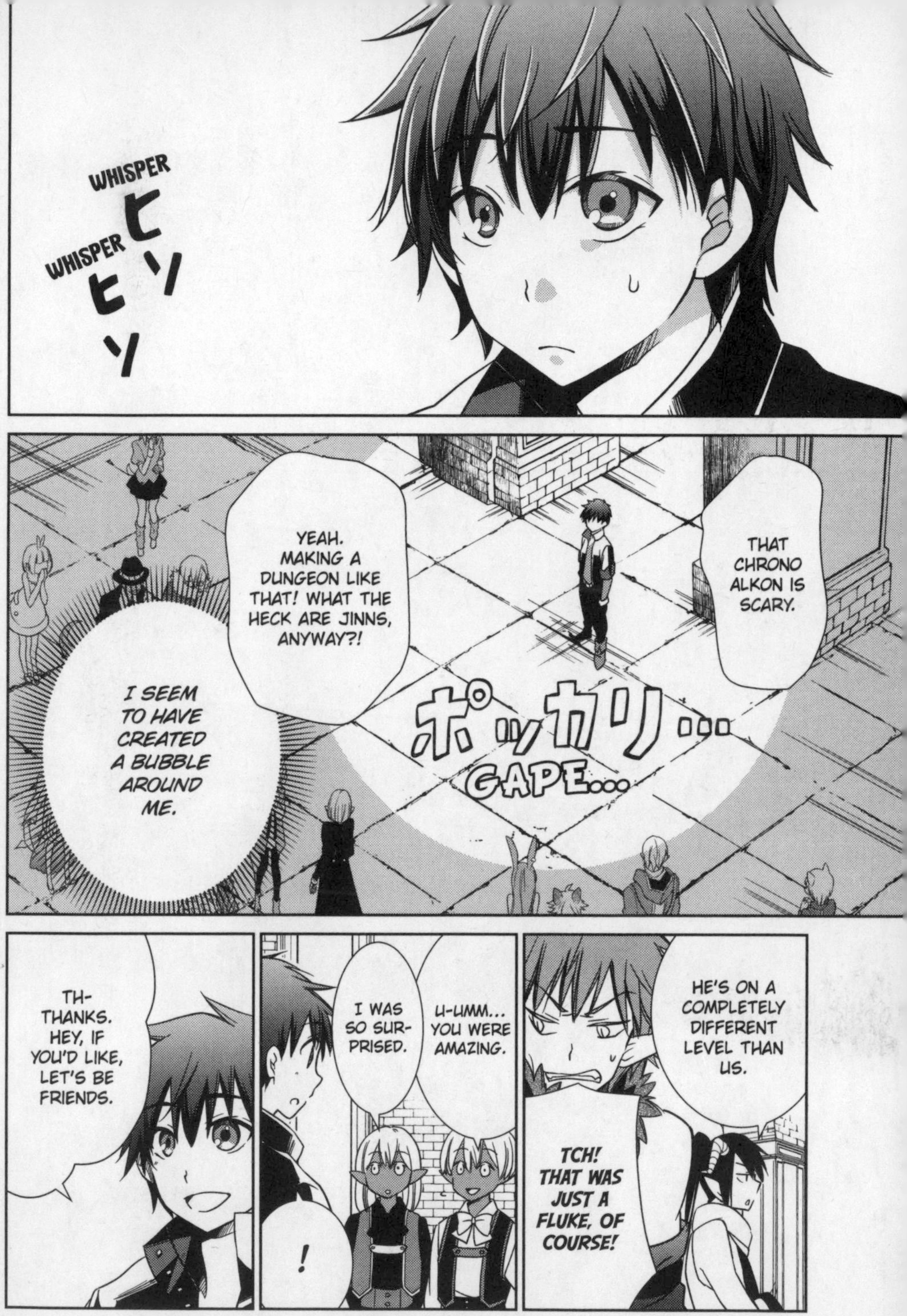
WHISPER
ヒソ
WHISPER
ヒソ
THAT CHRONO ALKON IS SCARY.
YEAH. MAKING A DUNGEON LIKE THAT! WHAT THE HECK ARE JINNS, ANYWAY?!
ポッカリ…
GAPE…
I SEEM TO HAVE CREATED A BUBBLE AROUND ME.
HE'S ON A COMPLETELY DIFFERENT LEVEL THAN US.
TCH! THAT WAS JUST A FLUKE, OF COURSE!
U-UMM… YOU WERE AMAZING.
I WAS SO SUR-PRISED.
!
TH-THANKS. HEY, IF YOU'D LIKE, LET'S BE FRIENDS.

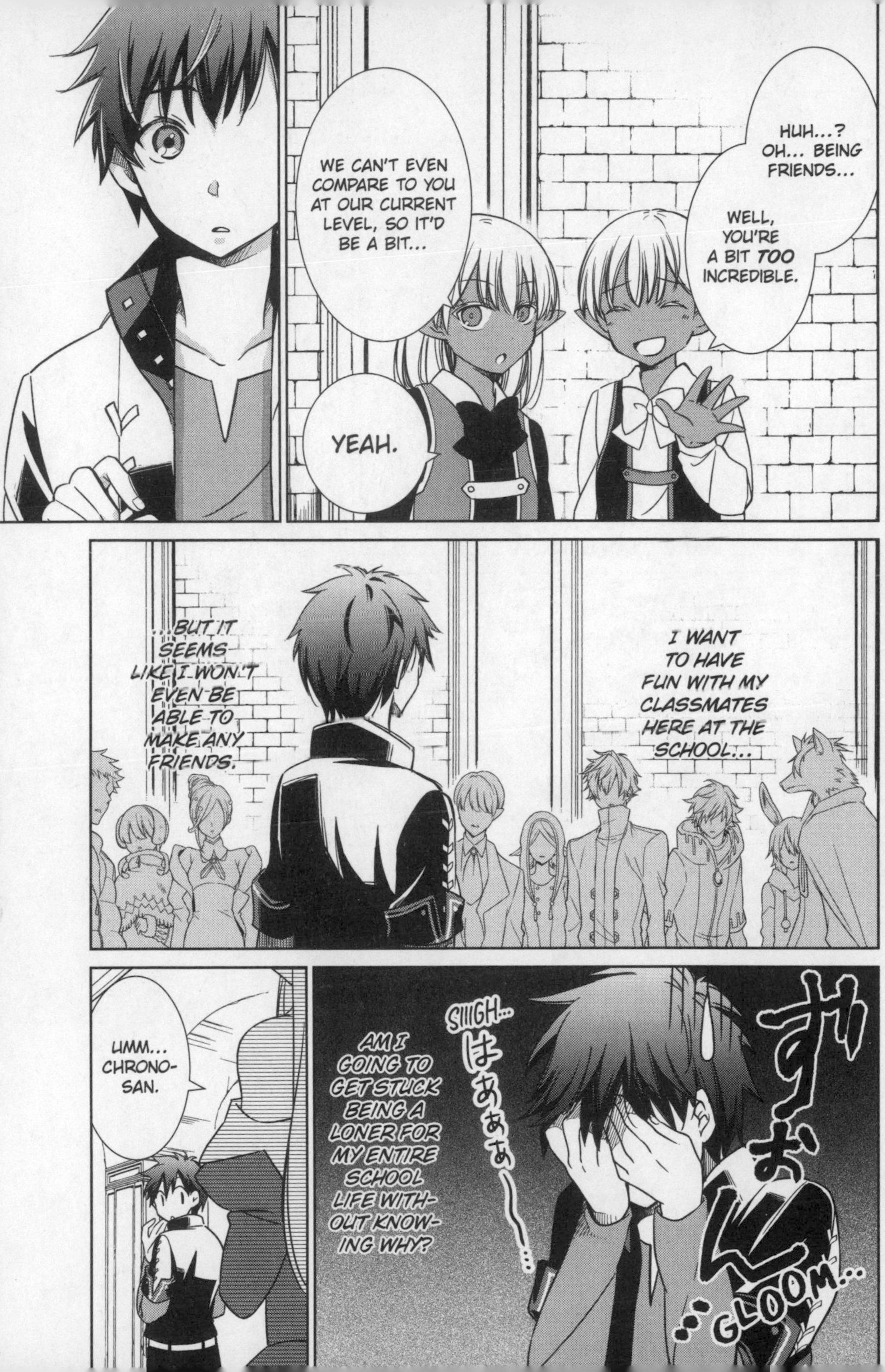
HUH...? OH... BEING FRIENDS...
WELL, YOU'RE A BIT *TOO* INCREDIBLE.
WE CAN'T EVEN COMPARE TO YOU AT OUR CURRENT LEVEL, SO IT'D BE A BIT...
YEAH.
I WANT TO HAVE FUN WITH MY CLASSMATES HERE AT THE SCHOOL...
...BUT IT SEEMS LIKE I WON'T EVEN BE ABLE TO MAKE ANY FRIENDS.
...GLOOM...
SIIIGH...
AM I GOING TO GET STUCK BEING A LONER FOR MY ENTIRE SCHOOL LIFE WITHOUT KNOWING WHY?
UMM... CHRONO-SAN.

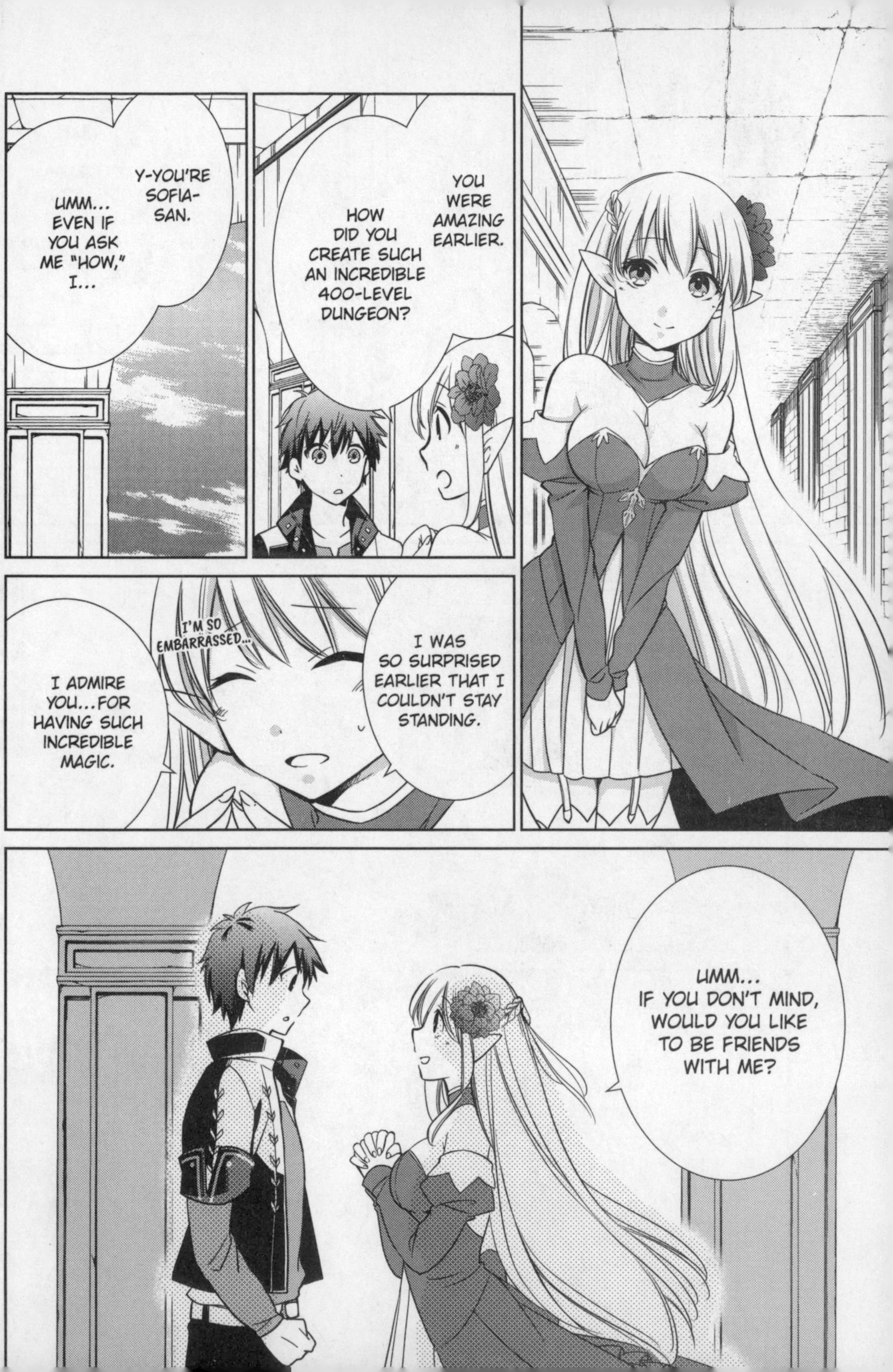
YOU WERE AMAZING EARLIER.
HOW DID YOU CREATE SUCH AN INCREDIBLE 400-LEVEL DUNGEON?
Y-YOU'RE SOFIA-SAN.
UMM... EVEN IF YOU ASK ME "HOW," I...
I WAS SO SURPRISED EARLIER THAT I COULDN'T STAY STANDING.
I'M SO EMBARRASSED...
I ADMIRE YOU...FOR HAVING SUCH INCREDIBLE MAGIC.
UMM... IF YOU DON'T MIND, WOULD YOU LIKE TO BE FRIENDS WITH ME?

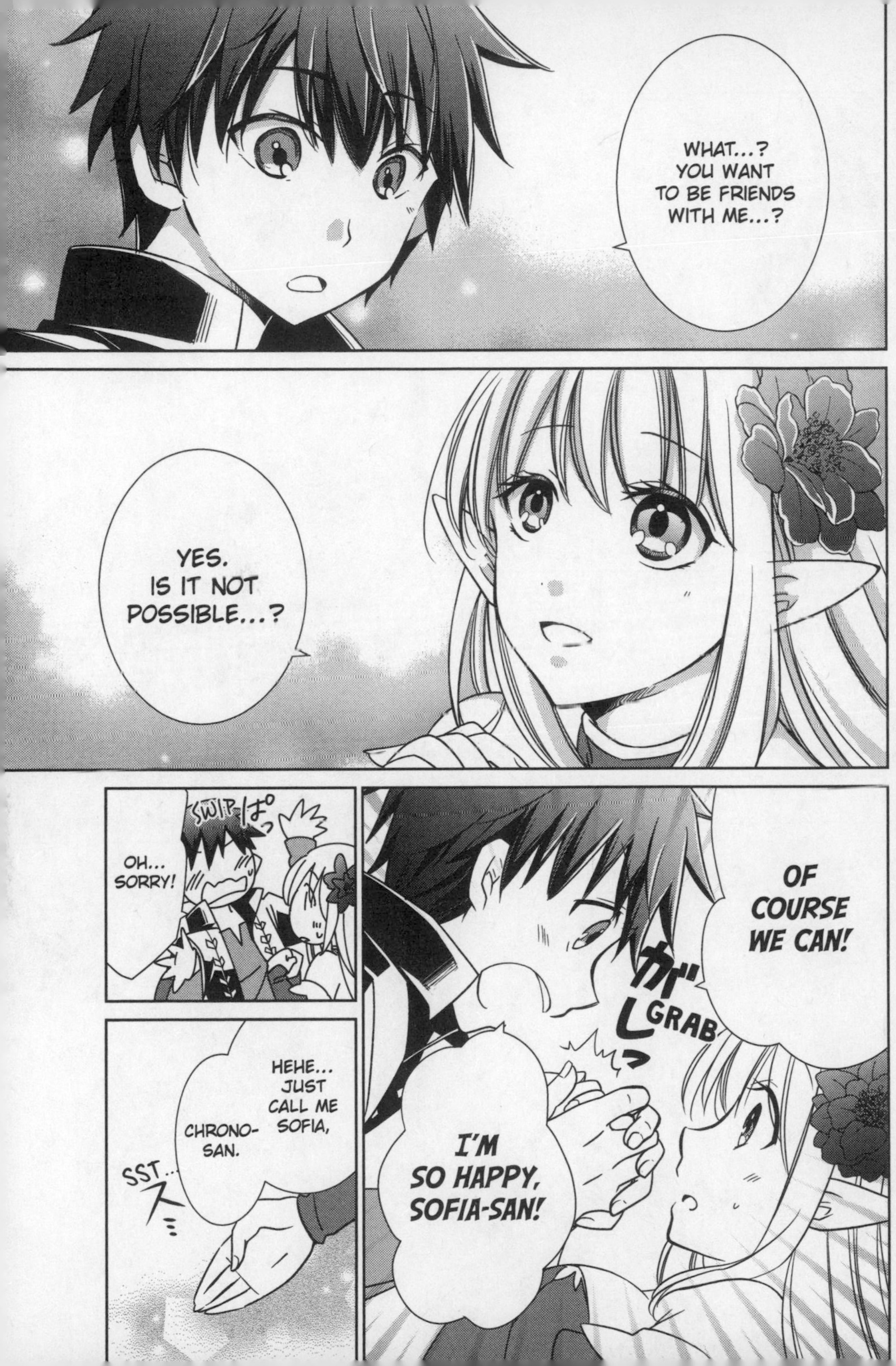
WHAT...? YOU WANT TO BE FRIENDS WITH ME...?
YES. IS IT NOT POSSIBLE...?
OF COURSE WE CAN!
がし GRAB
I'M SO HAPPY, SOFIA-SAN!
SWIP ぱっ
OH... SORRY!
HEHE... JUST CALL ME SOFIA,
CHRONO-SAN.
SST... ス

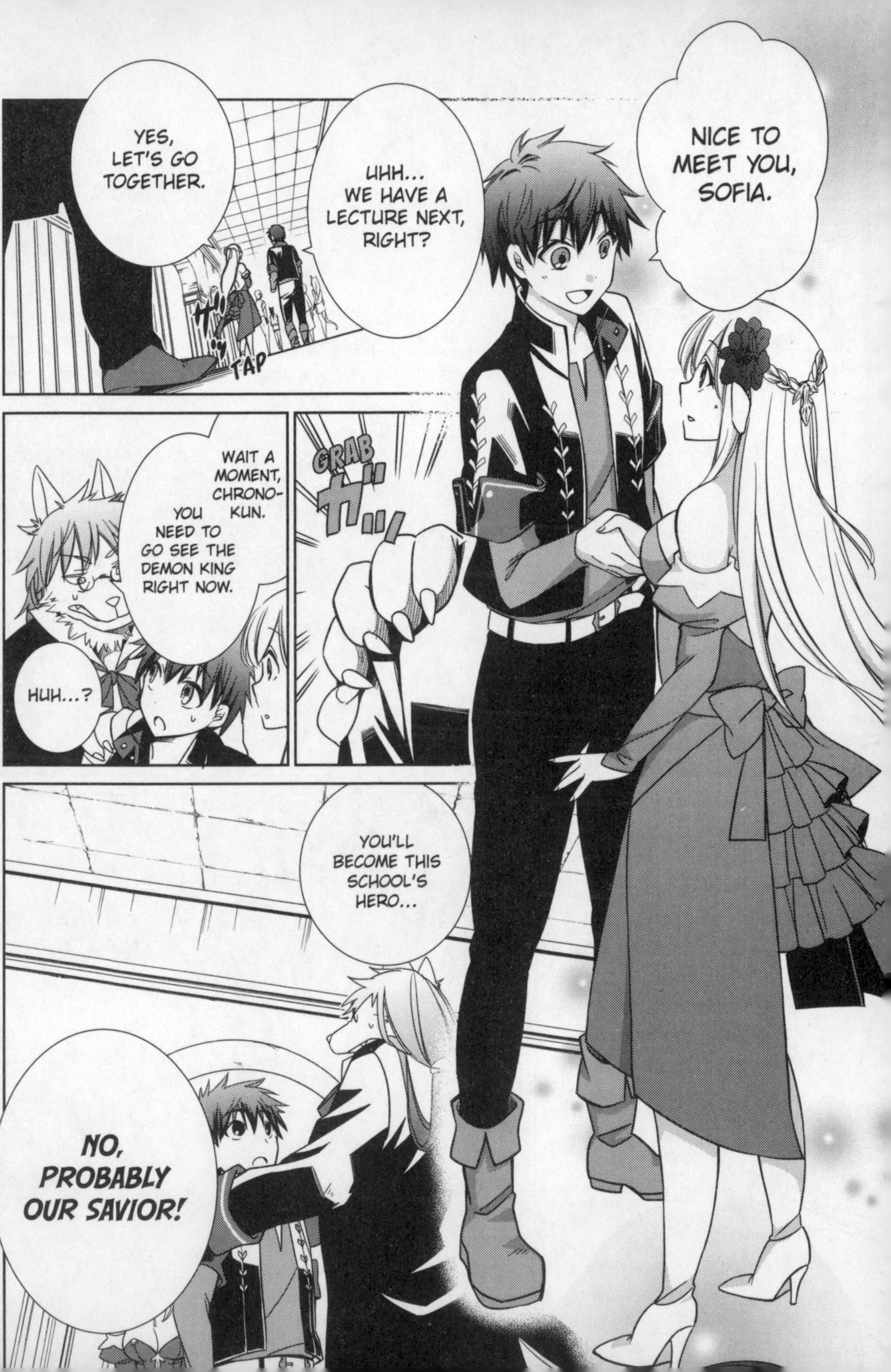
NICE TO MEET YOU, SOFIA.
UHH... WE HAVE A LECTURE NEXT, RIGHT?
YES, LET'S GO TOGETHER.
TAP
GRAB
WAIT A MOMENT, CHRONO-KUN. YOU NEED TO GO SEE THE DEMON KING RIGHT NOW.
HUH...?
YOU'LL BECOME THIS SCHOOL'S HERO...
NO, PROBABLY OUR SAVIOR!

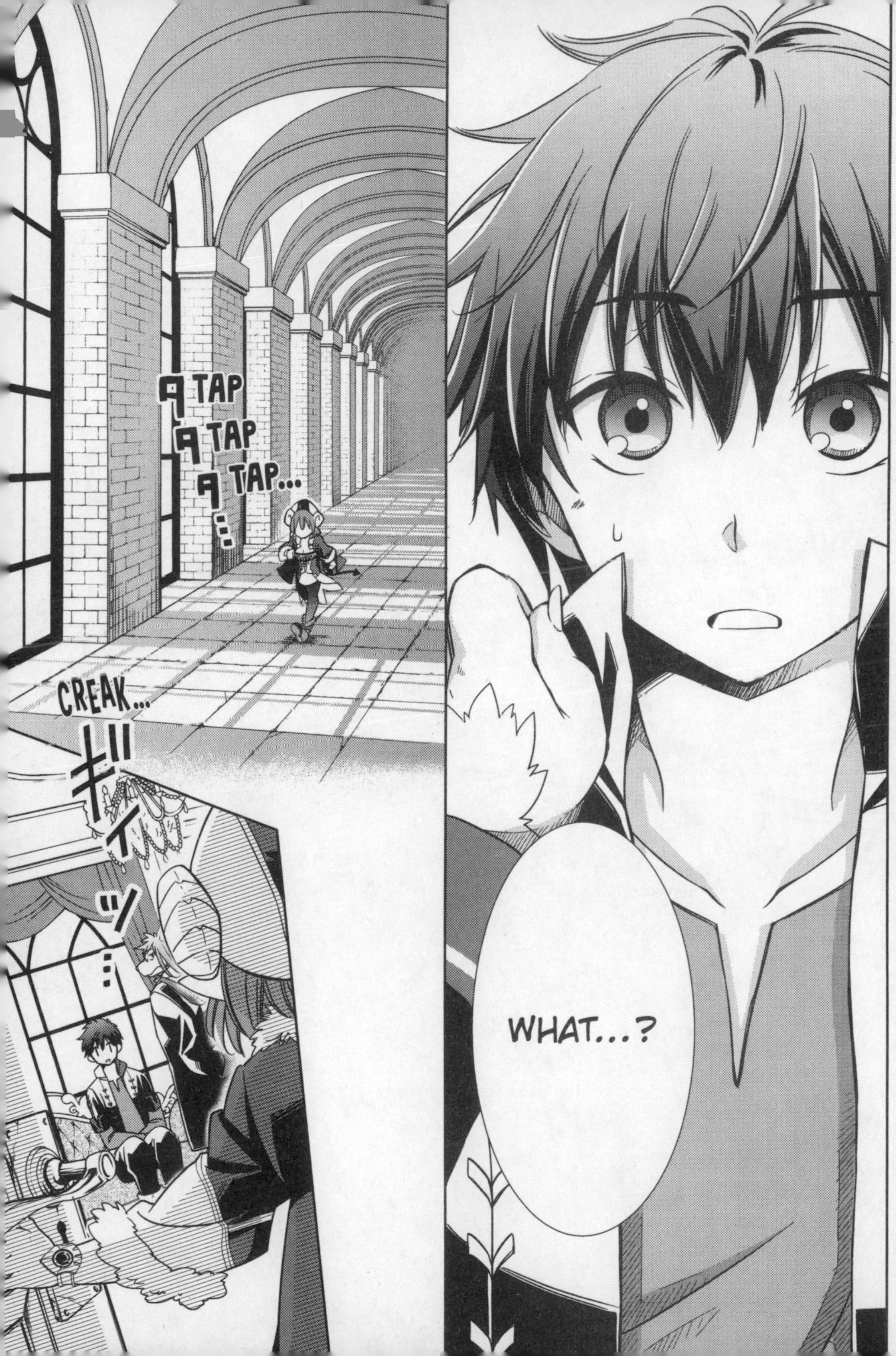
WHAT...?
TAP
TAP
TAP...
CREAK...

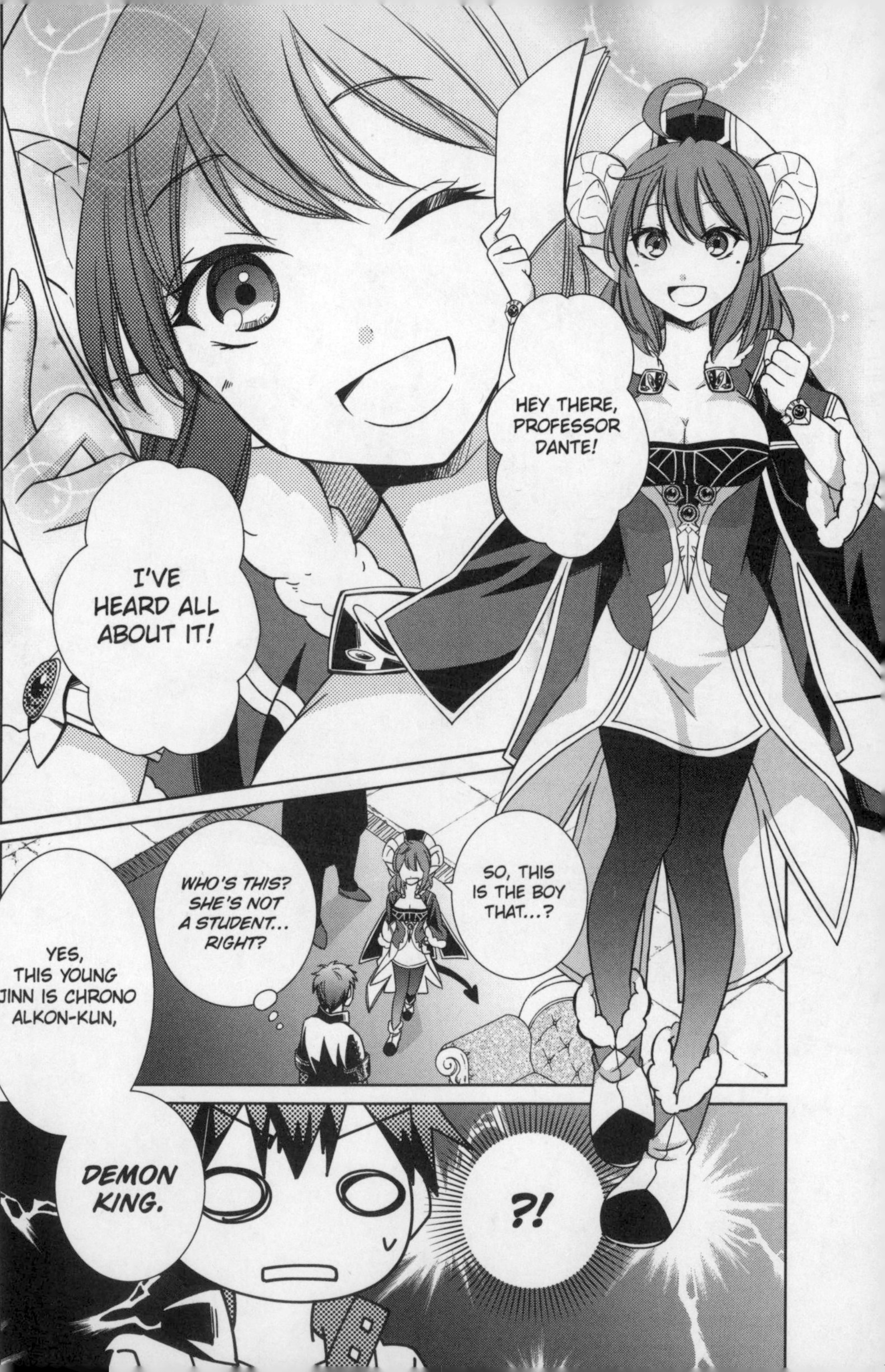
HEY THERE, PROFESSOR DANTE!
I'VE HEARD ALL ABOUT IT!
SO, THIS IS THE BOY THAT...?
WHO'S THIS? SHE'S NOT A STUDENT... RIGHT?
YES, THIS YOUNG JINN IS CHRONO ALKON-KUN,
DEMON KING.
?!

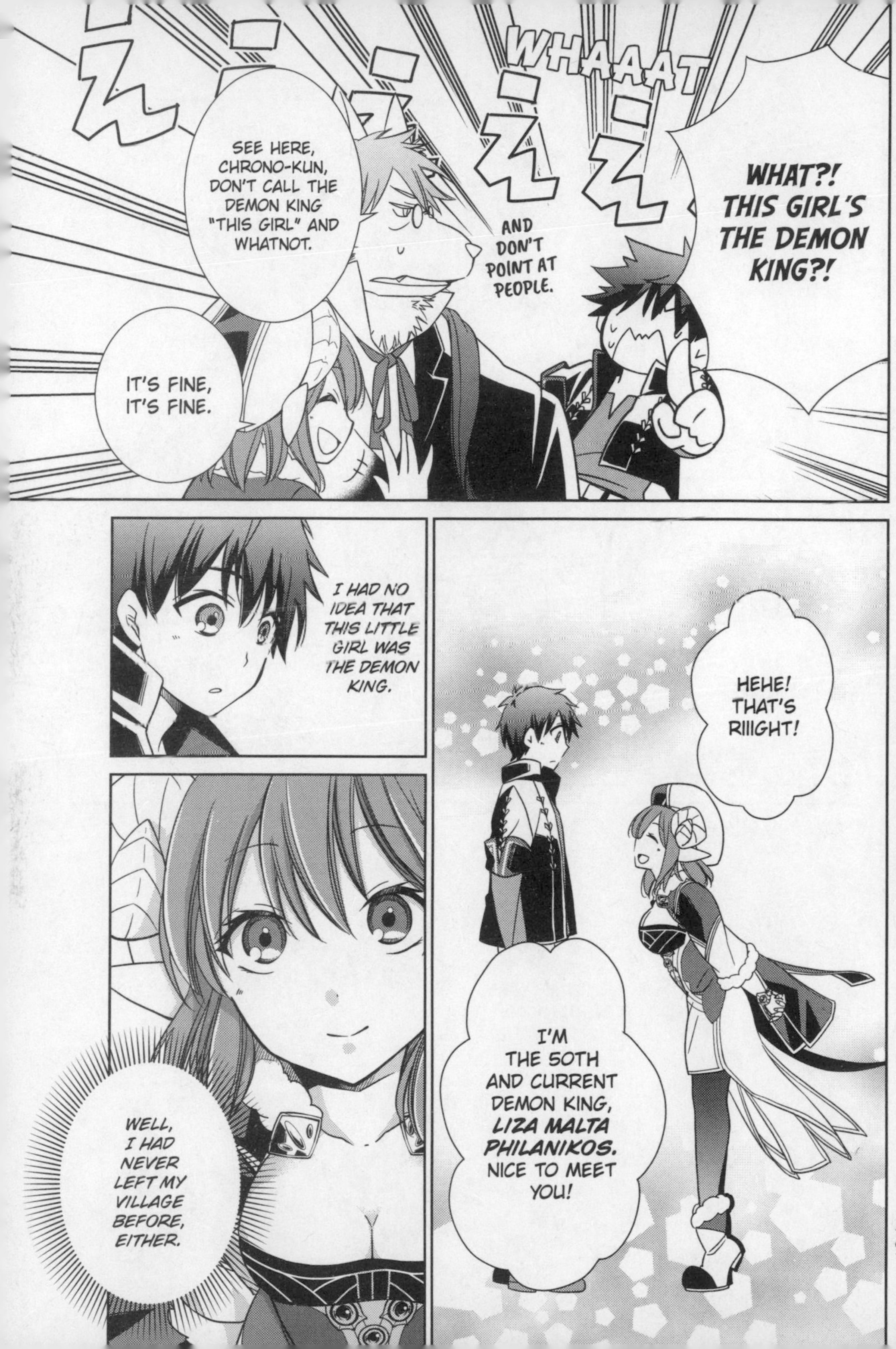
WHAT?! THIS GIRL'S THE DEMON KING?!
WHAAAT
AND DON'T POINT AT PEOPLE.
SEE HERE, CHRONO-KUN, DON'T CALL THE DEMON KING "THIS GIRL" AND WHATNOT.
IT'S FINE, IT'S FINE.
HEHE! THAT'S RIIIGHT!
I'M THE 50TH AND CURRENT DEMON KING, LIZA MALTA PHILANIKOS. NICE TO MEET YOU!
I HAD NO IDEA THAT THIS LITTLE GIRL WAS THE DEMON KING.
WELL, I HAD NEVER LEFT MY VILLAGE BEFORE, EITHER.

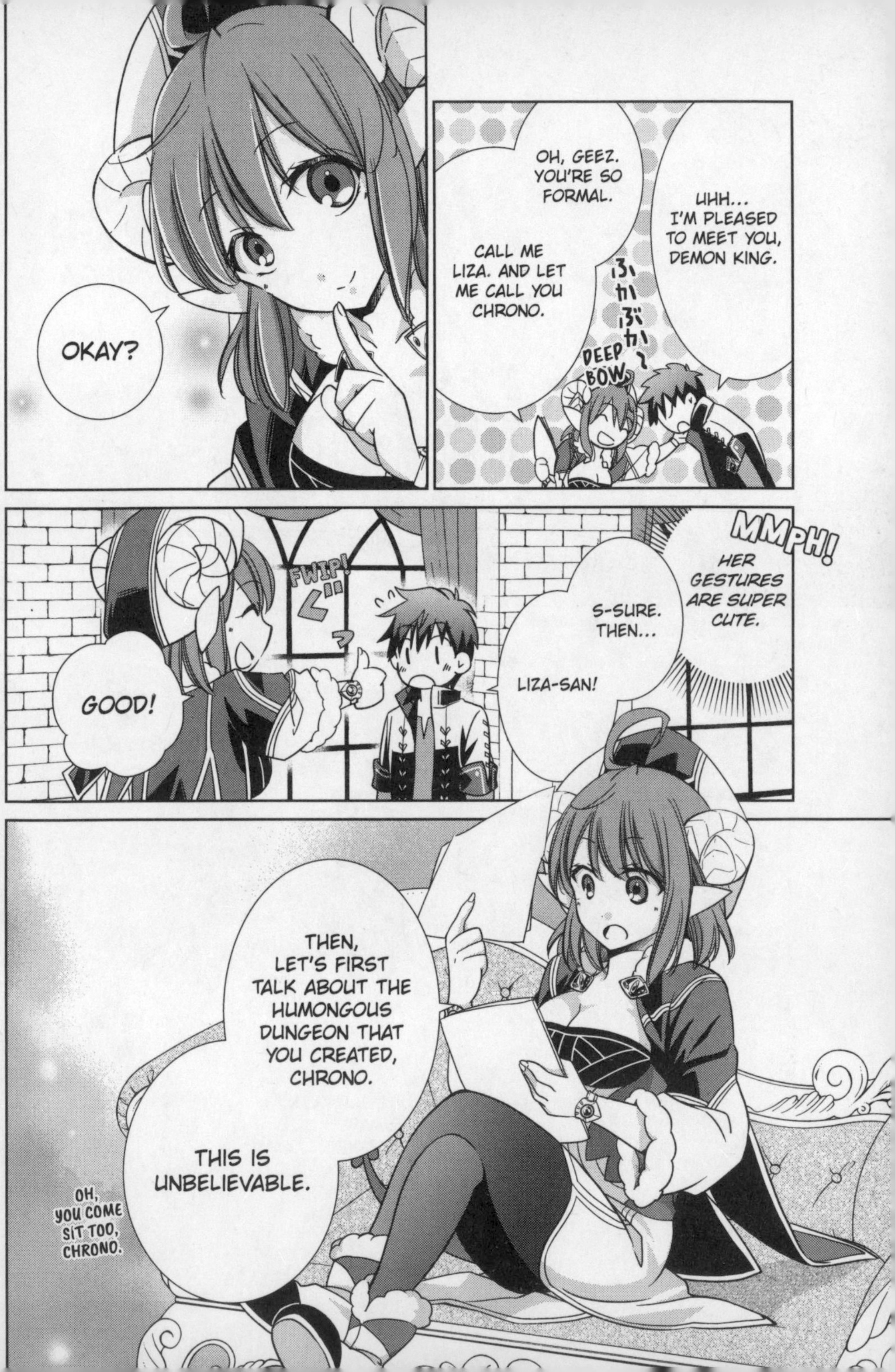
UHH... I'M PLEASED TO MEET YOU, DEMON KING.
ふかぶか~
DEEP BOW
OH, GEEZ. YOU'RE SO FORMAL.
CALL ME LIZA. AND LET ME CALL YOU CHRONO.
OKAY?
MMPH!
HER GESTURES ARE SUPER CUTE.
S-SURE. THEN...
LIZA-SAN!
FWIP!
GOOD!
THEN, LET'S FIRST TALK ABOUT THE HUMONGOUS DUNGEON THAT YOU CREATED, CHRONO.
THIS IS UNBELIEVABLE.
OH, YOU COME SIT TOO, CHRONO.

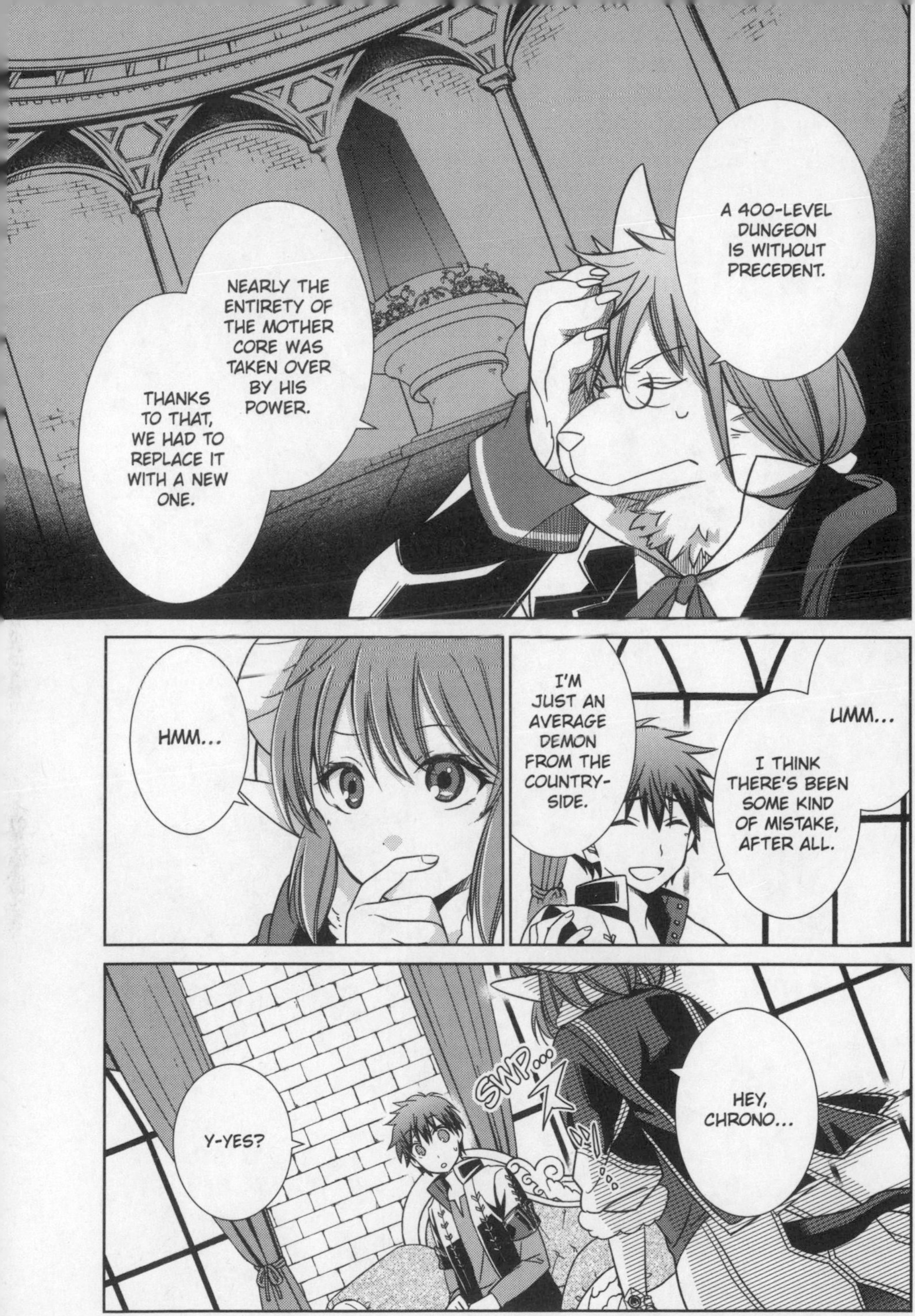
A 400-LEVEL DUNGEON IS WITHOUT PRECEDENT.
NEARLY THE ENTIRETY OF THE MOTHER CORE WAS TAKEN OVER BY HIS POWER.
THANKS TO THAT, WE HAD TO REPLACE IT WITH A NEW ONE.
UMM...
I THINK THERE'S BEEN SOME KIND OF MISTAKE, AFTER ALL.
I'M JUST AN AVERAGE DEMON FROM THE COUNTRY-SIDE.
HMM...
HEY, CHRONO...
SWP...
Y-YES?

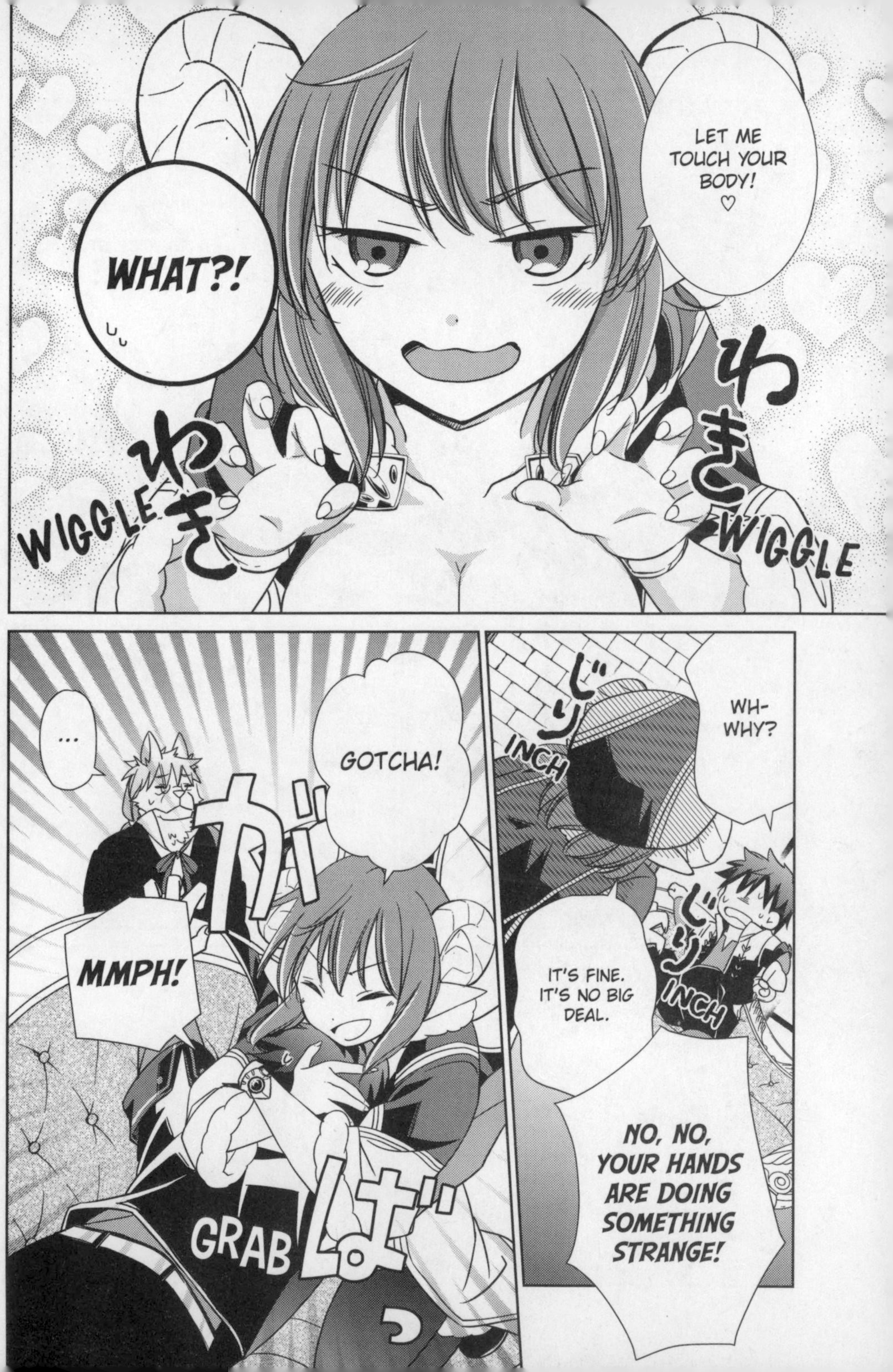

LET ME TOUCH YOUR BODY! ♡
WHAT?!
わき
WIGGLE
わき
WIGGLE
WH- WHY?
じり
INCH
IT'S FINE. IT'S NO BIG DEAL.
じり
INCH
NO, NO, YOUR HANDS ARE DOING SOMETHING STRANGE!
GOTCHA!
...
MMPH!
GRAB

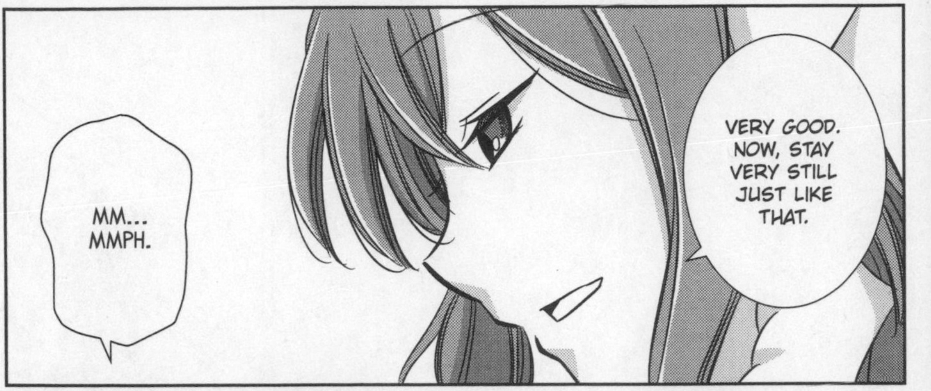
VERY GOOD. NOW, STAY VERY STILL JUST LIKE THAT.
MM... MMPH.

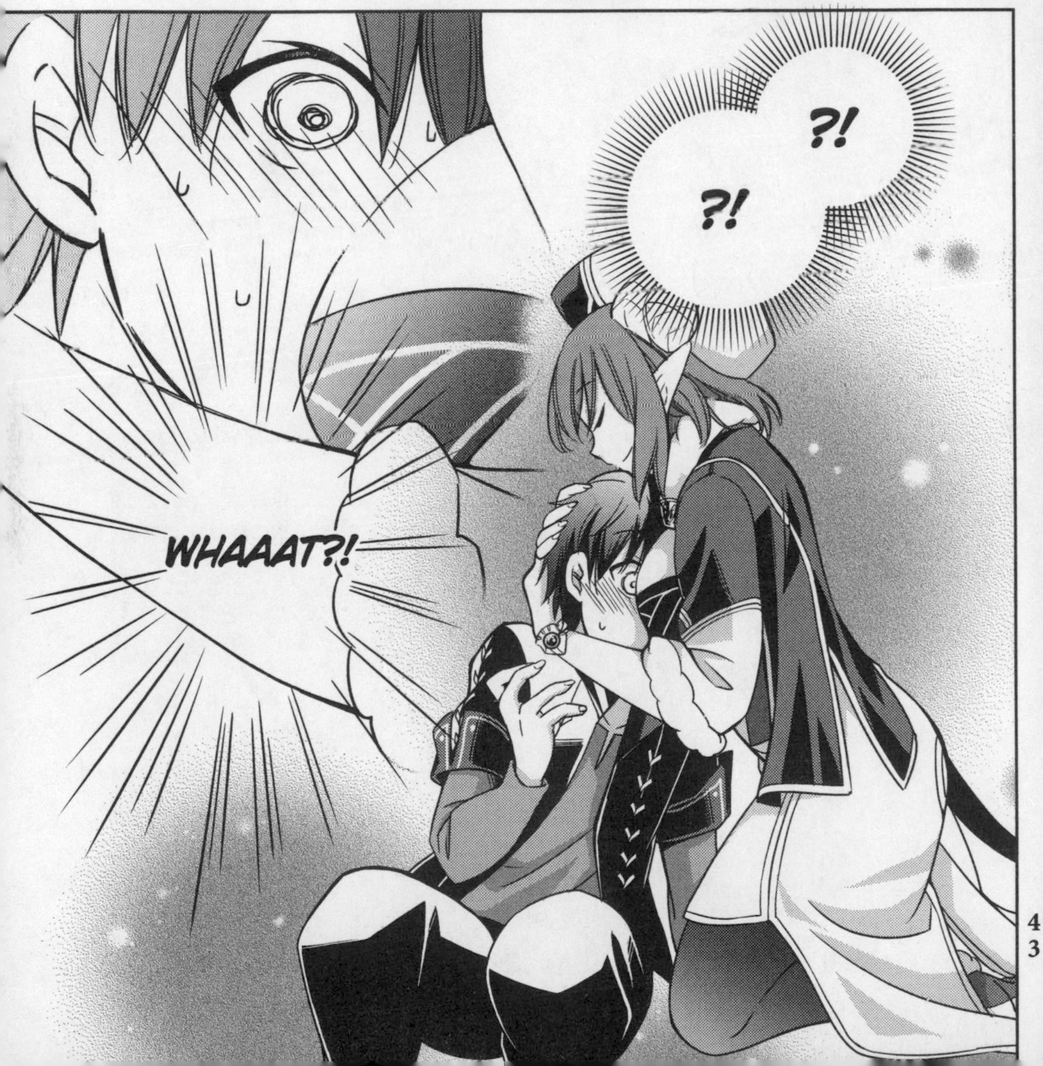
?!
?!
WHAAAT?!

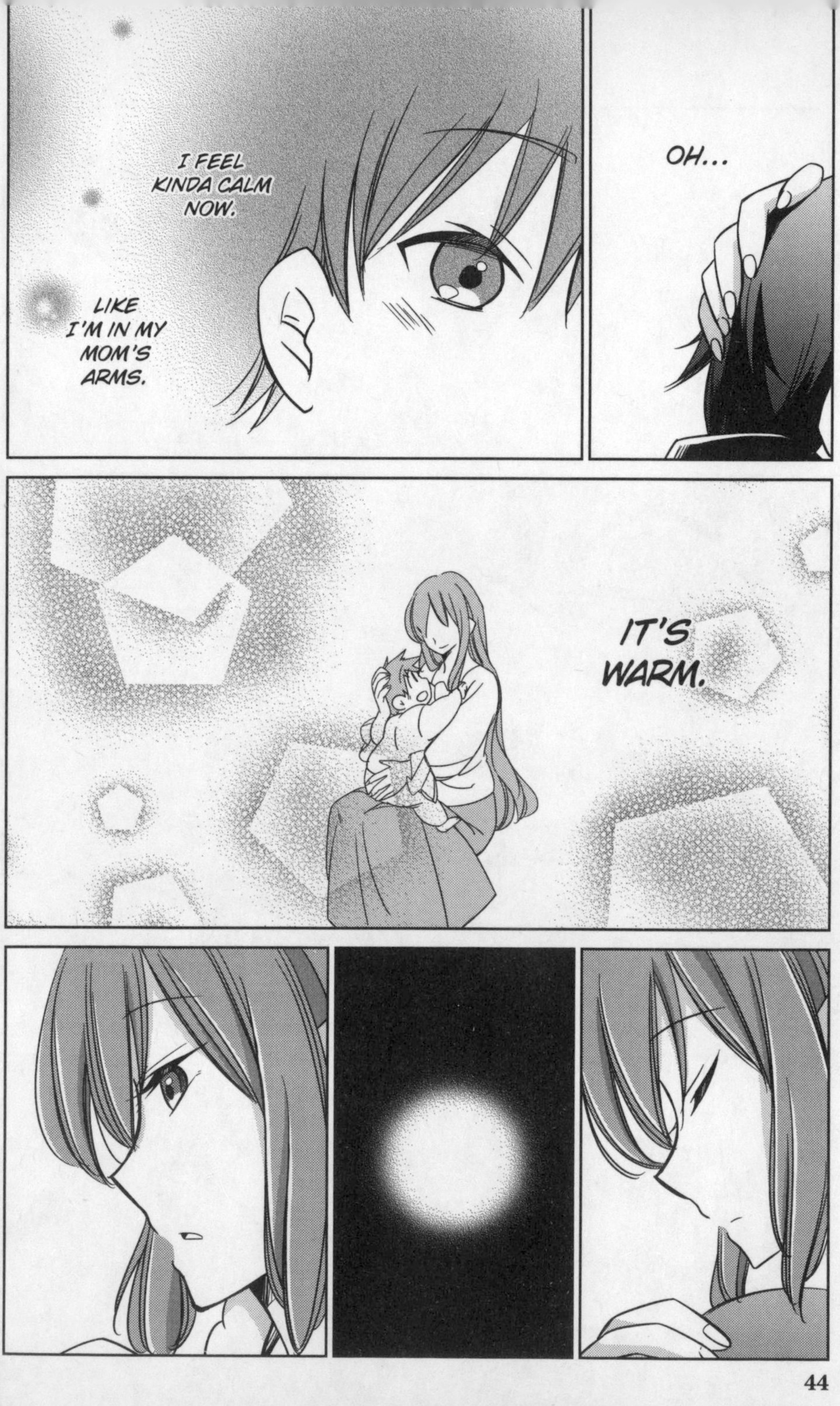
OH...
I FEEL KINDA CALM NOW.
LIKE I'M IN MY MOM'S ARMS.
IT'S WARM.

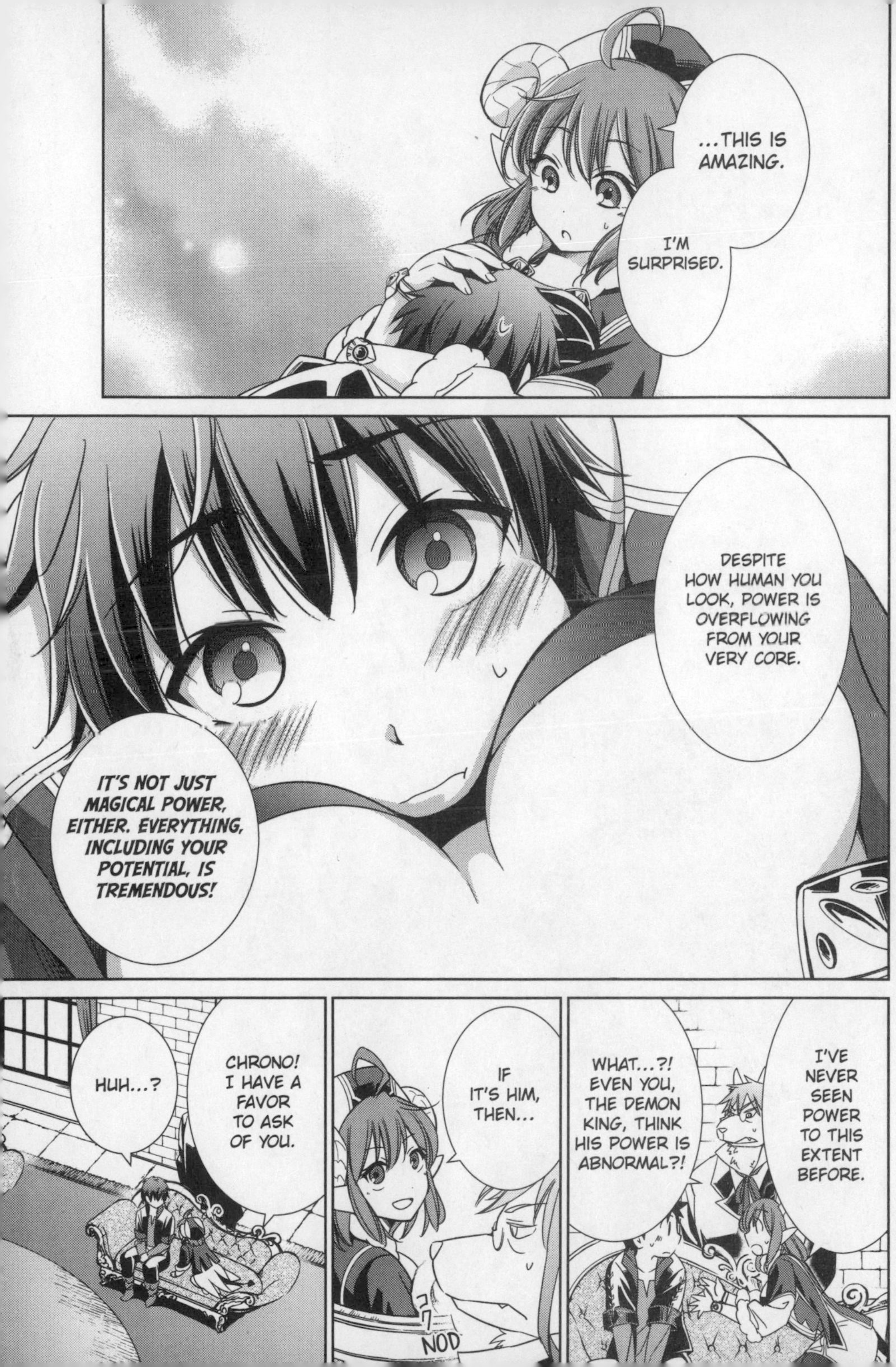
...THIS IS AMAZING.
I'M SURPRISED.
DESPITE HOW HUMAN YOU LOOK, POWER IS OVERFLOWING FROM YOUR VERY CORE.
IT'S NOT JUST MAGICAL POWER, EITHER. EVERYTHING, INCLUDING YOUR POTENTIAL, IS TREMENDOUS!
I'VE NEVER SEEN POWER TO THIS EXTENT BEFORE.
WHAT...?! EVEN YOU, THE DEMON KING, THINK HIS POWER IS ABNORMAL?!
IF IT'S HIM, THEN...
NOD
CHRONO! I HAVE A FAVOR TO ASK OF YOU.
HUH...?

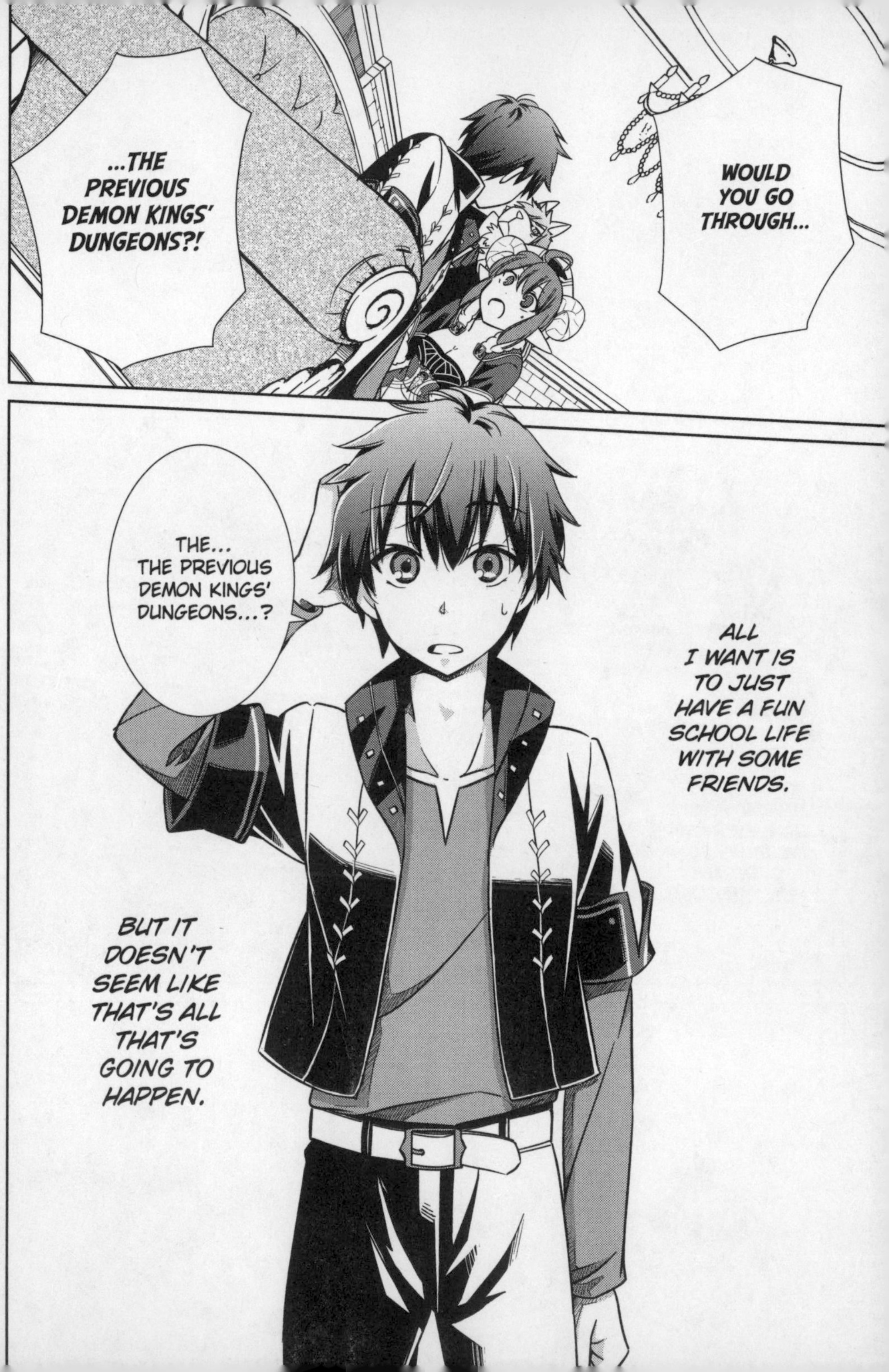
WOULD YOU GO THROUGH...
...THE PREVIOUS DEMON KINGS' DUNGEONS?!
THE... THE PREVIOUS DEMON KINGS' DUNGEONS...?
ALL I WANT IS TO JUST HAVE A FUN SCHOOL LIFE WITH SOME FRIENDS.
BUT IT DOESN'T SEEM LIKE THAT'S ALL THAT'S GOING TO HAPPEN.

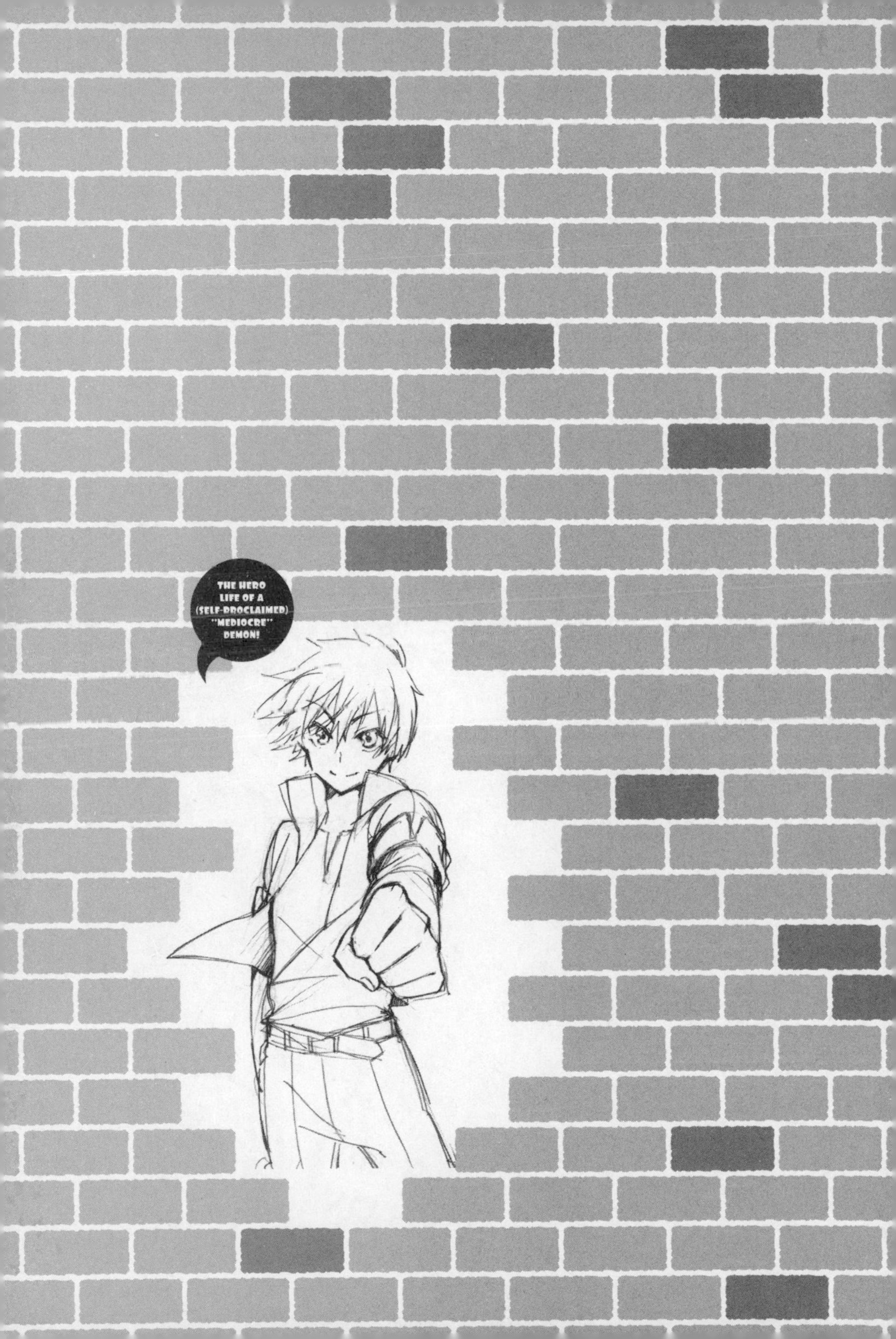
THE HERO LIFE OF A (SELF-PROCLAIMED) "MEDIOCRE" DEMON!

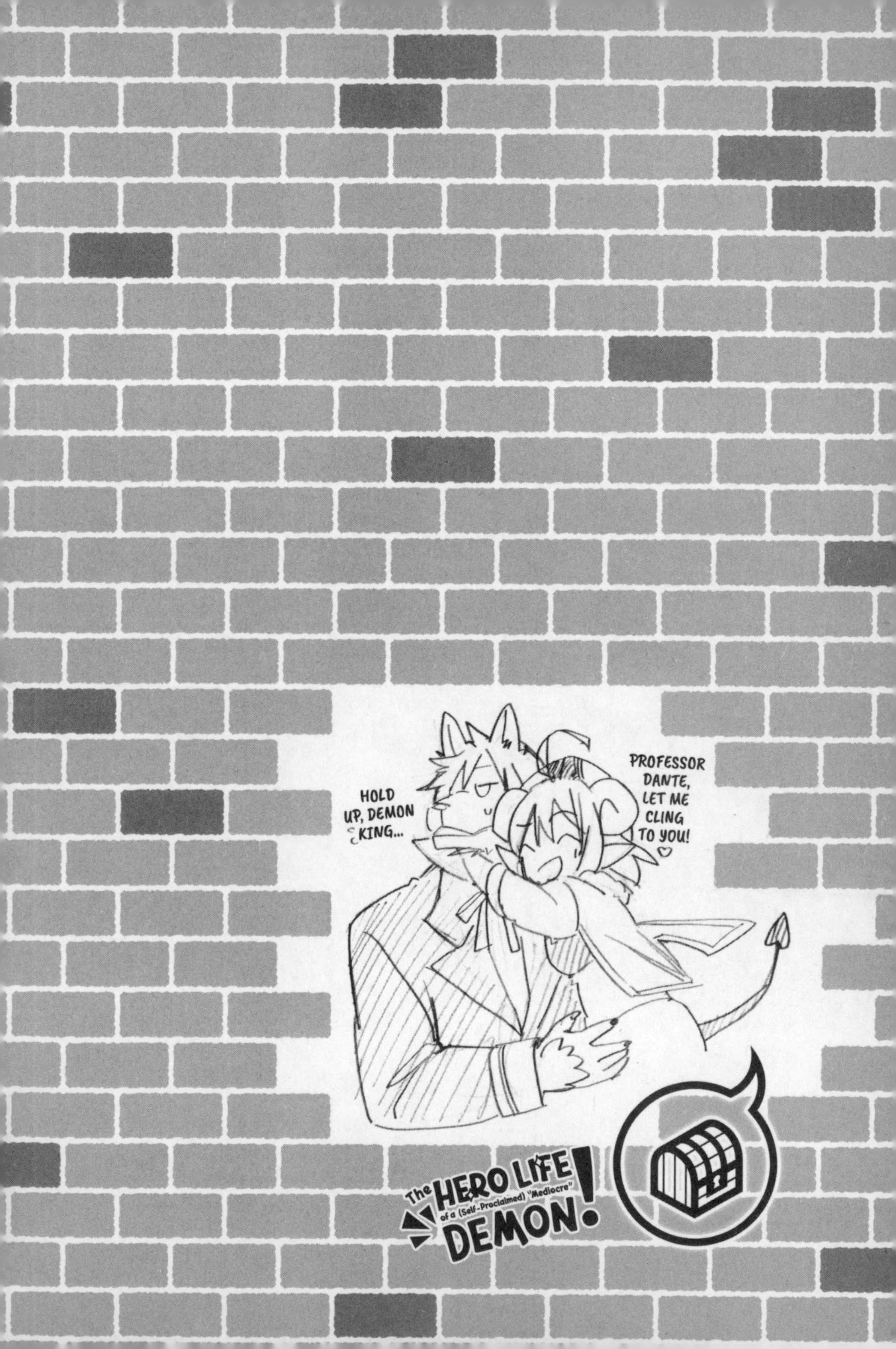
PROFESSOR DANTE, LET ME CLING TO YOU!
HOLD UP, DEMON KING...
The HERO LIFE of a (Self-Proclaimed) "Mediocre" DEMON!

CHAPTER 2 CHRONO JOINS AN EXPLORATION PARTY

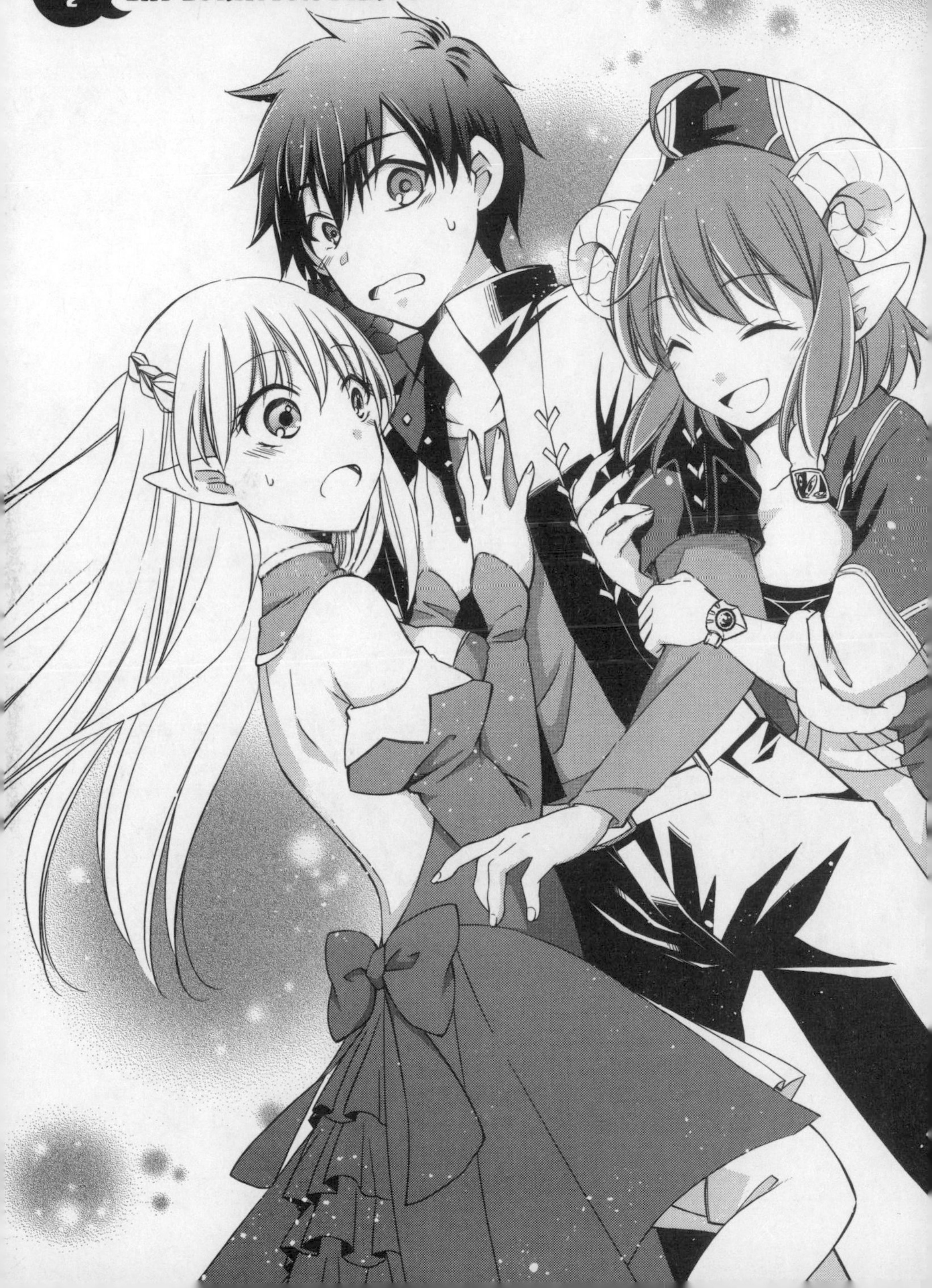

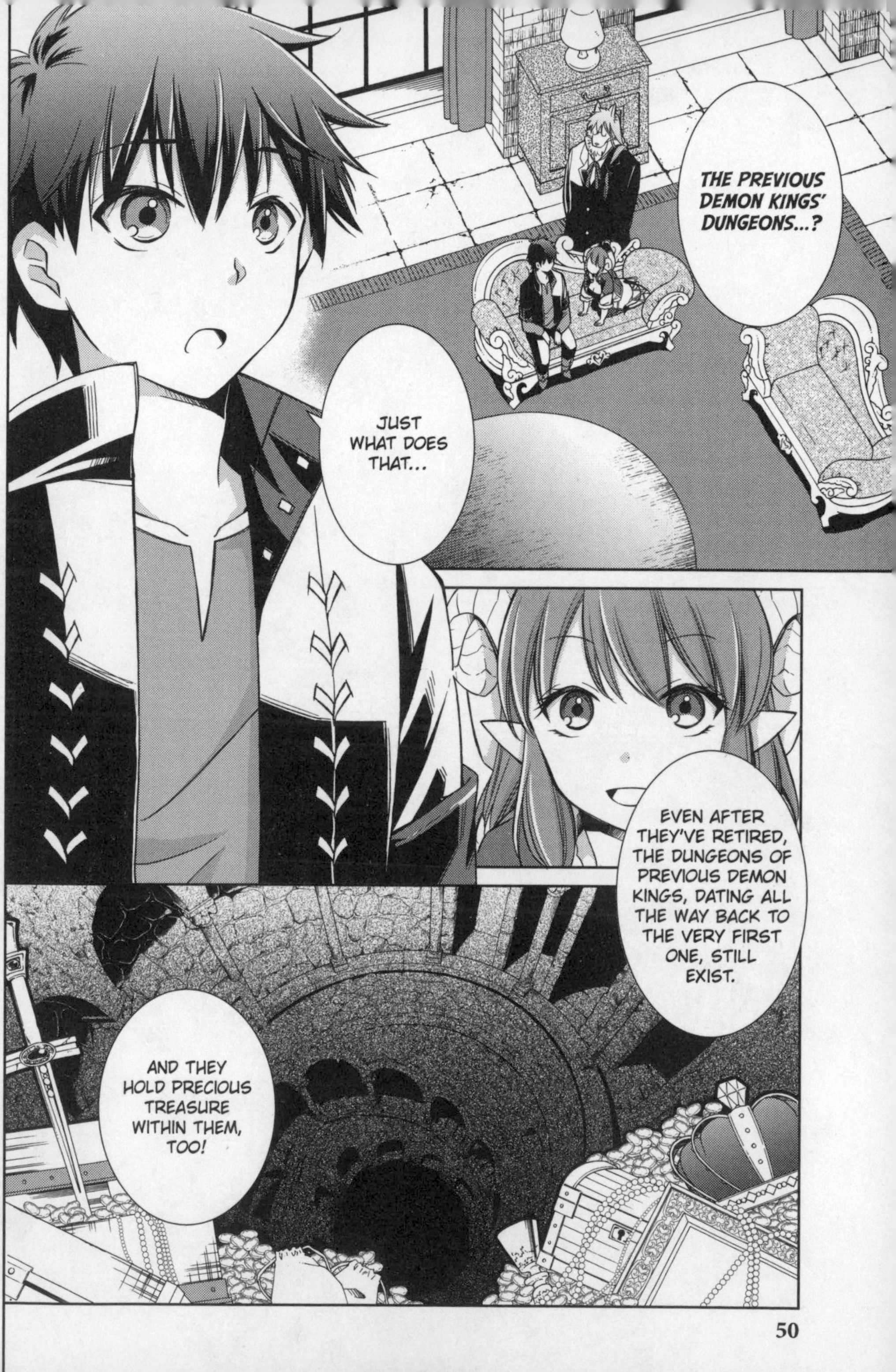

THE PREVIOUS DEMON KINGS' DUNGEONS...?
JUST WHAT DOES THAT...
EVEN AFTER THEY'VE RETIRED, THE DUNGEONS OF PREVIOUS DEMON KINGS, DATING ALL THE WAY BACK TO THE VERY FIRST ONE, STILL EXIST.
AND THEY HOLD PRECIOUS TREASURE WITHIN THEM, TOO!

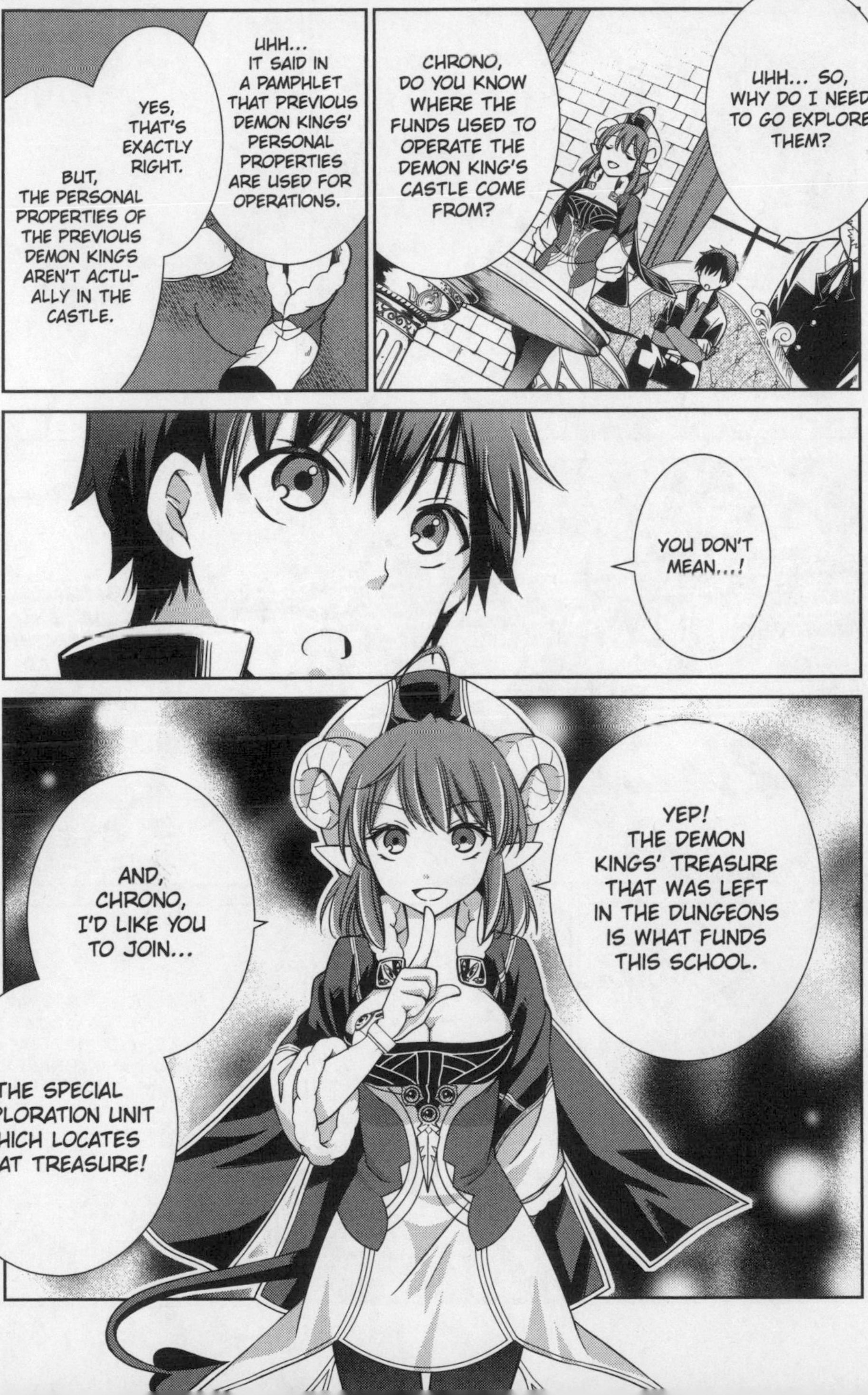
UHH... SO, WHY DO I NEED TO GO EXPLORE THEM?
CHRONO, DO YOU KNOW WHERE THE FUNDS USED TO OPERATE THE DEMON KING'S CASTLE COME FROM?
UHH... IT SAID IN A PAMPHLET THAT PREVIOUS DEMON KINGS' PERSONAL PROPERTIES ARE USED FOR OPERATIONS.
YES, THAT'S EXACTLY RIGHT.
BUT, THE PERSONAL PROPERTIES OF THE PREVIOUS DEMON KINGS AREN'T ACTU-ALLY IN THE CASTLE.
YOU DON'T MEAN...!
YEP! THE DEMON KINGS' TREASURE THAT WAS LEFT IN THE DUNGEONS IS WHAT FUNDS THIS SCHOOL.
AND, CHRONO, I'D LIKE YOU TO JOIN...
THE SPECIAL EXPLORATION UNIT WHICH LOCATES THAT TREASURE!

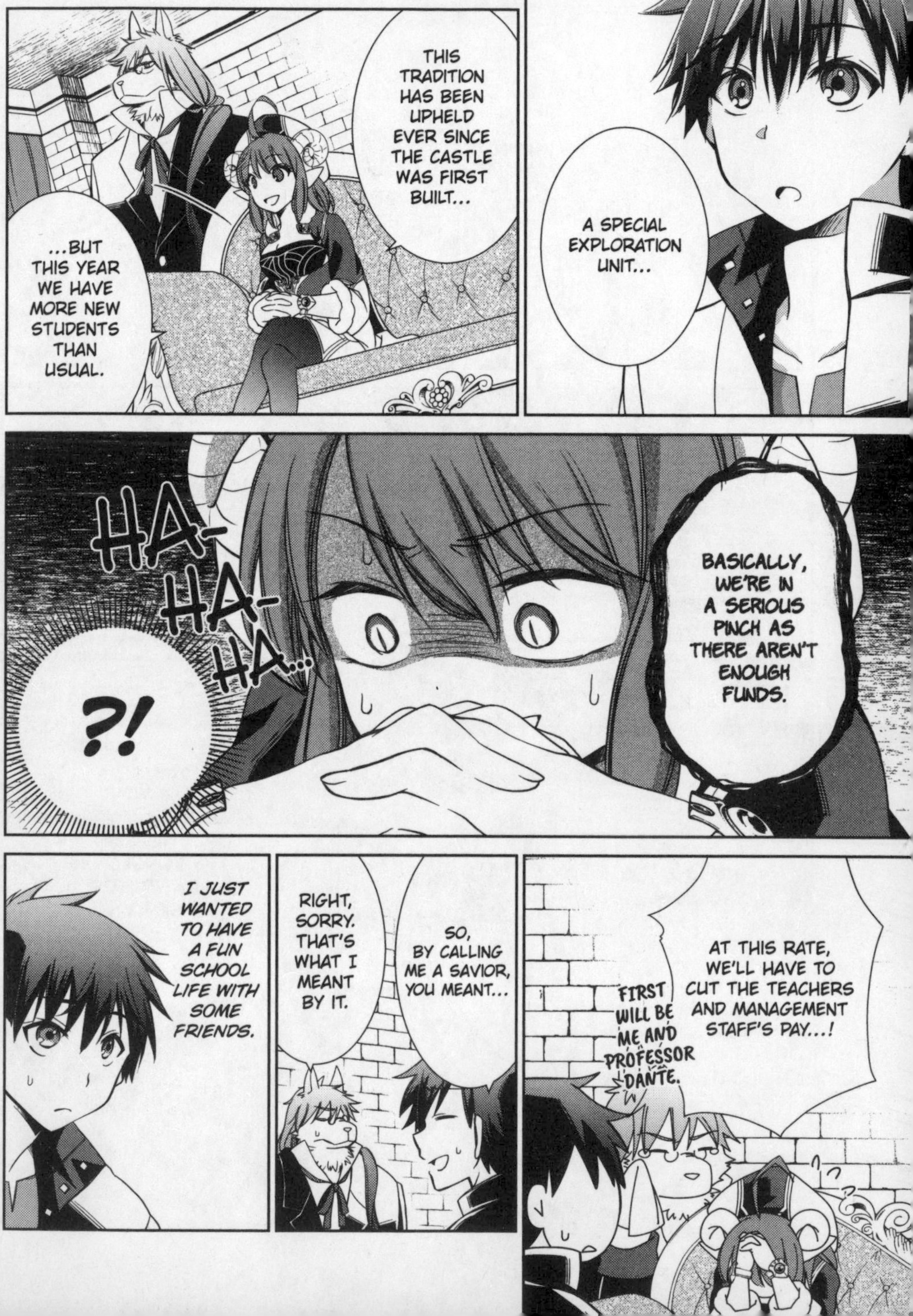
A SPECIAL EXPLORATION UNIT...
THIS TRADITION HAS BEEN UPHELD EVER SINCE THE CASTLE WAS FIRST BUILT...
...BUT THIS YEAR WE HAVE MORE NEW STUDENTS THAN USUAL.
BASICALLY, WE'RE IN A SERIOUS PINCH AS THERE AREN'T ENOUGH FUNDS.
HA-HA-HA...
?!
AT THIS RATE, WE'LL HAVE TO CUT THE TEACHERS AND MANAGEMENT STAFF'S PAY...!
FIRST WILL BE ME AND PROFESSOR DANTE.
SO, BY CALLING ME A SAVIOR, YOU MEANT...
RIGHT, SORRY. THAT'S WHAT I MEANT BY IT.
I JUST WANTED TO HAVE A FUN SCHOOL LIFE WITH SOME FRIENDS.

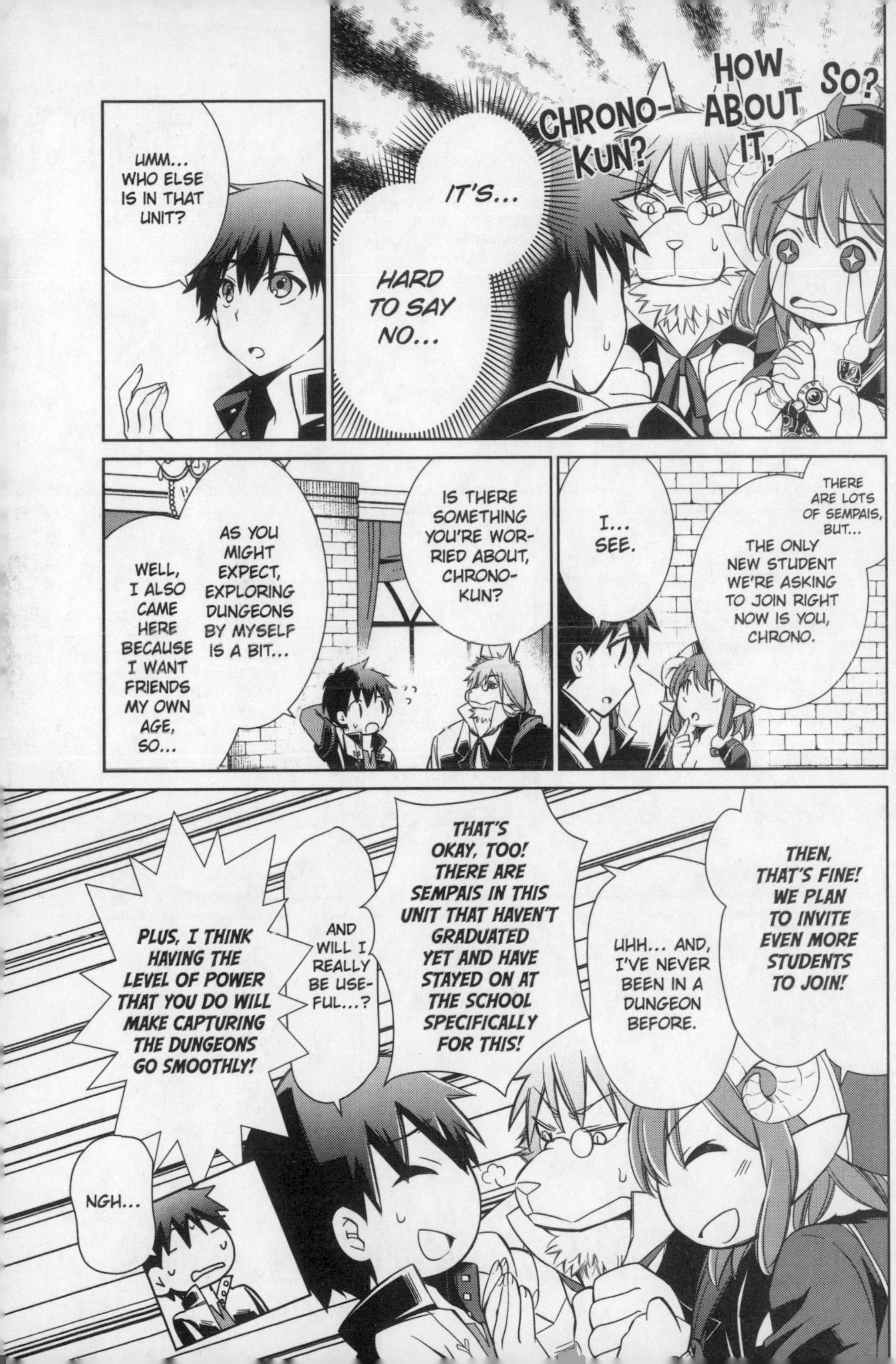
SO? HOW ABOUT IT, CHRONO-KUN?
IT'S... HARD TO SAY NO...
UMM... WHO ELSE IS IN THAT UNIT?
THERE ARE LOTS OF SEMPAIS, BUT...
THE ONLY NEW STUDENT WE'RE ASKING TO JOIN RIGHT NOW IS YOU, CHRONO.
I... SEE.
IS THERE SOMETHING YOU'RE WOR-RIED ABOUT, CHRONO-KUN?
AS YOU MIGHT EXPECT, EXPLORING DUNGEONS BY MYSELF IS A BIT...
WELL, I ALSO CAME HERE BECAUSE I WANT FRIENDS MY OWN AGE, SO...
THEN, THAT'S FINE! WE PLAN TO INVITE EVEN MORE STUDENTS TO JOIN!
UHH... AND, I'VE NEVER BEEN IN A DUNGEON BEFORE.
THAT'S OKAY, TOO! THERE ARE SEMPAIS IN THIS UNIT THAT HAVEN'T GRADUATED YET AND HAVE STAYED ON AT THE SCHOOL SPECIFICALLY FOR THIS!
AND WILL I REALLY BE USE-FUL...?
PLUS, I THINK HAVING THE LEVEL OF POWER THAT YOU DO WILL MAKE CAPTURING THE DUNGEONS GO SMOOTHLY!
NGH...

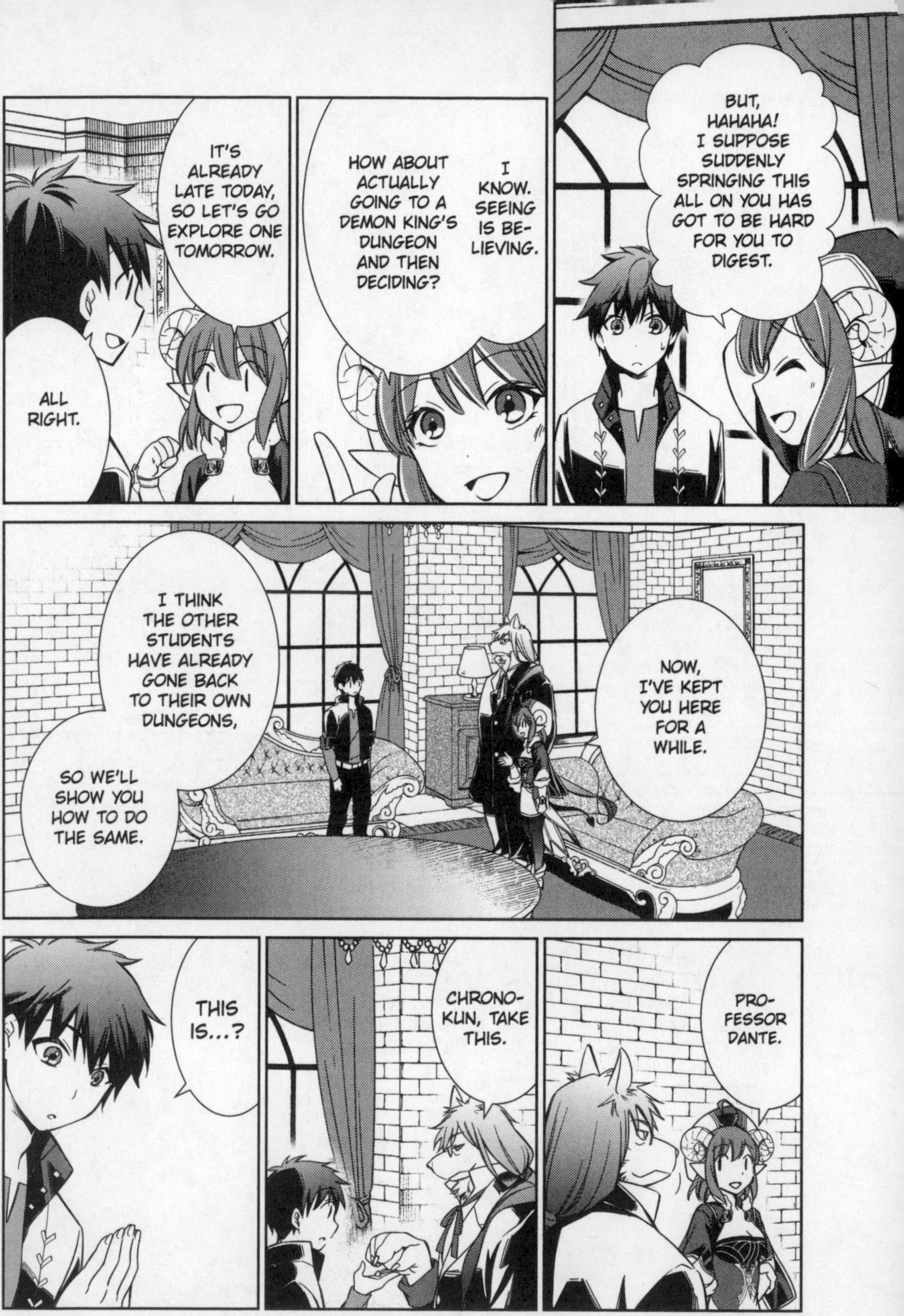
BUT, HAHAHA! I SUPPOSE SUDDENLY SPRINGING THIS ALL ON YOU HAS GOT TO BE HARD FOR YOU TO DIGEST.
I KNOW. SEEING IS BE-LIEVING.
HOW ABOUT ACTUALLY GOING TO A DEMON KING'S DUNGEON AND THEN DECIDING?
IT'S ALREADY LATE TODAY, SO LET'S GO EXPLORE ONE TOMORROW.
ALL RIGHT.
NOW, I'VE KEPT YOU HERE FOR A WHILE.
I THINK THE OTHER STUDENTS HAVE ALREADY GONE BACK TO THEIR OWN DUNGEONS,
SO WE'LL SHOW YOU HOW TO DO THE SAME.
PRO-FESSOR DANTE.
CHRONO-KUN, TAKE THIS.
THIS IS...?

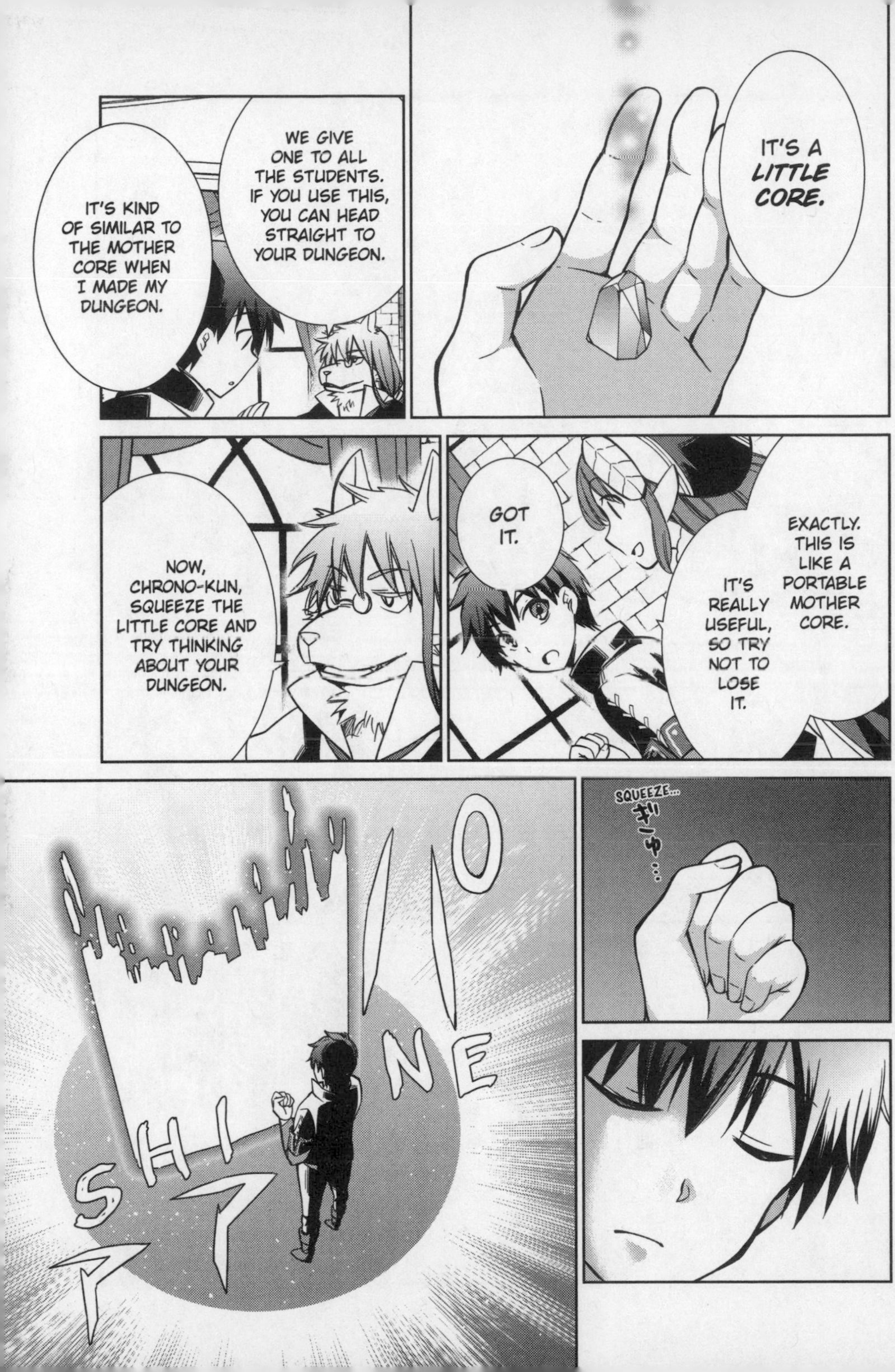

IT'S A LITTLE CORE.
WE GIVE ONE TO ALL THE STUDENTS. IF YOU USE THIS, YOU CAN HEAD STRAIGHT TO YOUR DUNGEON.
IT'S KIND OF SIMILAR TO THE MOTHER CORE WHEN I MADE MY DUNGEON.
EXACTLY. THIS IS LIKE A PORTABLE MOTHER CORE.
IT'S REALLY USEFUL, SO TRY NOT TO LOSE IT.
GOT IT.
NOW, CHRONO-KUN, SQUEEZE THE LITTLE CORE AND TRY THINKING ABOUT YOUR DUNGEON.
SQUEEZE...
ギュ…
SHINE

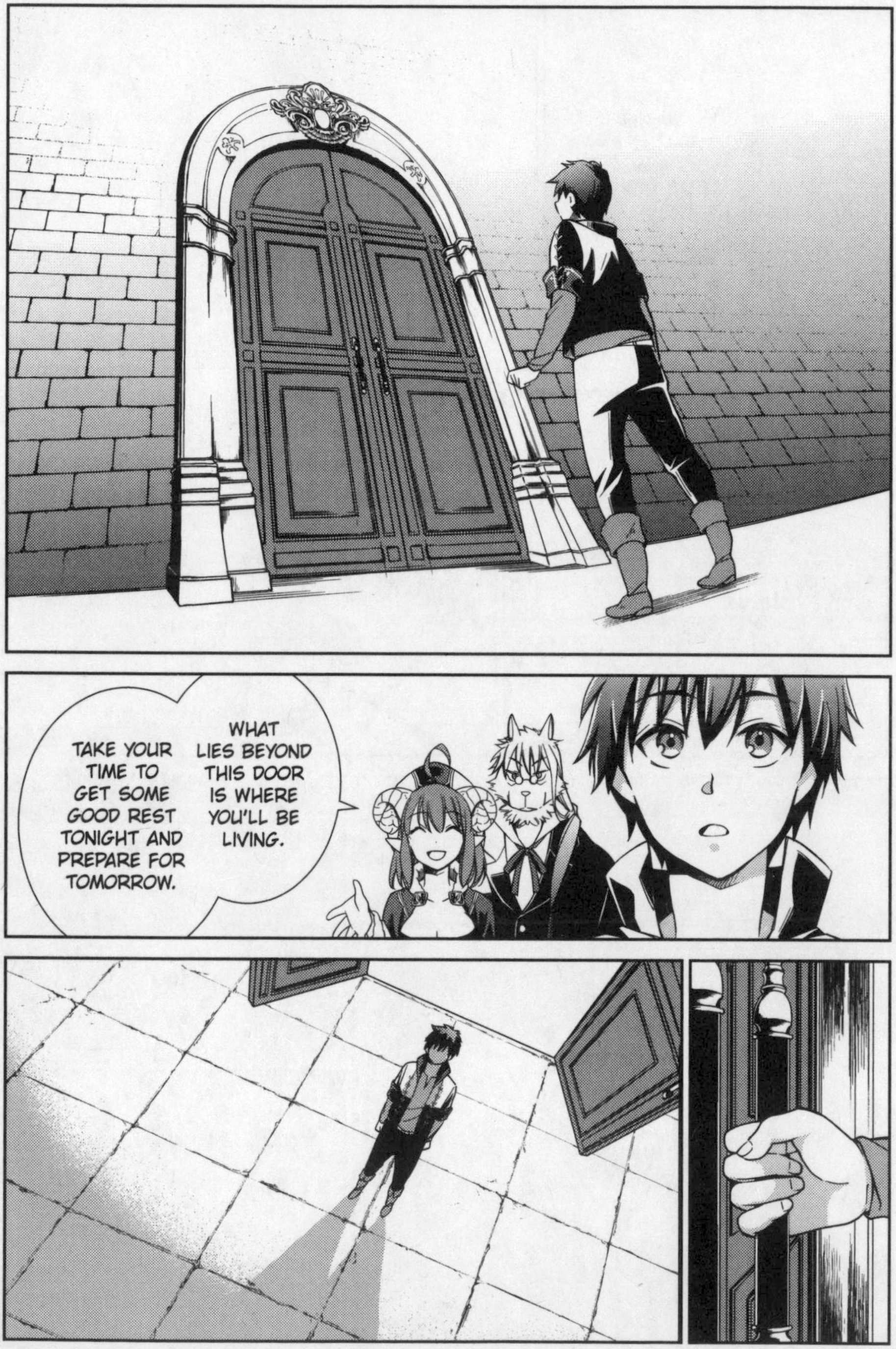
WHAT LIES BEYOND THIS DOOR IS WHERE YOU'LL BE LIVING.
TAKE YOUR TIME TO GET SOME GOOD REST TONIGHT AND PREPARE FOR TOMORROW.

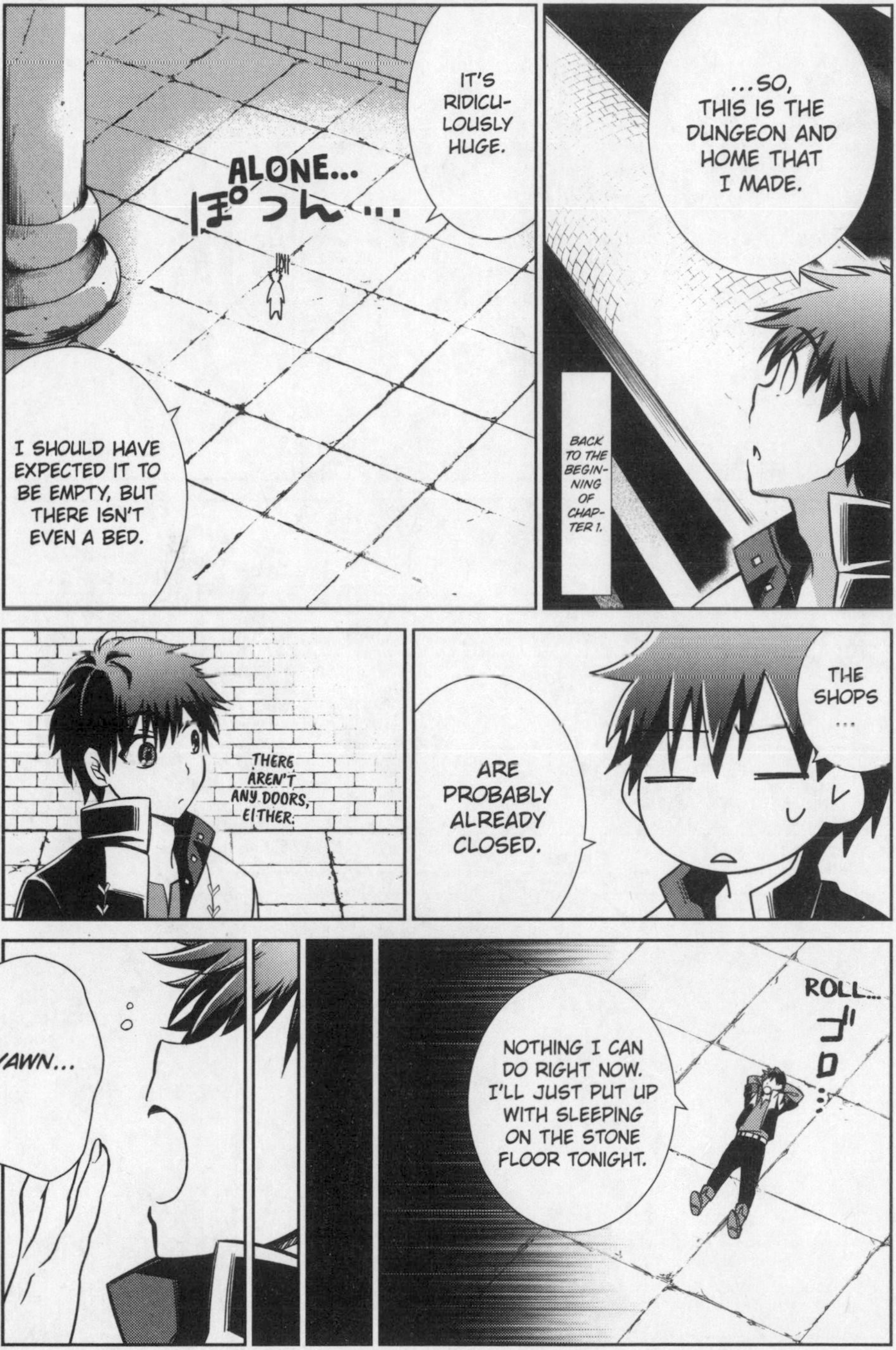
...SO, THIS IS THE DUNGEON AND HOME THAT I MADE.
BACK TO THE BEGINNING OF CHAPTER 1.
IT'S RIDICULOUSLY HUGE.
ALONE...
ぽつん...
I SHOULD HAVE EXPECTED IT TO BE EMPTY, BUT THERE ISN'T EVEN A BED.
THE SHOPS...
ARE PROBABLY ALREADY CLOSED.
THERE AREN'T ANY DOORS, EITHER.
ROLL...
ゴロ...
NOTHING I CAN DO RIGHT NOW. I'LL JUST PUT UP WITH SLEEPING ON THE STONE FLOOR TONIGHT.
YAWN...

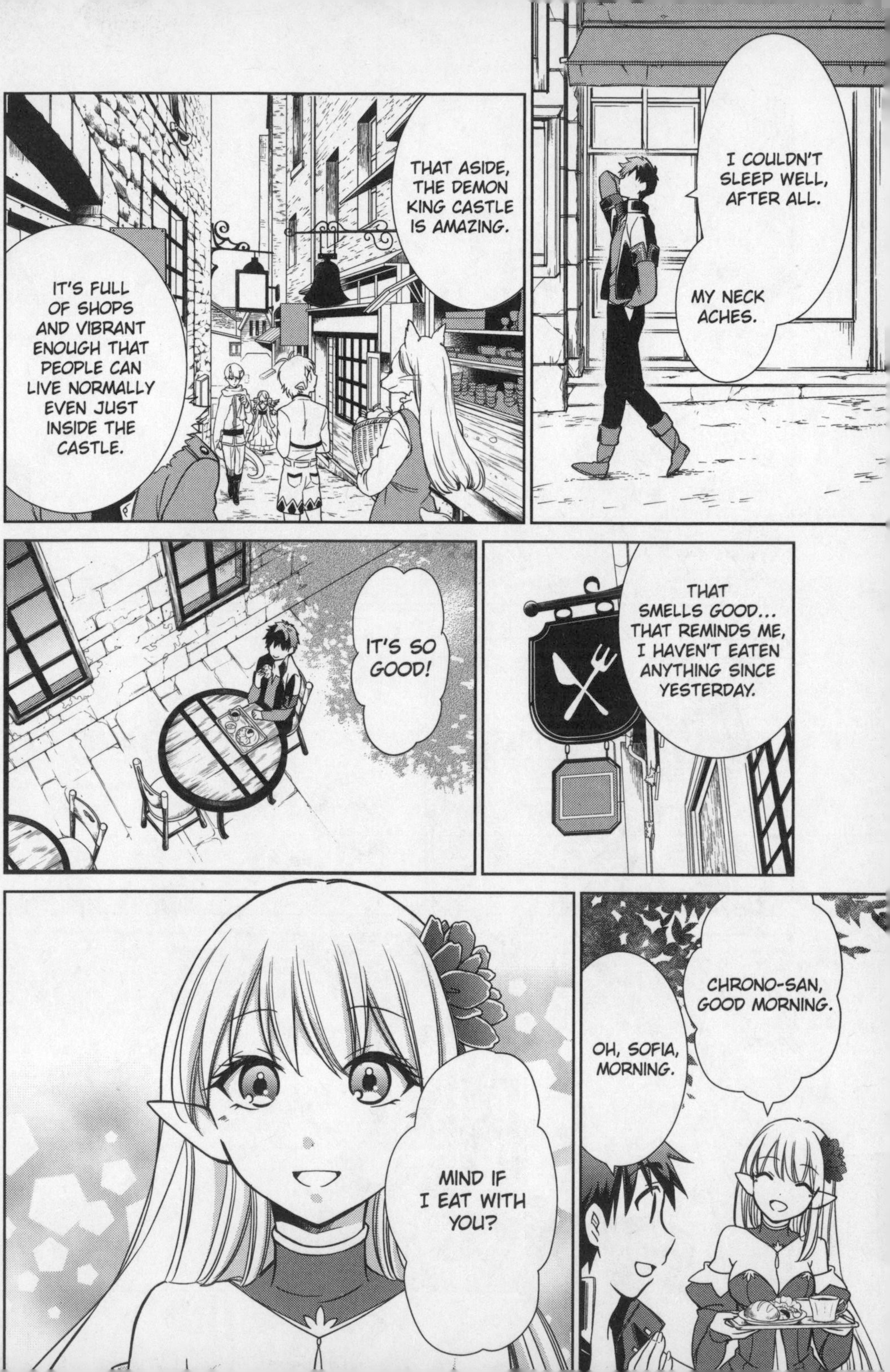
I COULDN'T SLEEP WELL, AFTER ALL.
MY NECK ACHES.
THAT ASIDE, THE DEMON KING CASTLE IS AMAZING.
IT'S FULL OF SHOPS AND VIBRANT ENOUGH THAT PEOPLE CAN LIVE NORMALLY EVEN JUST INSIDE THE CASTLE.
THAT SMELLS GOOD... THAT REMINDS ME, I HAVEN'T EATEN ANYTHING SINCE YESTERDAY.
IT'S SO GOOD!
CHRONO-SAN, GOOD MORNING.
OH, SOFIA, MORNING.
MIND IF I EAT WITH YOU?

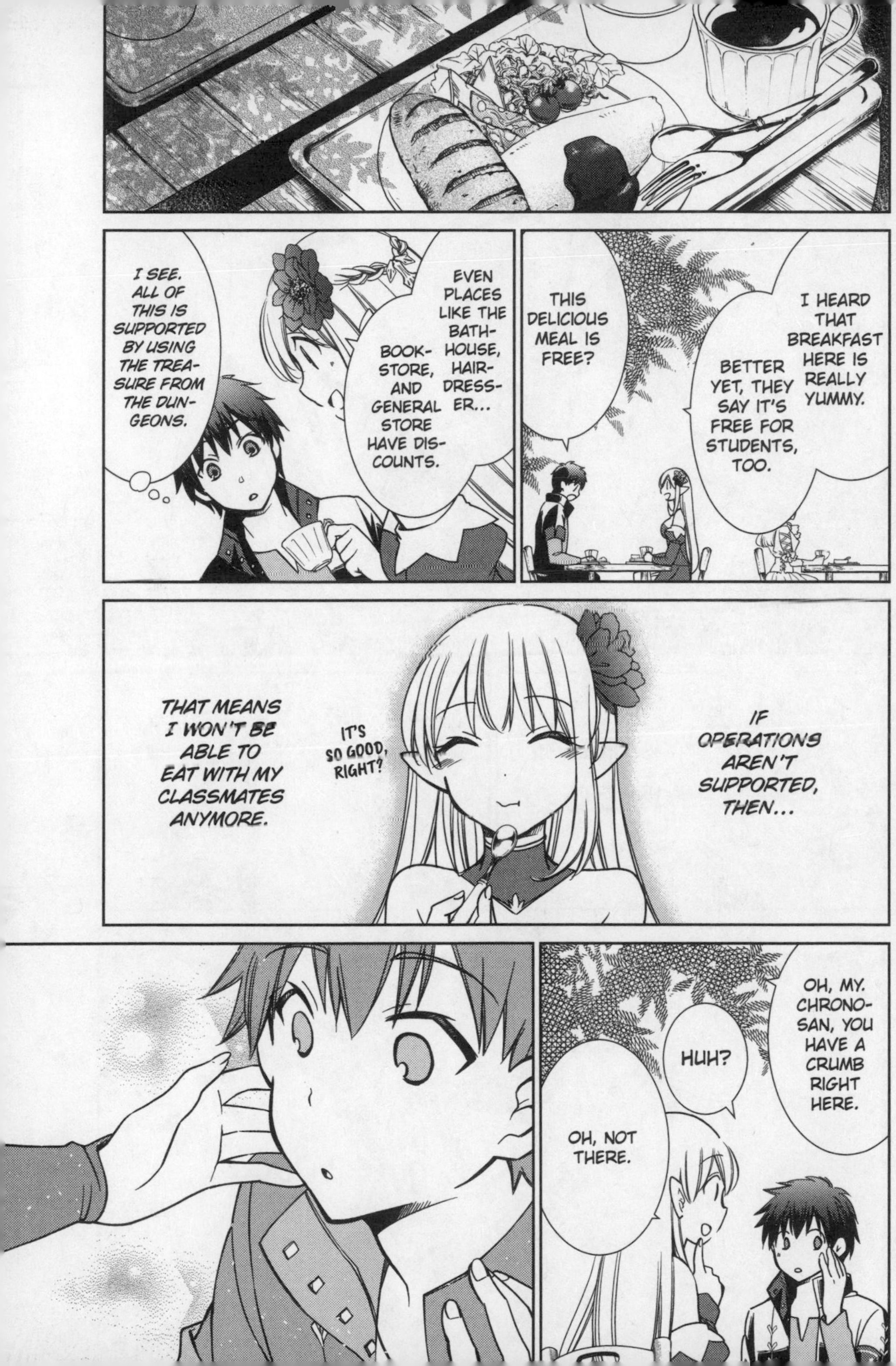
I HEARD THAT BREAKFAST HERE IS REALLY YUMMY.
BETTER YET, THEY SAY IT'S FREE FOR STUDENTS, TOO.
THIS DELICIOUS MEAL IS FREE?
EVEN PLACES LIKE THE BATH-HOUSE, HAIR-DRESSER...
BOOK-STORE, AND GENERAL STORE HAVE DIS-COUNTS.
I SEE. ALL OF THIS IS SUPPORTED BY USING THE TREA-SURE FROM THE DUN-GEONS.
IF OPERATIONS AREN'T SUPPORTED, THEN...
IT'S SO GOOD, RIGHT?
THAT MEANS I WON'T BE ABLE TO EAT WITH MY CLASSMATES ANYMORE.
OH, MY. CHRONO-SAN, YOU HAVE A CRUMB RIGHT HERE.
HUH?
OH, NOT THERE.

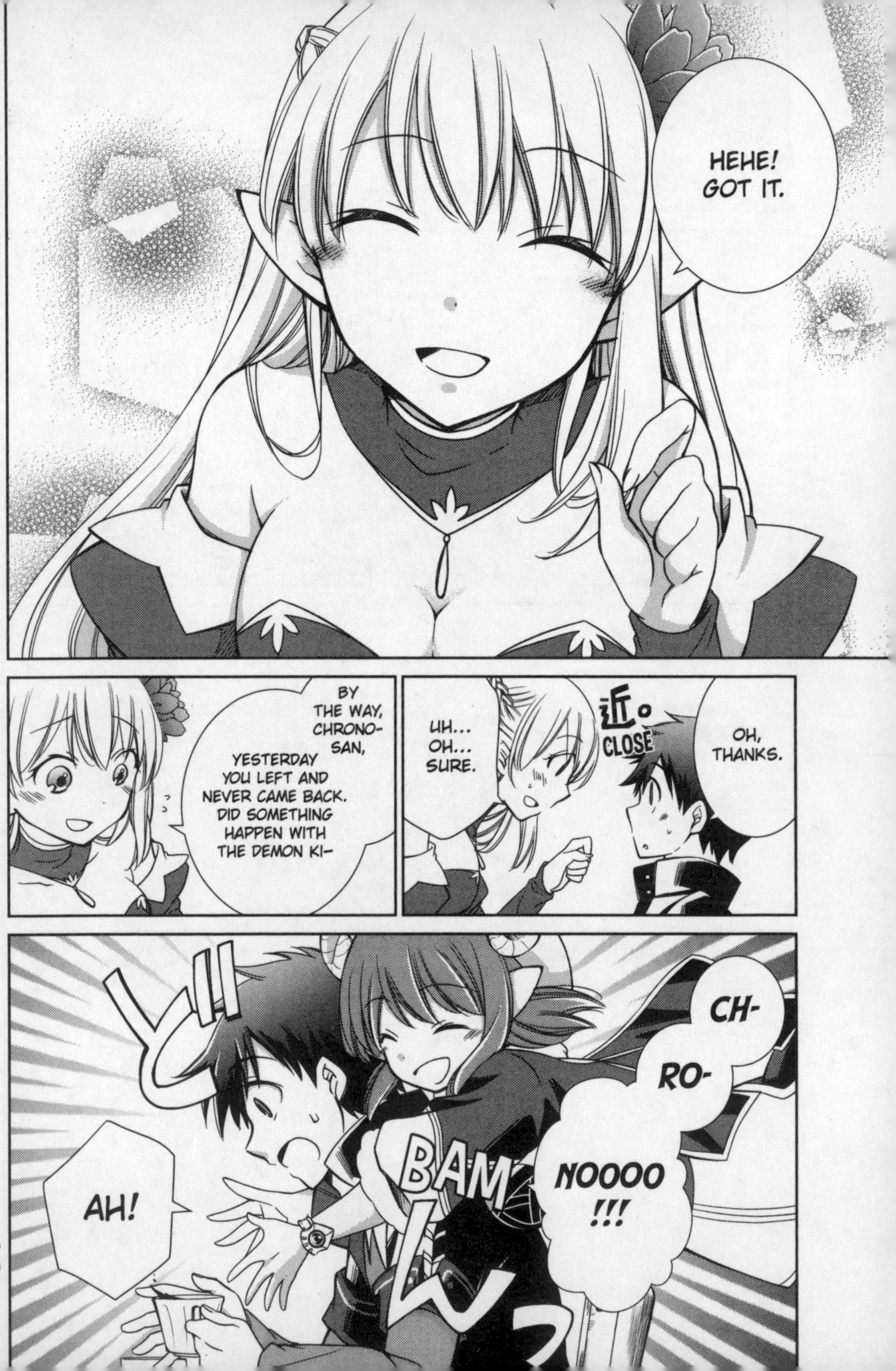
HEHE! GOT IT.
OH, THANKS.
近。 CLOSE
UH... OH... SURE.
BY THE WAY, CHRONO-SAN, YESTERDAY YOU LEFT AND NEVER CAME BACK. DID SOMETHING HAPPEN WITH THE DEMON KI-
CH- RO- NOOOO !!!
BAM
AH!

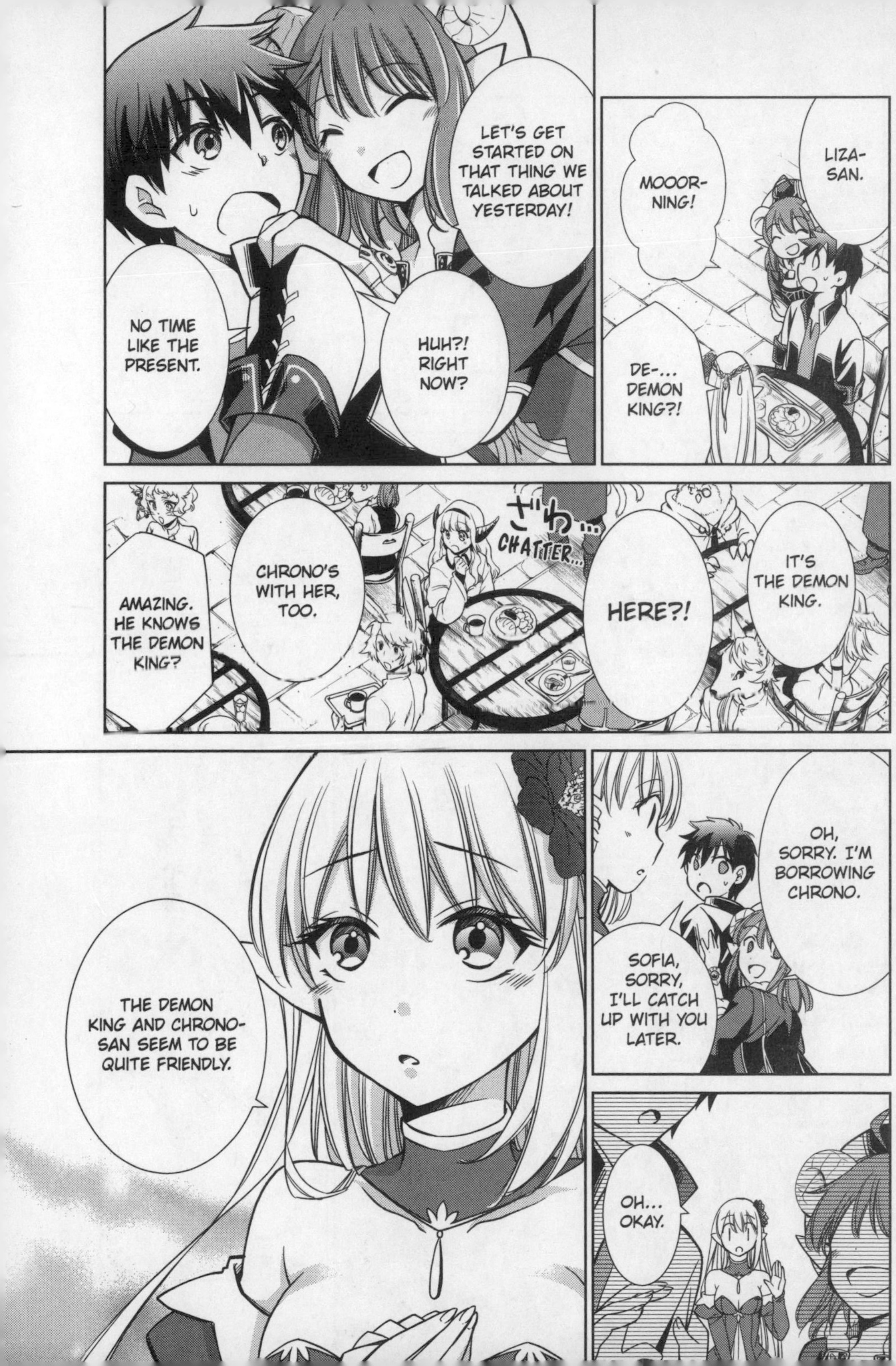
LIZA-SAN.
MOOOR-NING!
DE-... DEMON KING?!
LET'S GET STARTED ON THAT THING WE TALKED ABOUT YESTERDAY!
HUH?! RIGHT NOW?
NO TIME LIKE THE PRESENT.
IT'S THE DEMON KING.
HERE?!
ざわ… CHATTER...
CHRONO'S WITH HER, TOO.
AMAZING. HE KNOWS THE DEMON KING?
OH, SORRY. I'M BORROWING CHRONO.
SOFIA, SORRY, I'LL CATCH UP WITH YOU LATER.
OH... OKAY.
THE DEMON KING AND CHRONO-SAN SEEM TO BE QUITE FRIENDLY.

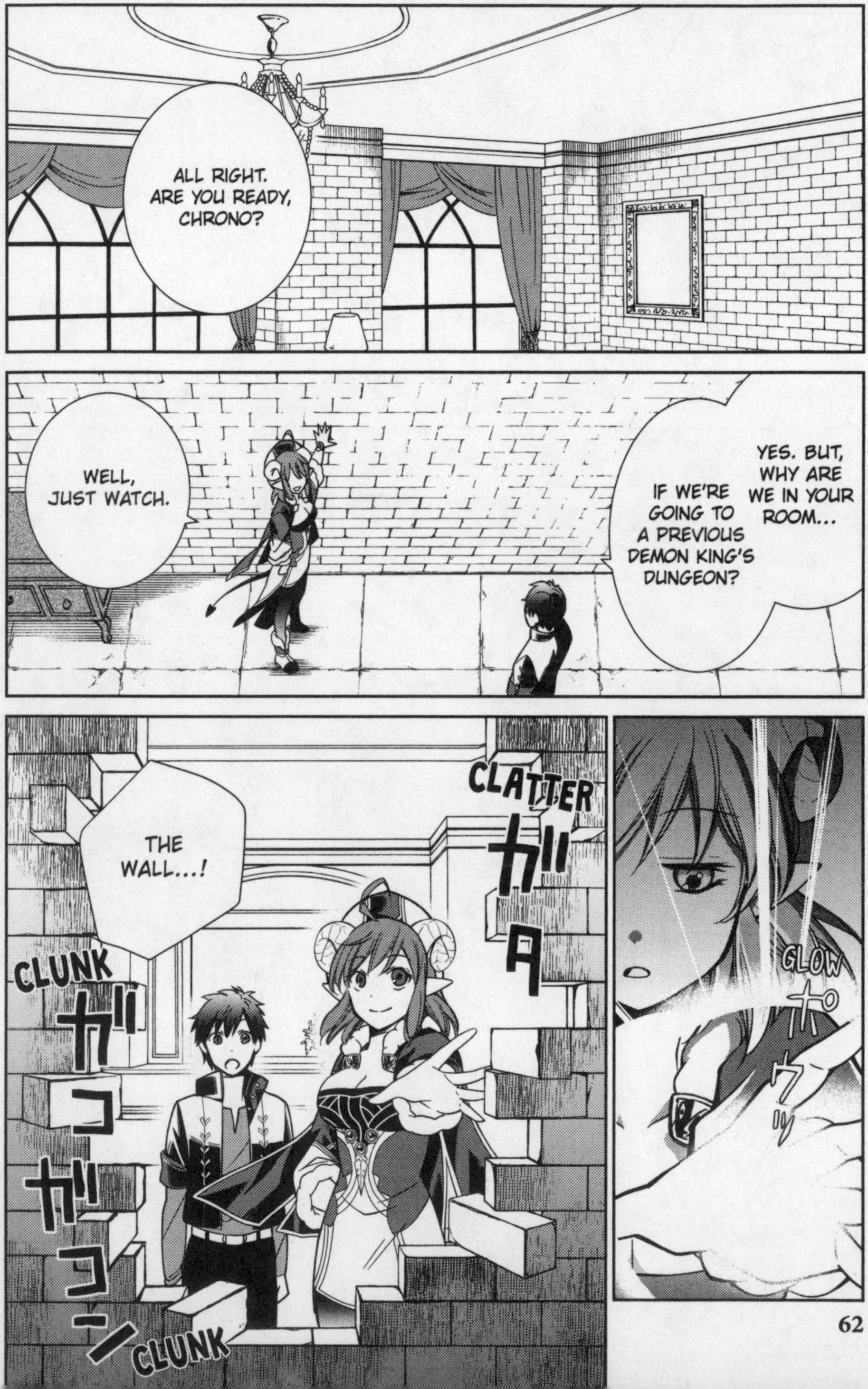
ALL RIGHT. ARE YOU READY, CHRONO?
YES. BUT, WHY ARE WE IN YOUR ROOM...
IF WE'RE GOING TO A PREVIOUS DEMON KING'S DUNGEON?
WELL, JUST WATCH.
GLOW
ポワッ
CLATTER
ガタ
THE WALL...!
CLUNK
ガコ
ガコン
CLUNK

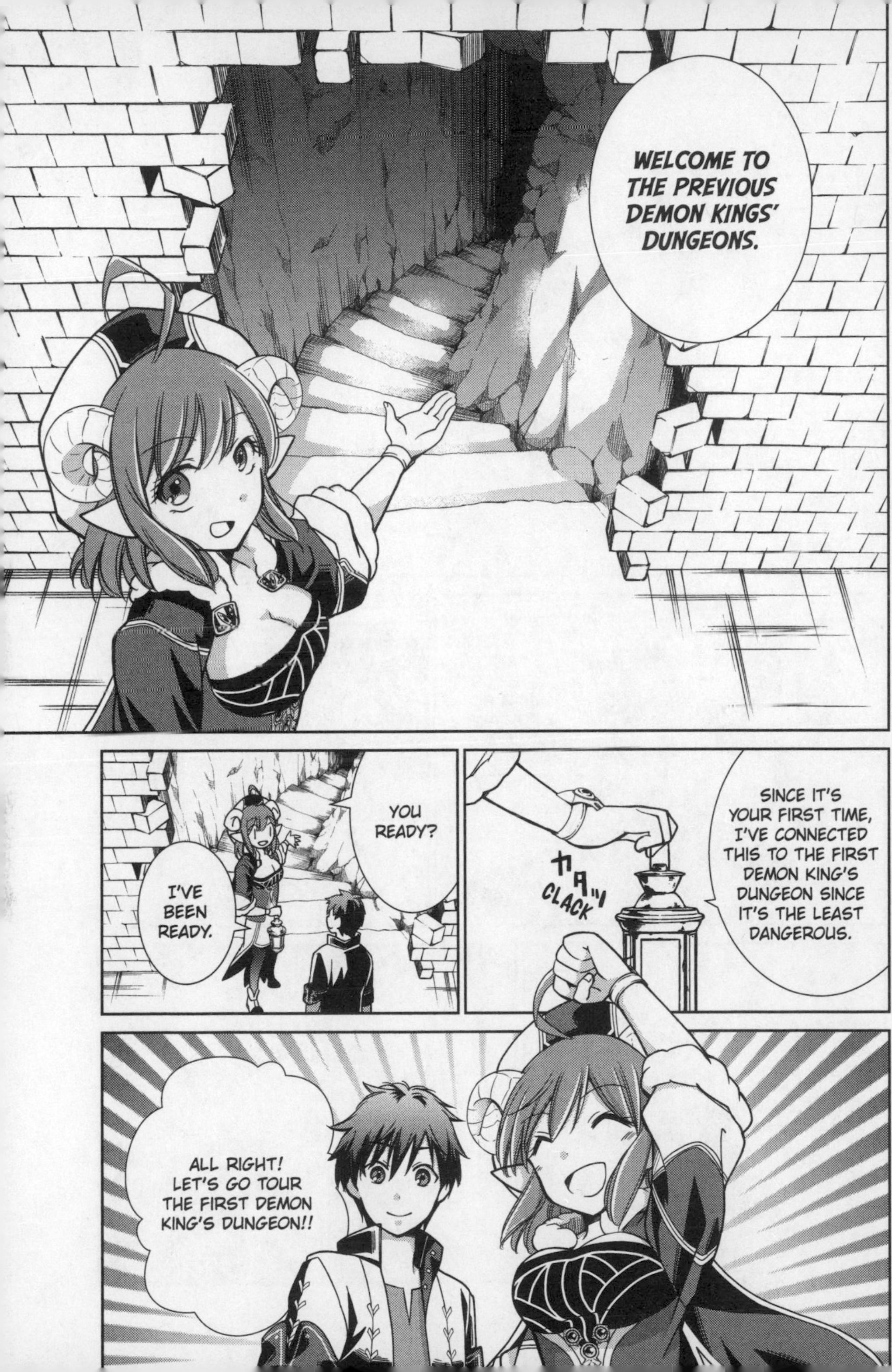
WELCOME TO THE PREVIOUS DEMON KINGS' DUNGEONS.
SINCE IT'S YOUR FIRST TIME, I'VE CONNECTED THIS TO THE FIRST DEMON KING'S DUNGEON SINCE IT'S THE LEAST DANGEROUS.
カタッ
CLACK
YOU READY?
I'VE BEEN READY.
ALL RIGHT! LET'S GO TOUR THE FIRST DEMON KING'S DUNGEON!!

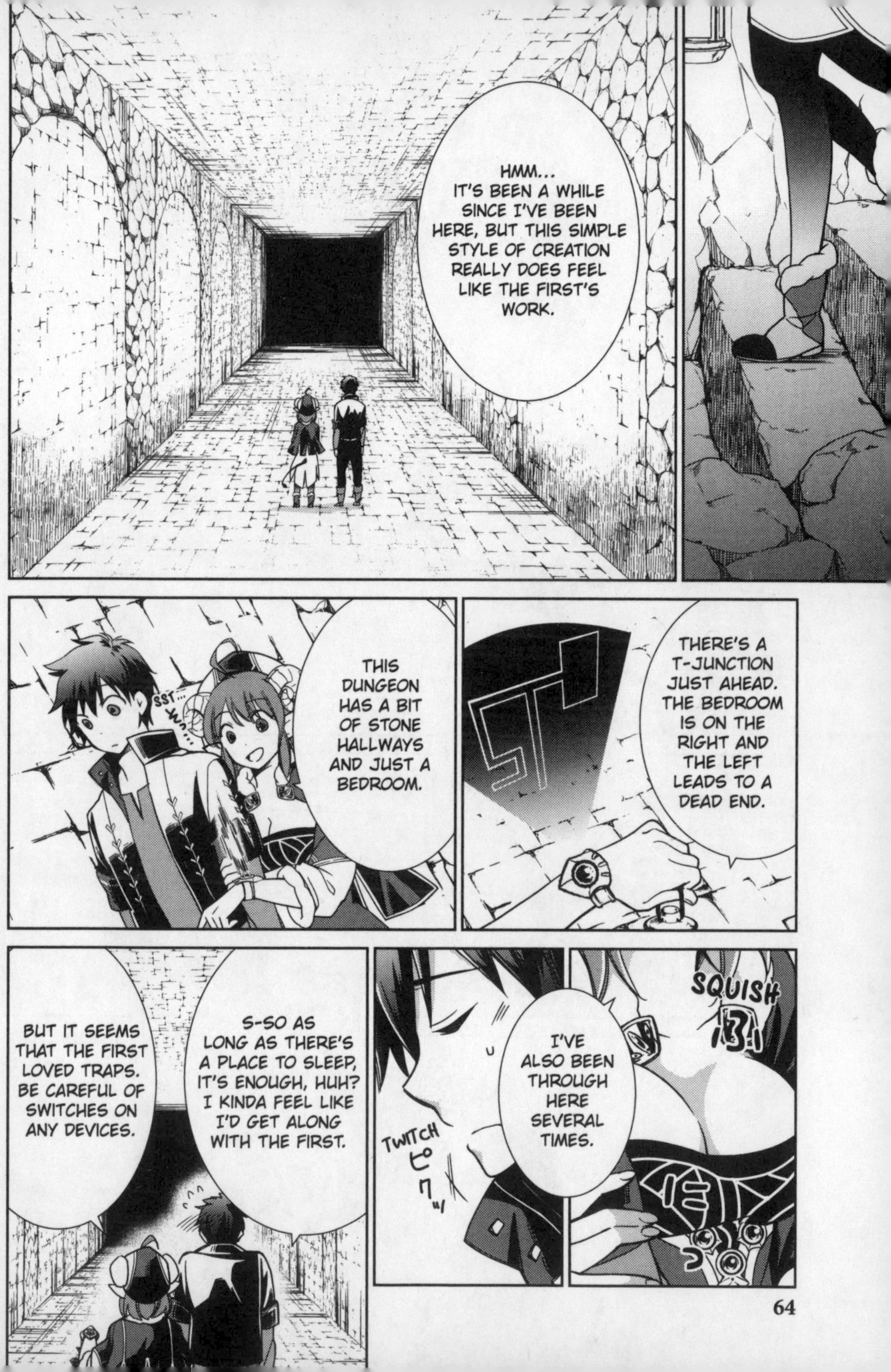

HMM... IT'S BEEN A WHILE SINCE I'VE BEEN HERE, BUT THIS SIMPLE STYLE OF CREATION REALLY DOES FEEL LIKE THE FIRST'S WORK.
THERE'S A T-JUNCTION JUST AHEAD. THE BEDROOM IS ON THE RIGHT AND THE LEFT LEADS TO A DEAD END.
SST...
THIS DUNGEON HAS A BIT OF STONE HALLWAYS AND JUST A BEDROOM.
SQUISH
I'VE ALSO BEEN THROUGH HERE SEVERAL TIMES.
TWITCH
S-SO AS LONG AS THERE'S A PLACE TO SLEEP, IT'S ENOUGH, HUH? I KINDA FEEL LIKE I'D GET ALONG WITH THE FIRST.
BUT IT SEEMS THAT THE FIRST LOVED TRAPS. BE CAREFUL OF SWITCHES ON ANY DEVICES.

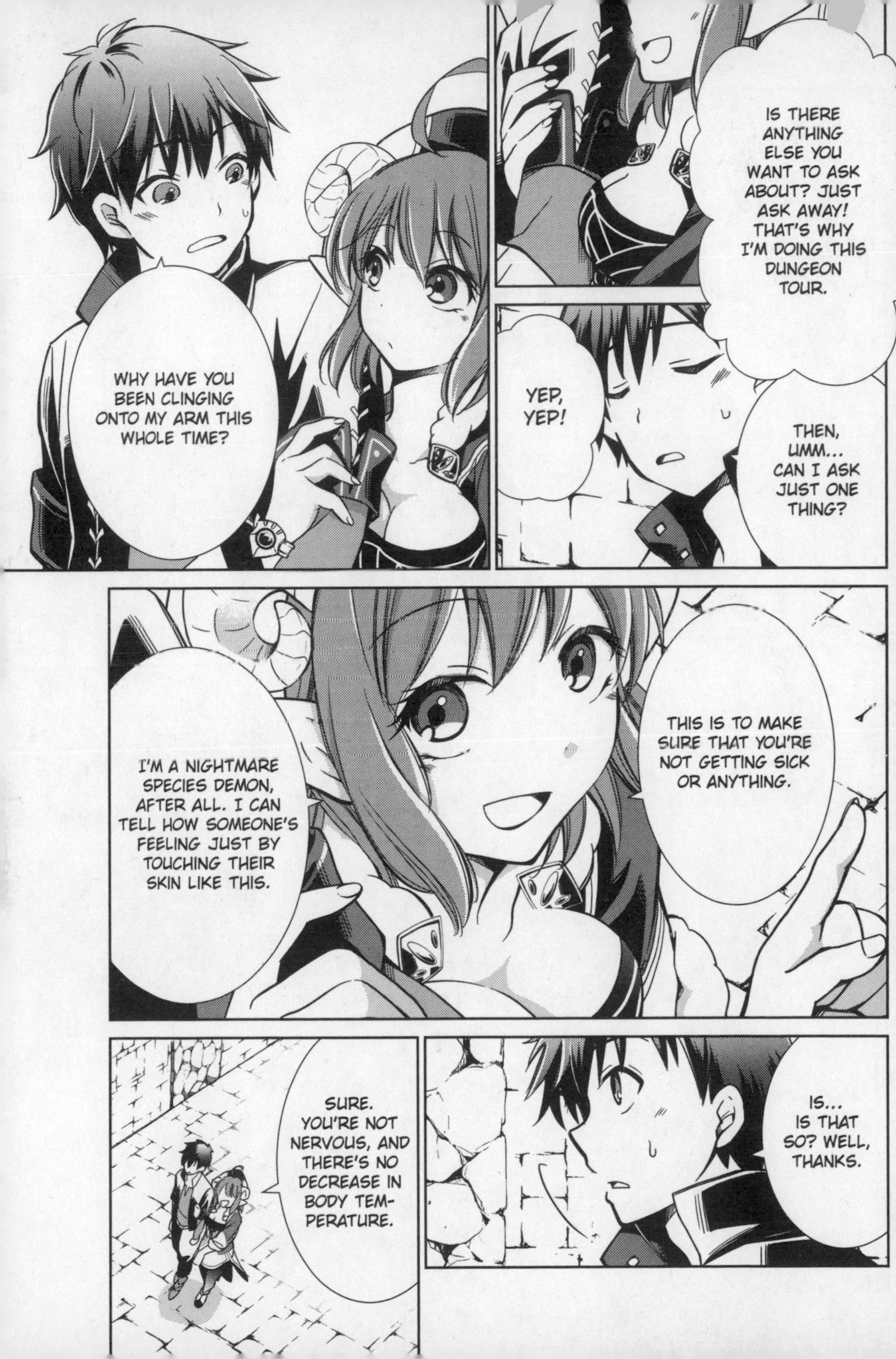
IS THERE ANYTHING ELSE YOU WANT TO ASK ABOUT? JUST ASK AWAY! THAT'S WHY I'M DOING THIS DUNGEON TOUR.
THEN, UMM... CAN I ASK JUST ONE THING?
YEP, YEP!
WHY HAVE YOU BEEN CLINGING ONTO MY ARM THIS WHOLE TIME?
THIS IS TO MAKE SURE THAT YOU'RE NOT GETTING SICK OR ANYTHING.
I'M A NIGHTMARE SPECIES DEMON, AFTER ALL. I CAN TELL HOW SOMEONE'S FEELING JUST BY TOUCHING THEIR SKIN LIKE THIS.
IS... IS THAT SO? WELL, THANKS.
SURE. YOU'RE NOT NERVOUS, AND THERE'S NO DECREASE IN BODY TEM-PERATURE.

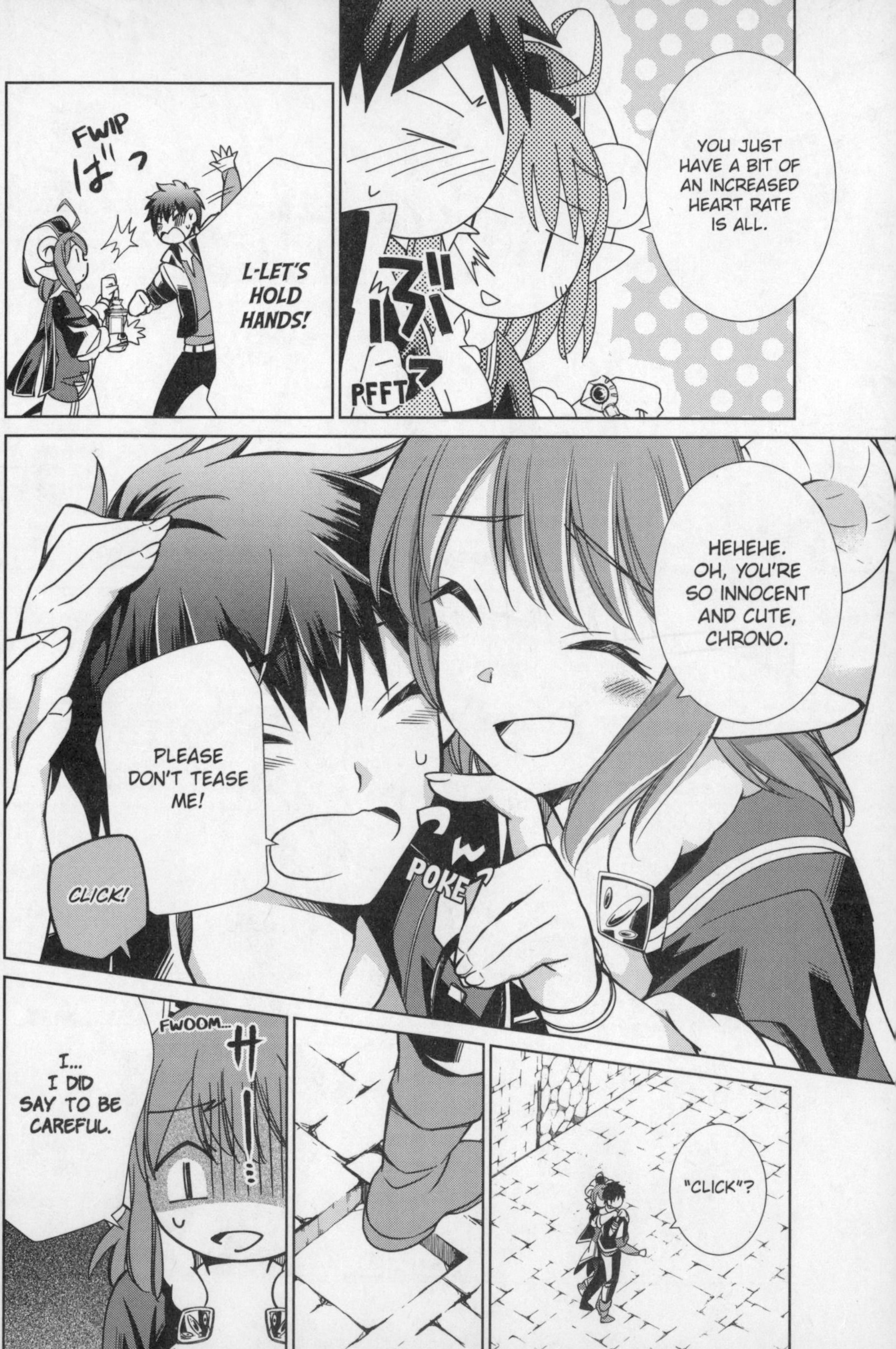
PFFT
YOU JUST HAVE A BIT OF AN INCREASED HEART RATE IS ALL.
FWIP
ばっ
L-LET'S HOLD HANDS!
HEHEHE. OH, YOU'RE SO INNOCENT AND CUTE, CHRONO.
PLEASE DON'T TEASE ME!
POKE
CLICK!
"CLICK"?
FWOOM...
I... I DID SAY TO BE CAREFUL.

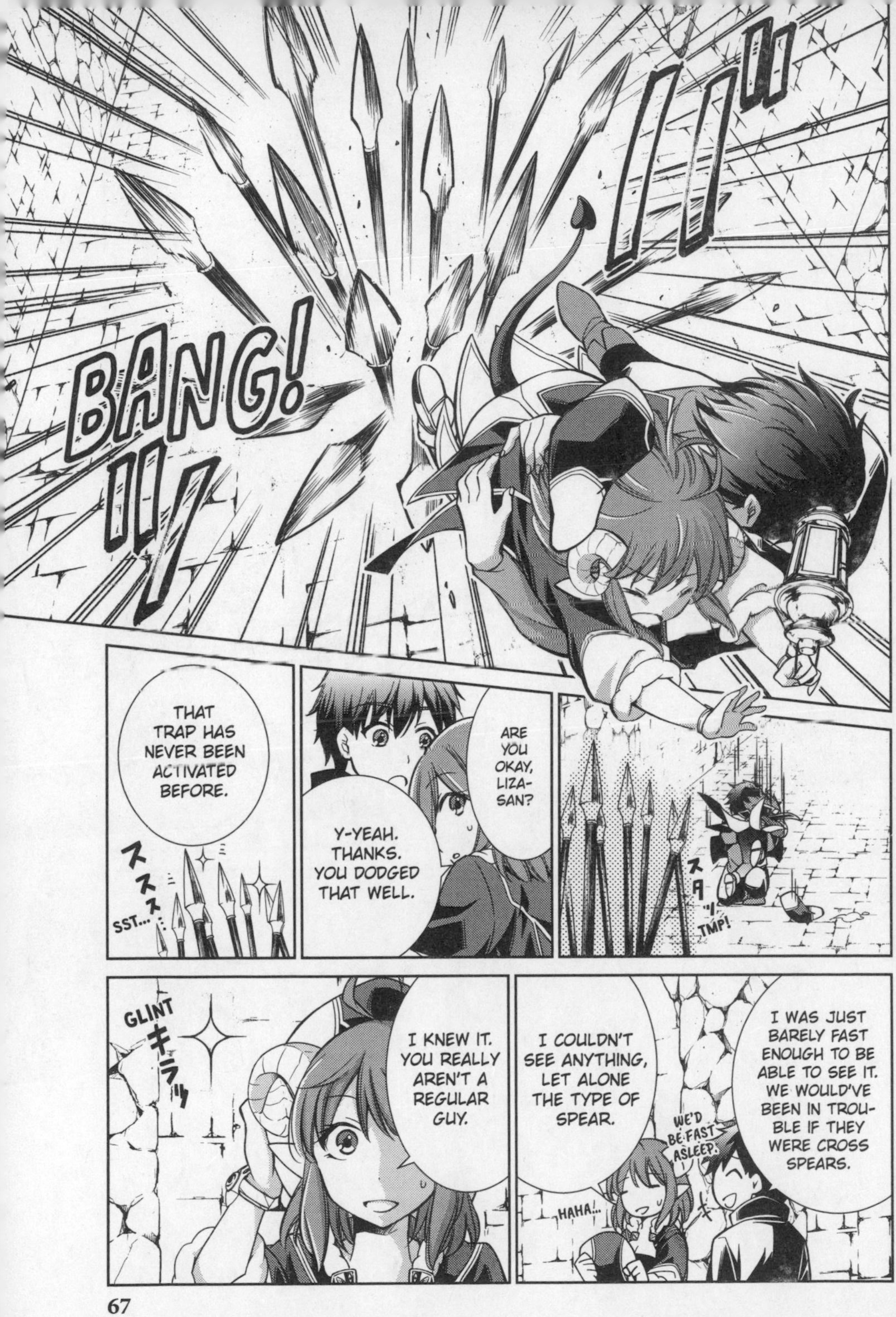
BANG!!
スタッ
TMP!
ARE YOU OKAY, LIZA-SAN?
Y-YEAH. THANKS. YOU DODGED THAT WELL.
THAT TRAP HAS NEVER BEEN ACTIVATED BEFORE.
ススス
SST...
I WAS JUST BARELY FAST ENOUGH TO BE ABLE TO SEE IT. WE WOULD'VE BEEN IN TROUBLE IF THEY WERE CROSS SPEARS.
I COULDN'T SEE ANYTHING, LET ALONE THE TYPE OF SPEAR.
WE'D BE FAST ASLEEP.
HAHA!..
I KNEW IT. YOU REALLY AREN'T A REGULAR GUY.
GLINT
キラッ

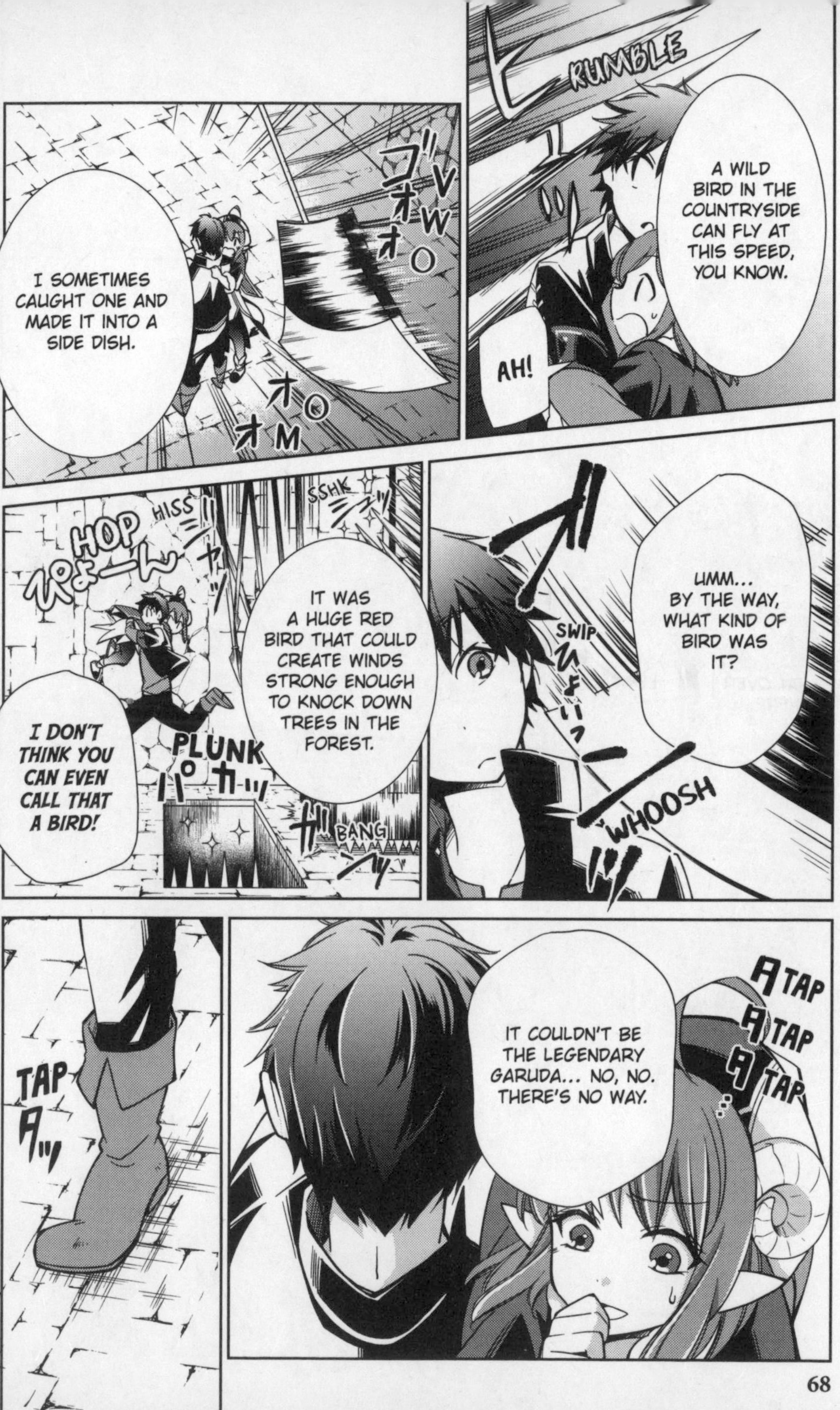
RUMBLE
A WILD BIRD IN THE COUNTRYSIDE CAN FLY AT THIS SPEED, YOU KNOW.
AH!
VWOOM
I SOMETIMES CAUGHT ONE AND MADE IT INTO A SIDE DISH.
UMM... BY THE WAY, WHAT KIND OF BIRD WAS IT?
SWIP
WHOOSH
SSHK
HISS
HOP
ぴょーん
IT WAS A HUGE RED BIRD THAT COULD CREATE WINDS STRONG ENOUGH TO KNOCK DOWN TREES IN THE FOREST.
PLUNK
BANG
I DON'T THINK YOU CAN EVEN CALL THAT A BIRD!
IT COULDN'T BE THE LEGENDARY GARUDA... NO, NO. THERE'S NO WAY.
TAP
TAP
TAP
TAP

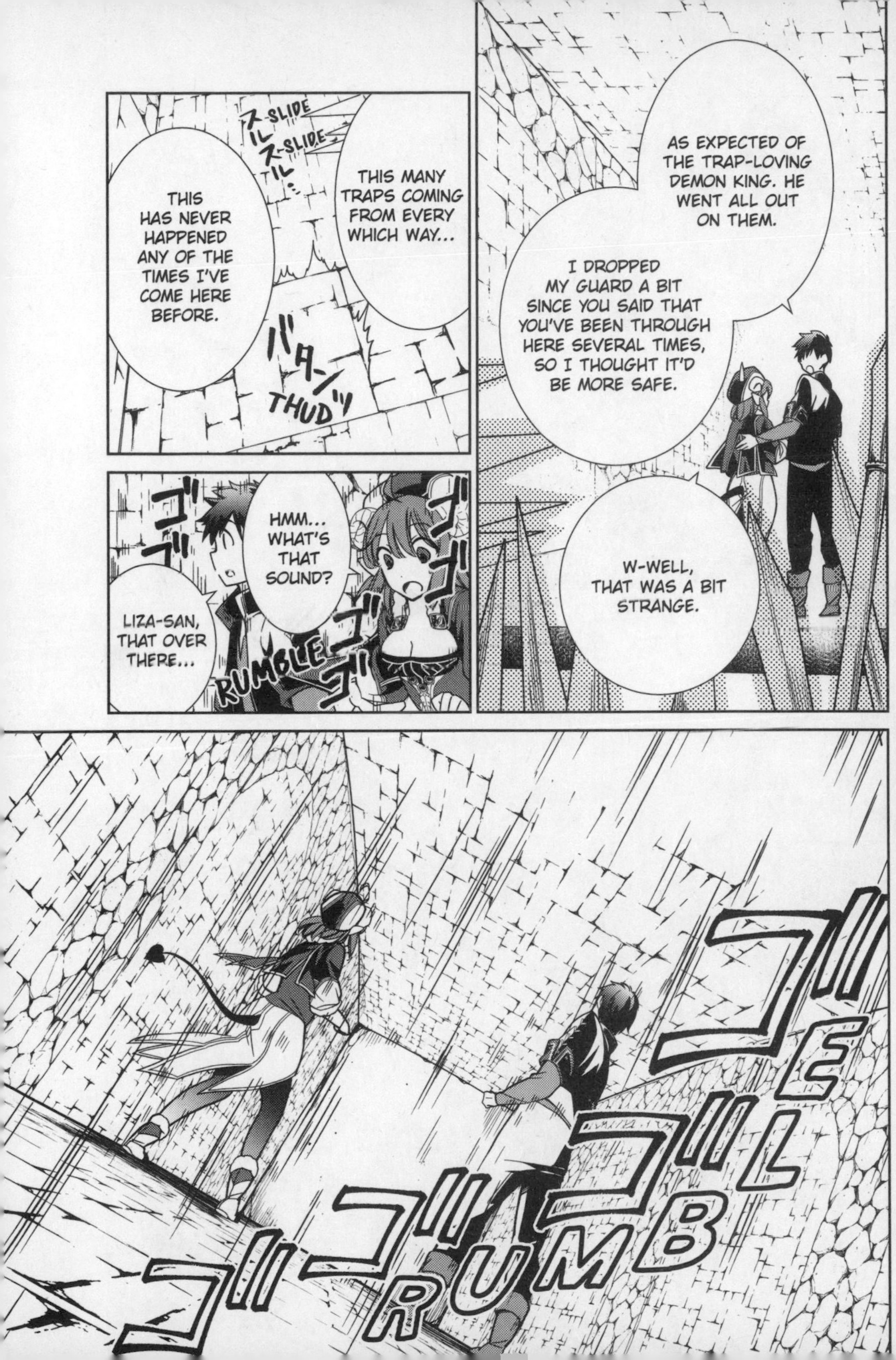
AS EXPECTED OF THE TRAP-LOVING DEMON KING. HE WENT ALL OUT ON THEM.
I DROPPED MY GUARD A BIT SINCE YOU SAID THAT YOU'VE BEEN THROUGH HERE SEVERAL TIMES, SO I THOUGHT IT'D BE MORE SAFE.
W-WELL, THAT WAS A BIT STRANGE.
スル SLIDE スル SLIDE
THIS MANY TRAPS COMING FROM EVERY WHICH WAY...
THIS HAS NEVER HAPPENED ANY OF THE TIMES I'VE COME HERE BEFORE.
バターンッ THUD
ゴゴゴ
HMM... WHAT'S THAT SOUND?
ゴゴ
LIZA-SAN, THAT OVER THERE...
ゴゴ RUMBLE
ゴゴゴゴゴ RUMBLE

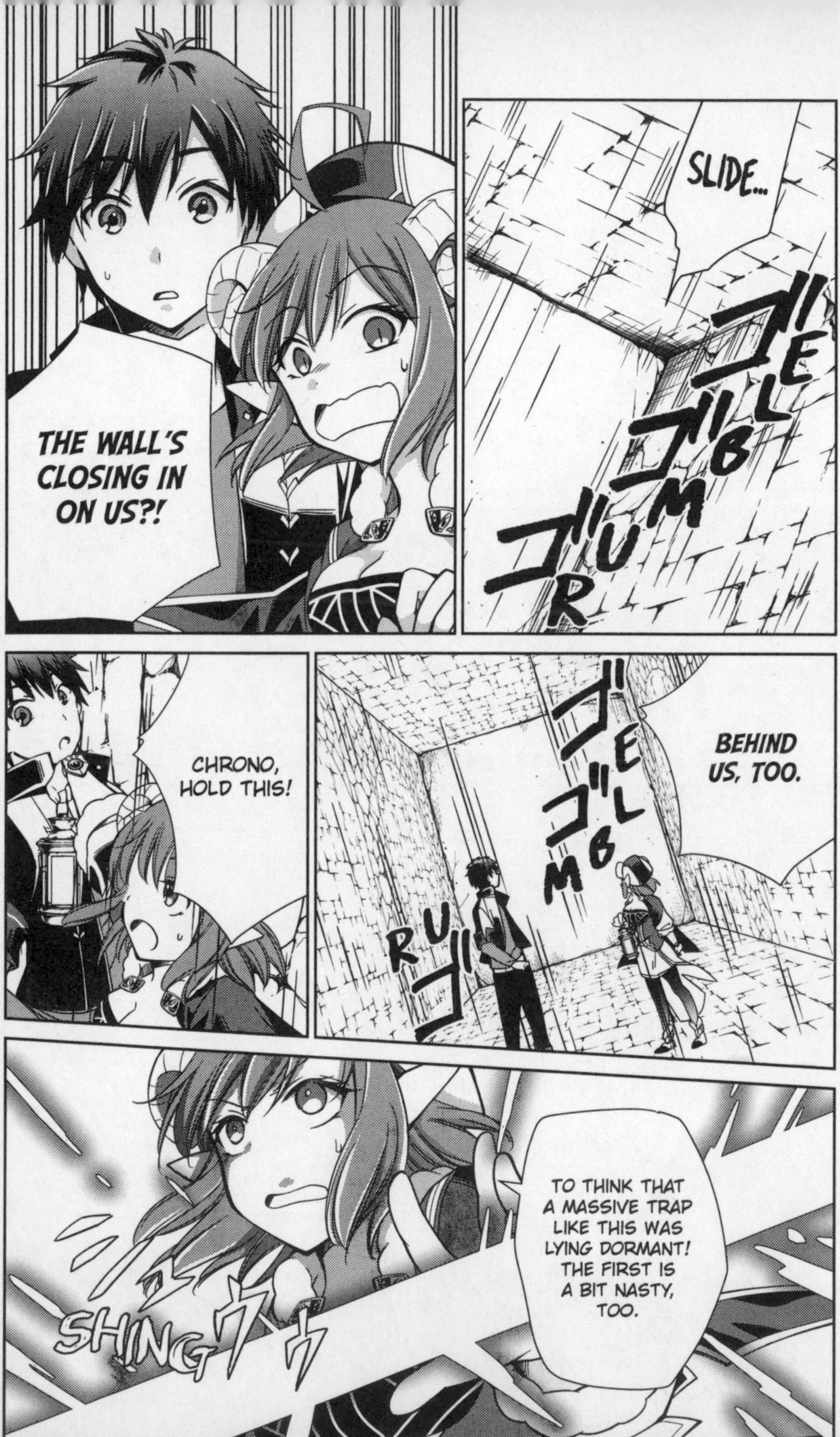
SLIDE...
RUMBLE
THE WALL'S CLOSING IN ON US?!
BEHIND US, TOO.
RUMBLE
CHRONO, HOLD THIS!
TO THINK THAT A MASSIVE TRAP LIKE THIS WAS LYING DORMANT! THE FIRST IS A BIT NASTY, TOO.
SHING

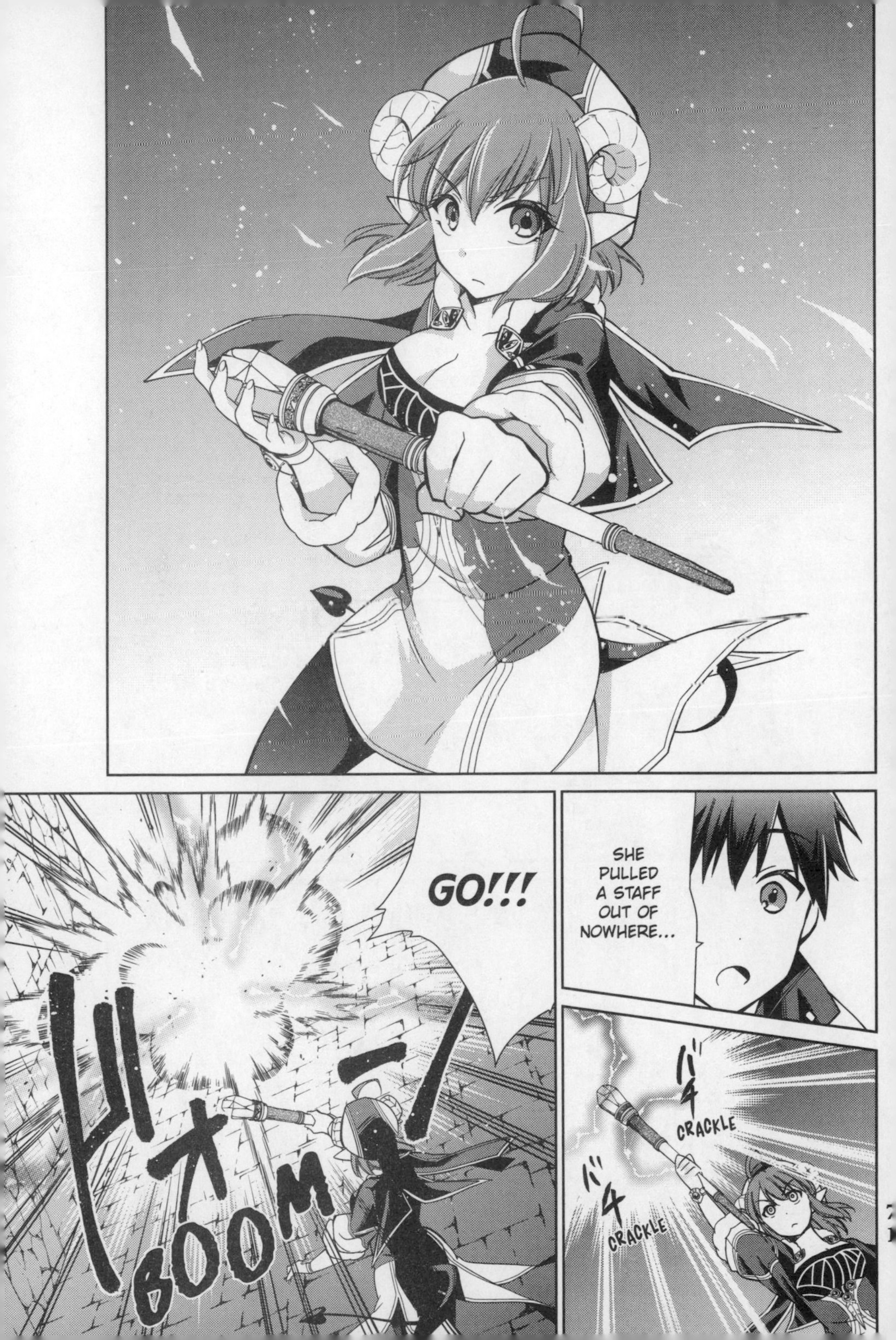
SHE PULLED A STAFF OUT OF NOWHERE...
バチ
CRACKLE
バチ
CRACKLE
GO!!!
ドオー
BOOM

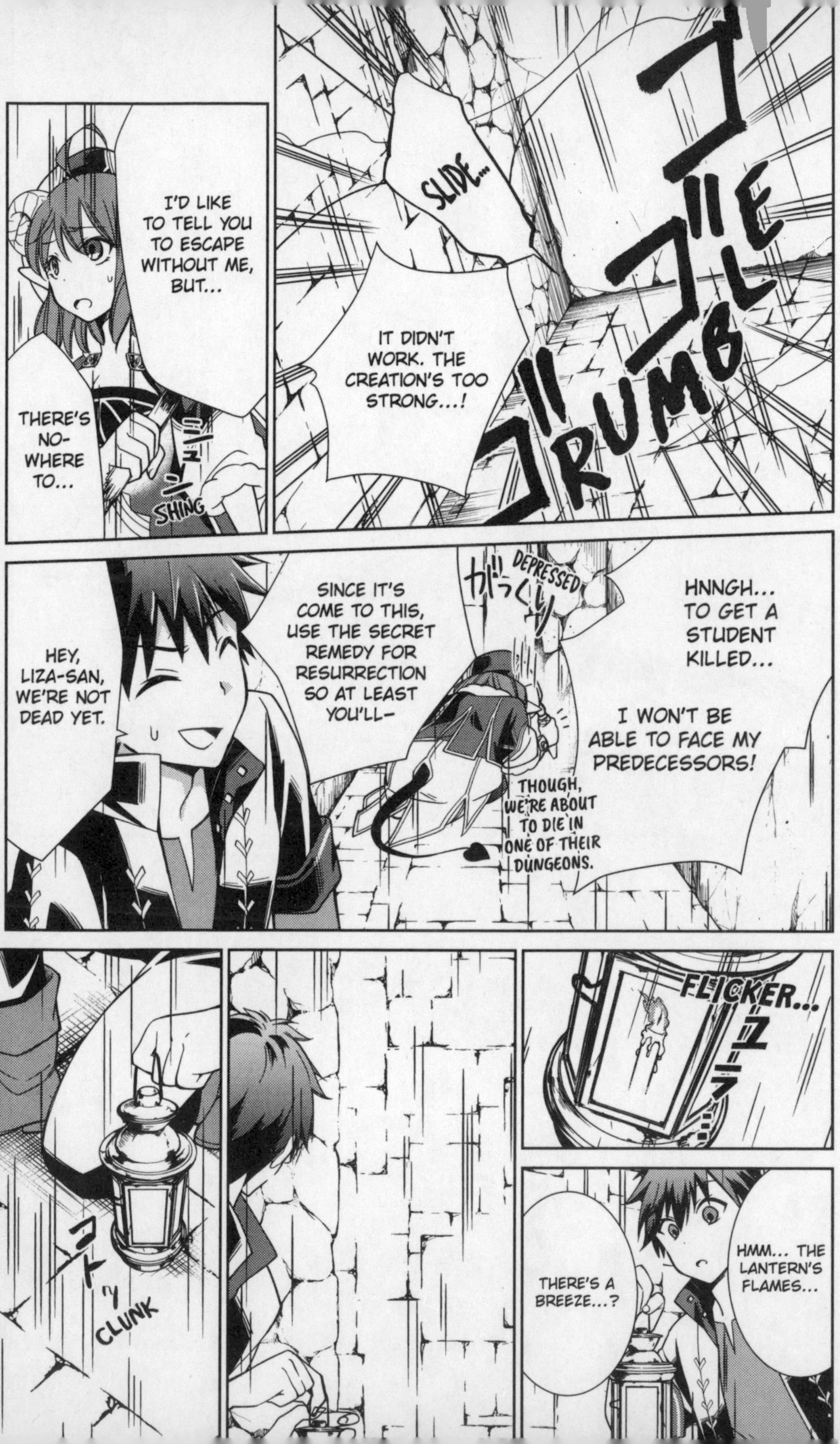
RUMBLE
SLIDE...
IT DIDN'T WORK. THE CREATION'S TOO STRONG...!
I'D LIKE TO TELL YOU TO ESCAPE WITHOUT ME, BUT...
THERE'S NO-WHERE TO...
SHING
HNNGH... TO GET A STUDENT KILLED...
I WON'T BE ABLE TO FACE MY PREDECESSORS!
DEPRESSED
THOUGH, WE'RE ABOUT TO DIE IN ONE OF THEIR DUNGEONS.
SINCE IT'S COME TO THIS, USE THE SECRET REMEDY FOR RESURRECTION SO AT LEAST YOU'LL-
HEY, LIZA-SAN, WE'RE NOT DEAD YET.
FLICKER...
HMM... THE LANTERN'S FLAMES...
THERE'S A BREEZE...?
CLUNK

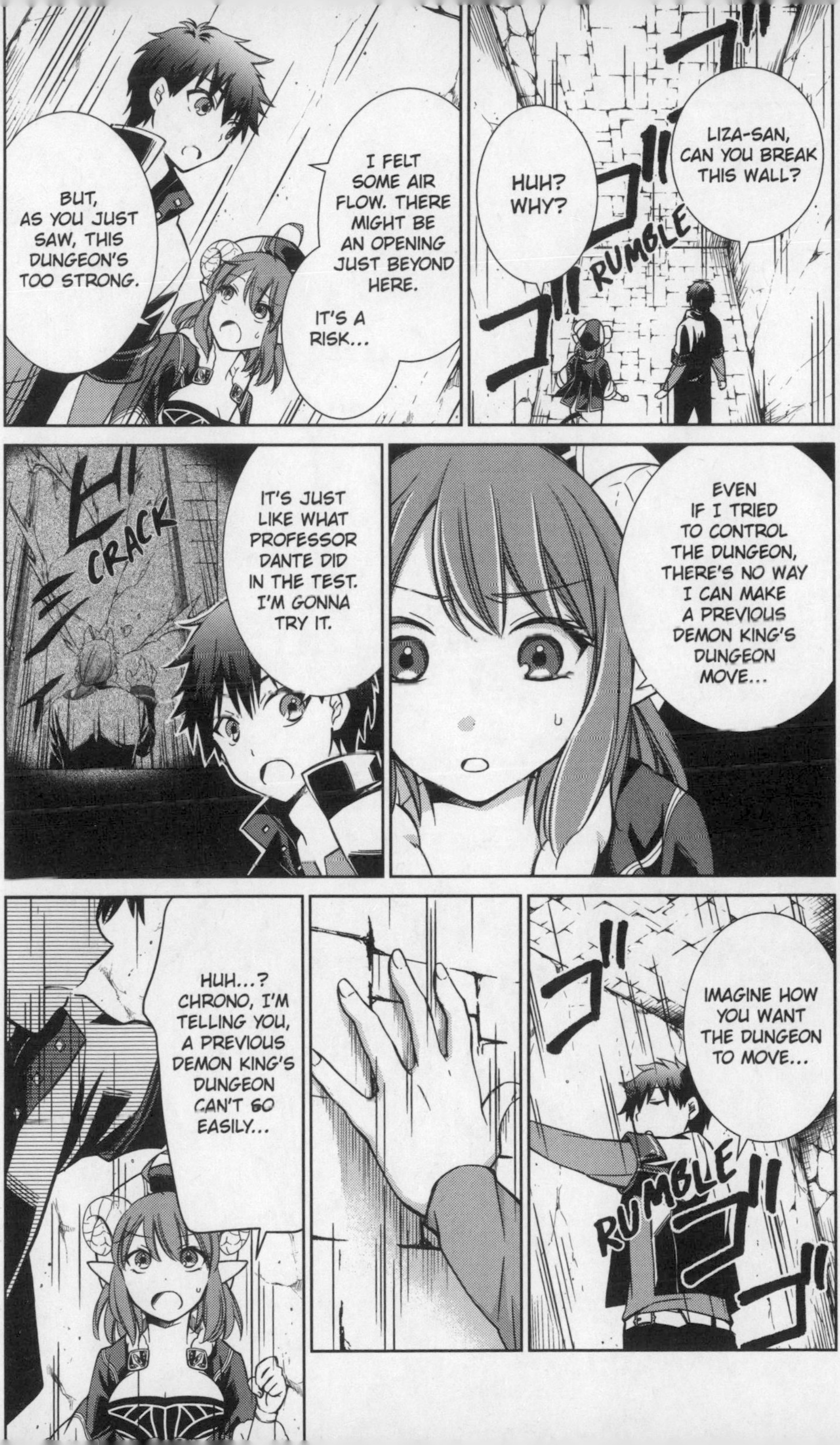
LIZA-SAN, CAN YOU BREAK THIS WALL?
HUH? WHY?
RUMBLE
I FELT SOME AIR FLOW. THERE MIGHT BE AN OPENING JUST BEYOND HERE.
BUT, AS YOU JUST SAW, THIS DUNGEON'S TOO STRONG.
IT'S A RISK...
EVEN IF I TRIED TO CONTROL THE DUNGEON, THERE'S NO WAY I CAN MAKE A PREVIOUS DEMON KING'S DUNGEON MOVE...
IT'S JUST LIKE WHAT PROFESSOR DANTE DID IN THE TEST. I'M GONNA TRY IT.
CRACK
IMAGINE HOW YOU WANT THE DUNGEON TO MOVE...
RUMBLE
HUH...? CHRONO, I'M TELLING YOU, A PREVIOUS DEMON KING'S DUNGEON CAN'T GO EASILY...

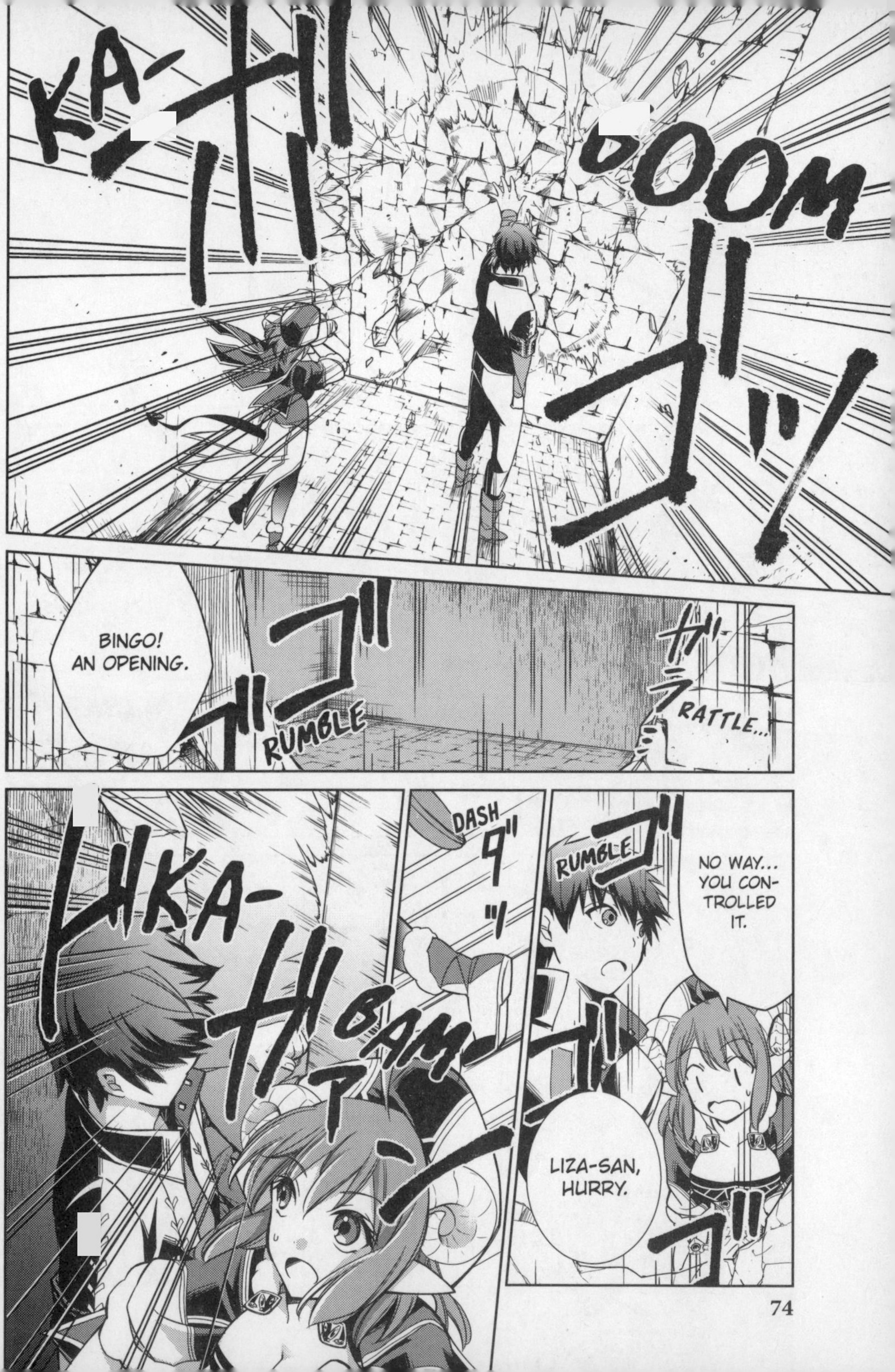
BOOM
ゴッ!
KA-
ガラ
RATTLE...
BINGO! AN OPENING.
ゴ
RUMBLE
RUMBLE
ゴ
NO WAY... YOU CON-TROLLED IT.
LIZA-SAN, HURRY.
DASH
ダッ
KA-
BAM-

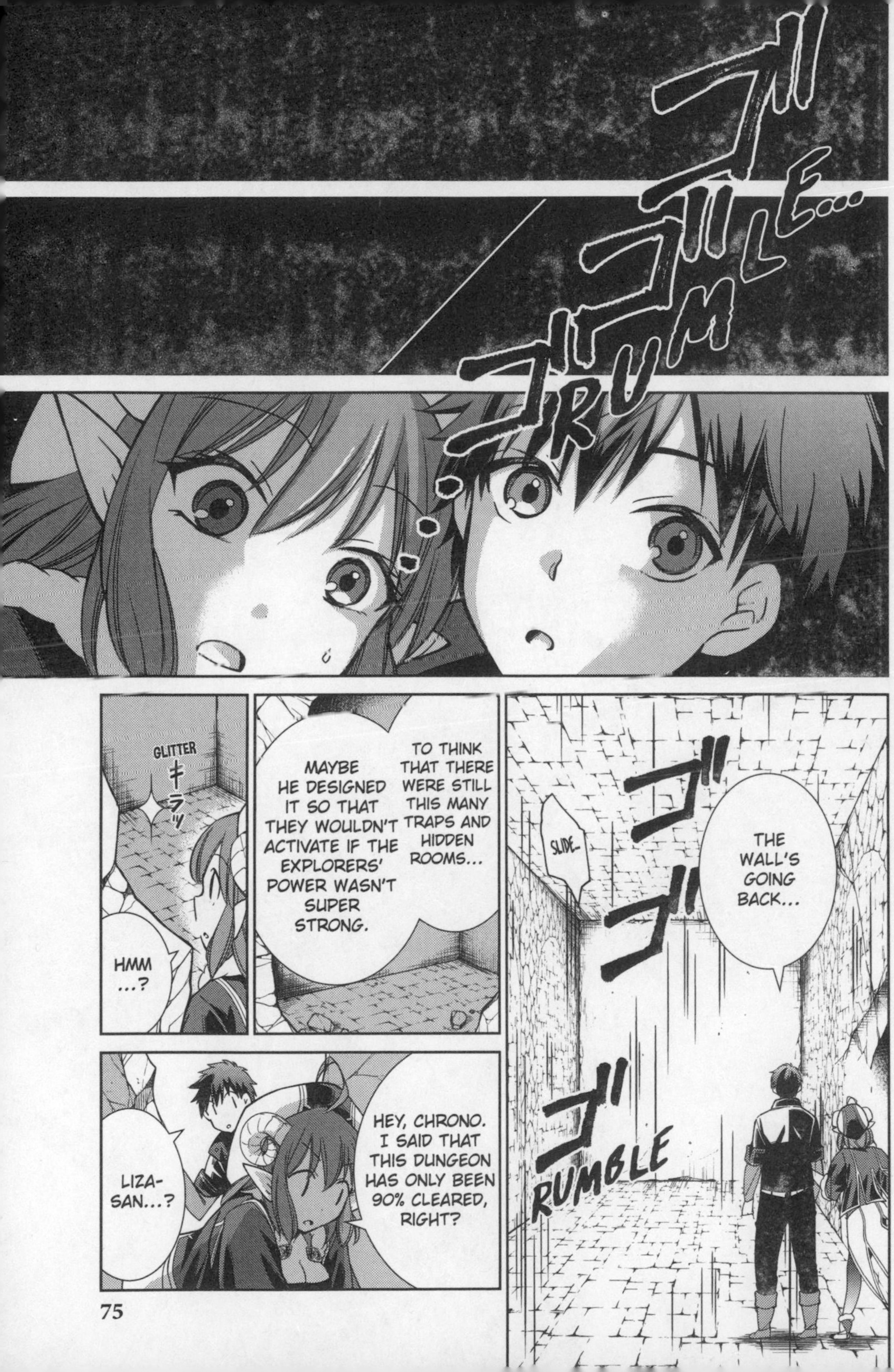

ゴゴゴ
RUMBLE...
THE WALL'S GOING BACK...
SLIDE...
ゴゴゴ
RUMBLE
TO THINK THAT THERE WERE STILL THIS MANY TRAPS AND HIDDEN ROOMS...
MAYBE HE DESIGNED IT SO THAT THEY WOULDN'T ACTIVATE IF THE EXPLORERS' POWER WASN'T SUPER STRONG.
GLITTER
キラッ
HMM ...?
HEY, CHRONO. I SAID THAT THIS DUNGEON HAS ONLY BEEN 90% CLEARED, RIGHT?
LIZA-SAN...?

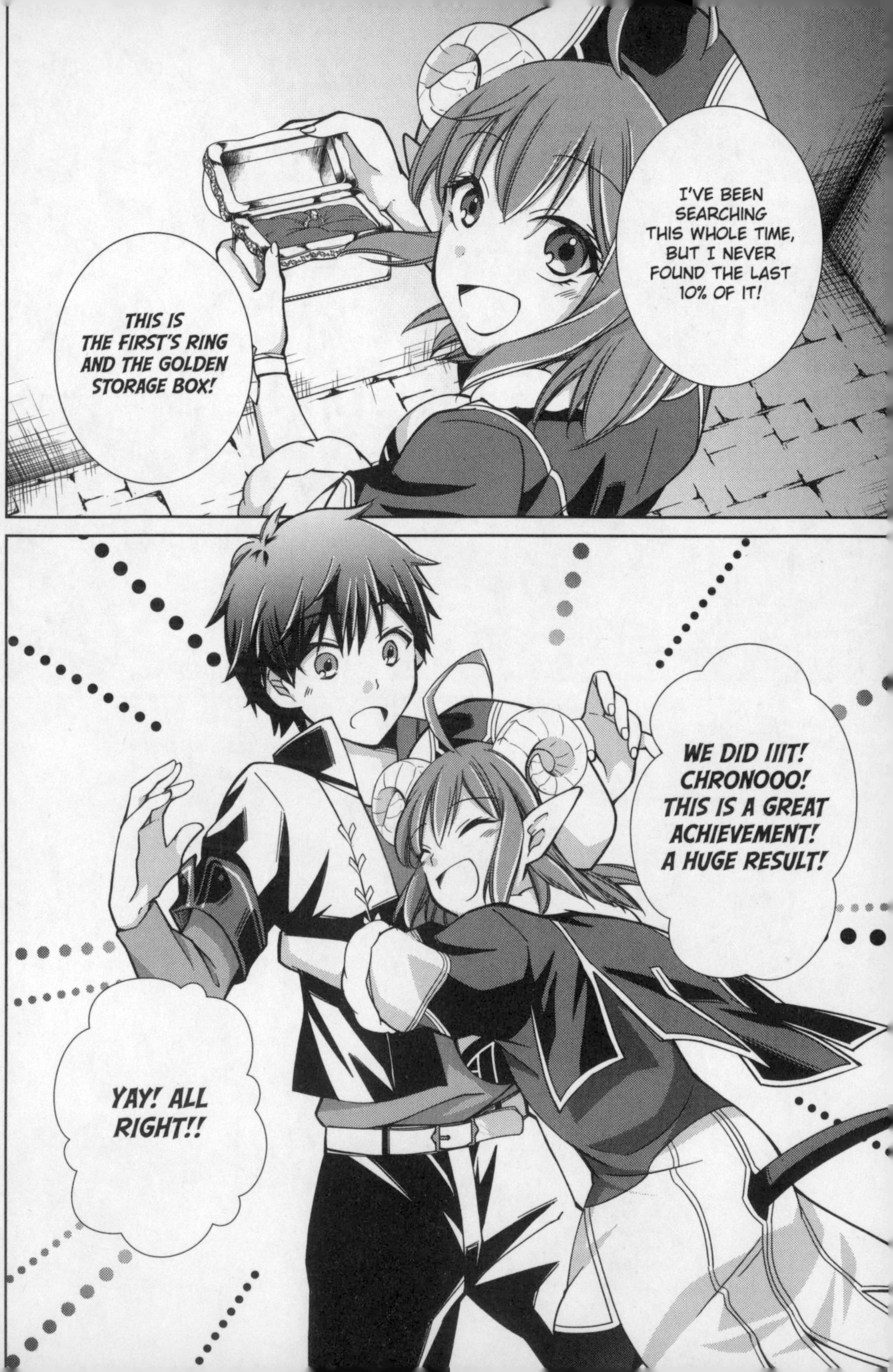
I'VE BEEN SEARCHING THIS WHOLE TIME, BUT I NEVER FOUND THE LAST 10% OF IT!
THIS IS THE FIRST'S RING AND THE GOLDEN STORAGE BOX!
WE DID IIIT! CHRONOOO! THIS IS A GREAT ACHIEVEMENT! A HUGE RESULT!
YAY! ALL RIGHT!!

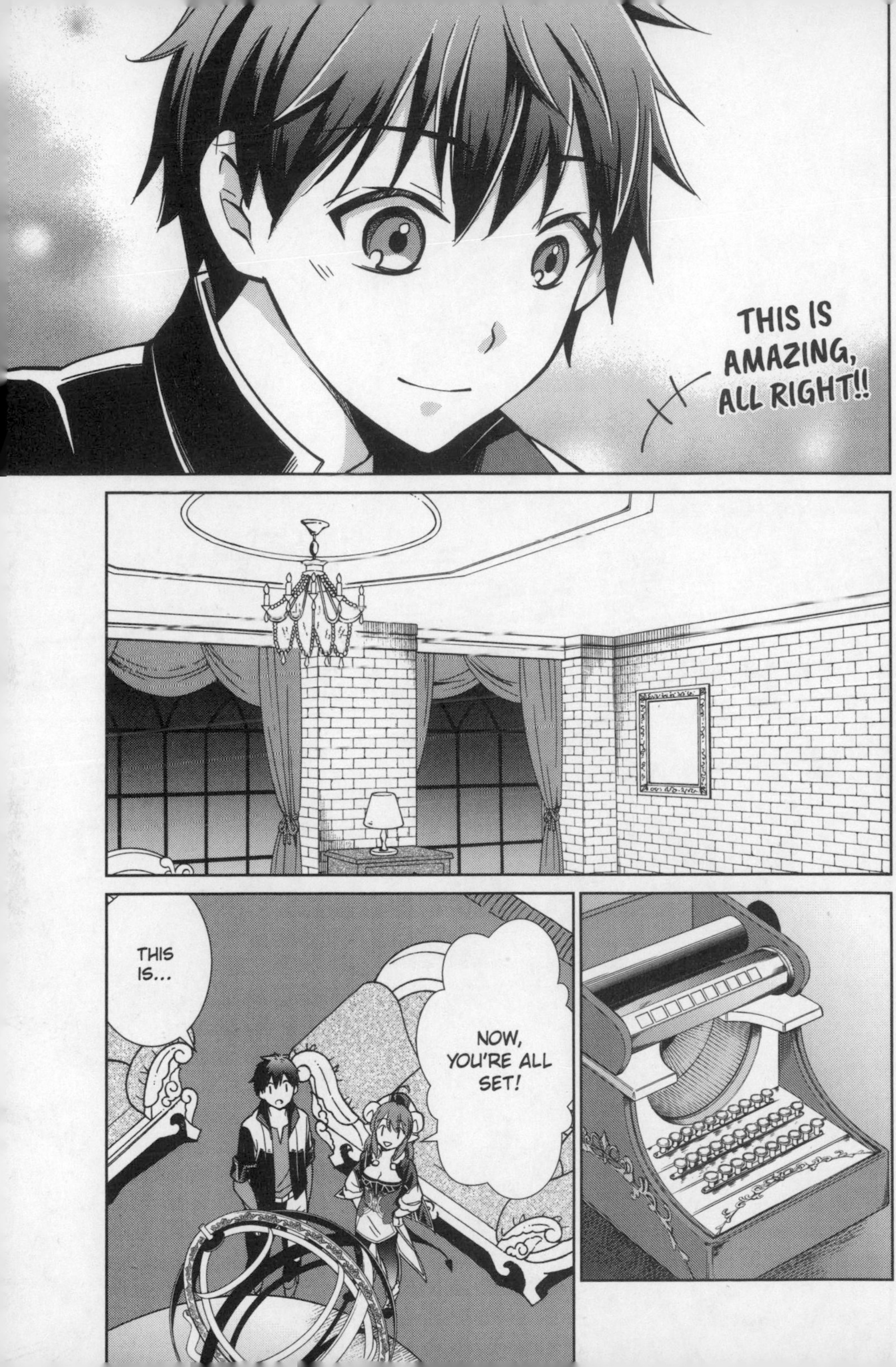
THIS IS AMAZING, ALL RIGHT!!
NOW, YOU'RE ALL SET!
THIS IS...

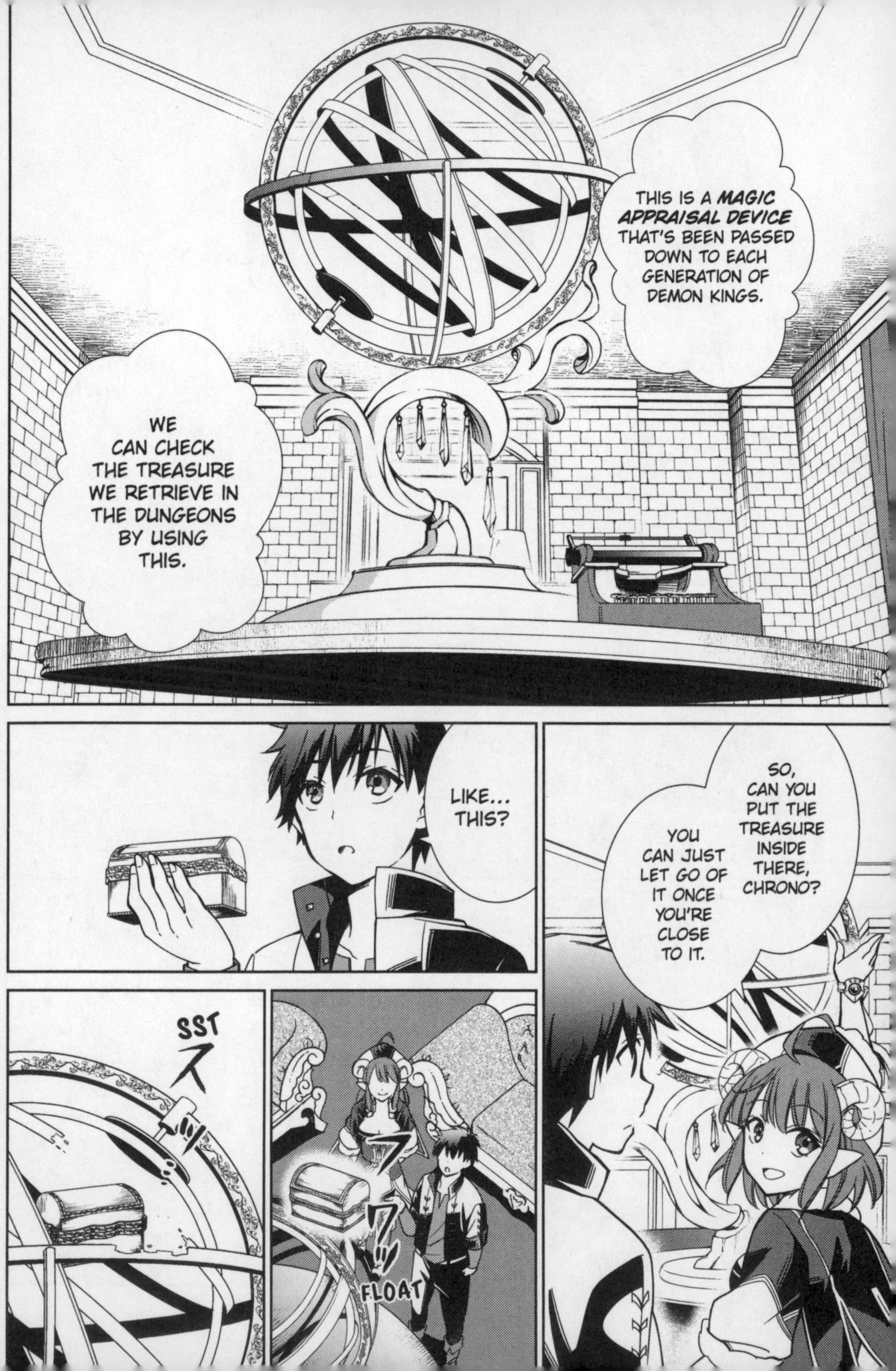
THIS IS A ***MAGIC APPRAISAL DEVICE*** THAT'S BEEN PASSED DOWN TO EACH GENERATION OF DEMON KINGS.
WE CAN CHECK THE TREASURE WE RETRIEVE IN THE DUNGEONS BY USING THIS.
SO, CAN YOU PUT THE TREASURE INSIDE THERE, CHRONO?
YOU CAN JUST LET GO OF IT ONCE YOU'RE CLOSE TO IT.
LIKE... THIS?
FLOAT
SST

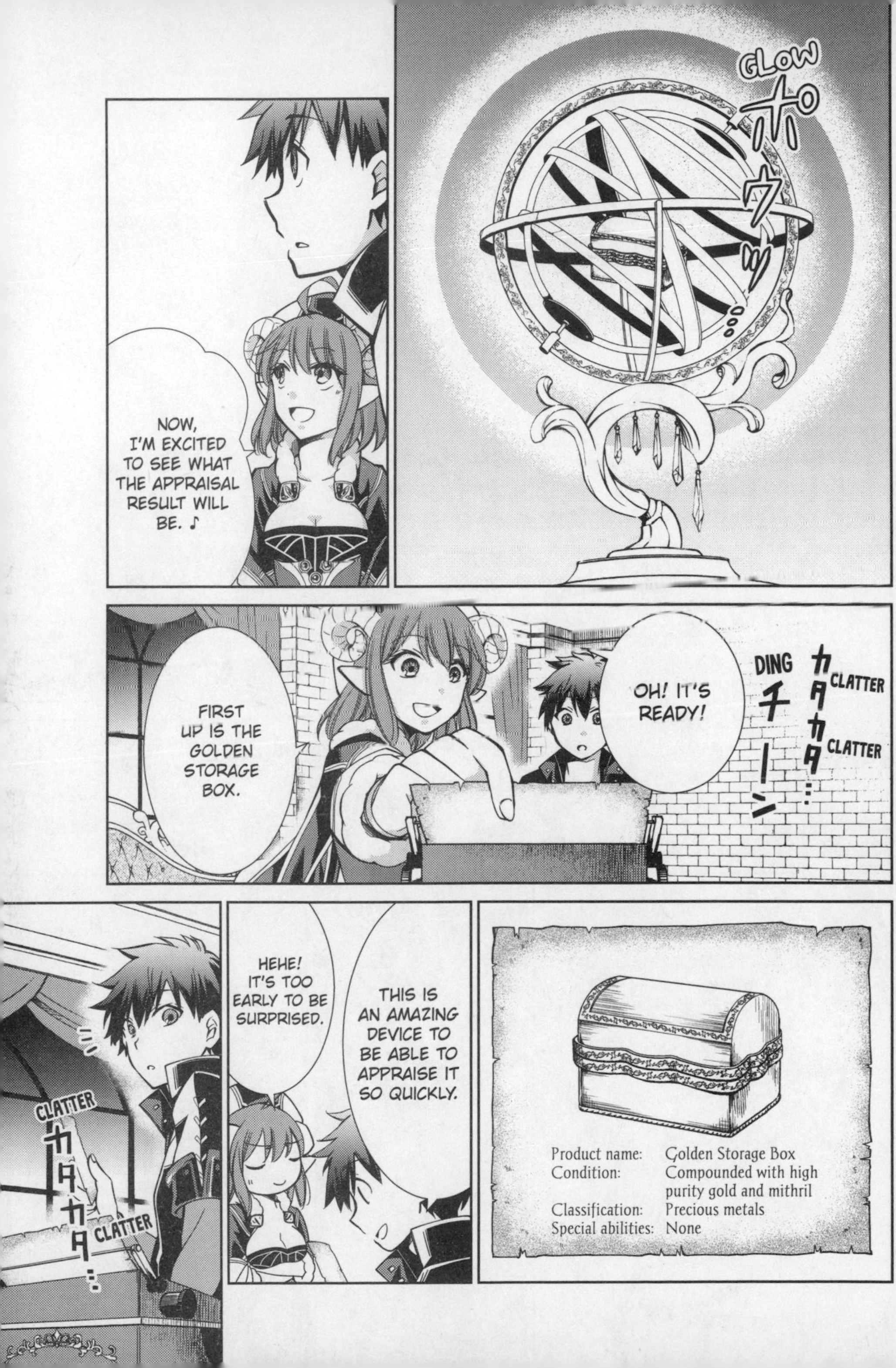
GLOW
ポウッ…
NOW, I'M EXCITED TO SEE WHAT THE APPRAISAL RESULT WILL BE. ♪
CLATTER
CLATTER
カタカタ…
DING
チーン
OH! IT'S READY!
FIRST UP IS THE GOLDEN STORAGE BOX.
Product name: Golden Storage Box
Condition: Compounded with high purity gold and mithril
Classification: Precious metals
Special abilities: None
THIS IS AN AMAZING DEVICE TO BE ABLE TO APPRAISE IT SO QUICKLY.
HEHE! IT'S TOO EARLY TO BE SURPRISED.
CLATTER
カタカタ…
CLATTER

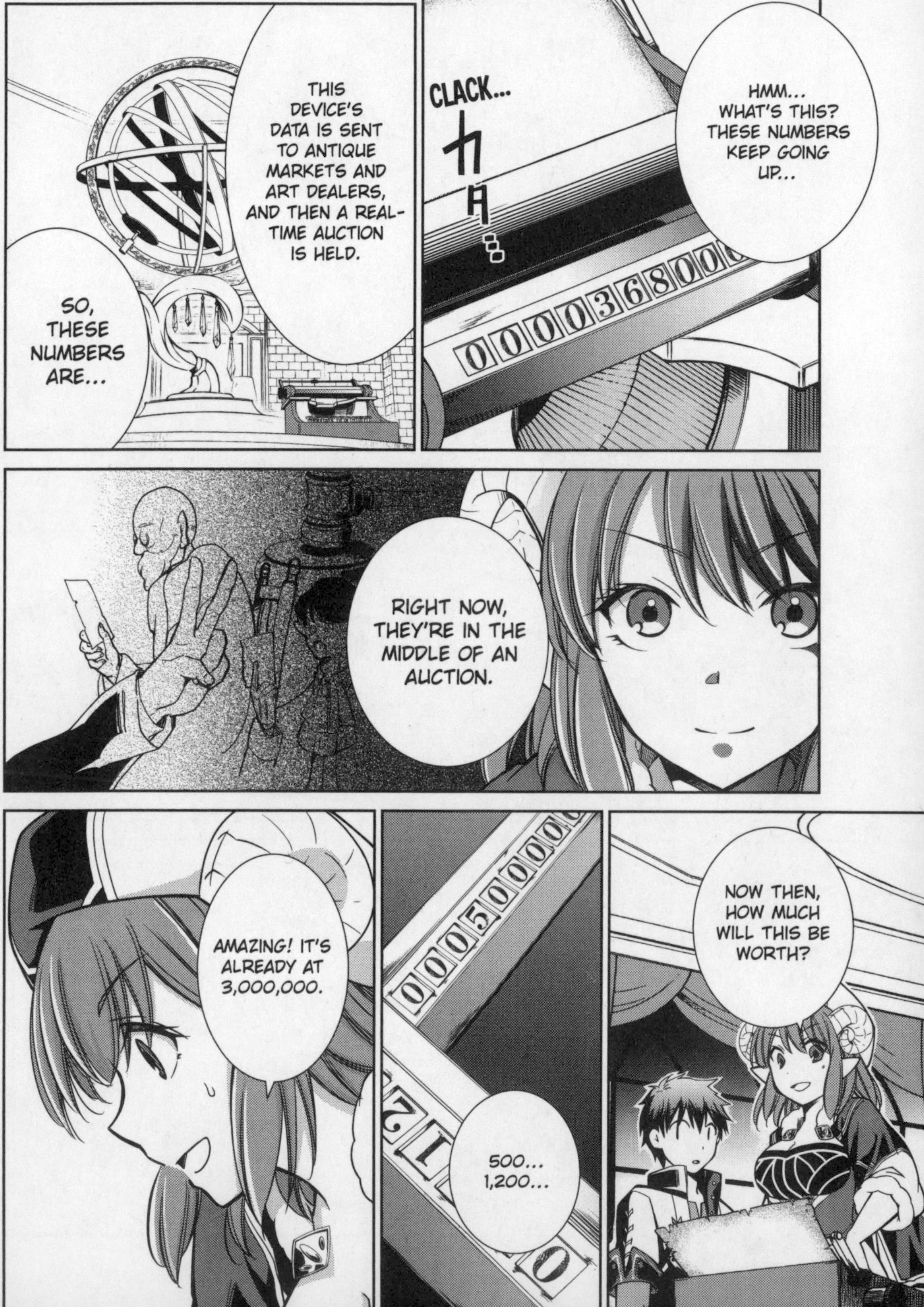
HMM... WHAT'S THIS? THESE NUMBERS KEEP GOING UP...
CLACK...
カタ...
THIS DEVICE'S DATA IS SENT TO ANTIQUE MARKETS AND ART DEALERS, AND THEN A REAL-TIME AUCTION IS HELD.
SO, THESE NUMBERS ARE...
RIGHT NOW, THEY'RE IN THE MIDDLE OF AN AUCTION.
NOW THEN, HOW MUCH WILL THIS BE WORTH?
500... 1,200...
AMAZING! IT'S ALREADY AT 3,000,000.

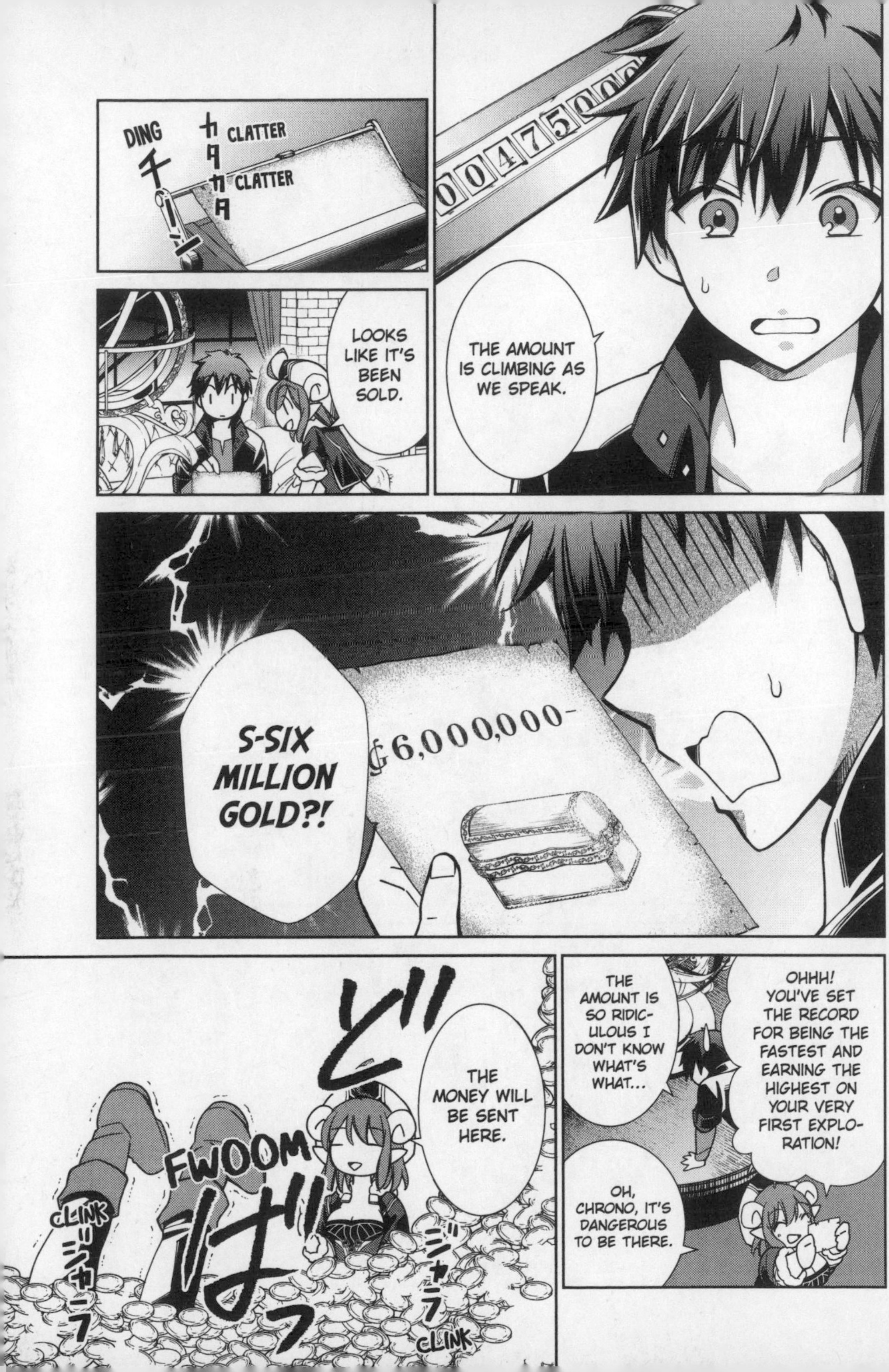

THE AMOUNT IS CLIMBING AS WE SPEAK.
00475000
DING
チーン
CLATTER
カタカタ
CLATTER
LOOKS LIKE IT'S BEEN SOLD.
S-SIX MILLION GOLD?!
₲6,000,000-
OHHH! YOU'VE SET THE RECORD FOR BEING THE FASTEST AND EARNING THE HIGHEST ON YOUR VERY FIRST EXPLORATION!
THE AMOUNT IS SO RIDICULOUS I DON'T KNOW WHAT'S WHAT...
OH, CHRONO, IT'S DANGEROUS TO BE THERE.
THE MONEY WILL BE SENT HERE.
FWOOM
ばっ
CLINK
ジャラ
CLINK

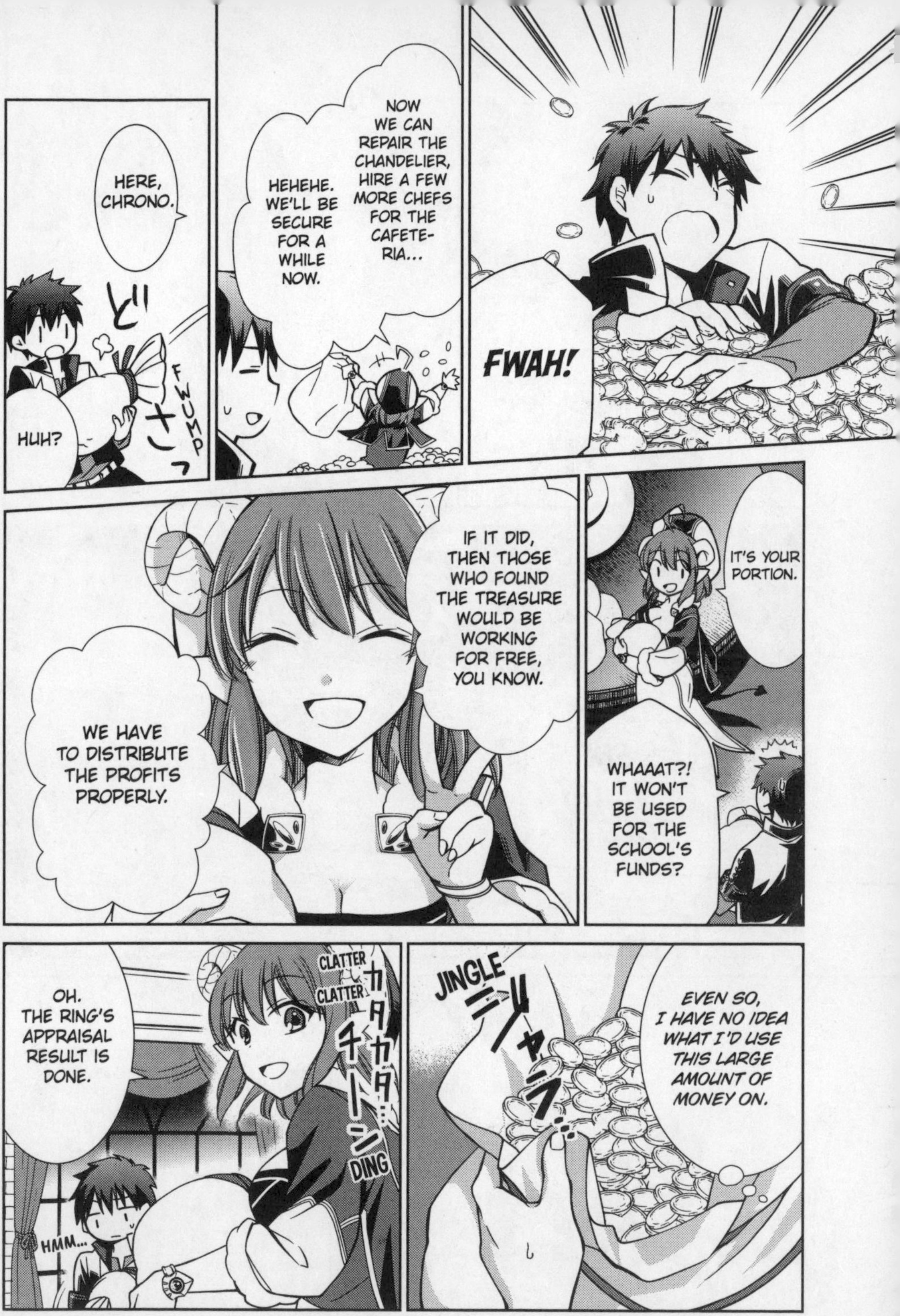
FWAH!
NOW WE CAN REPAIR THE CHANDELIER, HIRE A FEW MORE CHEFS FOR THE CAFETE-RIA...
HEHEHE. WE'LL BE SECURE FOR A WHILE NOW.
HERE, CHRONO.
FWUMP
HUH?
IT'S YOUR PORTION.
WHAAAT?! IT WON'T BE USED FOR THE SCHOOL'S FUNDS?
IF IT DID, THEN THOSE WHO FOUND THE TREASURE WOULD BE WORKING FOR FREE, YOU KNOW.
WE HAVE TO DISTRIBUTE THE PROFITS PROPERLY.
JINGLE
EVEN SO, I HAVE NO IDEA WHAT I'D USE THIS LARGE AMOUNT OF MONEY ON.
CLATTER
CLATTER
DING
OH. THE RING'S APPRAISAL RESULT IS DONE.
HMM...

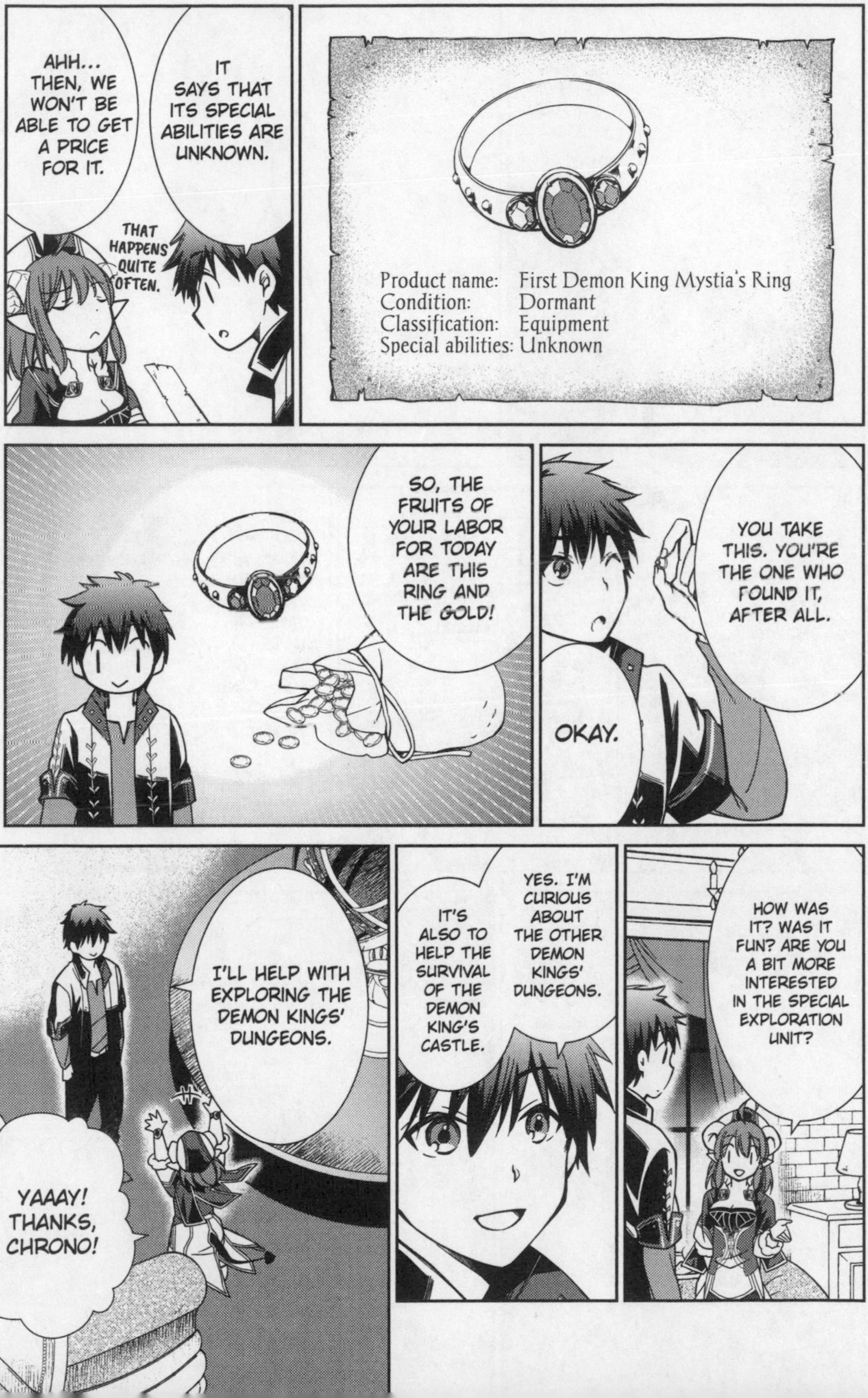
Product name: First Demon King Mystia's Ring
Condition: Dormant
Classification: Equipment
Special abilities: Unknown
IT SAYS THAT ITS SPECIAL ABILITIES ARE UNKNOWN.
AHH... THEN, WE WON'T BE ABLE TO GET A PRICE FOR IT.
THAT HAPPENS QUITE OFTEN.
YOU TAKE THIS. YOU'RE THE ONE WHO FOUND IT, AFTER ALL.
OKAY.
SO, THE FRUITS OF YOUR LABOR FOR TODAY ARE THIS RING AND THE GOLD!
HOW WAS IT? WAS IT FUN? ARE YOU A BIT MORE INTERESTED IN THE SPECIAL EXPLORATION UNIT?
YES. I'M CURIOUS ABOUT THE OTHER DEMON KINGS' DUNGEONS.
IT'S ALSO TO HELP THE SURVIVAL OF THE DEMON KING'S CASTLE.
I'LL HELP WITH EXPLORING THE DEMON KINGS' DUNGEONS.
YAAAY! THANKS, CHRONO!

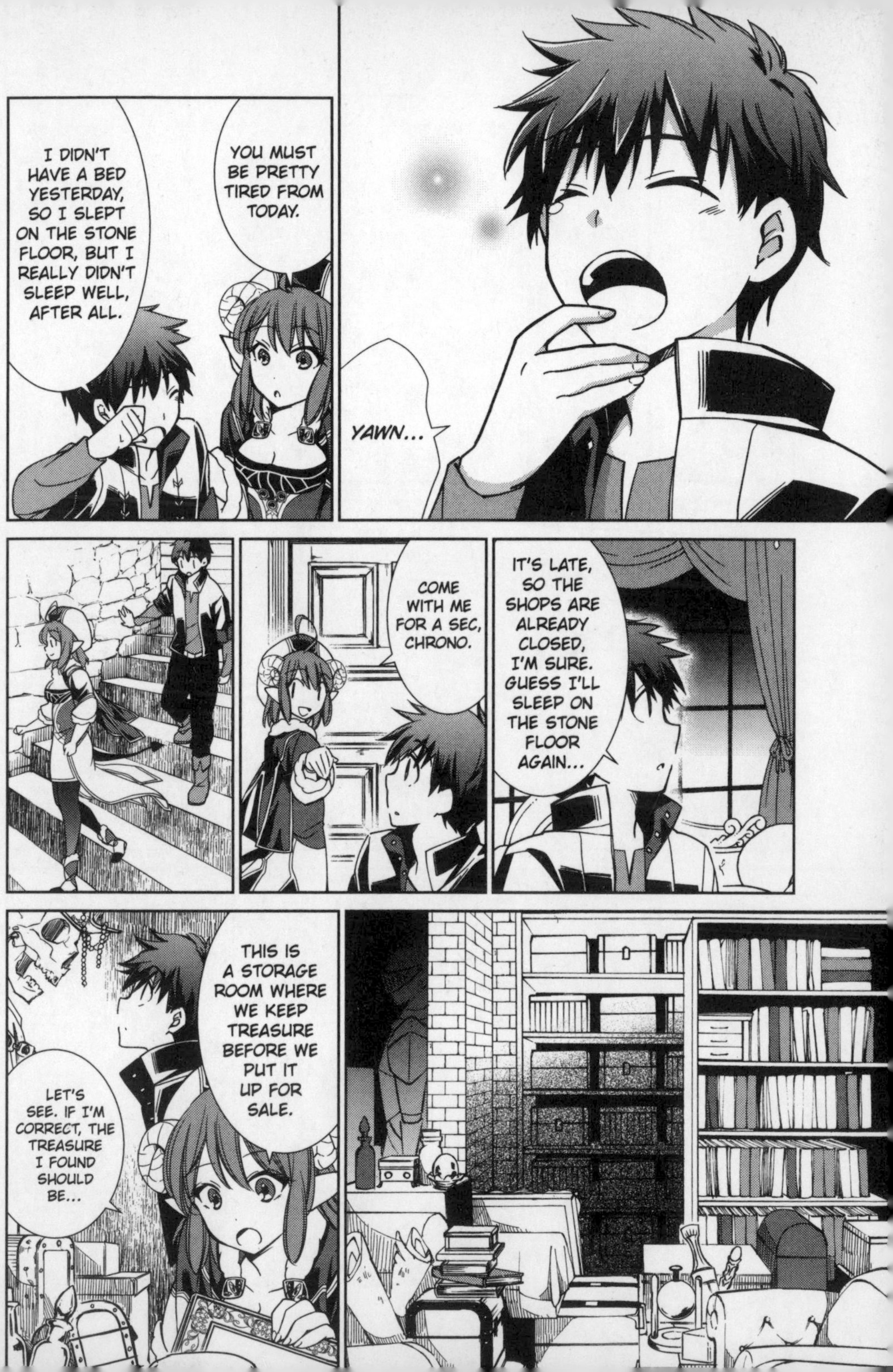
YAWN...
YOU MUST BE PRETTY TIRED FROM TODAY.
I DIDN'T HAVE A BED YESTERDAY, SO I SLEPT ON THE STONE FLOOR, BUT I REALLY DIDN'T SLEEP WELL, AFTER ALL.
IT'S LATE, SO THE SHOPS ARE ALREADY CLOSED, I'M SURE. GUESS I'LL SLEEP ON THE STONE FLOOR AGAIN...
COME WITH ME FOR A SEC, CHRONO.
THIS IS A STORAGE ROOM WHERE WE KEEP TREASURE BEFORE WE PUT IT UP FOR SALE.
LET'S SEE. IF I'M CORRECT, THE TREASURE I FOUND SHOULD BE...

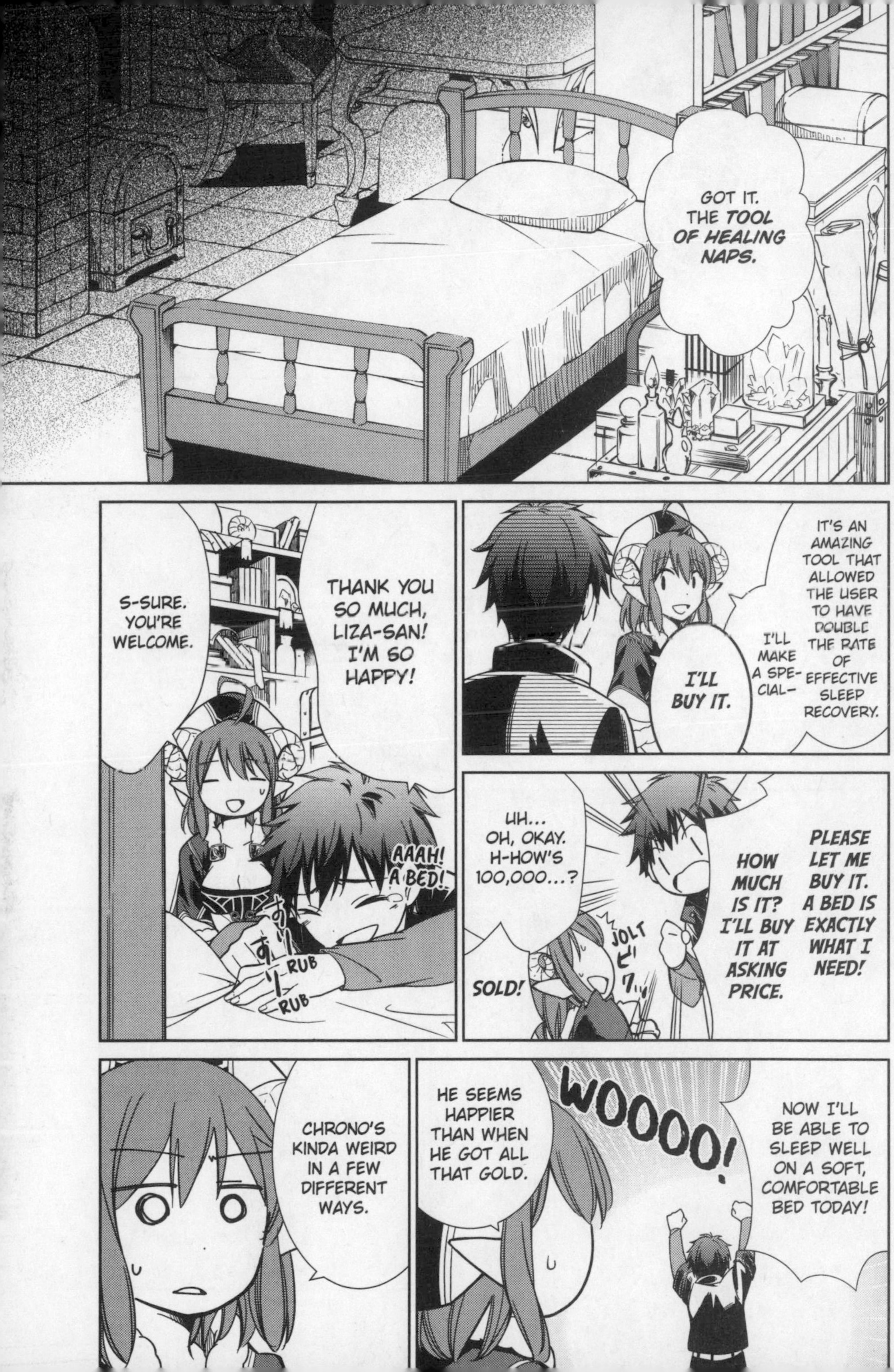
GOT IT. THE TOOL OF HEALING NAPS.
IT'S AN AMAZING TOOL THAT ALLOWED THE USER TO HAVE DOUBLE THE RATE OF EFFECTIVE SLEEP RECOVERY.
I'LL MAKE A SPE-CIAL-
I'LL BUY IT.
PLEASE LET ME BUY IT. A BED IS EXACTLY WHAT I NEED!
HOW MUCH IS IT? I'LL BUY IT AT ASKING PRICE.
UH... OH, OKAY. H-HOW'S 100,000...?
JOLT
SOLD!
THANK YOU SO MUCH, LIZA-SAN! I'M SO HAPPY!
S-SURE. YOU'RE WELCOME.
AAAH! A BED!
RUB
RUB
NOW I'LL BE ABLE TO SLEEP WELL ON A SOFT, COMFORTABLE BED TODAY!
WOOOOO!
HE SEEMS HAPPIER THAN WHEN HE GOT ALL THAT GOLD.
CHRONO'S KINDA WEIRD IN A FEW DIFFERENT WAYS.

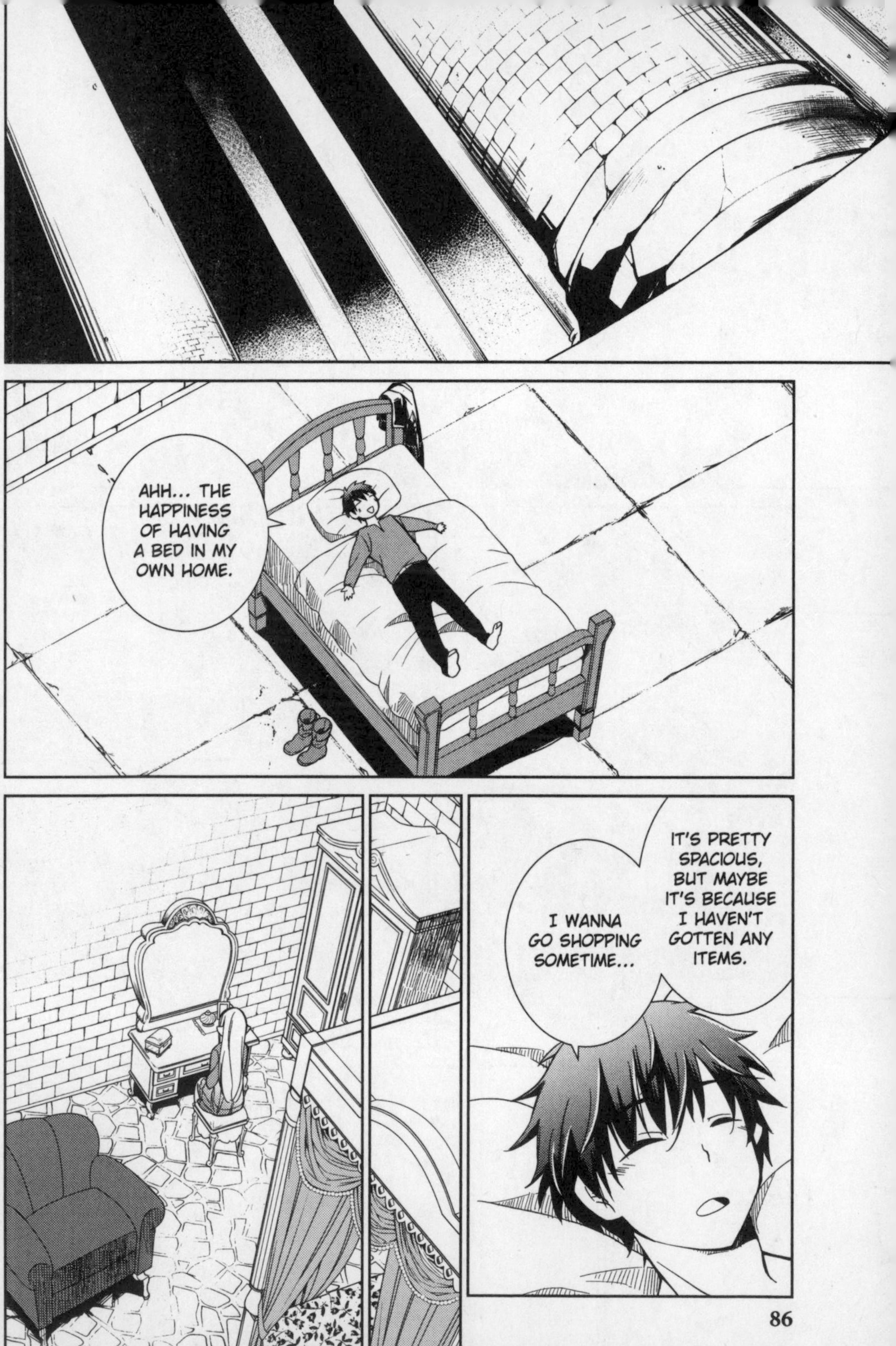
AHH... THE HAPPINESS OF HAVING A BED IN MY OWN HOME.
IT'S PRETTY SPACIOUS, BUT MAYBE IT'S BECAUSE I HAVEN'T GOTTEN ANY ITEMS.
I WANNA GO SHOPPING SOMETIME...

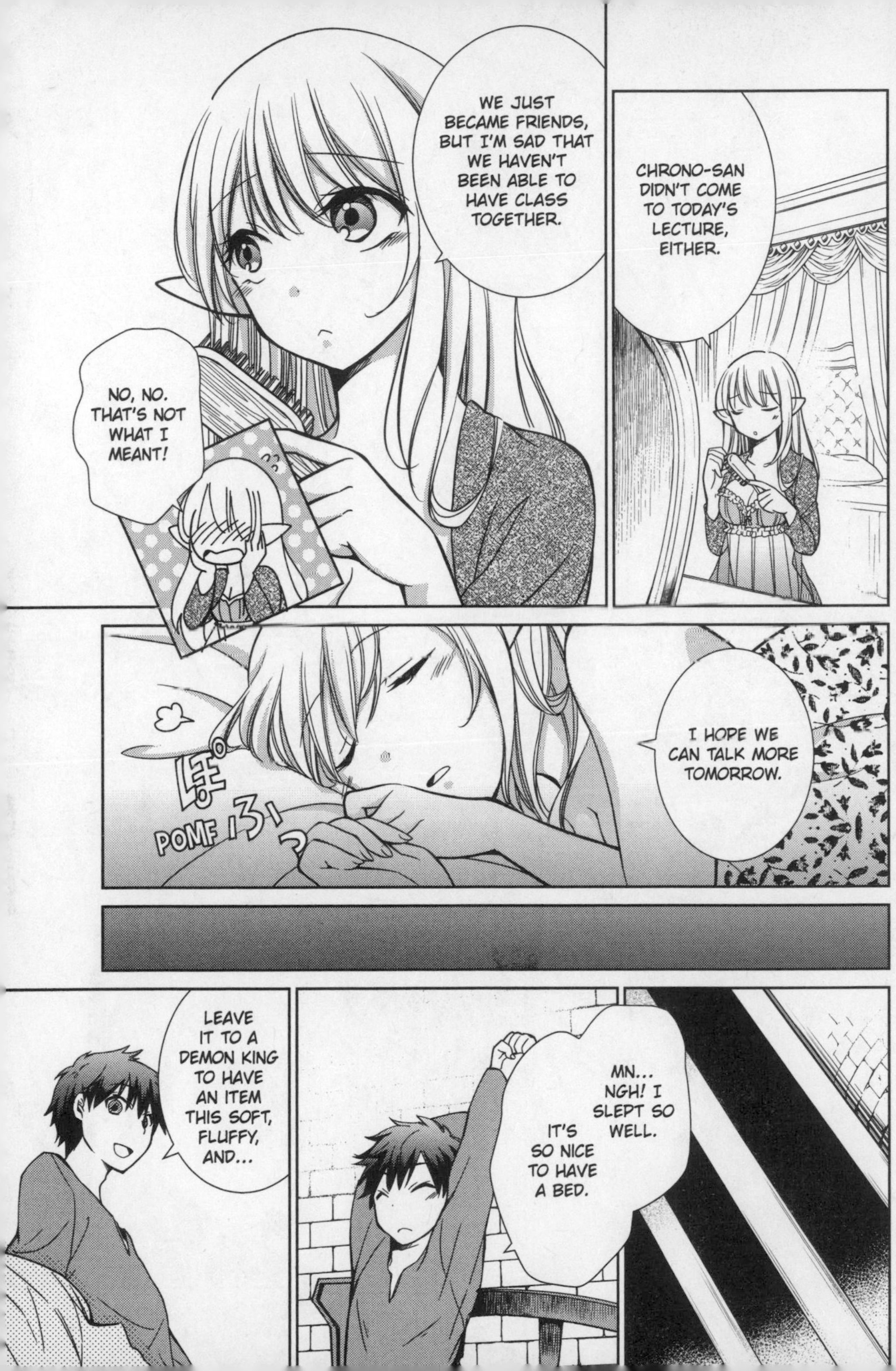
CHRONO-SAN DIDN'T COME TO TODAY'S LECTURE, EITHER.
WE JUST BECAME FRIENDS, BUT I'M SAD THAT WE HAVEN'T BEEN ABLE TO HAVE CLASS TOGETHER.
NO, NO. THAT'S NOT WHAT I MEANT!
I HOPE WE CAN TALK MORE TOMORROW.
POMF
MN... NGH! I SLEPT SO WELL.
IT'S SO NICE TO HAVE A BED.
LEAVE IT TO A DEMON KING TO HAVE AN ITEM THIS SOFT, FLUFFY, AND...

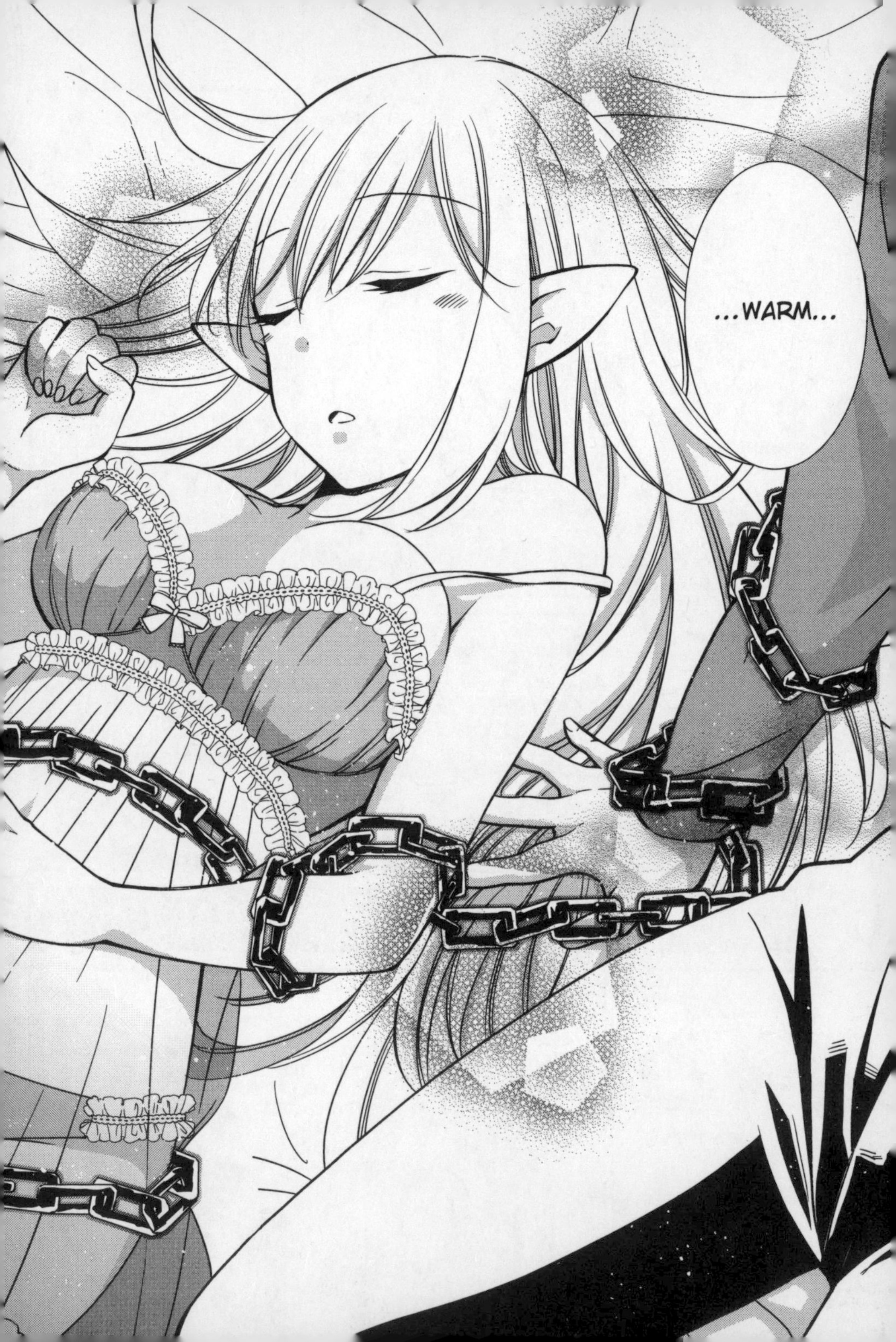
...WARM...

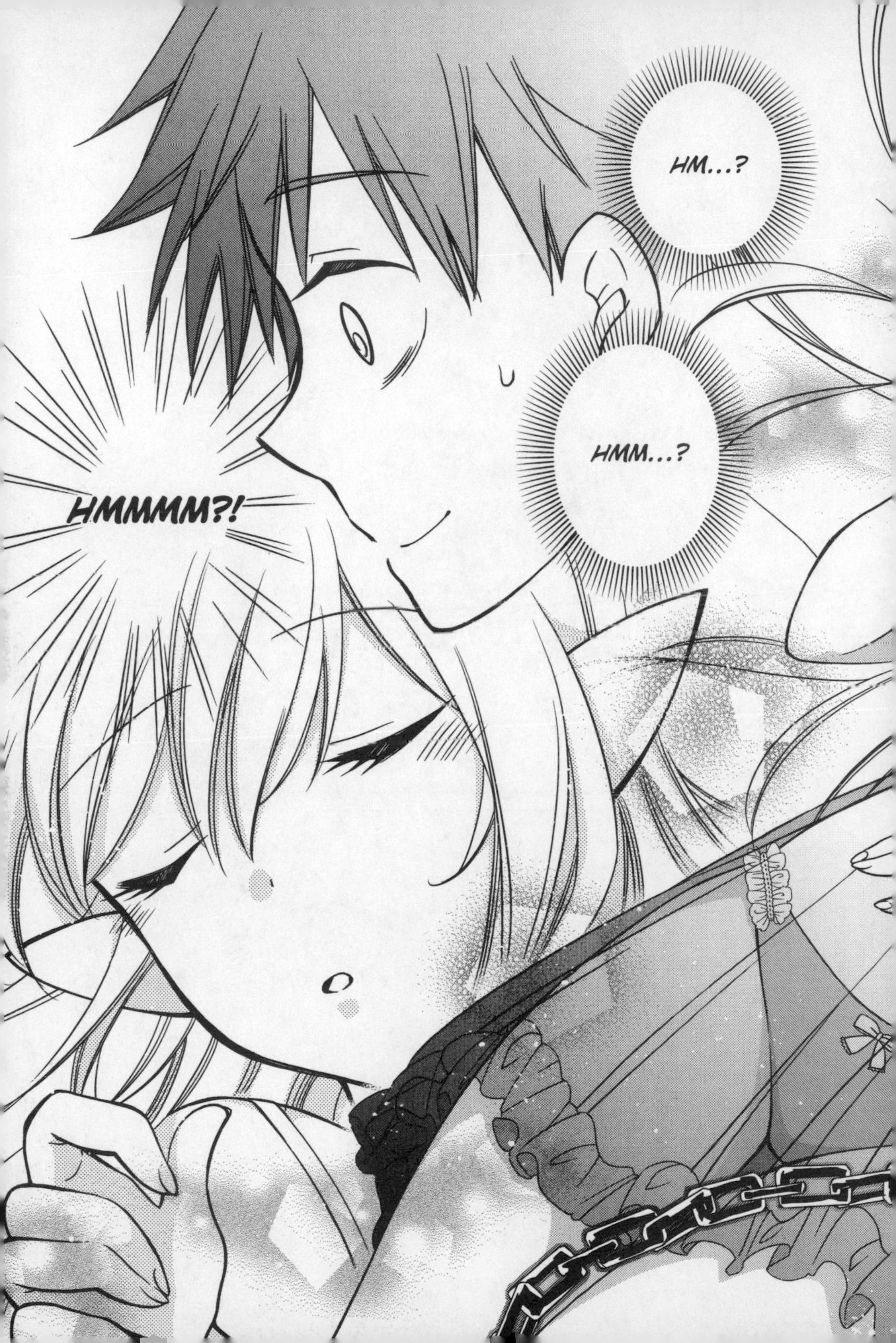
HM...?
HMM...?
HMMMM?!

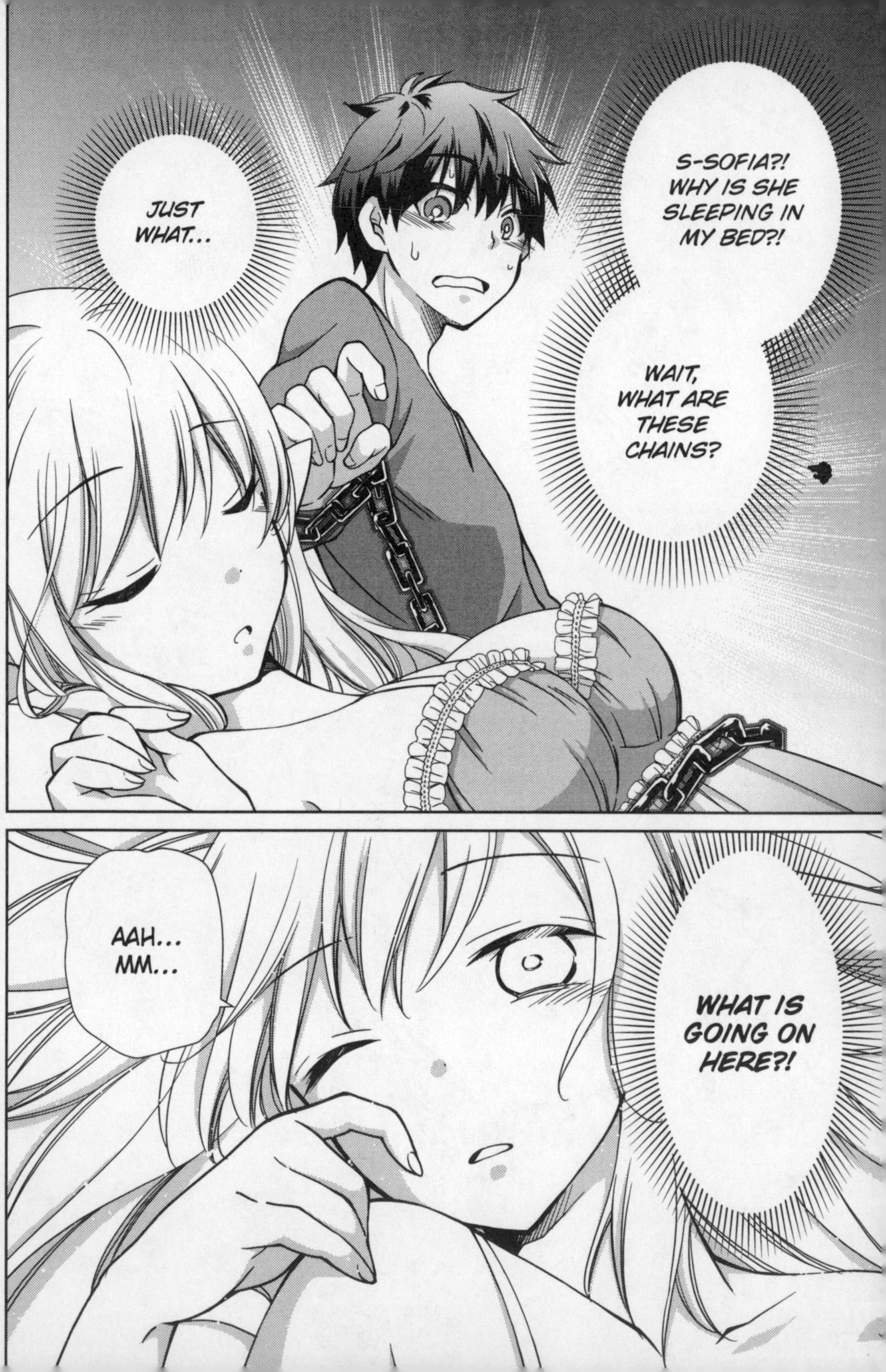
S-SOFIA?! WHY IS SHE SLEEPING IN MY BED?!
JUST WHAT...
WAIT, WHAT ARE THESE CHAINS?
WHAT IS GOING ON HERE?!
AAH... MM...

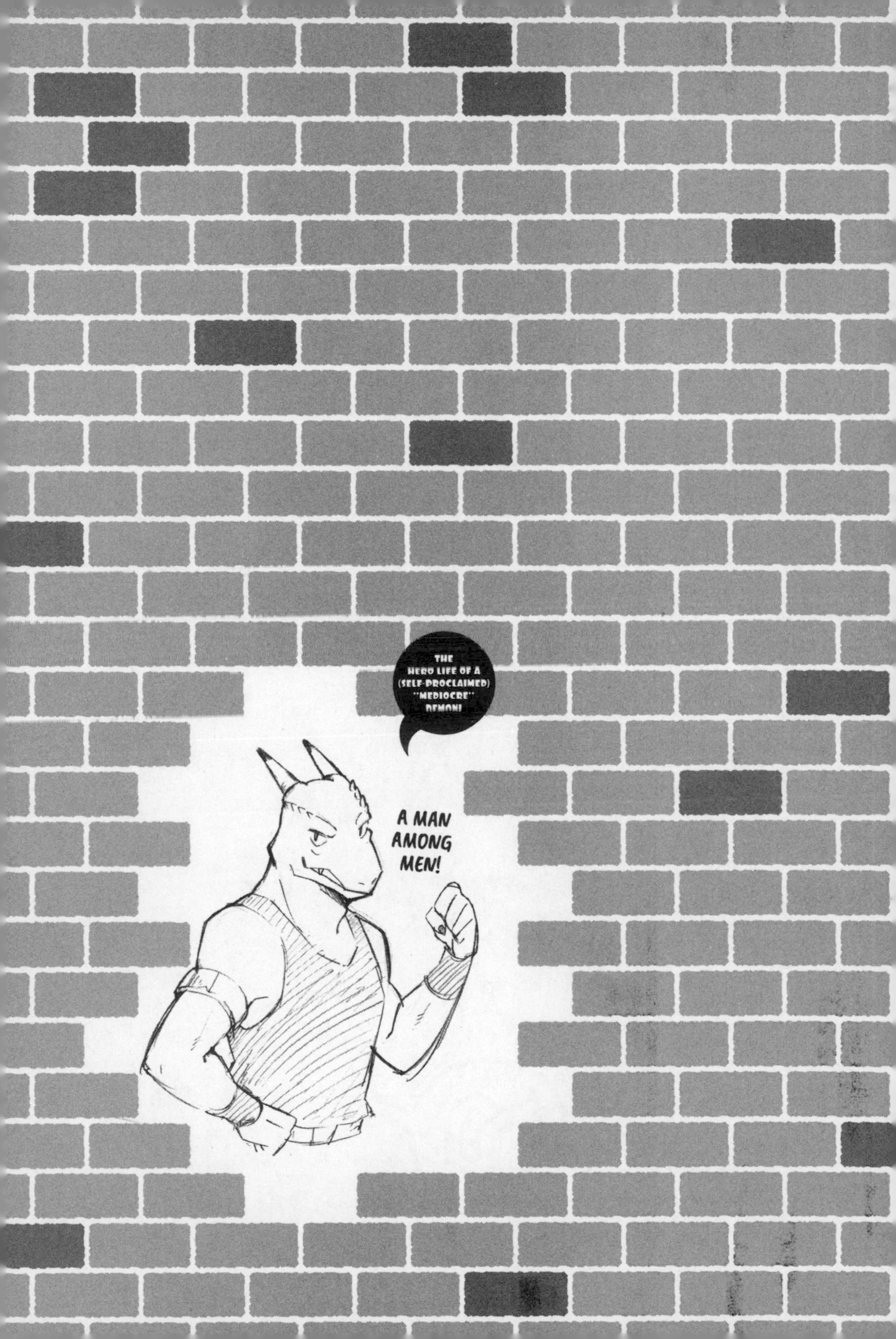
THE HERO LIFE OF A (SELF-PROCLAIMED) "MEDIOCRE" DEMON!
A MAN AMONG MEN!

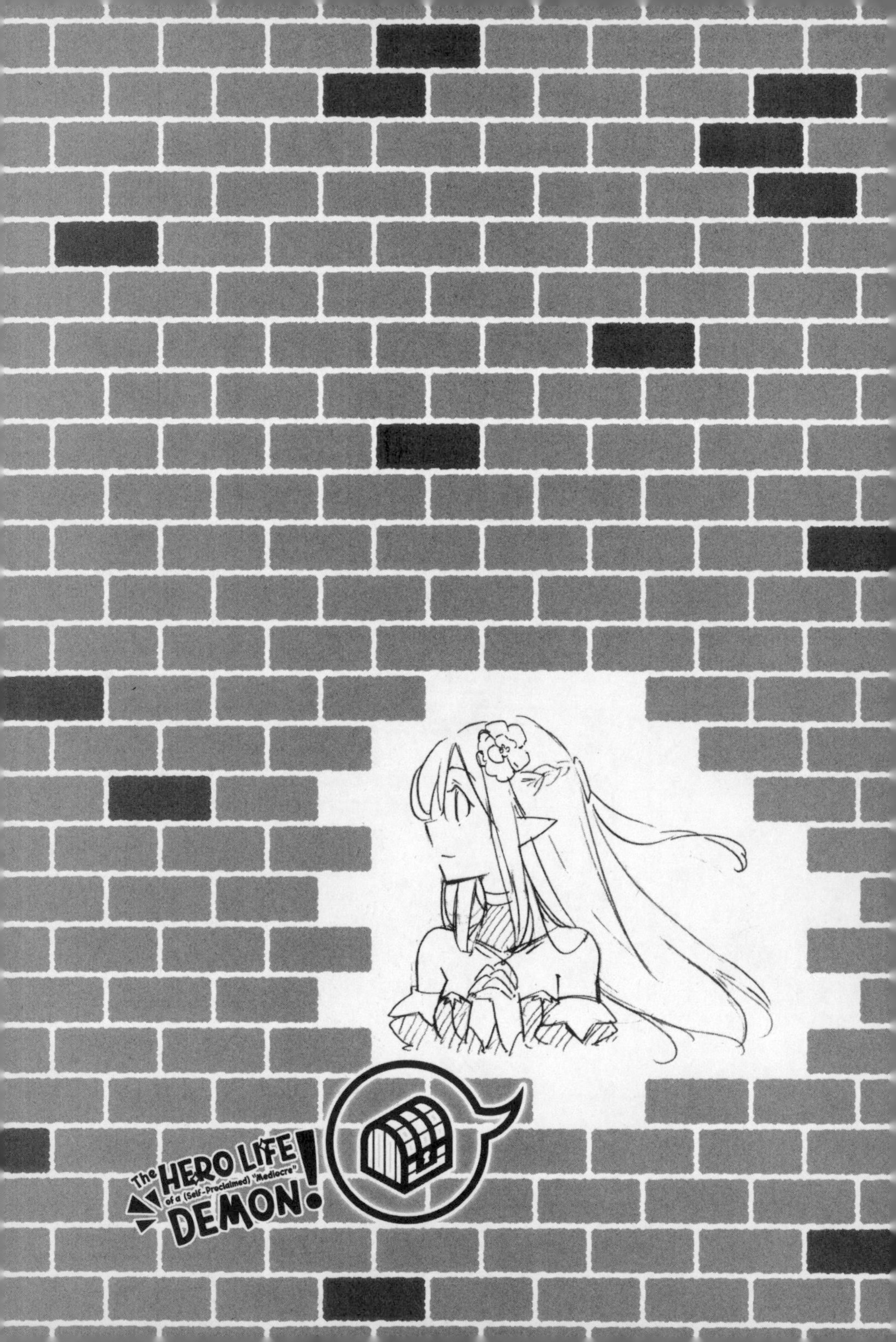
The HERO LIFE of a (Self-Proclaimed) "Mediocre" DEMON!

CHAPTER 3 CHRONO STICKS WITH SOFIA

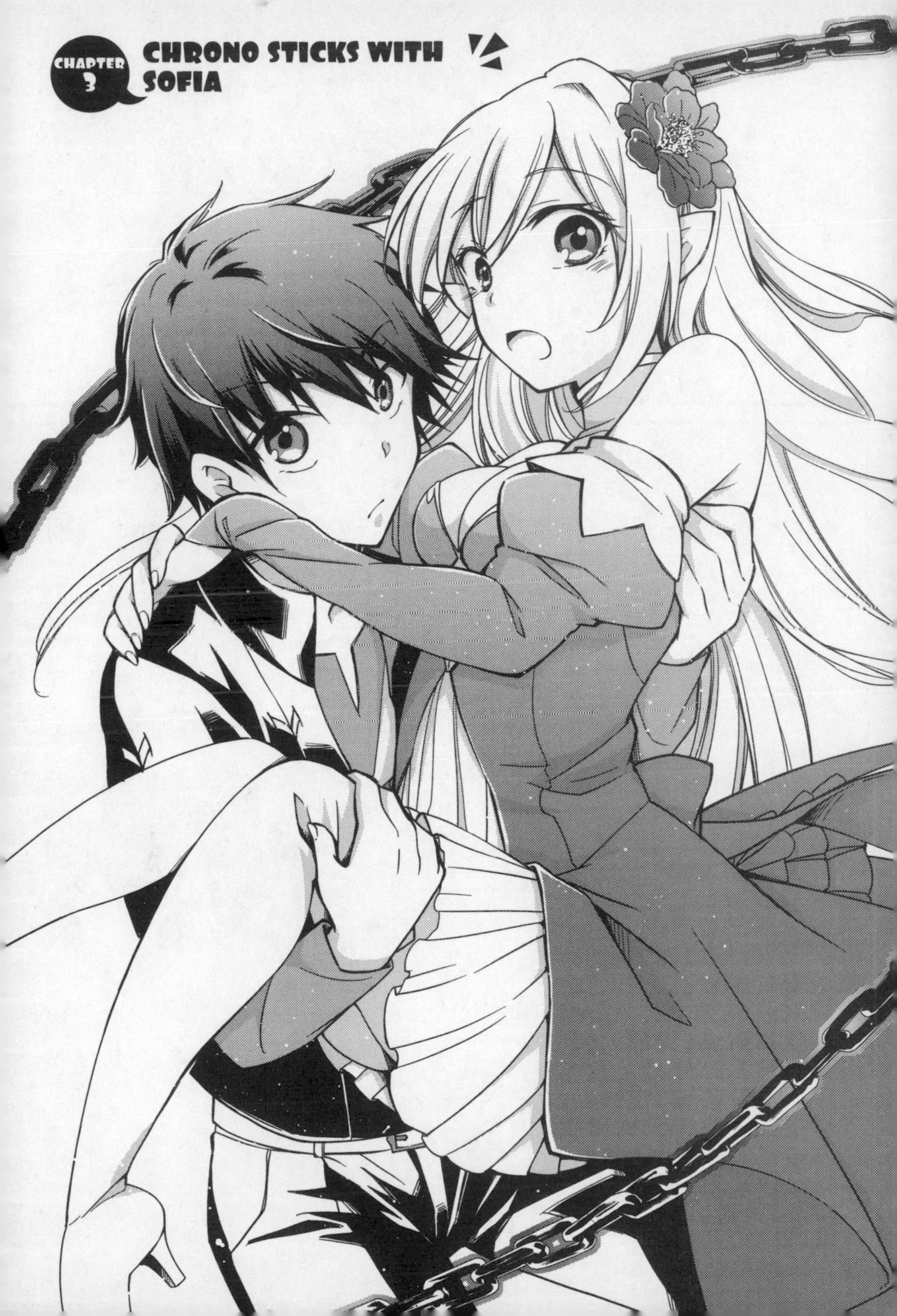

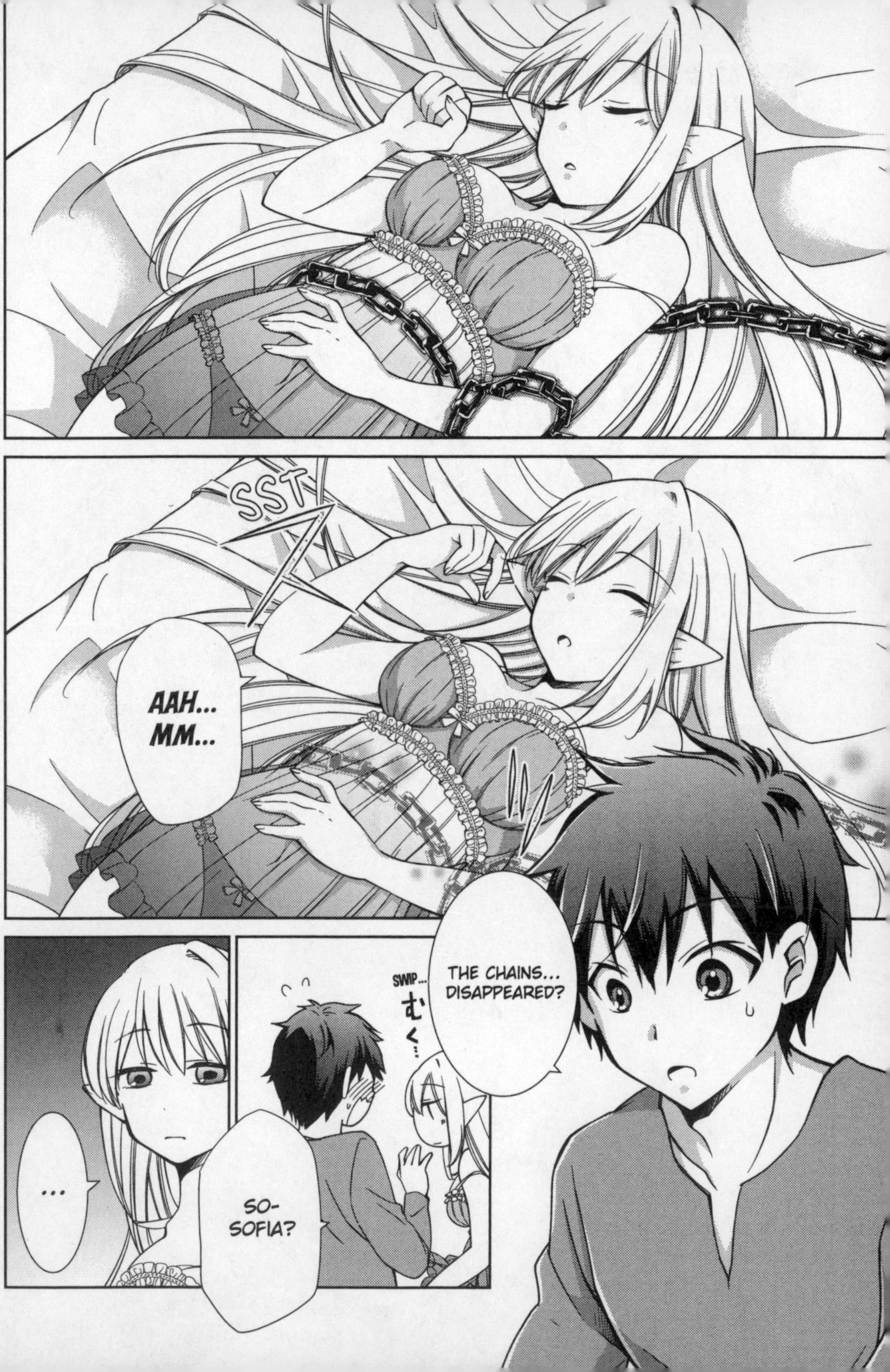
SST
AAH... MM...
THE CHAINS... DISAPPEARED?
SWIP...
むく...
SO-SOFIA?
...

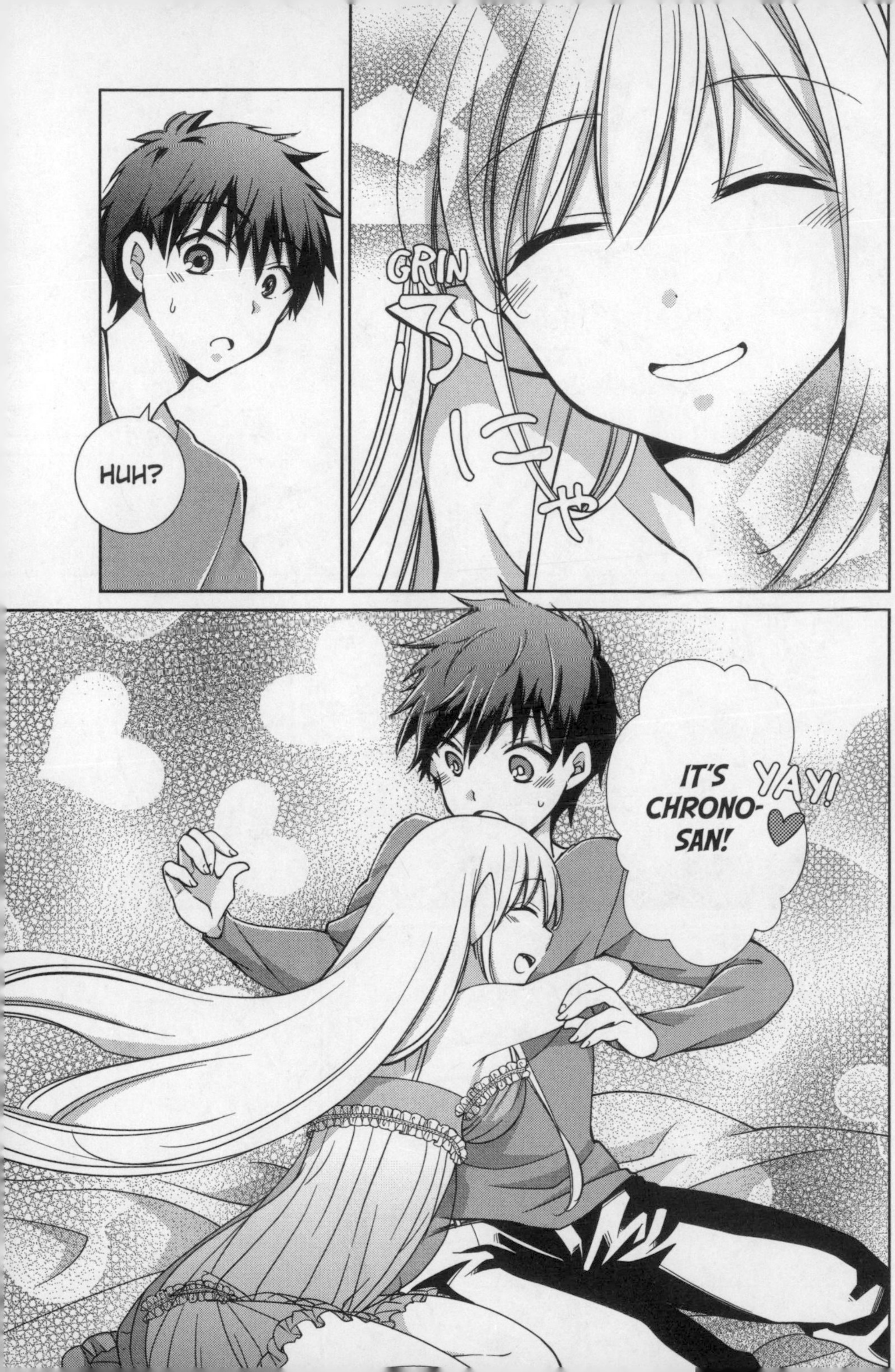
GRIN
HUH?
IT'S CHRONO-SAN!
YAY!

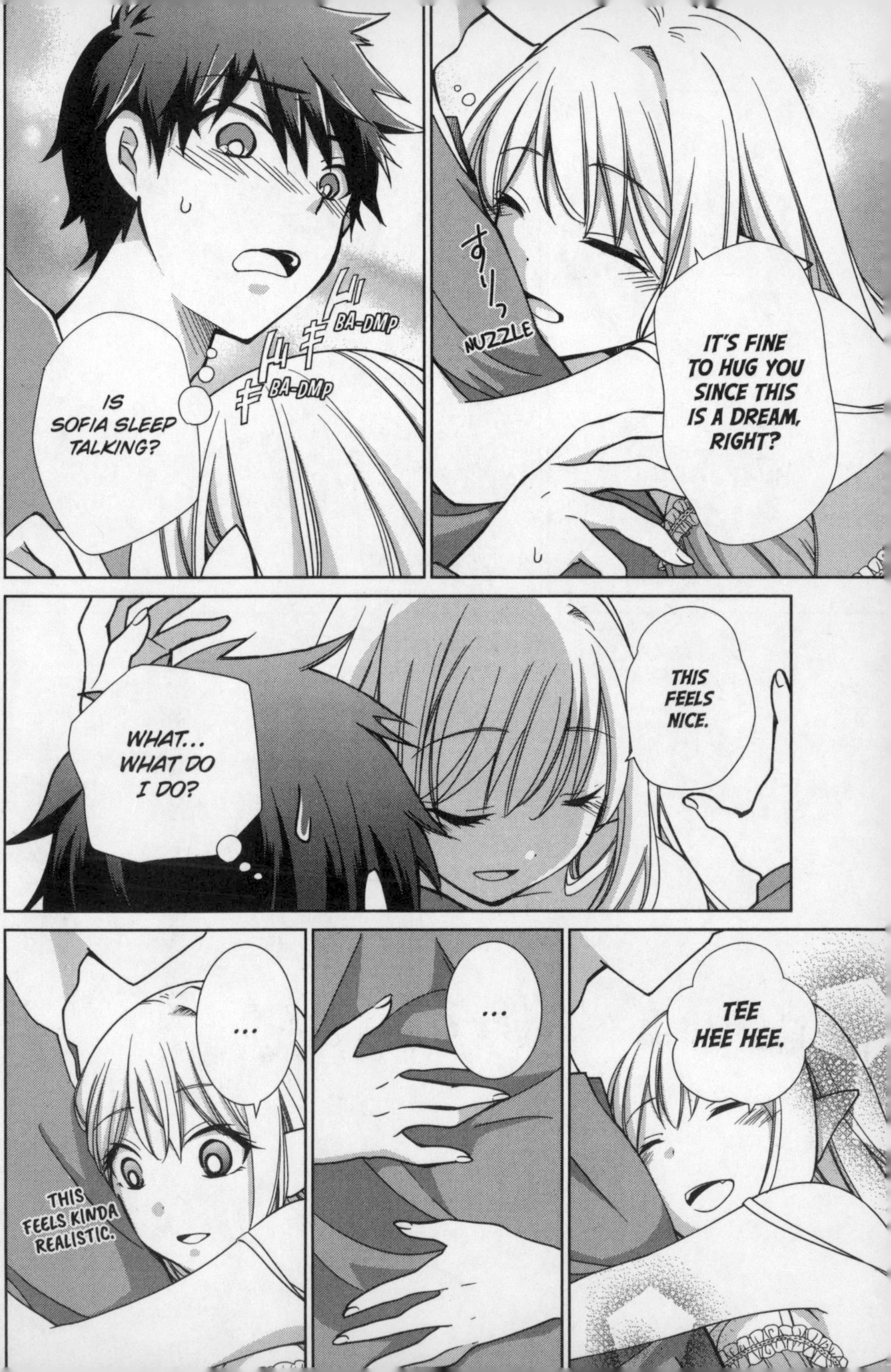
すりっ
NUZZLE
IT'S FINE TO HUG YOU SINCE THIS IS A DREAM, RIGHT?
ドキ
BA-DMP
ドキ
BA-DMP
IS SOFIA SLEEP TALKING?
THIS FEELS NICE.
WHAT... WHAT DO I DO?
TEE HEE HEE.
...
...
THIS FEELS KINDA REALISTIC.

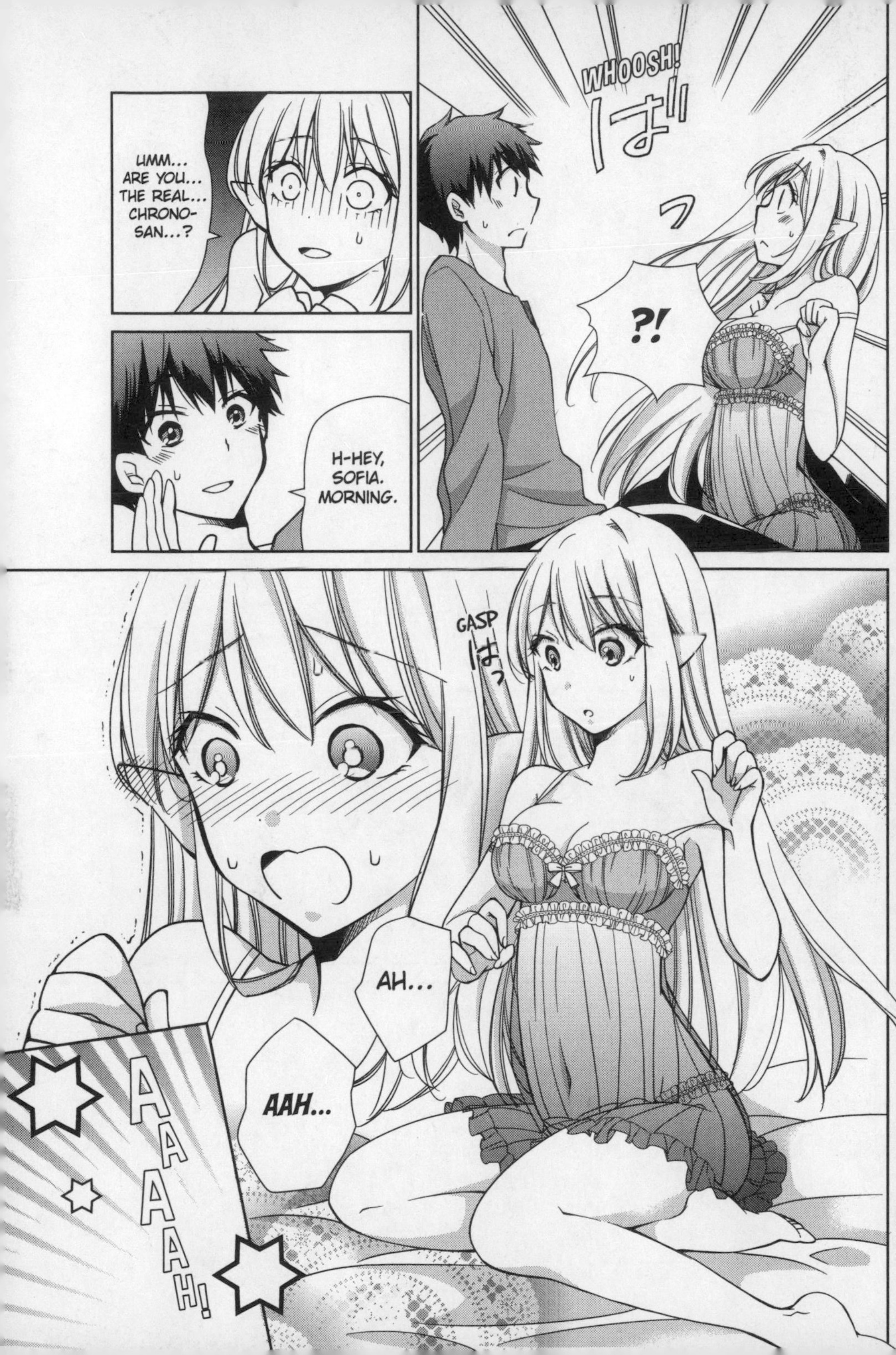
WHOOSH!
ばッ
っ
?!
UMM... ARE YOU... THE REAL... CHRONO-SAN...?
H-HEY, SOFIA. MORNING.
GASP
はっ
AH...
AAH...
AAAAAH!

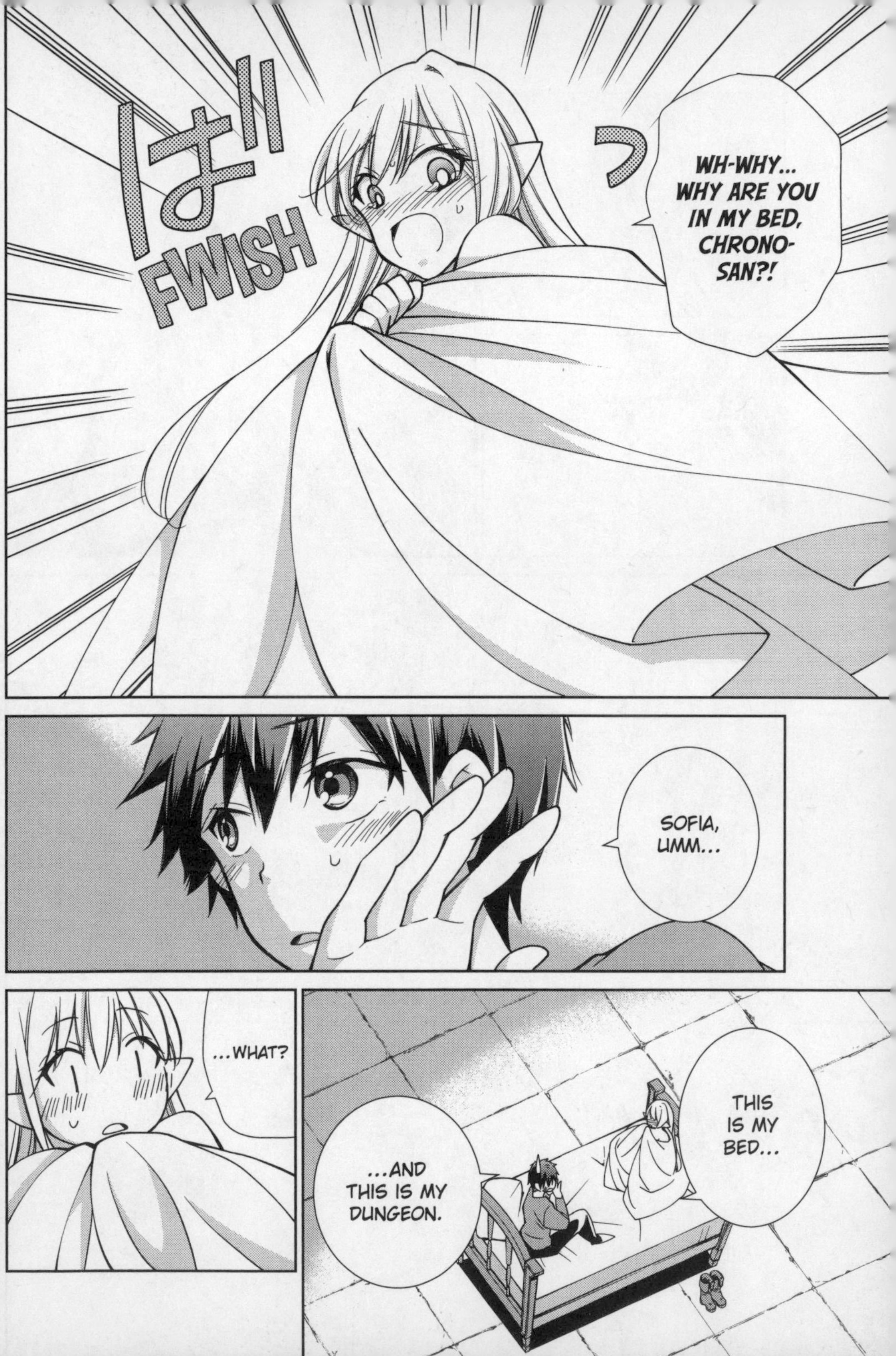
WH-WHY... WHY ARE YOU IN MY BED, CHRONO-SAN?!
はっ
FWISH
SOFIA, UMM...
THIS IS MY BED...
...AND THIS IS MY DUNGEON.
...WHAT?

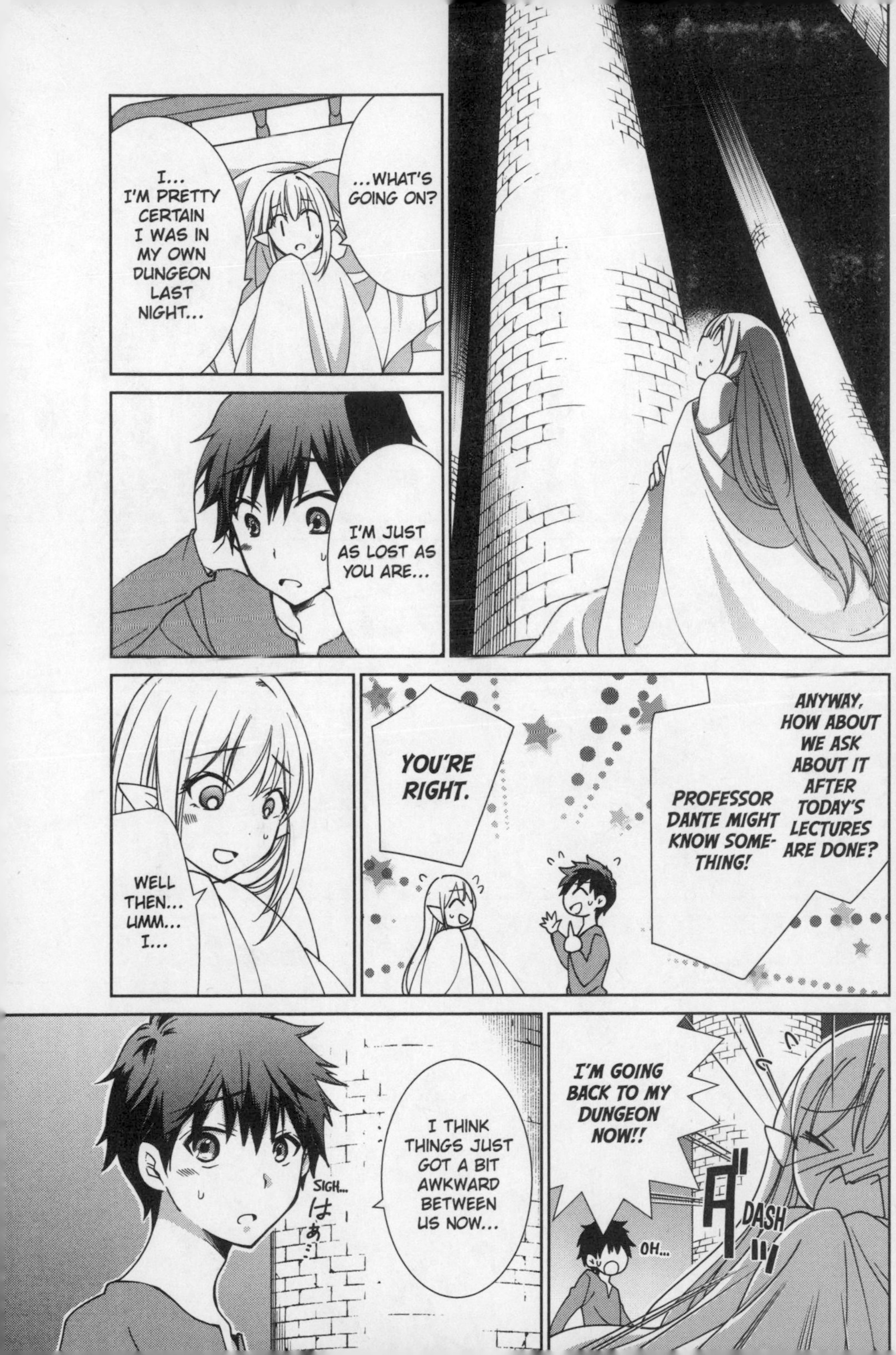
...WHAT'S GOING ON?
I... I'M PRETTY CERTAIN I WAS IN MY OWN DUNGEON LAST NIGHT...
I'M JUST AS LOST AS YOU ARE...
ANYWAY, HOW ABOUT WE ASK ABOUT IT AFTER TODAY'S LECTURES ARE DONE?
PROFESSOR DANTE MIGHT KNOW SOME-THING!
YOU'RE RIGHT.
WELL THEN... UMM... I...
I'M GOING BACK TO MY DUNGEON NOW!!
DASH
OH...
I THINK THINGS JUST GOT A BIT AWKWARD BETWEEN US NOW...
SIGH...
はぁ…

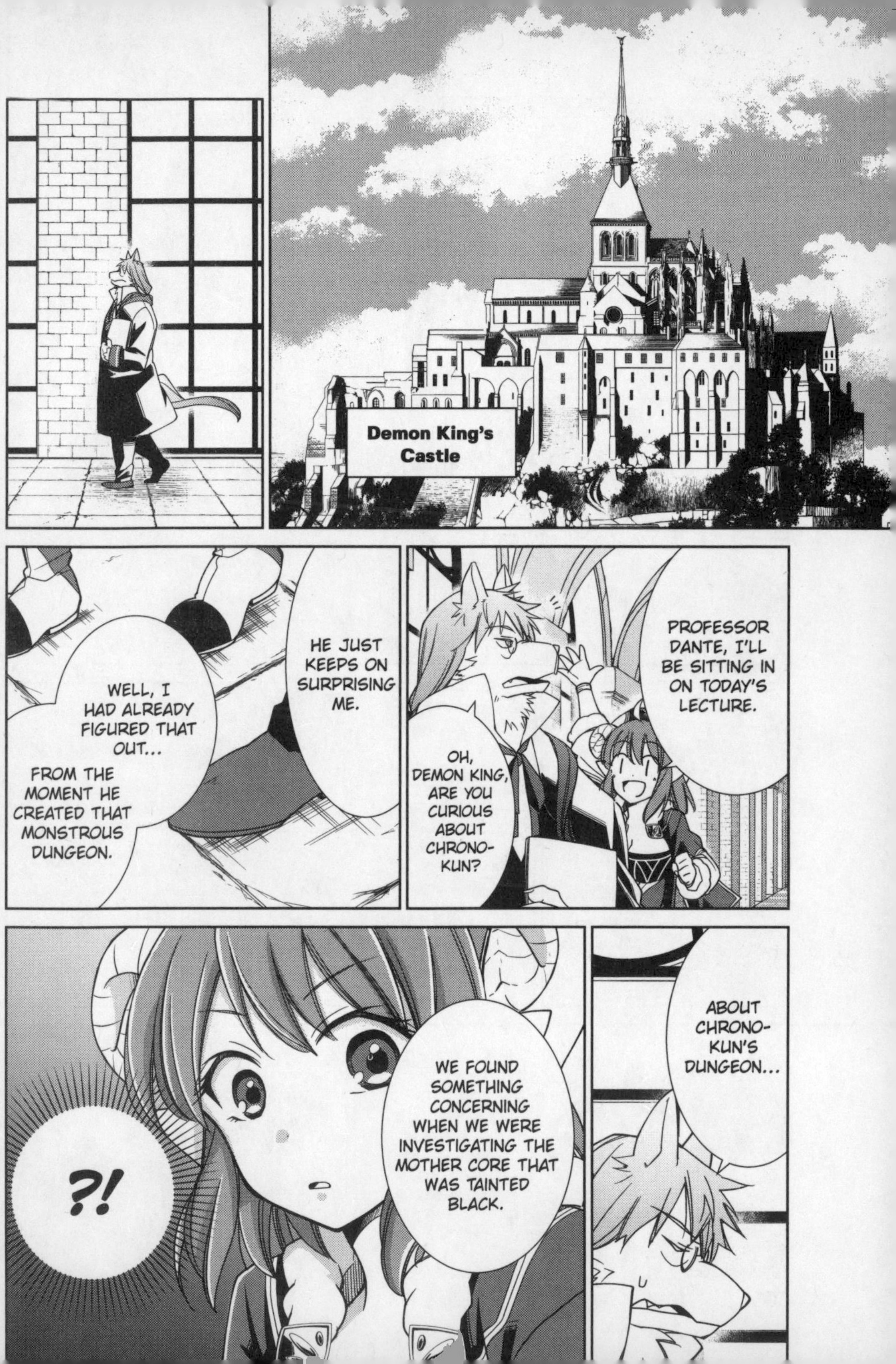
Demon King's Castle
PROFESSOR DANTE, I'LL BE SITTING IN ON TODAY'S LECTURE.
OH, DEMON KING, ARE YOU CURIOUS ABOUT CHRONO-KUN?
HE JUST KEEPS ON SURPRISING ME.
WELL, I HAD ALREADY FIGURED THAT OUT...
FROM THE MOMENT HE CREATED THAT MONSTROUS DUNGEON.
ABOUT CHRONO-KUN'S DUNGEON...
WE FOUND SOMETHING CONCERNING WHEN WE WERE INVESTIGATING THE MOTHER CORE THAT WAS TAINTED BLACK.
?!

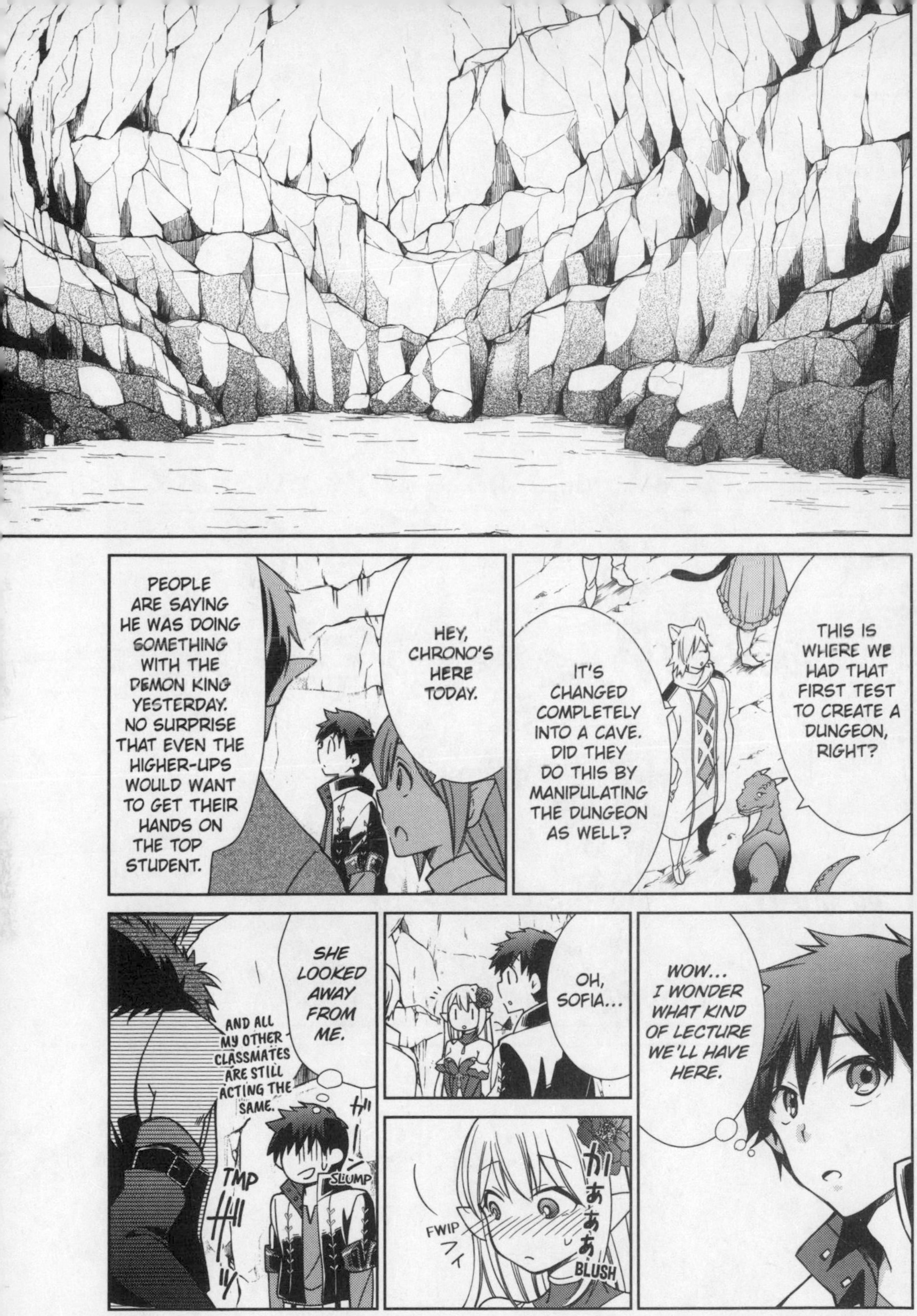
THIS IS WHERE WE HAD THAT FIRST TEST TO CREATE A DUNGEON, RIGHT?
IT'S CHANGED COMPLETELY INTO A CAVE. DID THEY DO THIS BY MANIPULATING THE DUNGEON AS WELL?
HEY, CHRONO'S HERE TODAY.
PEOPLE ARE SAYING HE WAS DOING SOMETHING WITH THE DEMON KING YESTERDAY. NO SURPRISE THAT EVEN THE HIGHER-UPS WOULD WANT TO GET THEIR HANDS ON THE TOP STUDENT.
WOW... I WONDER WHAT KIND OF LECTURE WE'LL HAVE HERE.
OH, SOFIA...
かあああ
BLUSH
フイ
FWIP
SHE LOOKED AWAY FROM ME.
AND ALL MY OTHER CLASSMATES ARE STILL ACTING THE SAME.
SLUMP
TMP

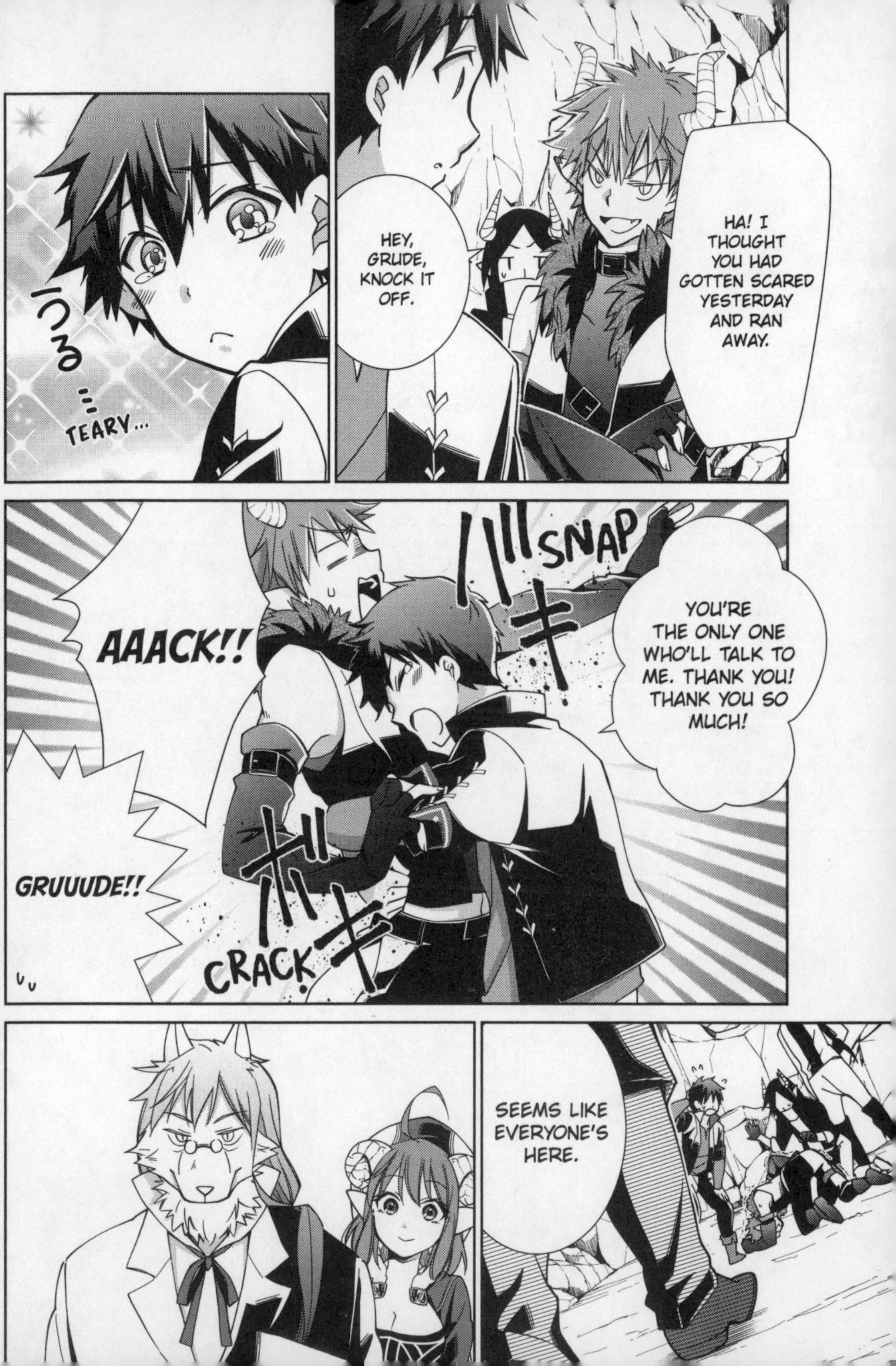
HA! I THOUGHT YOU HAD GOTTEN SCARED YESTERDAY AND RAN AWAY.
HEY, GRUDE, KNOCK IT OFF.
うる
TEARY...
SNAP
YOU'RE THE ONLY ONE WHO'LL TALK TO ME. THANK YOU! THANK YOU SO MUCH!
AAACK!!
GRUUUDE!!
CRACK
SEEMS LIKE EVERYONE'S HERE.

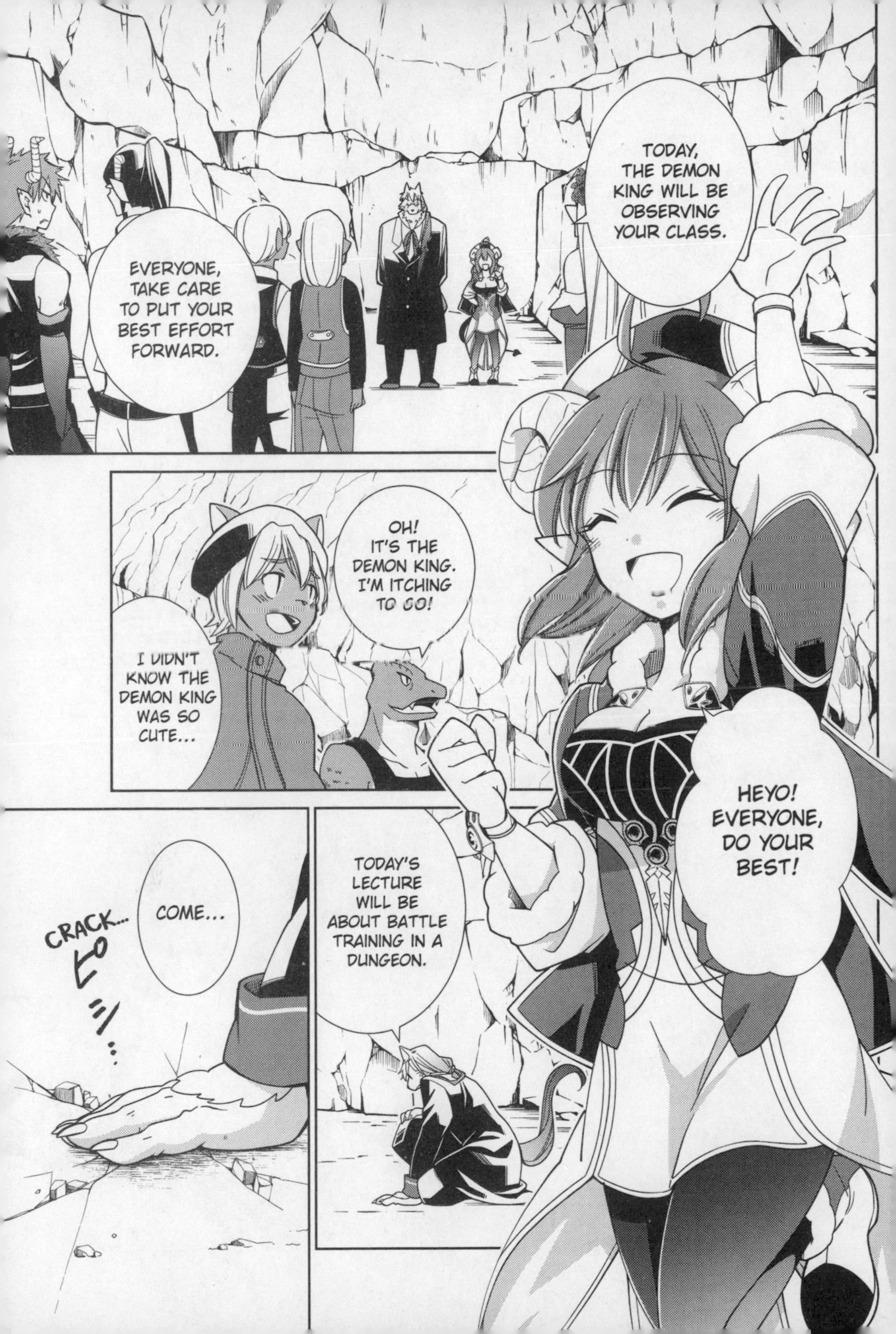
TODAY, THE DEMON KING WILL BE OBSERVING YOUR CLASS.
EVERYONE, TAKE CARE TO PUT YOUR BEST EFFORT FORWARD.
HEYO! EVERYONE, DO YOUR BEST!
OH! IT'S THE DEMON KING. I'M ITCHING TO GO!
I DIDN'T KNOW THE DEMON KING WAS SO CUTE...
TODAY'S LECTURE WILL BE ABOUT BATTLE TRAINING IN A DUNGEON.
COME...
CRACK...

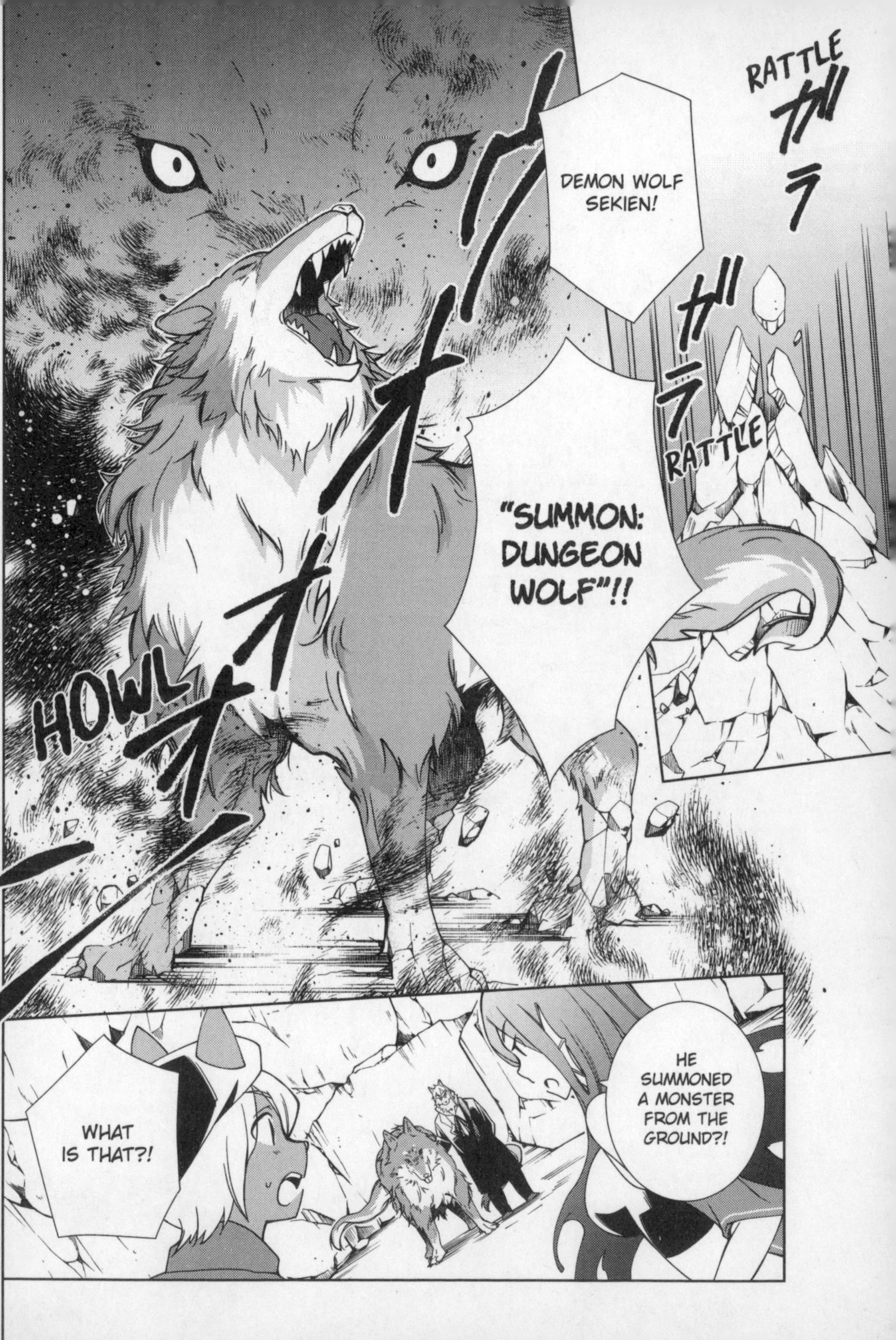
RATTLE
ガラ
DEMON WOLF SEKIEN!
ガラ
RATTLE
"SUMMON: DUNGEON WOLF"!!
HOWL
HE SUMMONED A MONSTER FROM THE GROUND?!
WHAT IS THAT?!

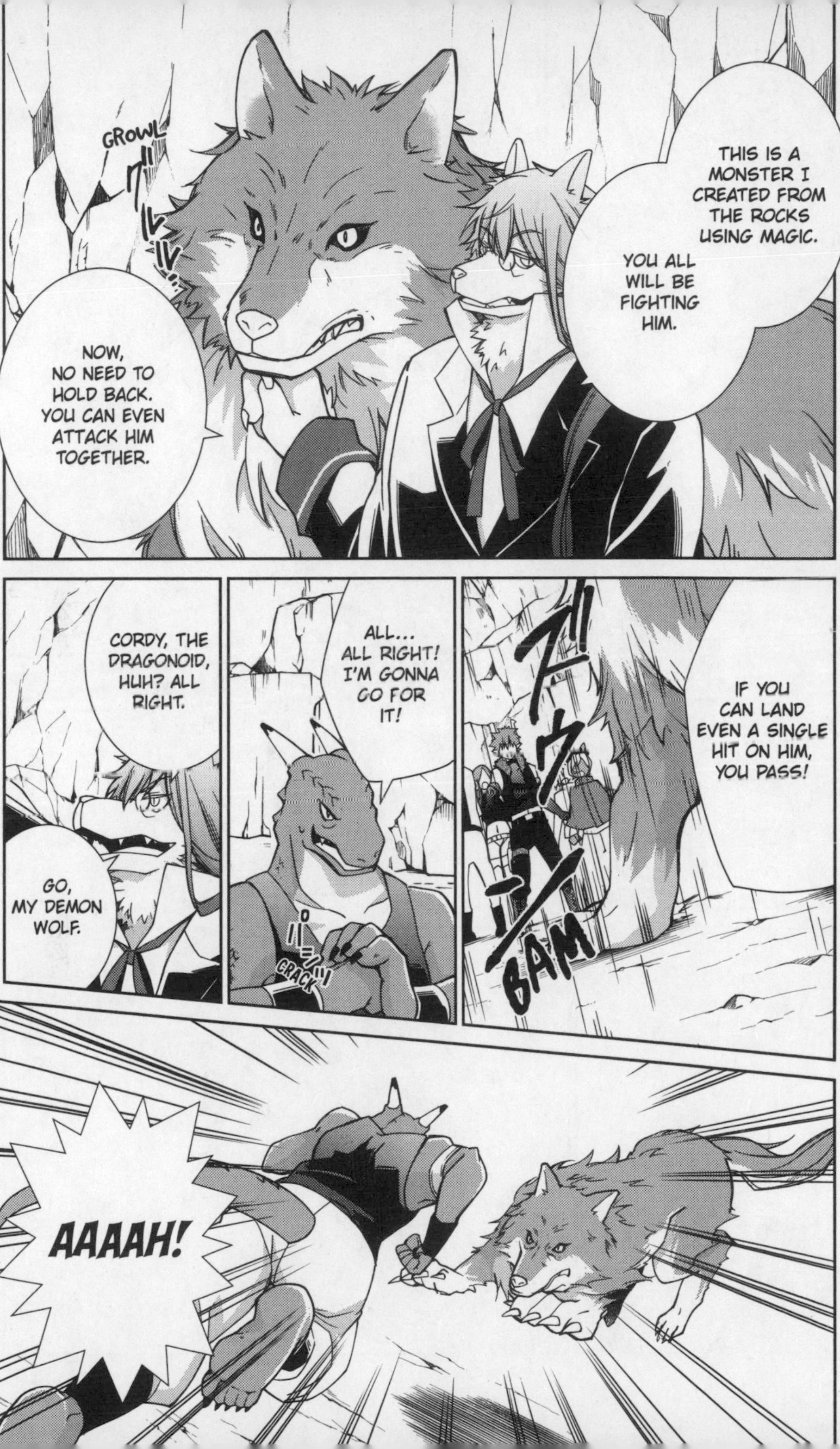

THIS IS A MONSTER I CREATED FROM THE ROCKS USING MAGIC.
YOU ALL WILL BE FIGHTING HIM.
GROWL
NOW, NO NEED TO HOLD BACK. YOU CAN EVEN ATTACK HIM TOGETHER.
IF YOU CAN LAND EVEN A SINGLE HIT ON HIM, YOU PASS!
BAM
ALL... ALL RIGHT! I'M GONNA GO FOR IT!
CRACK
CORDY, THE DRAGONOID, HUH? ALL RIGHT.
GO, MY DEMON WOLF.
AAAAH!

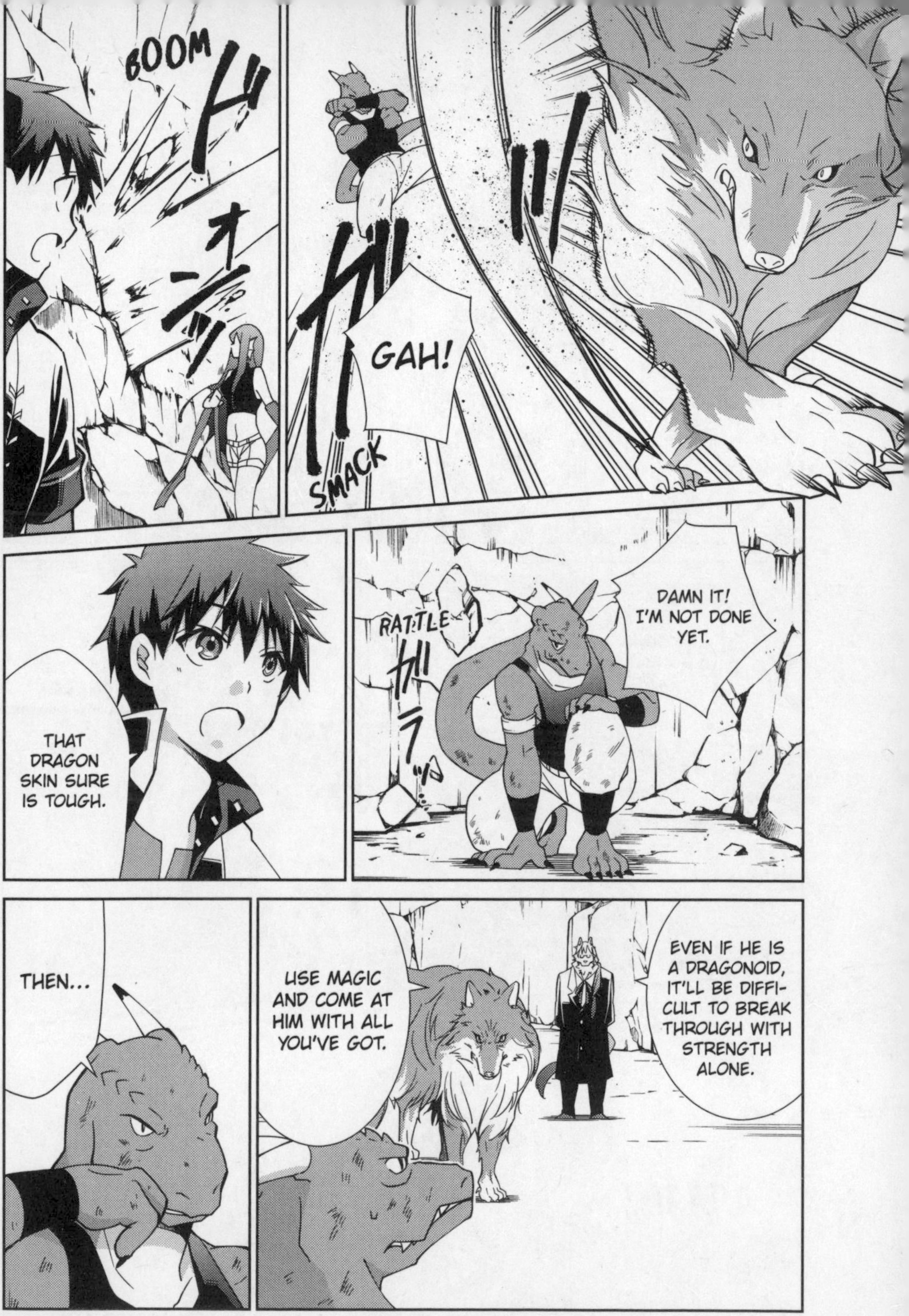
GAH!
SMACK
BOOM
RATTLE
DAMN IT! I'M NOT DONE YET.
THAT DRAGON SKIN SURE IS TOUGH.
EVEN IF HE IS A DRAGONOID, IT'LL BE DIFFICULT TO BREAK THROUGH WITH STRENGTH ALONE.
USE MAGIC AND COME AT HIM WITH ALL YOU'VE GOT.
THEN...

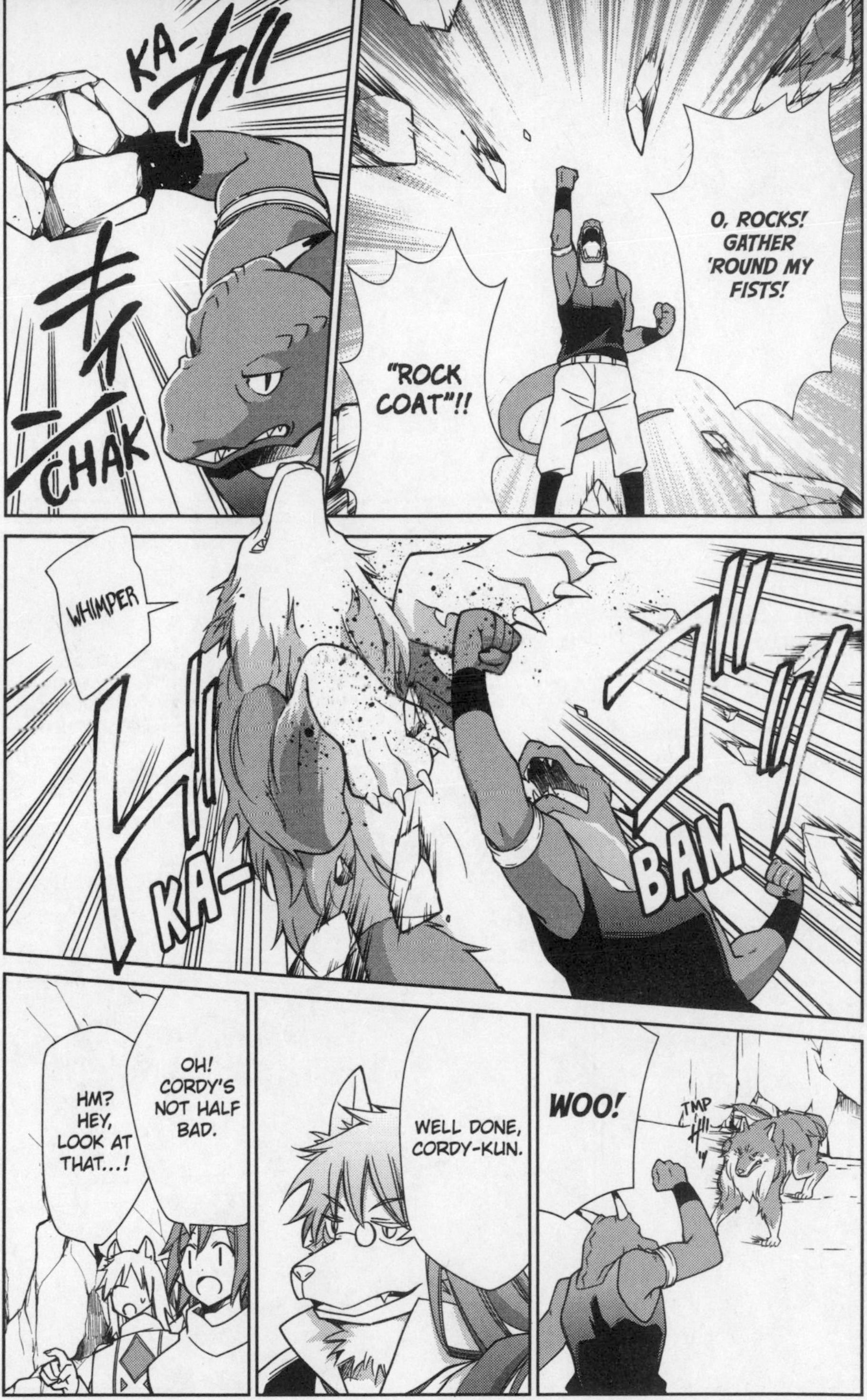
O, ROCKS! GATHER 'ROUND MY FISTS!
"ROCK COAT"!!
KA-
CHAK
BAM
WHIMPER
KA-
WOO!
TMP
WELL DONE, CORDY-KUN.
OH! CORDY'S NOT HALF BAD.
HM? HEY, LOOK AT THAT...!

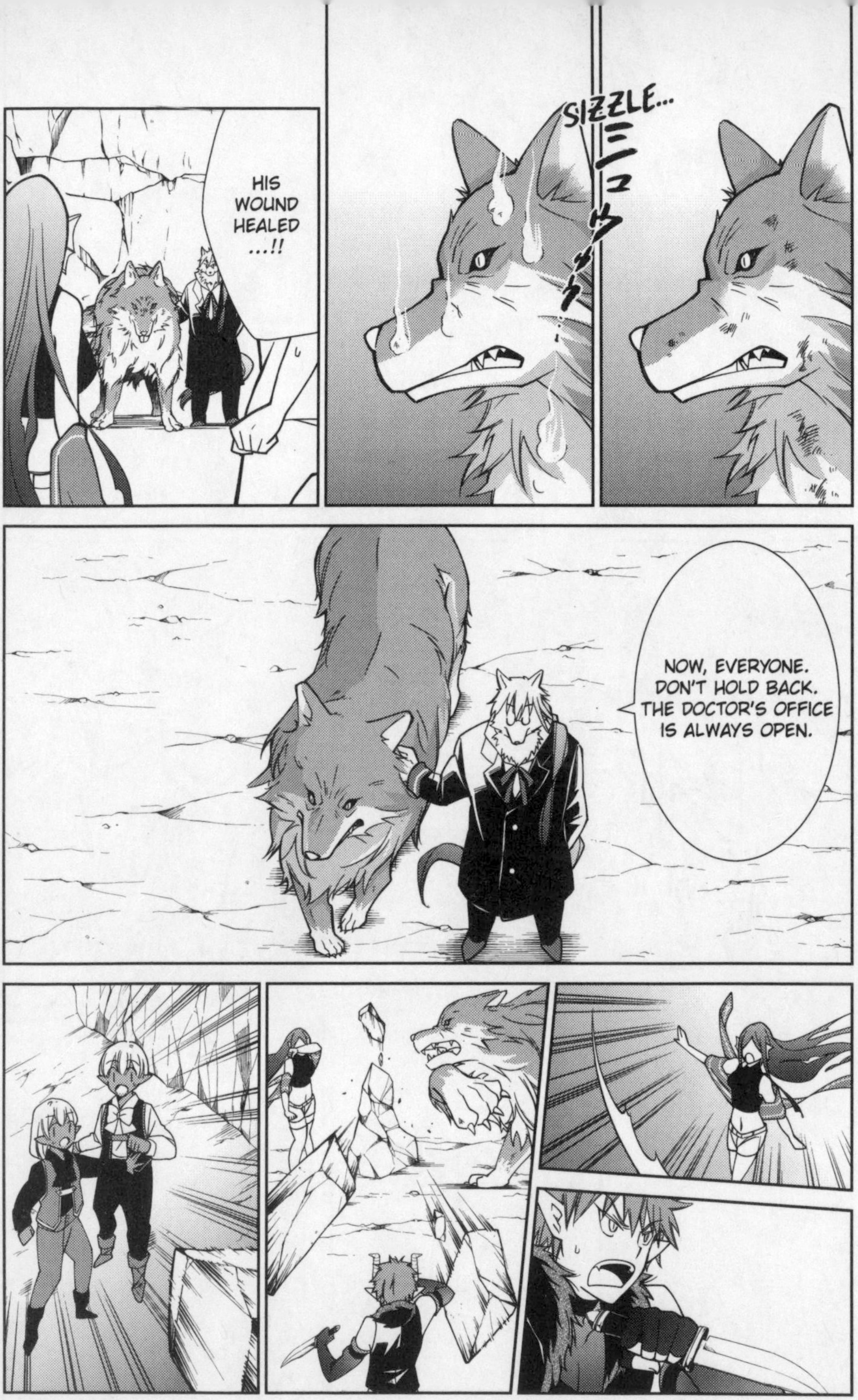
SIZZLE...
HIS WOUND HEALED ...!!
NOW, EVERYONE. DON'T HOLD BACK. THE DOCTOR'S OFFICE IS ALWAYS OPEN.

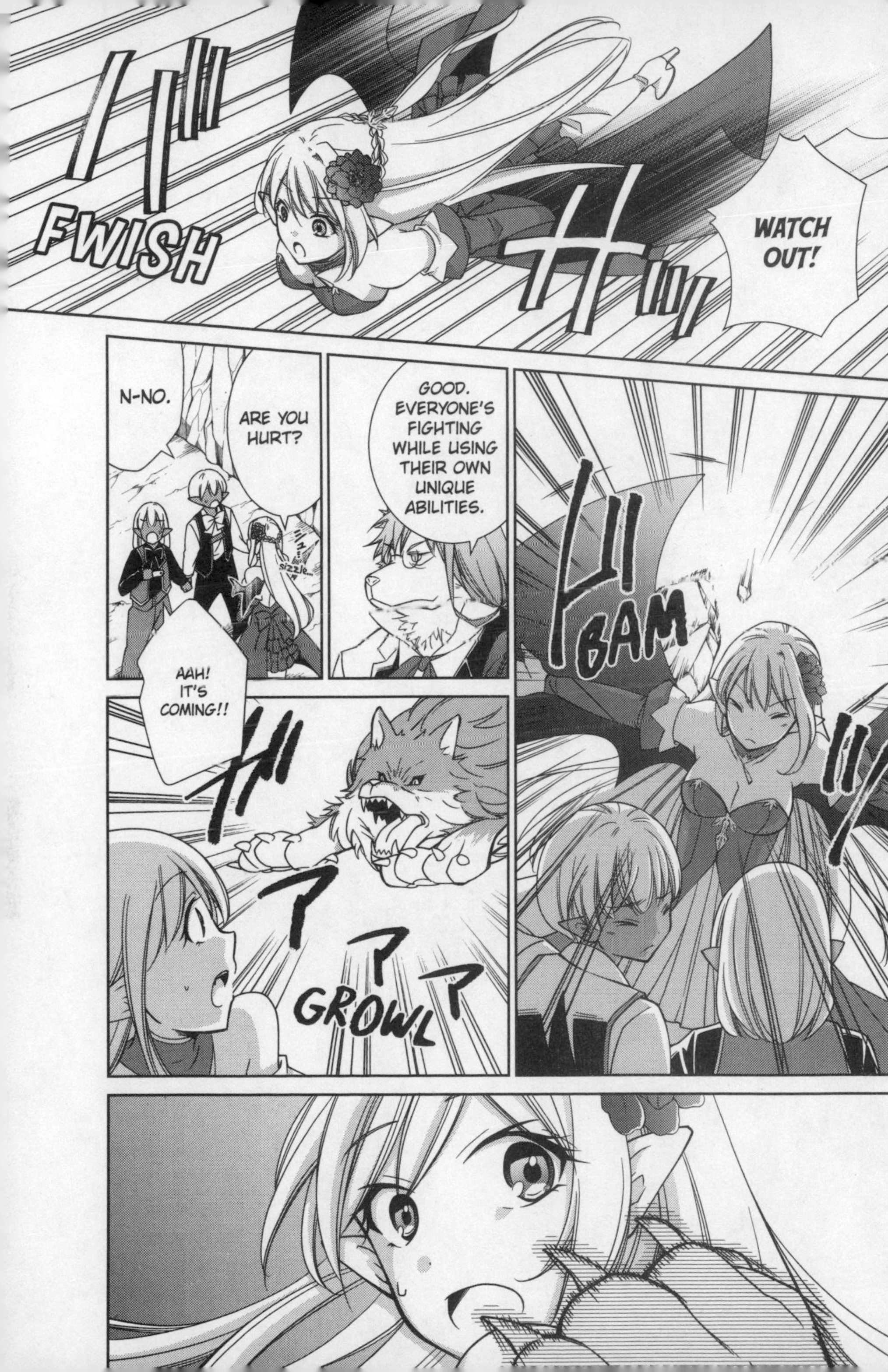
WATCH OUT!
FWISH
BAM
GOOD. EVERYONE'S FIGHTING WHILE USING THEIR OWN UNIQUE ABILITIES.
ARE YOU HURT?
N-NO.
sizzle...
AAH! IT'S COMING!!
GROWL

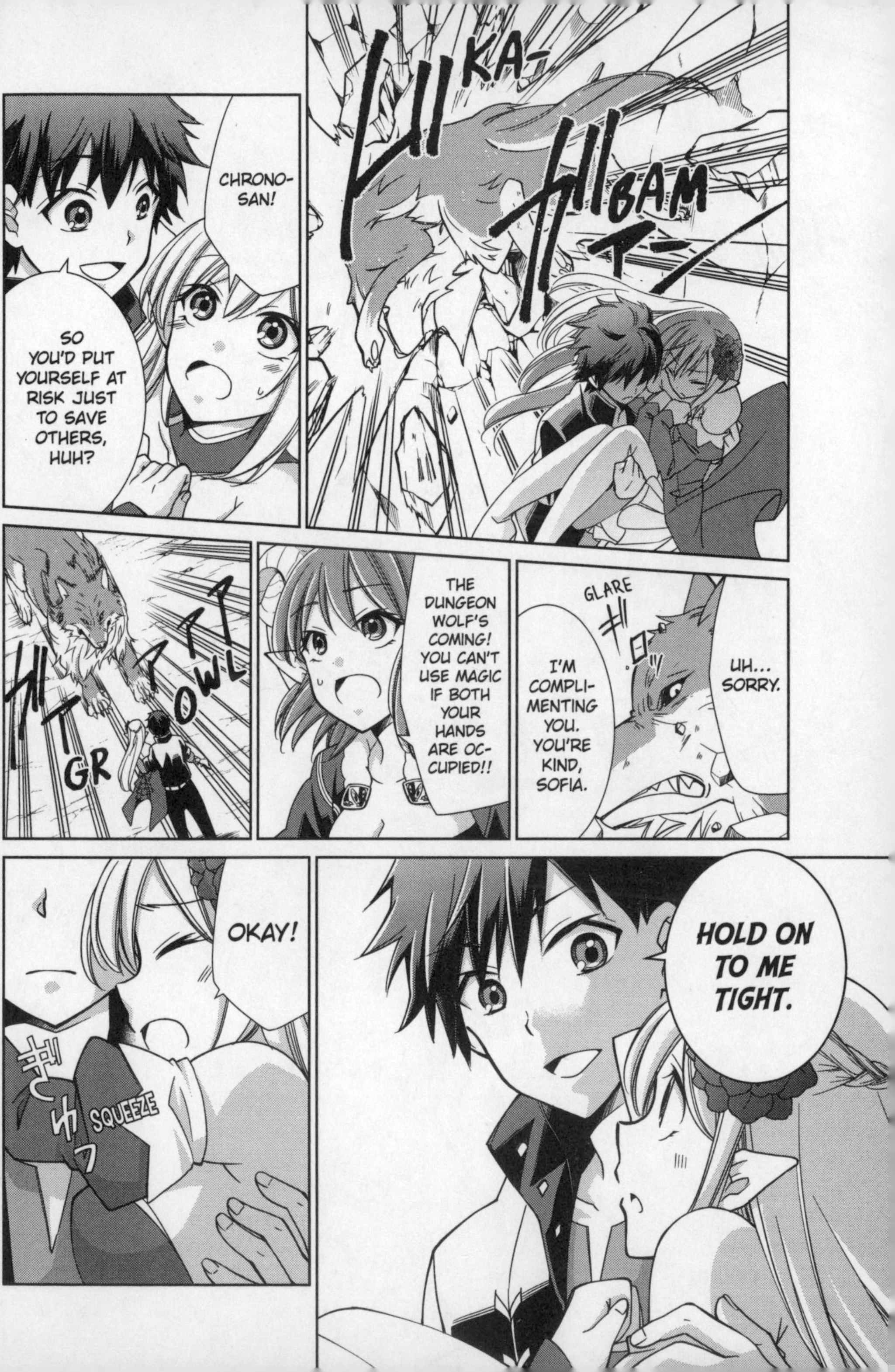
KA-BAM
CHRONO-SAN!
SO YOU'D PUT YOURSELF AT RISK JUST TO SAVE OTHERS, HUH?
GLARE
UH... SORRY.
I'M COMPLI-MENTING YOU. YOU'RE KIND, SOFIA.
THE DUNGEON WOLF'S COMING! YOU CAN'T USE MAGIC IF BOTH YOUR HANDS ARE OC-CUPIED!!
GR
OWL
HOLD ON TO ME TIGHT.
OKAY!
SQUEEZE

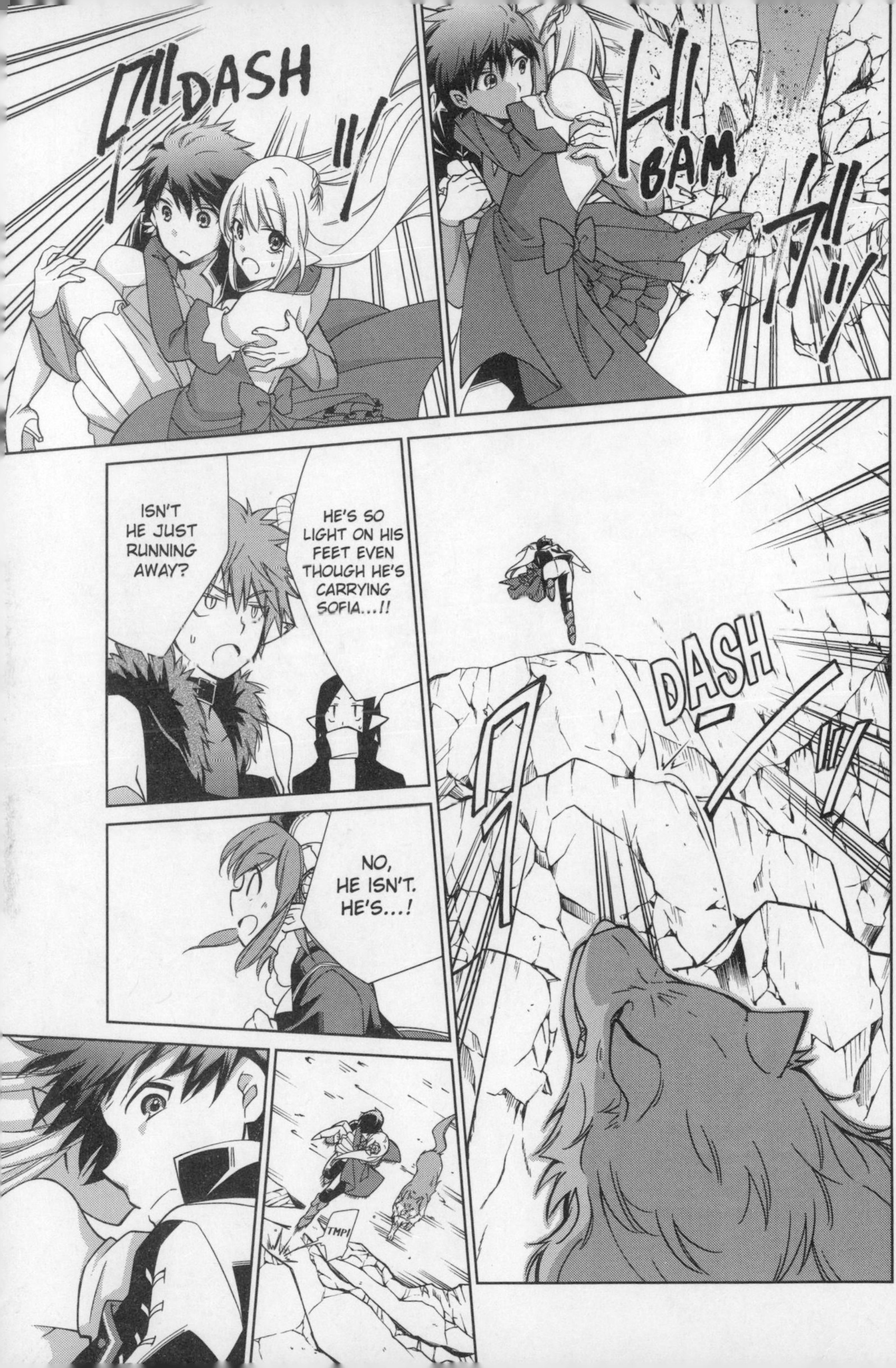
BAM
DASH
DASH
HE'S SO LIGHT ON HIS FEET EVEN THOUGH HE'S CARRYING SOFIA...!!
ISN'T HE JUST RUNNING AWAY?
NO, HE ISN'T. HE'S...!
TMP!

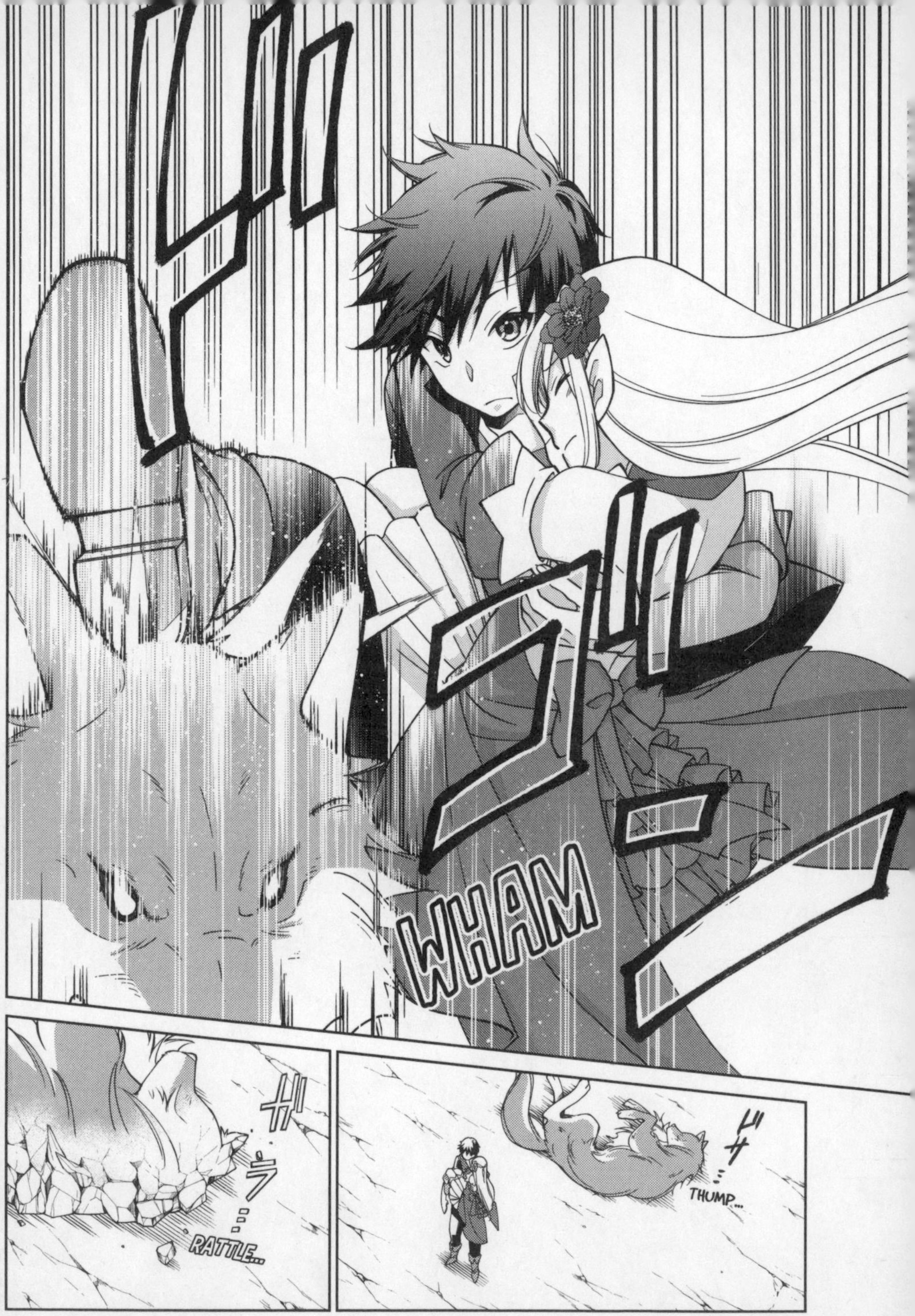
WHAM
ドサ…
THUMP...
ガラ…
RATTLE...

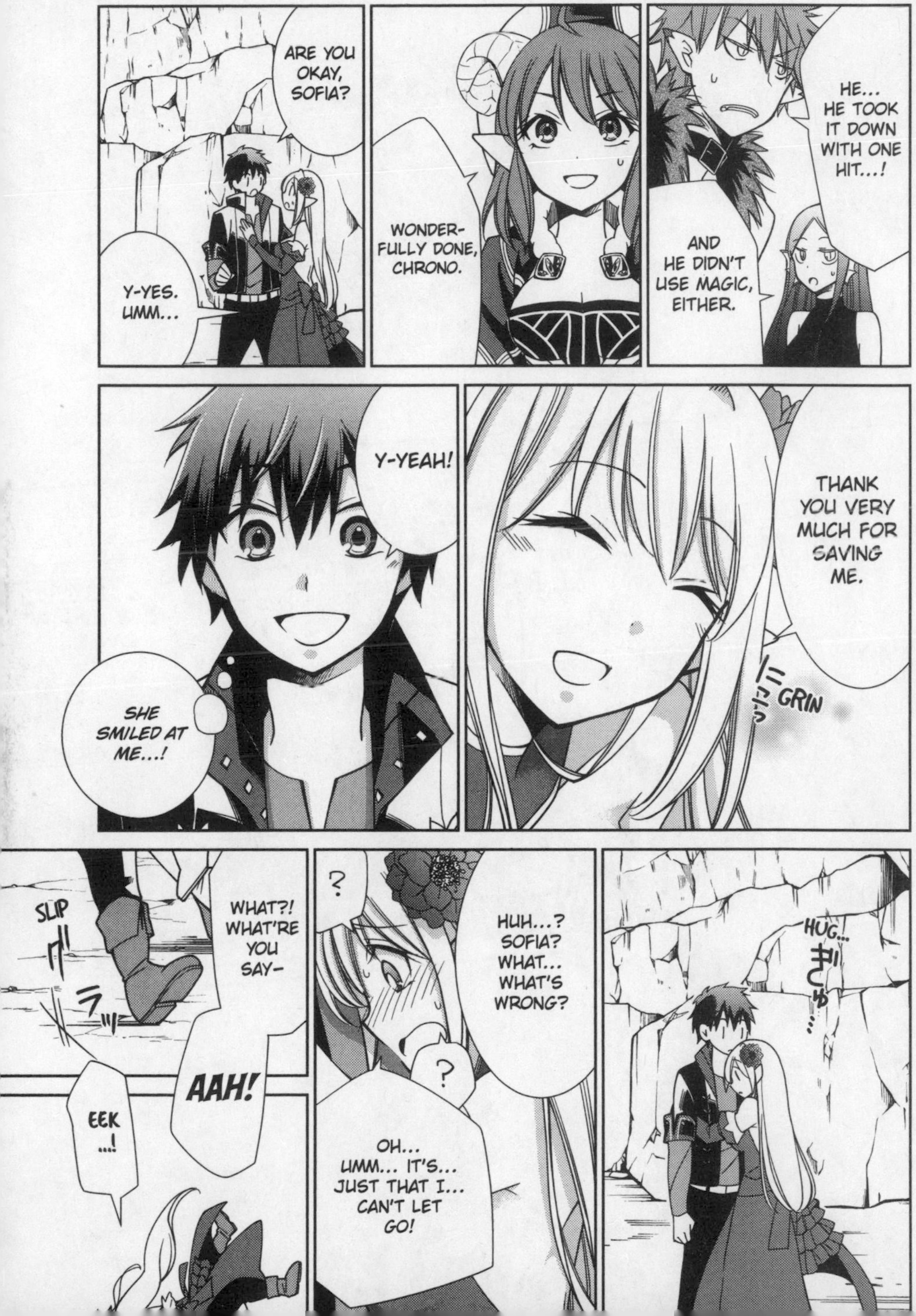
HE... HE TOOK IT DOWN WITH ONE HIT...!
AND HE DIDN'T USE MAGIC, EITHER.
WONDERFULLY DONE, CHRONO.
ARE YOU OKAY, SOFIA?
Y-YES. UMM...
THANK YOU VERY MUCH FOR SAVING ME.
GRIN
Y-YEAH!
SHE SMILED AT ME...!
HUG...
?
HUH...? SOFIA? WHAT... WHAT'S WRONG?
?
OH... UMM... IT'S... JUST THAT I... CAN'T LET GO!
SLIP
WHAT?! WHAT'RE YOU SAY-
AAH!
EEK...!

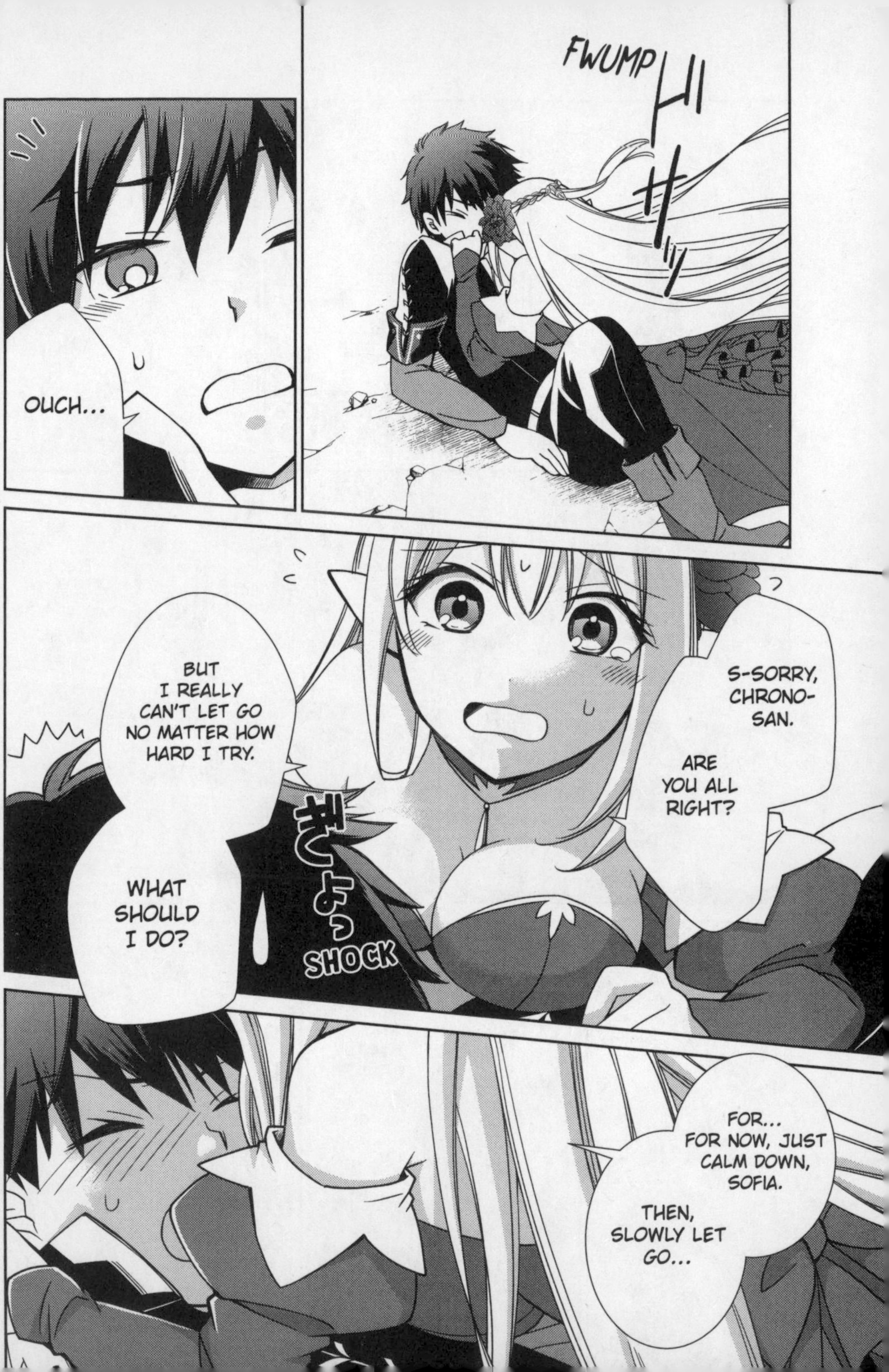
FWUMP
OUCH...
S-SORRY, CHRONO-SAN.
ARE YOU ALL RIGHT?
BUT I REALLY CAN'T LET GO NO MATTER HOW HARD I TRY.
WHAT SHOULD I DO?
SHOCK
FOR... FOR NOW, JUST CALM DOWN, SOFIA.
THEN, SLOWLY LET GO...

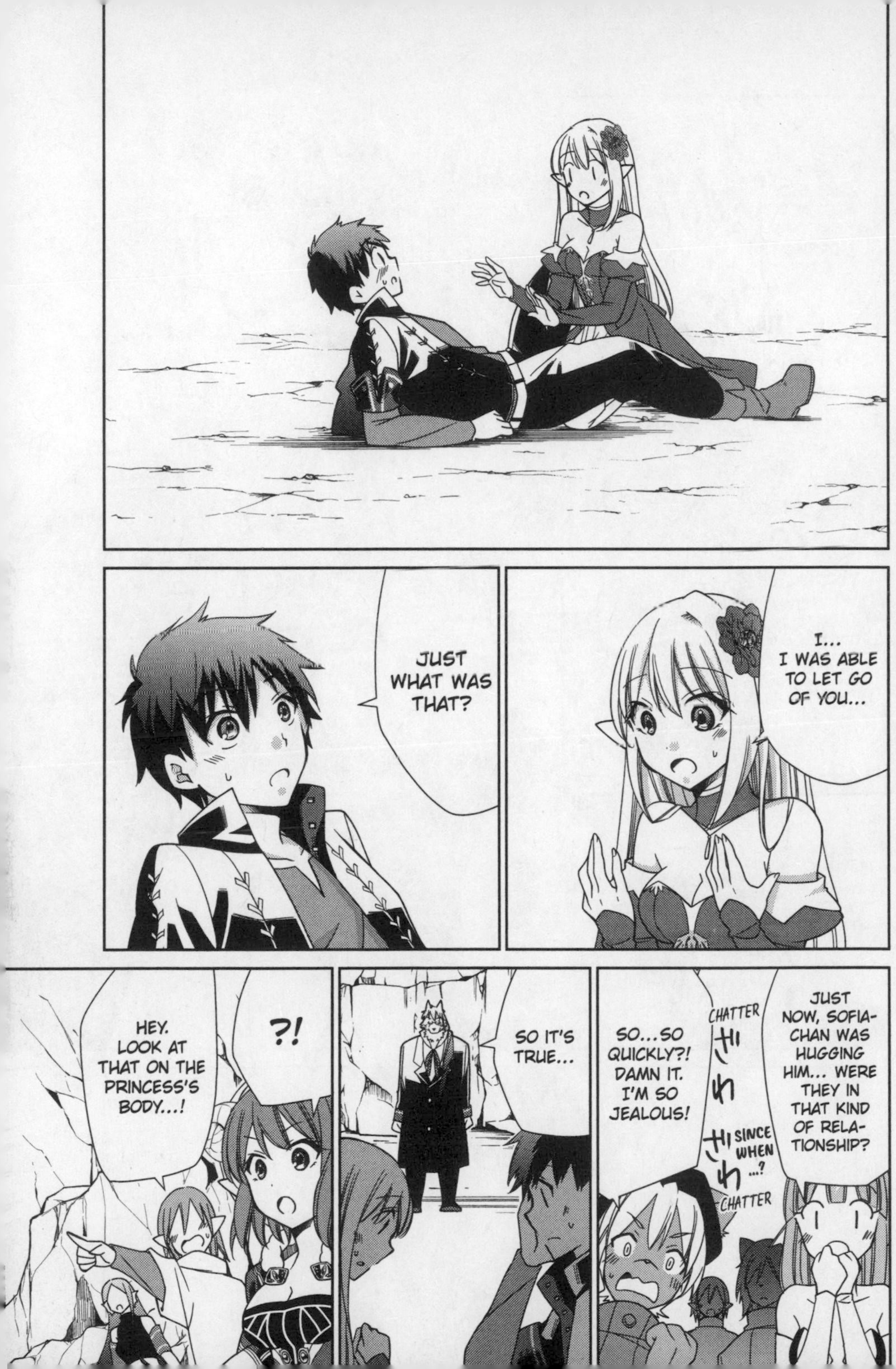
I... I WAS ABLE TO LET GO OF YOU...
JUST WHAT WAS THAT?
JUST NOW, SOFIA-CHAN WAS HUGGING HIM... WERE THEY IN THAT KIND OF RELA-TIONSHIP?
CHATTER
ざわ
SO...SO QUICKLY?! DAMN IT. I'M SO JEALOUS!
SINCE WHEN...?
ざわ
CHATTER
SO IT'S TRUE...
?!
HEY. LOOK AT THAT ON THE PRINCESS'S BODY...!

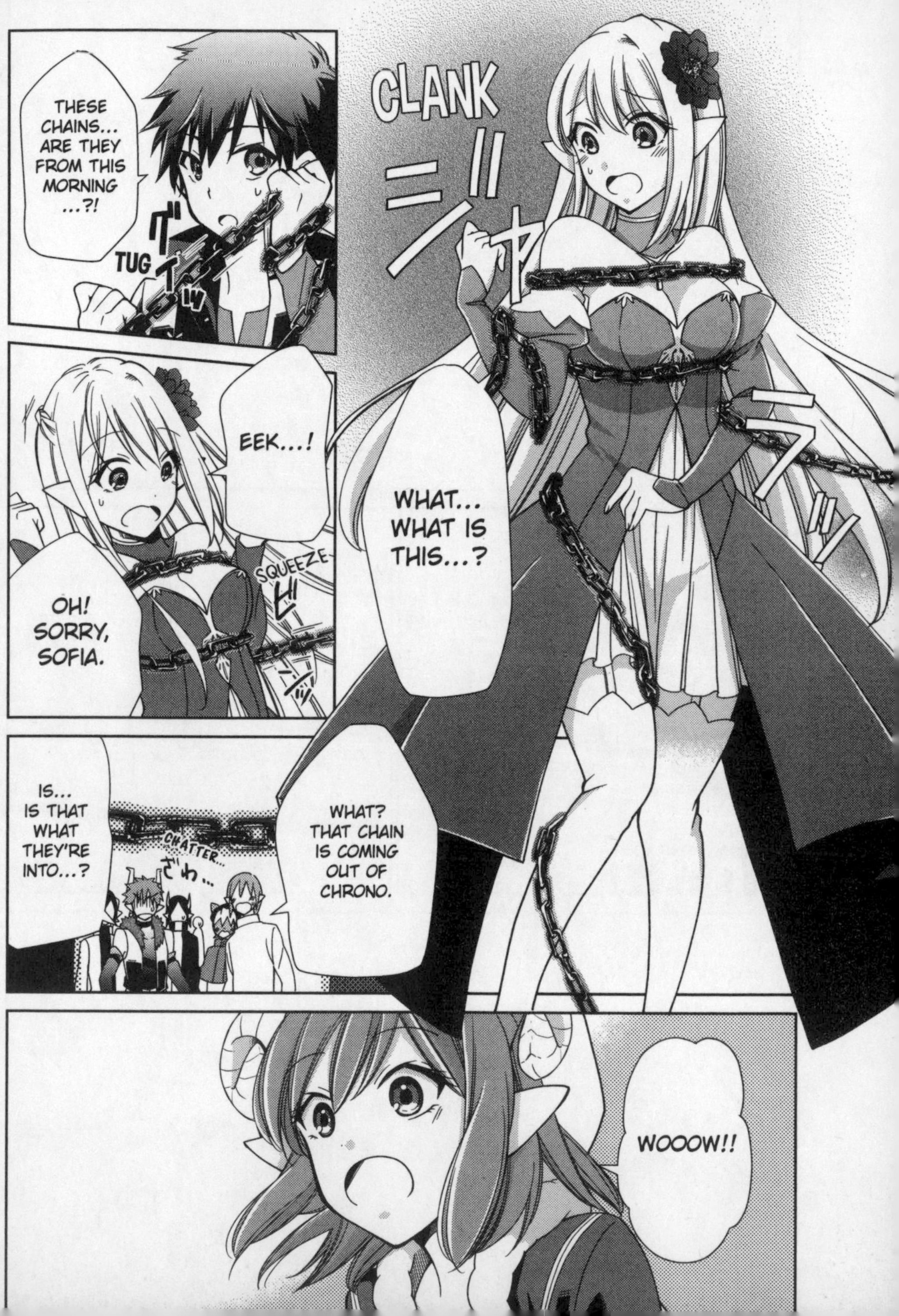
CLANK
WHAT... WHAT IS THIS...?
THESE CHAINS... ARE THEY FROM THIS MORNING ...?!
TUG
EEK...!
SQUEEZE
OH! SORRY, SOFIA.
WHAT? THAT CHAIN IS COMING OUT OF CHRONO.
CHATTER...
IS... IS THAT WHAT THEY'RE INTO...?
WOOOW!!

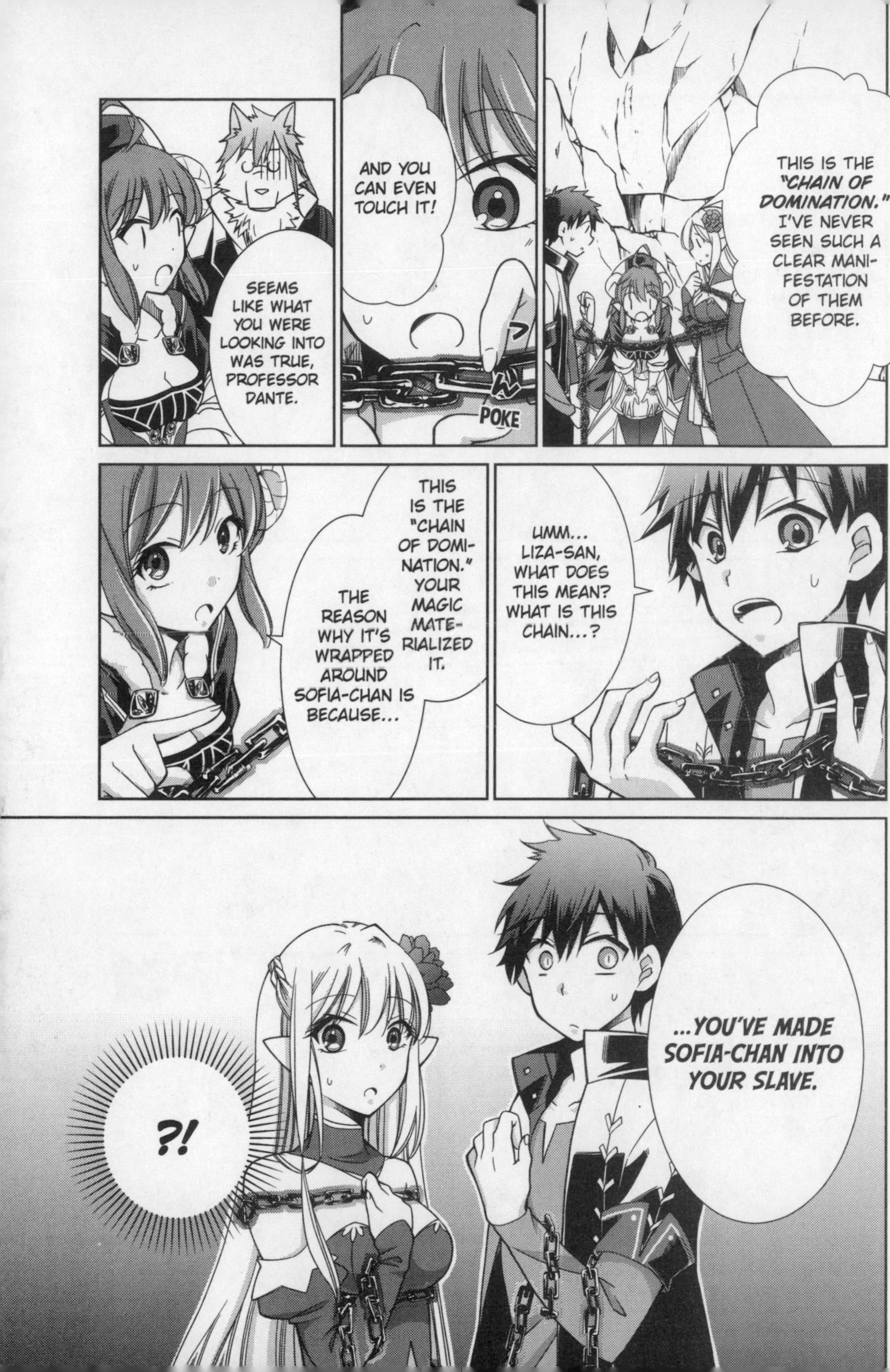
THIS IS THE "CHAIN OF DOMINATION." I'VE NEVER SEEN SUCH A CLEAR MANI-FESTATION OF THEM BEFORE.
AND YOU CAN EVEN TOUCH IT!
POKE
SEEMS LIKE WHAT YOU WERE LOOKING INTO WAS TRUE, PROFESSOR DANTE.
UMM... LIZA-SAN, WHAT DOES THIS MEAN? WHAT IS THIS CHAIN...?
THIS IS THE "CHAIN OF DOMI-NATION." YOUR MAGIC MATE-RIALIZED IT.
THE REASON WHY IT'S WRAPPED AROUND SOFIA-CHAN IS BECAUSE...
...YOU'VE MADE SOFIA-CHAN INTO YOUR SLAVE.
?!

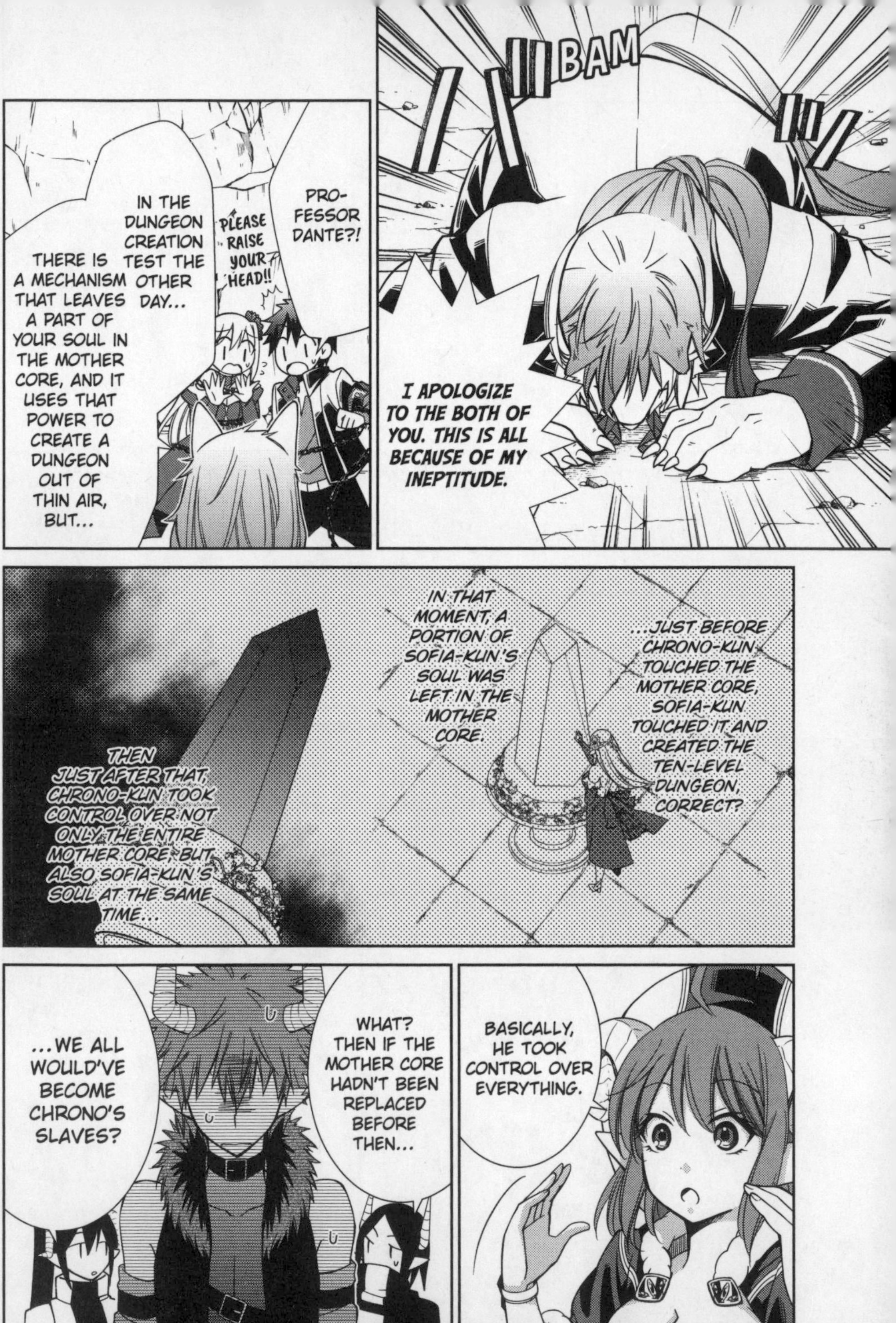
BAM
I APOLOGIZE TO THE BOTH OF YOU. THIS IS ALL BECAUSE OF MY INEPTITUDE.
PRO-FESSOR DANTE?!
PLEASE RAISE YOUR HEAD!!
IN THE DUNGEON CREATION TEST THE OTHER DAY...
THERE IS A MECHANISM THAT LEAVES A PART OF YOUR SOUL IN THE MOTHER CORE, AND IT USES THAT POWER TO CREATE A DUNGEON OUT OF THIN AIR, BUT...
...JUST BEFORE CHRONO-KUN TOUCHED THE MOTHER CORE, SOFIA-KUN TOUCHED IT AND CREATED THE TEN-LEVEL DUNGEON, CORRECT?
IN THAT MOMENT, A PORTION OF SOFIA-KUN'S SOUL WAS LEFT IN THE MOTHER CORE.
THEN JUST AFTER THAT, CHRONO-KUN TOOK CONTROL OVER NOT ONLY THE ENTIRE MOTHER CORE, BUT ALSO SOFIA-KUN'S SOUL AT THE SAME TIME...
BASICALLY, HE TOOK CONTROL OVER EVERYTHING.
WHAT? THEN IF THE MOTHER CORE HADN'T BEEN REPLACED BEFORE THEN...
...WE ALL WOULD'VE BECOME CHRONO'S SLAVES?

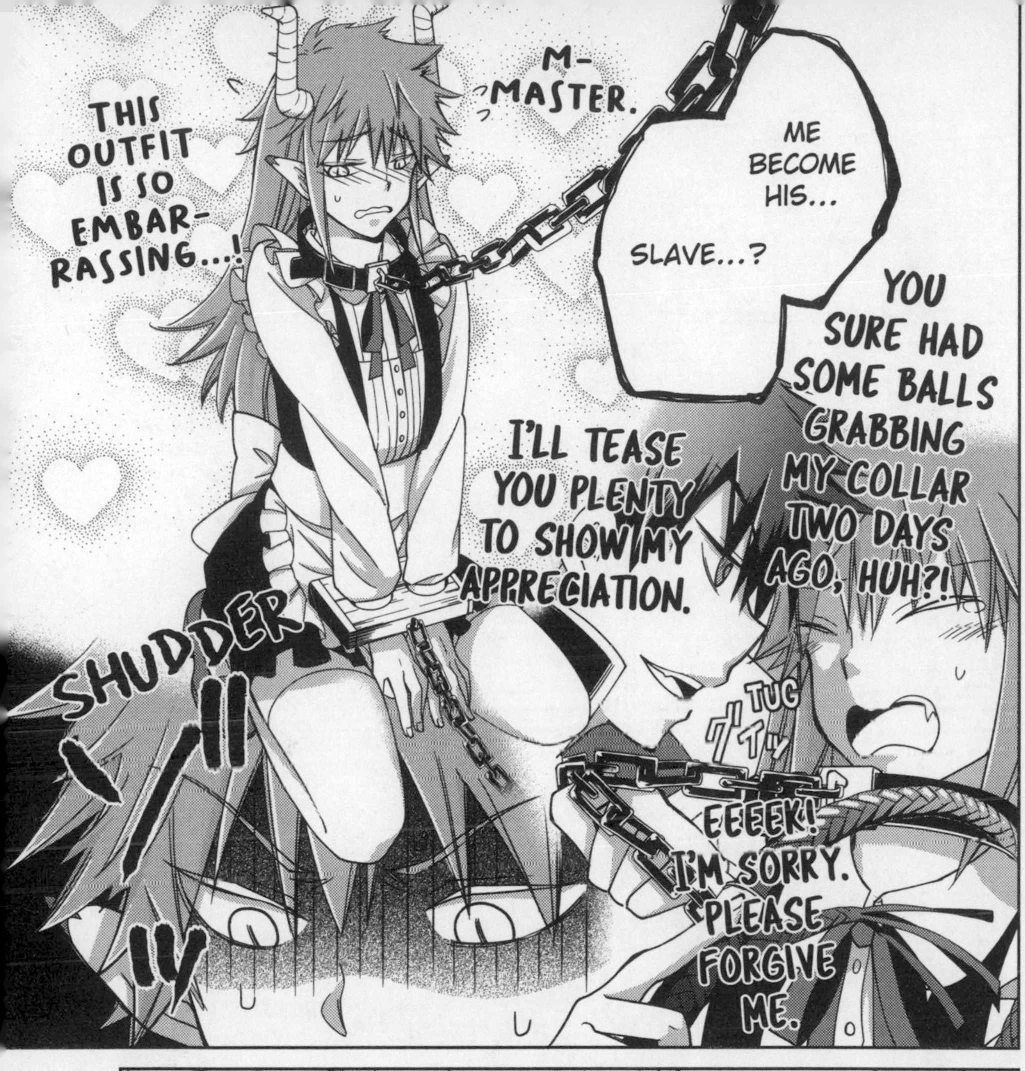
ME BECOME HIS... SLAVE...?
YOU SURE HAD SOME BALLS GRABBING MY COLLAR TWO DAYS AGO, HUH?!
M-MASTER.
THIS OUTFIT IS SO EMBARRASSING...!
I'LL TEASE YOU PLENTY TO SHOW MY APPRECIATION.
SHUDDER
TUG
EEEEK! I'M SORRY. PLEASE FORGIVE ME.
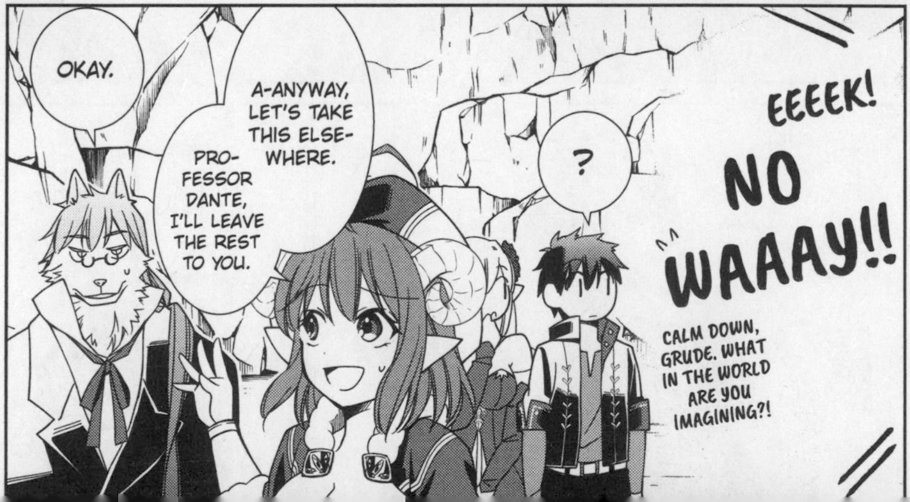
EEEEK!
NO WAAAY!!
CALM DOWN, GRUDE. WHAT IN THE WORLD ARE YOU IMAGINING?!
?
A-ANYWAY, LET'S TAKE THIS ELSEWHERE.
PROFESSOR DANTE, I'LL LEAVE THE REST TO YOU.
OKAY.

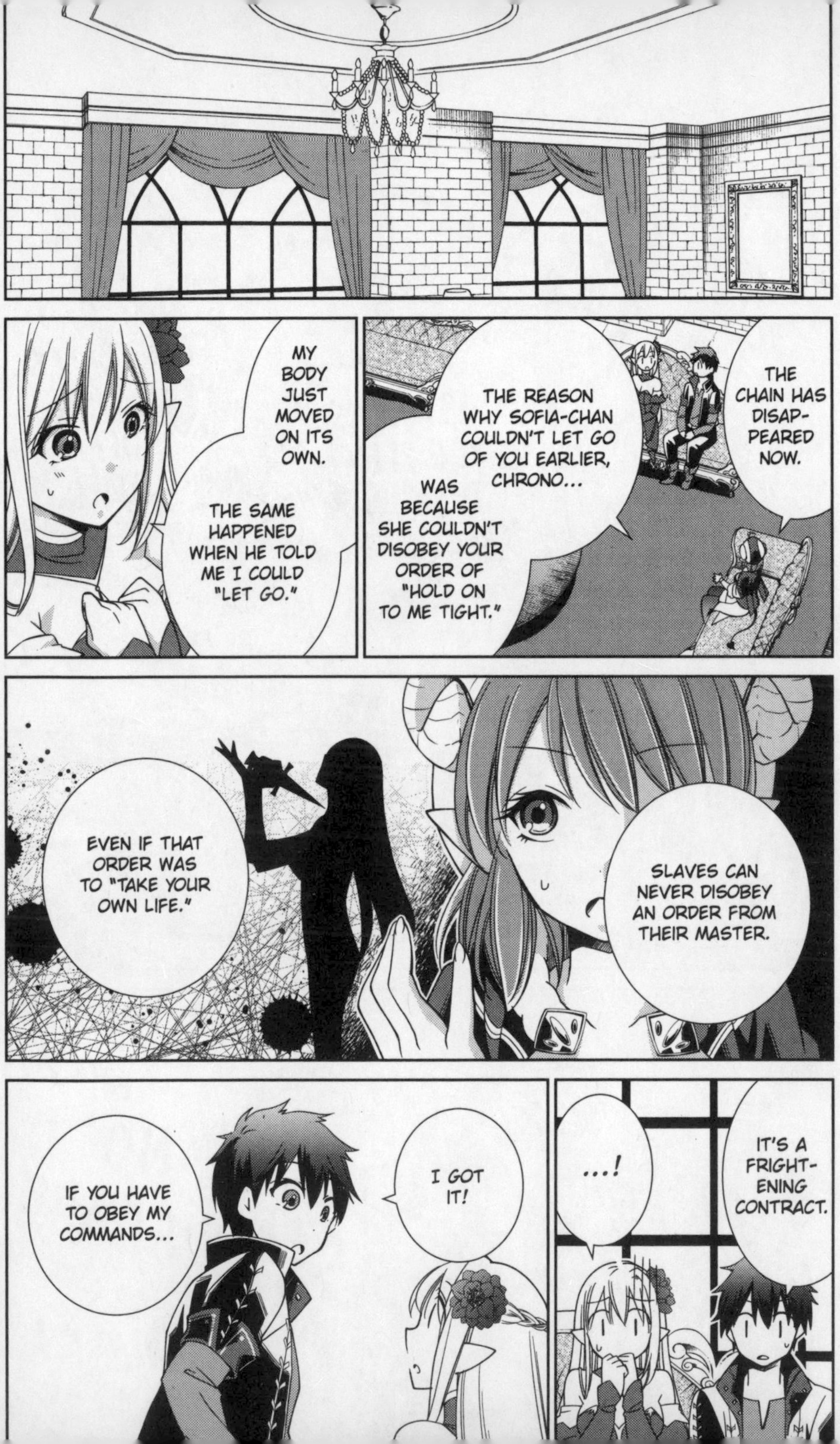
THE CHAIN HAS DISAPPEARED NOW.
THE REASON WHY SOFIA-CHAN COULDN'T LET GO OF YOU EARLIER, CHRONO...
WAS BECAUSE SHE COULDN'T DISOBEY YOUR ORDER OF "HOLD ON TO ME TIGHT."
MY BODY JUST MOVED ON ITS OWN.
THE SAME HAPPENED WHEN HE TOLD ME I COULD "LET GO."
SLAVES CAN NEVER DISOBEY AN ORDER FROM THEIR MASTER.
EVEN IF THAT ORDER WAS TO "TAKE YOUR OWN LIFE."
IT'S A FRIGHTENING CONTRACT.
...!
I GOT IT!
IF YOU HAVE TO OBEY MY COMMANDS...

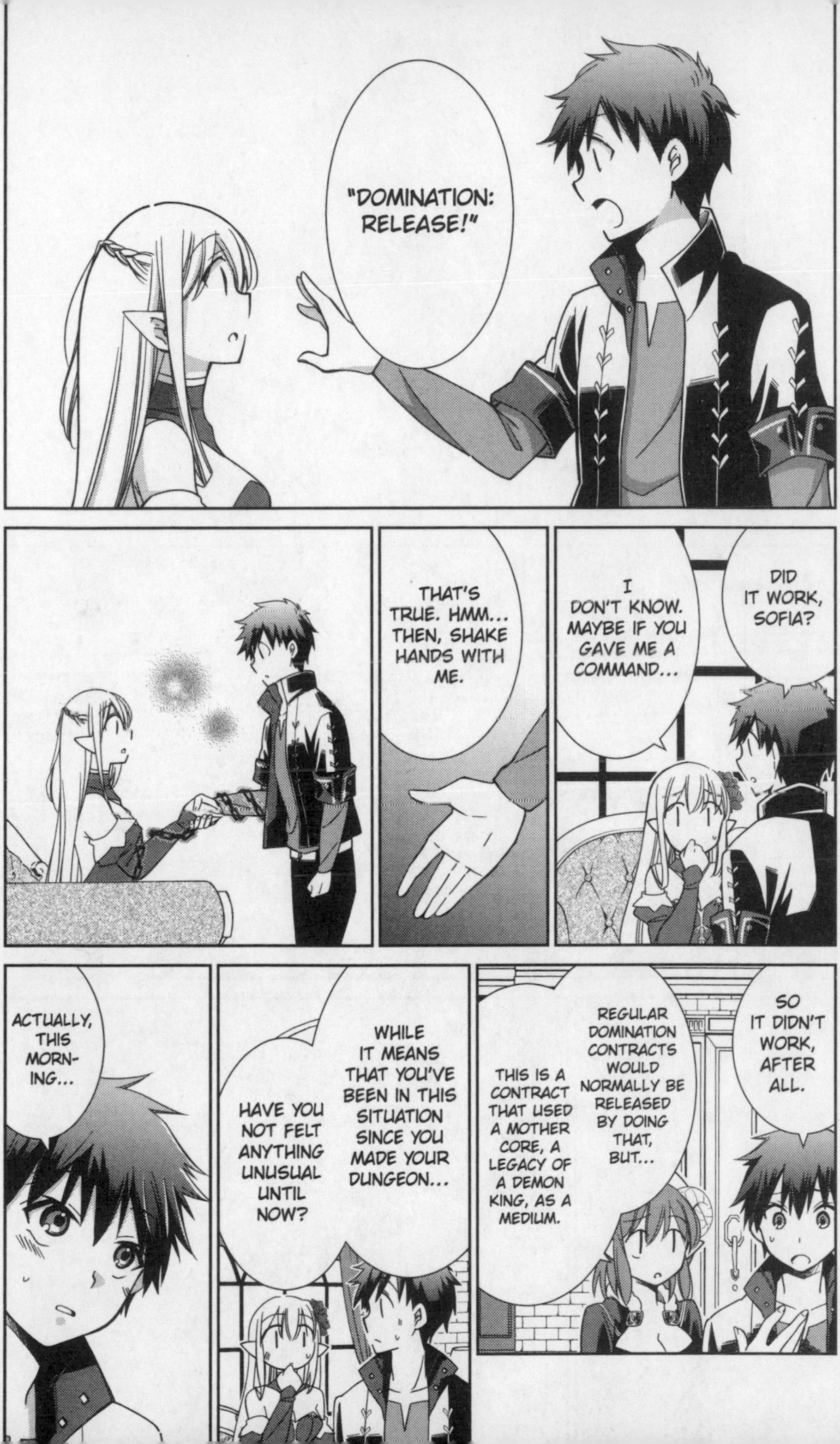
"DOMINATION: RELEASE!"
DID IT WORK, SOFIA?
I DON'T KNOW. MAYBE IF YOU GAVE ME A COMMAND...
THAT'S TRUE. HMM... THEN, SHAKE HANDS WITH ME.
SO IT DIDN'T WORK, AFTER ALL.
REGULAR DOMINATION CONTRACTS WOULD NORMALLY BE RELEASED BY DOING THAT, BUT...
THIS IS A CONTRACT THAT USED A MOTHER CORE, A LEGACY OF A DEMON KING, AS A MEDIUM.
WHILE IT MEANS THAT YOU'VE BEEN IN THIS SITUATION SINCE YOU MADE YOUR DUNGEON...
HAVE YOU NOT FELT ANYTHING UNUSUAL UNTIL NOW?
ACTUALLY, THIS MORNING-ING...

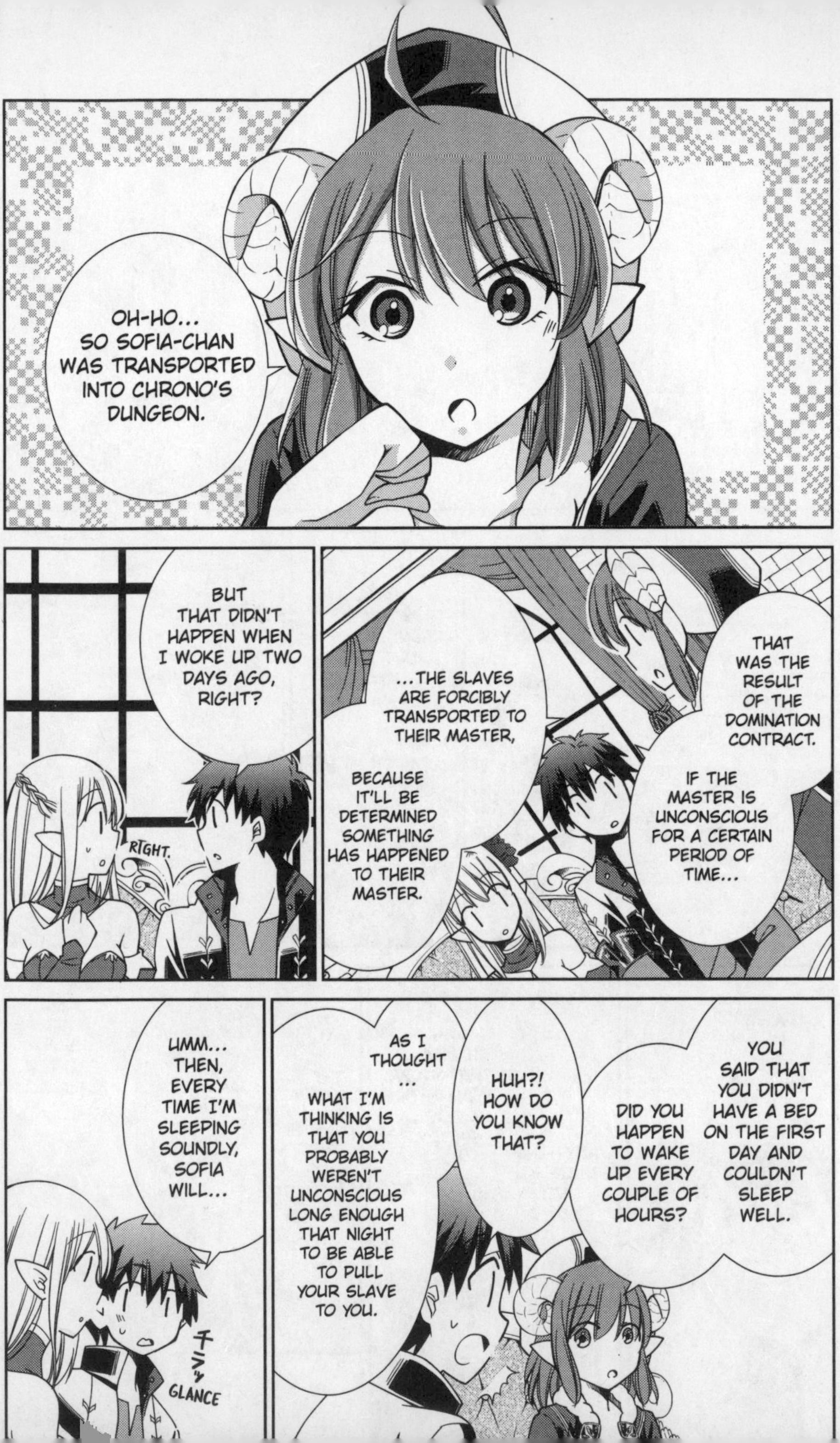
OH-HO... SO SOFIA-CHAN WAS TRANSPORTED INTO CHRONO'S DUNGEON.
THAT WAS THE RESULT OF THE DOMINATION CONTRACT.
IF THE MASTER IS UNCONSCIOUS FOR A CERTAIN PERIOD OF TIME...
...THE SLAVES ARE FORCIBLY TRANSPORTED TO THEIR MASTER,
BECAUSE IT'LL BE DETERMINED SOMETHING HAS HAPPENED TO THEIR MASTER.
BUT THAT DIDN'T HAPPEN WHEN I WOKE UP TWO DAYS AGO, RIGHT?
RIGHT.
YOU SAID THAT YOU DIDN'T HAVE A BED ON THE FIRST DAY AND COULDN'T SLEEP WELL.
DID YOU HAPPEN TO WAKE UP EVERY COUPLE OF HOURS?
HUH?! HOW DO YOU KNOW THAT?
AS I THOUGHT...
WHAT I'M THINKING IS THAT YOU PROBABLY WEREN'T UNCONSCIOUS LONG ENOUGH THAT NIGHT TO BE ABLE TO PULL YOUR SLAVE TO YOU.
UMM... THEN, EVERY TIME I'M SLEEPING SOUNDLY, SOFIA WILL...
チラッ
GLANCE

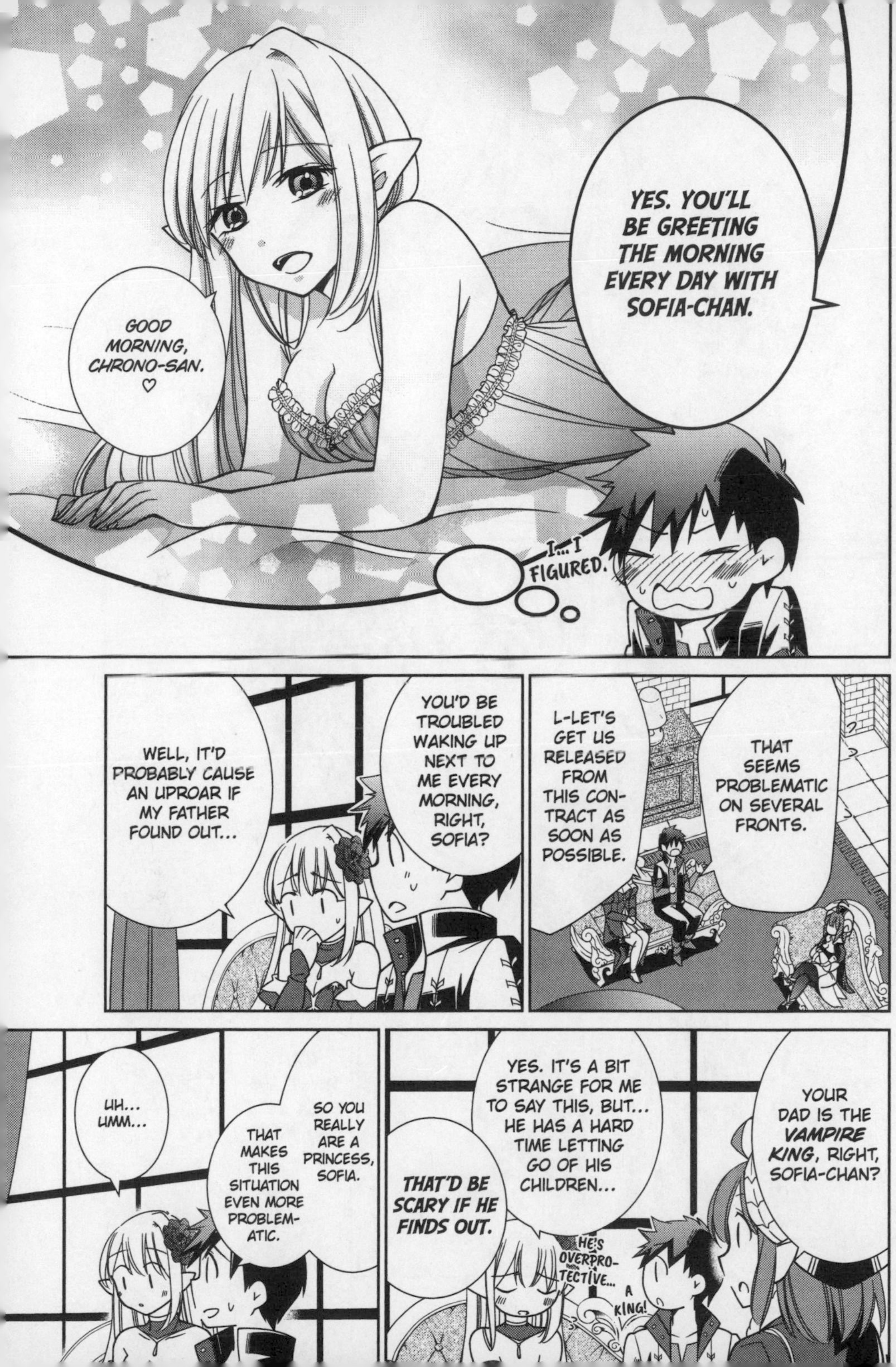
YES. YOU'LL BE GREETING THE MORNING EVERY DAY WITH SOFIA-CHAN.
GOOD MORNING, CHRONO-SAN. ♡
I... I FIGURED.
THAT SEEMS PROBLEMATIC ON SEVERAL FRONTS.
L-LET'S GET US RELEASED FROM THIS CONTRACT AS SOON AS POSSIBLE.
YOU'D BE TROUBLED WAKING UP NEXT TO ME EVERY MORNING, RIGHT, SOFIA?
WELL, IT'D PROBABLY CAUSE AN UPROAR IF MY FATHER FOUND OUT...
YOUR DAD IS THE *VAMPIRE KING*, RIGHT, SOFIA-CHAN?
YES. IT'S A BIT STRANGE FOR ME TO SAY THIS, BUT... HE HAS A HARD TIME LETTING GO OF HIS CHILDREN...
HE'S OVERPROTECTIVE...
A KING!
THAT'D BE SCARY IF HE FINDS OUT.
SO YOU REALLY ARE A PRINCESS, SOFIA.
THAT MAKES THIS SITUATION EVEN MORE PROBLEMATIC.
UH... UMM...

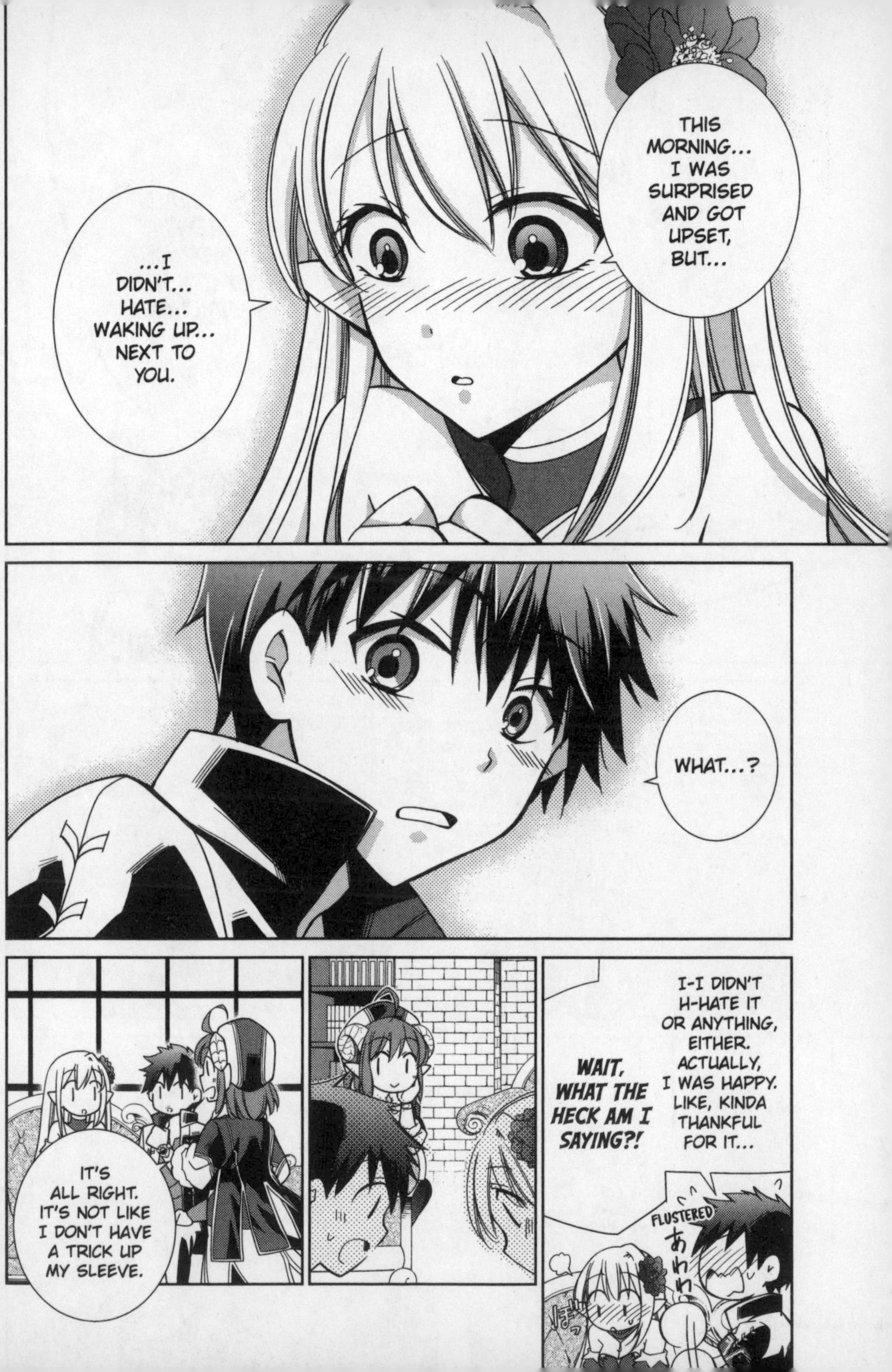
THIS MORNING... I WAS SURPRISED AND GOT UPSET, BUT...
...I DIDN'T... HATE... WAKING UP... NEXT TO YOU.
WHAT...?
I-I DIDN'T H-HATE IT OR ANYTHING, EITHER. ACTUALLY, I WAS HAPPY. LIKE, KINDA THANKFUL FOR IT...
WAIT, WHAT THE HECK AM I SAYING?!
FLUSTERED
あわわ
IT'S ALL RIGHT. IT'S NOT LIKE I DON'T HAVE A TRICK UP MY SLEEVE.

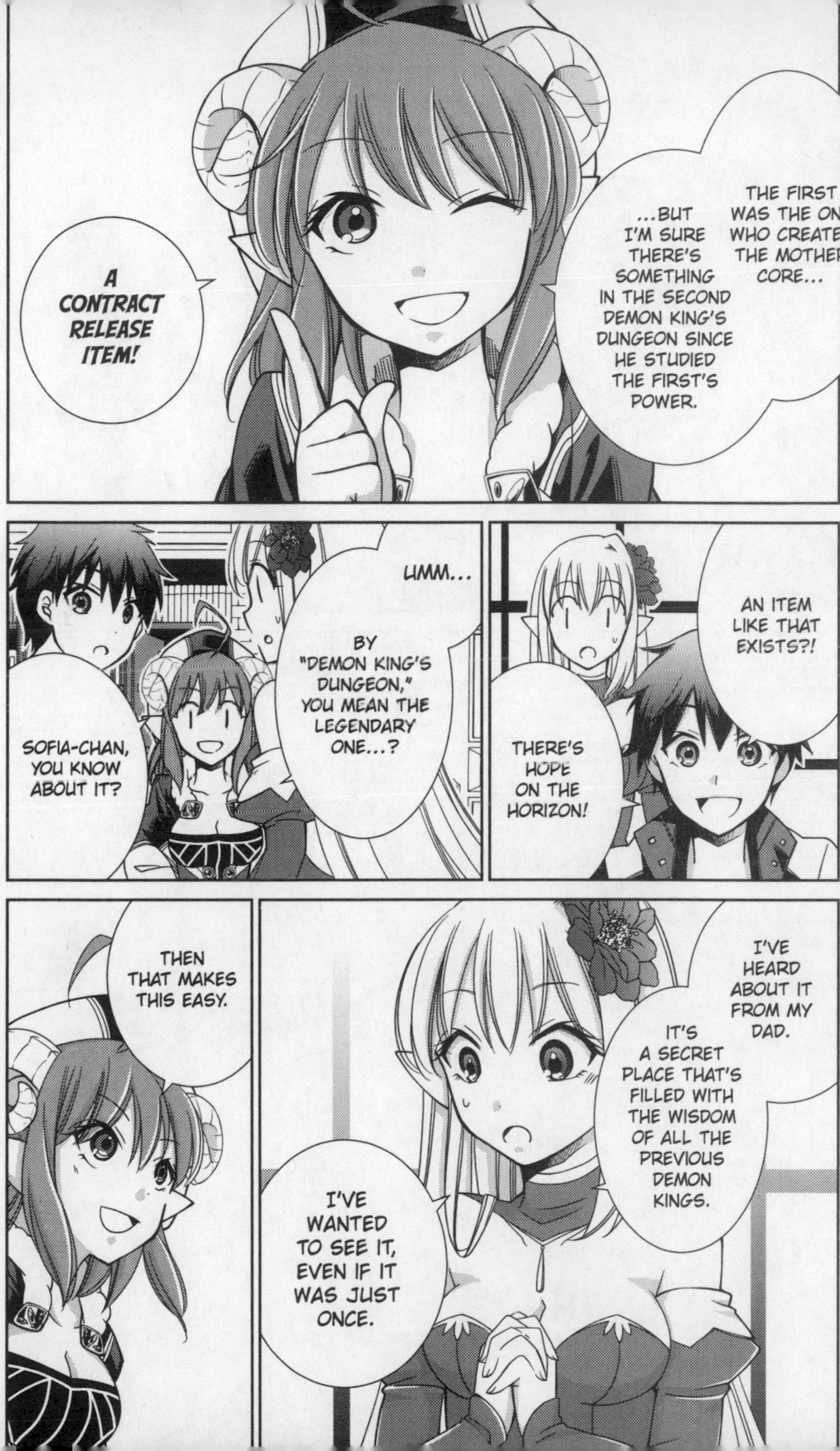
THE FIRST WAS THE ONE WHO CREATED THE MOTHER CORE...
...BUT I'M SURE THERE'S SOMETHING IN THE SECOND DEMON KING'S DUNGEON SINCE HE STUDIED THE FIRST'S POWER.
A CONTRACT RELEASE ITEM!
AN ITEM LIKE THAT EXISTS?!
THERE'S HOPE ON THE HORIZON!
UMM...
BY "DEMON KING'S DUNGEON," YOU MEAN THE LEGENDARY ONE...?
SOFIA-CHAN, YOU KNOW ABOUT IT?
I'VE HEARD ABOUT IT FROM MY DAD.
IT'S A SECRET PLACE THAT'S FILLED WITH THE WISDOM OF ALL THE PREVIOUS DEMON KINGS.
I'VE WANTED TO SEE IT, EVEN IF IT WAS JUST ONCE.
THEN THAT MAKES THIS EASY.

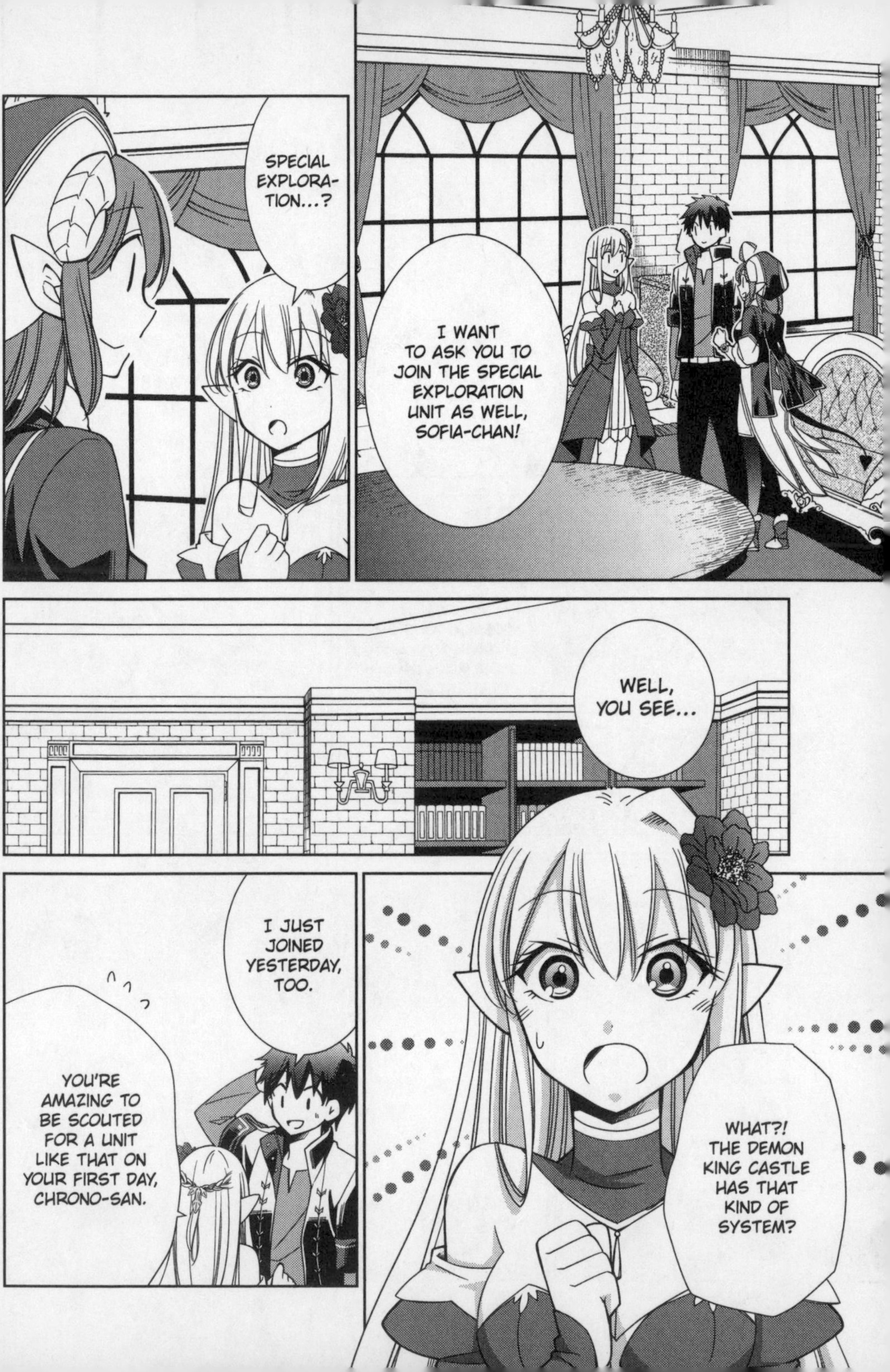
I WANT TO ASK YOU TO JOIN THE SPECIAL EXPLORATION UNIT AS WELL, SOFIA-CHAN!
SPECIAL EXPLORA-TION...?
WELL, YOU SEE...
WHAT?! THE DEMON KING CASTLE HAS THAT KIND OF SYSTEM?
I JUST JOINED YESTERDAY, TOO.
YOU'RE AMAZING TO BE SCOUTED FOR A UNIT LIKE THAT ON YOUR FIRST DAY, CHRONO-SAN.

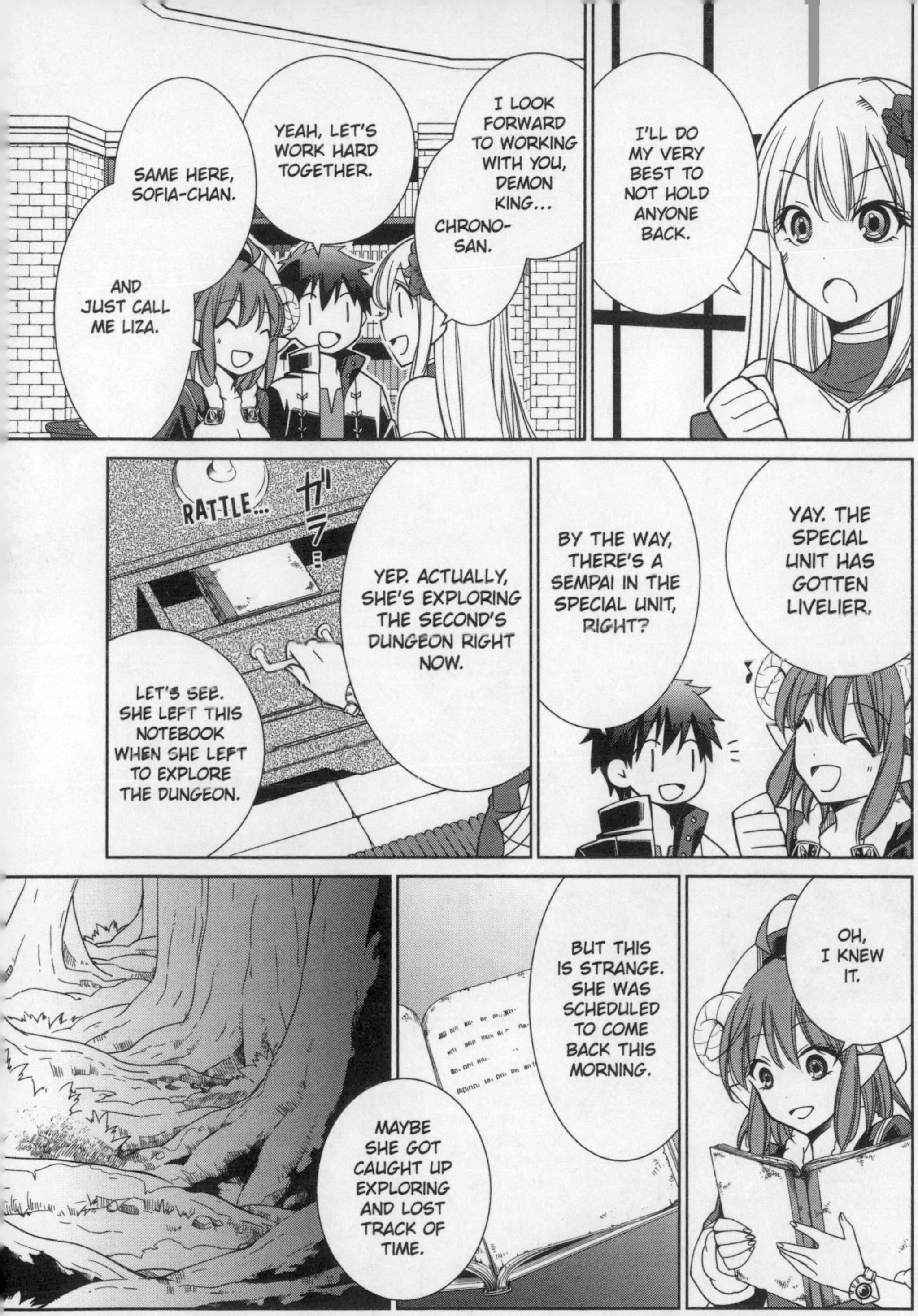
I'LL DO MY VERY BEST TO NOT HOLD ANYONE BACK.
I LOOK FORWARD TO WORKING WITH YOU, DEMON KING… CHRONO-SAN.
YEAH, LET'S WORK HARD TOGETHER.
SAME HERE, SOFIA-CHAN.
AND JUST CALL ME LIZA.
YAY. THE SPECIAL UNIT HAS GOTTEN LIVELIER.
BY THE WAY, THERE'S A SEMPAI IN THE SPECIAL UNIT, RIGHT?
YEP. ACTUALLY, SHE'S EXPLORING THE SECOND'S DUNGEON RIGHT NOW.
ガラ…
RATTLE…
LET'S SEE. SHE LEFT THIS NOTEBOOK WHEN SHE LEFT TO EXPLORE THE DUNGEON.
OH, I KNEW IT.
BUT THIS IS STRANGE. SHE WAS SCHEDULED TO COME BACK THIS MORNING.
MAYBE SHE GOT CAUGHT UP EXPLORING AND LOST TRACK OF TIME.

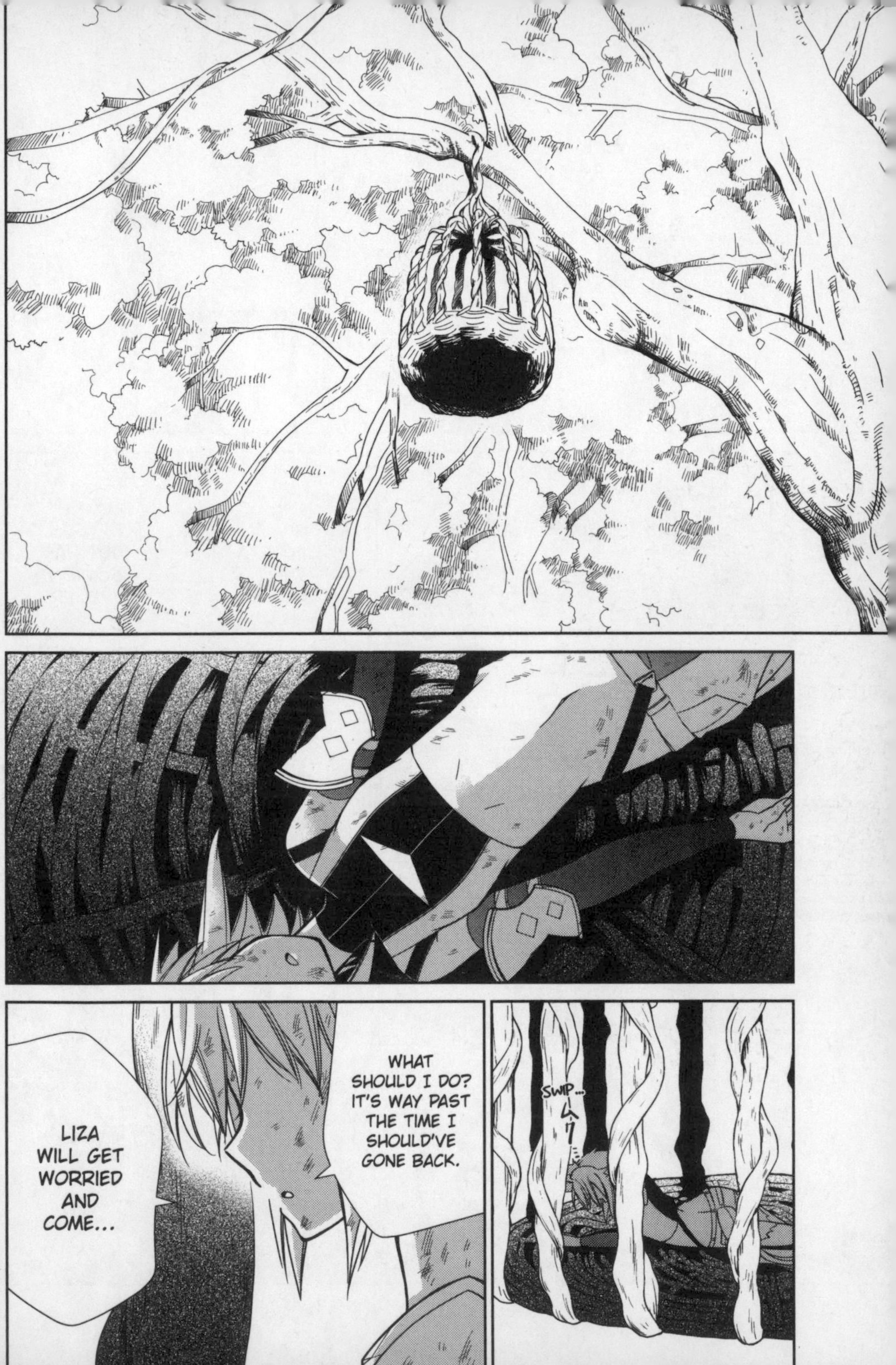
SWIP...
ムク...
WHAT SHOULD I DO? IT'S WAY PAST THE TIME I SHOULD'VE GONE BACK.
LIZA WILL GET WORRIED AND COME...

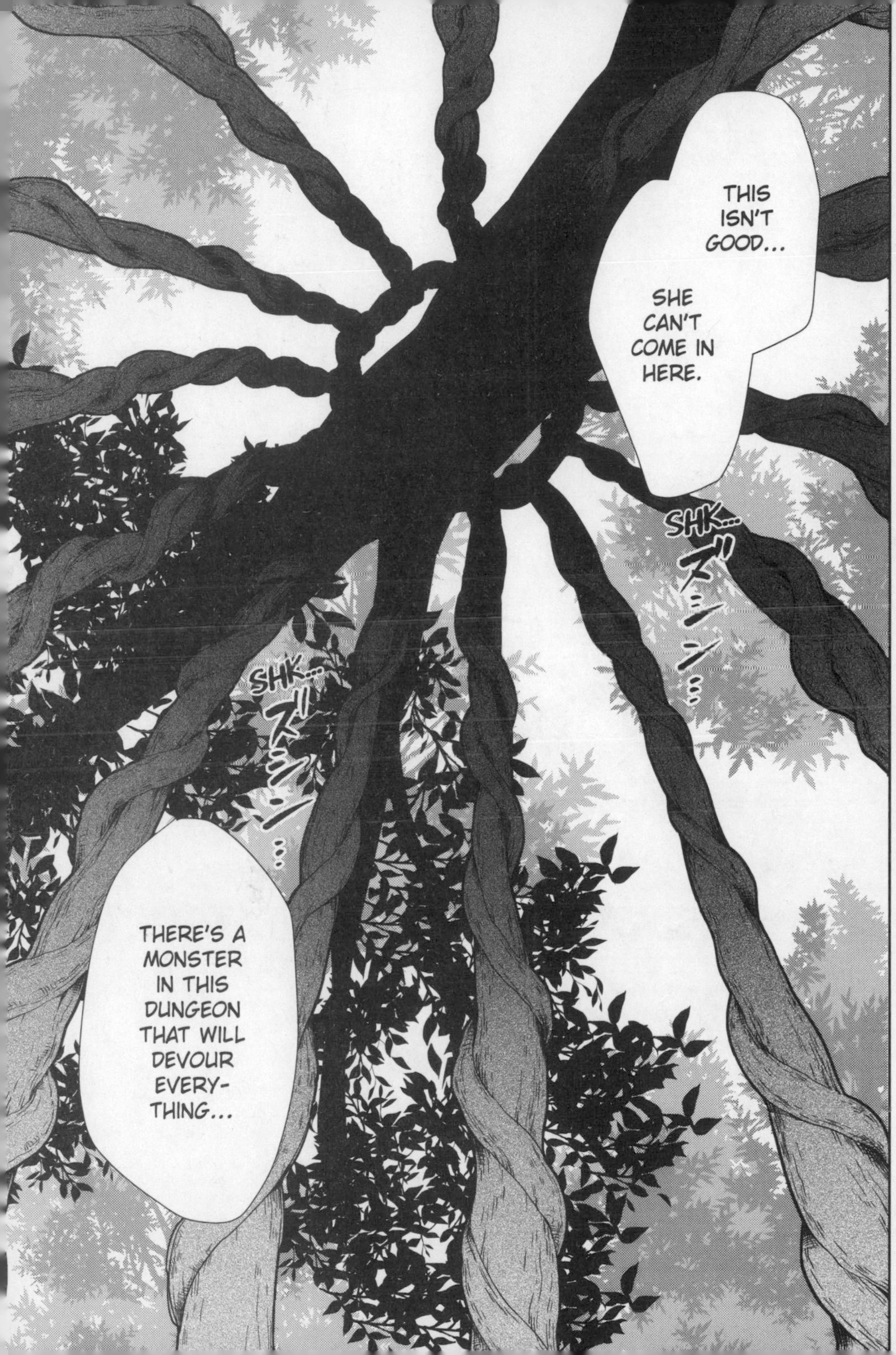
THIS ISN'T GOOD...
SHE CAN'T COME IN HERE.
SHK...
ズシン…
SHK...
ズシン…
THERE'S A MONSTER IN THIS DUNGEON THAT WILL DEVOUR EVERY-THING...

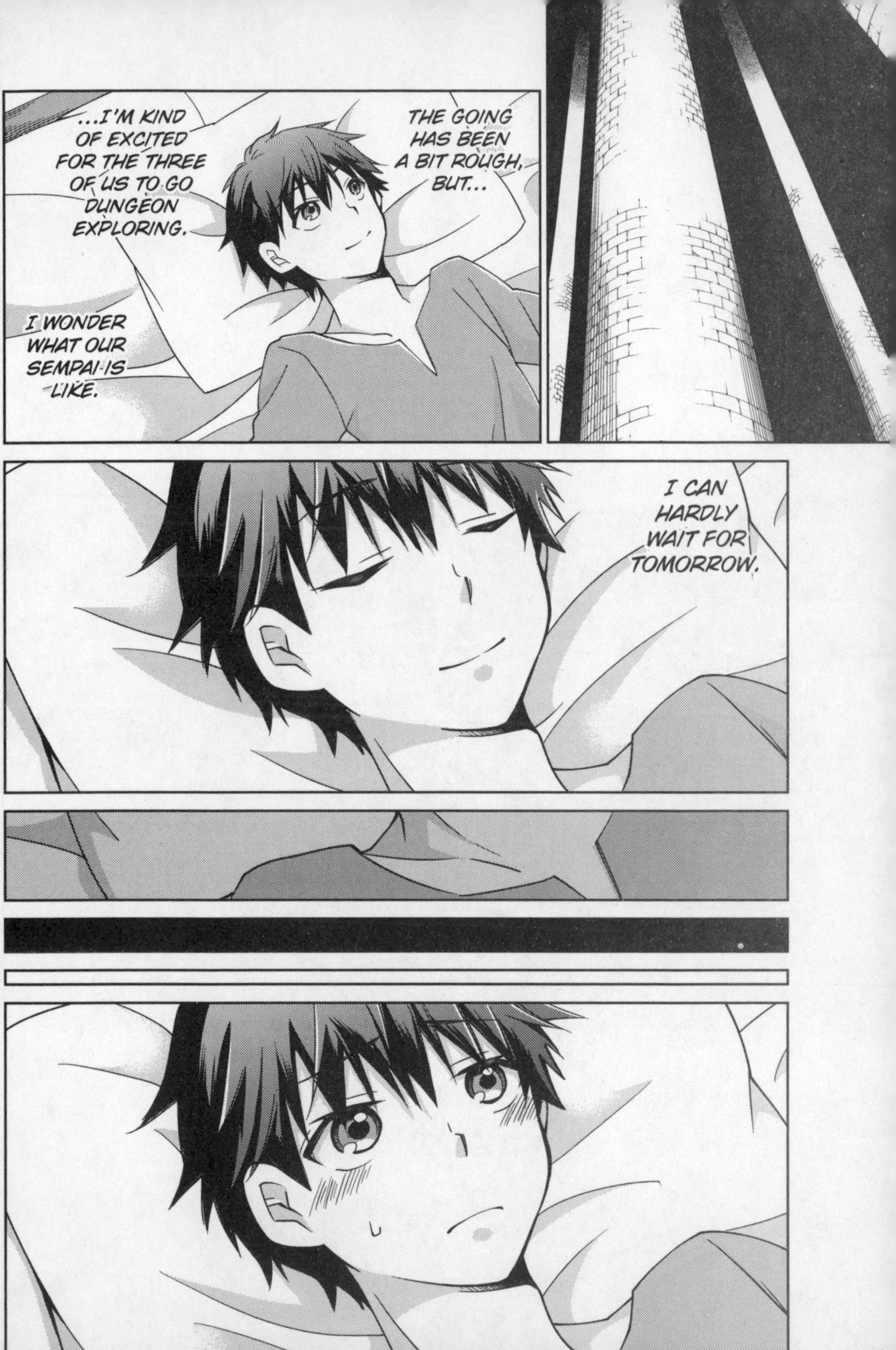
THE GOING HAS BEEN A BIT ROUGH, BUT...
...I'M KIND OF EXCITED FOR THE THREE OF US TO GO DUNGEON EXPLORING.
I WONDER WHAT OUR SEMPAI IS LIKE.
I CAN HARDLY WAIT FOR TOMORROW.

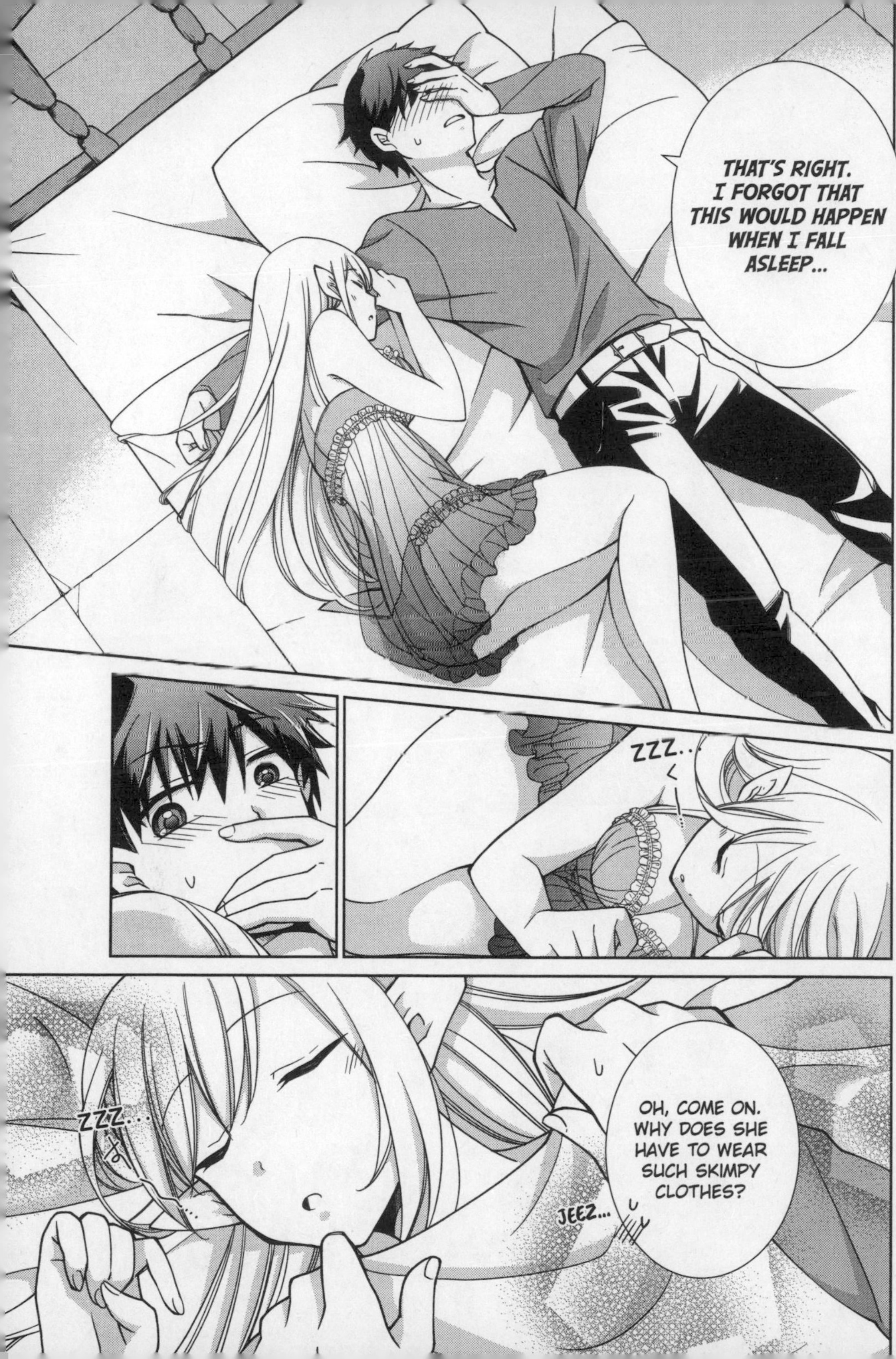
THAT'S RIGHT. I FORGOT THAT THIS WOULD HAPPEN WHEN I FALL ASLEEP...
ZZZ...
OH, COME ON. WHY DOES SHE HAVE TO WEAR SUCH SKIMPY CLOTHES?
JEEZ...
ZZZ...

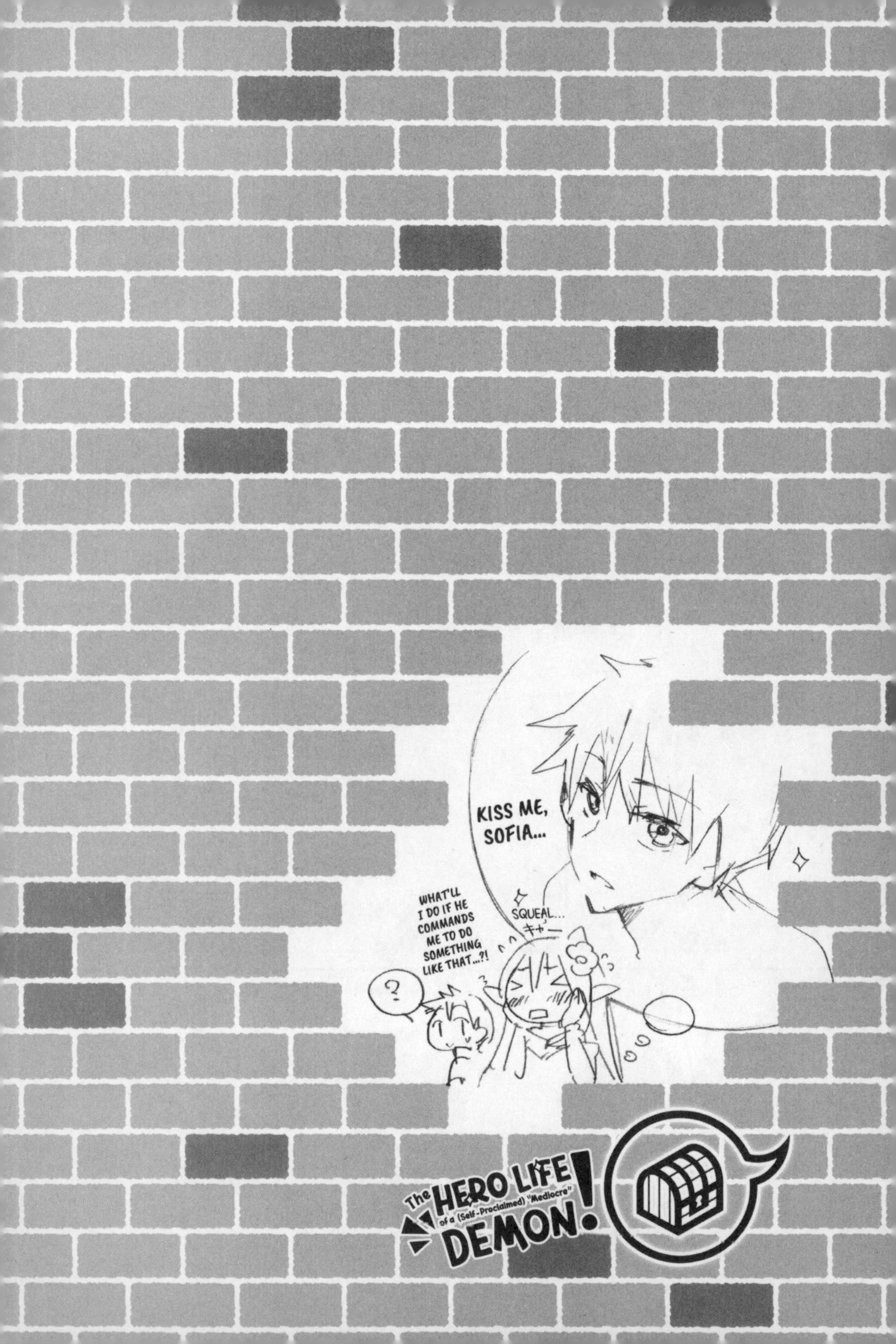
KISS ME, SOFIA...
SQUEAL... キャー
WHAT'LL I DO IF HE COMMANDS ME TO DO SOMETHING LIKE THAT...?!
The HERO LIFE of a (Self-Proclaimed) "Mediocre" DEMON!

Chapter 4
Chrono Dives into the Second's Dungeon

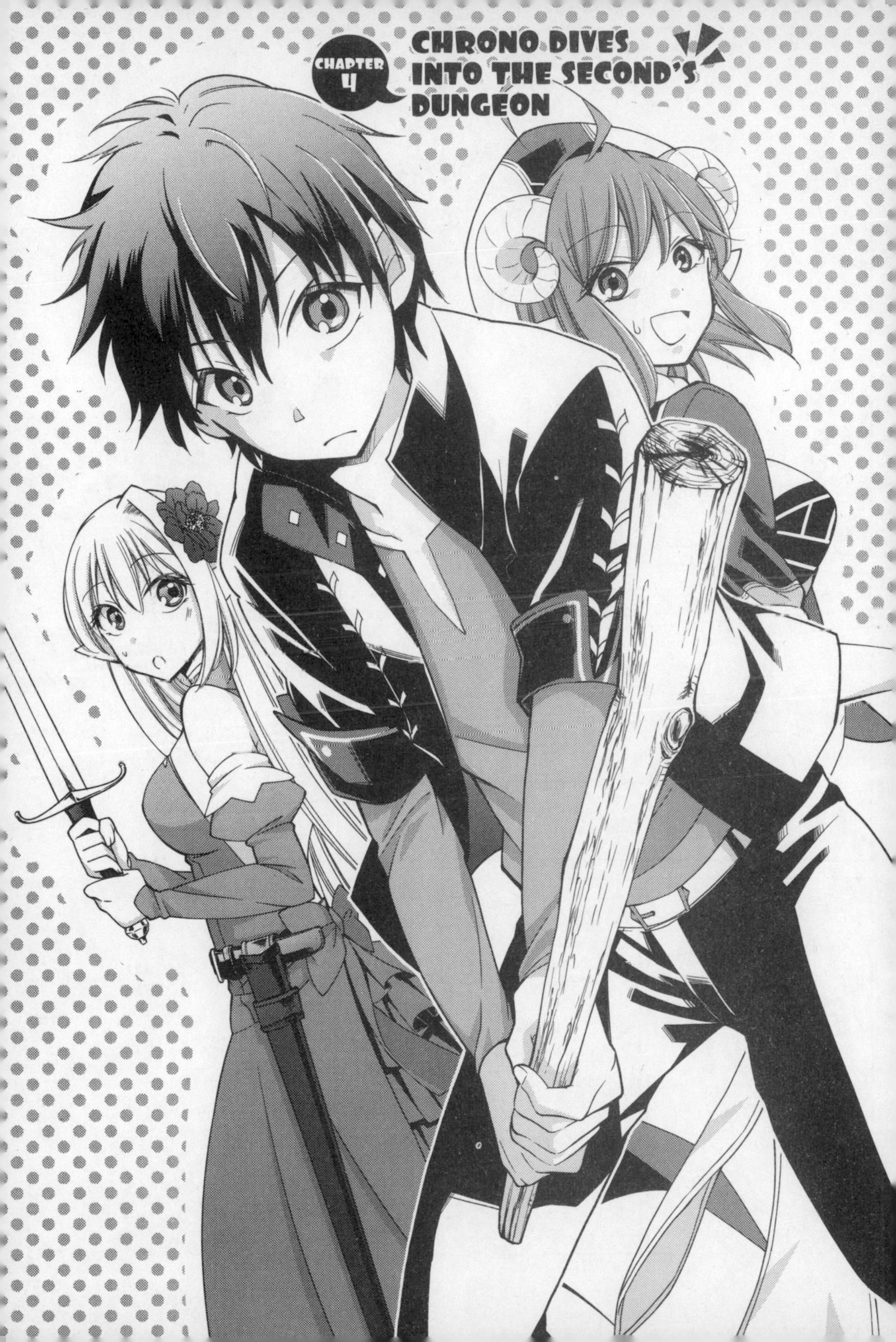

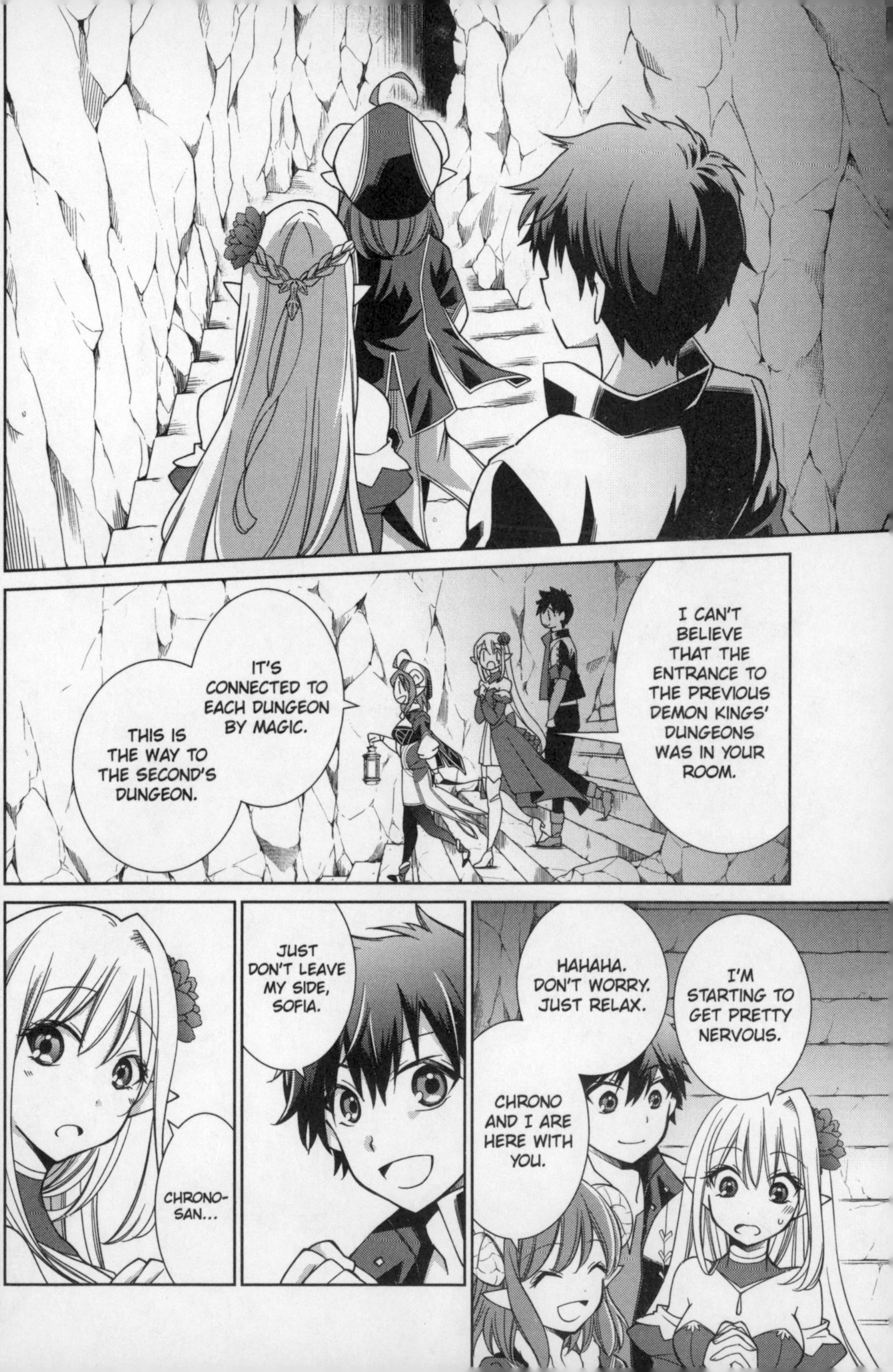
I CAN'T BELIEVE THAT THE ENTRANCE TO THE PREVIOUS DEMON KINGS' DUNGEONS WAS IN YOUR ROOM.
IT'S CONNECTED TO EACH DUNGEON BY MAGIC.
THIS IS THE WAY TO THE SECOND'S DUNGEON.
I'M STARTING TO GET PRETTY NERVOUS.
HAHAHA. DON'T WORRY. JUST RELAX.
CHRONO AND I ARE HERE WITH YOU.
JUST DON'T LEAVE MY SIDE, SOFIA.
CHRONO-SAN...

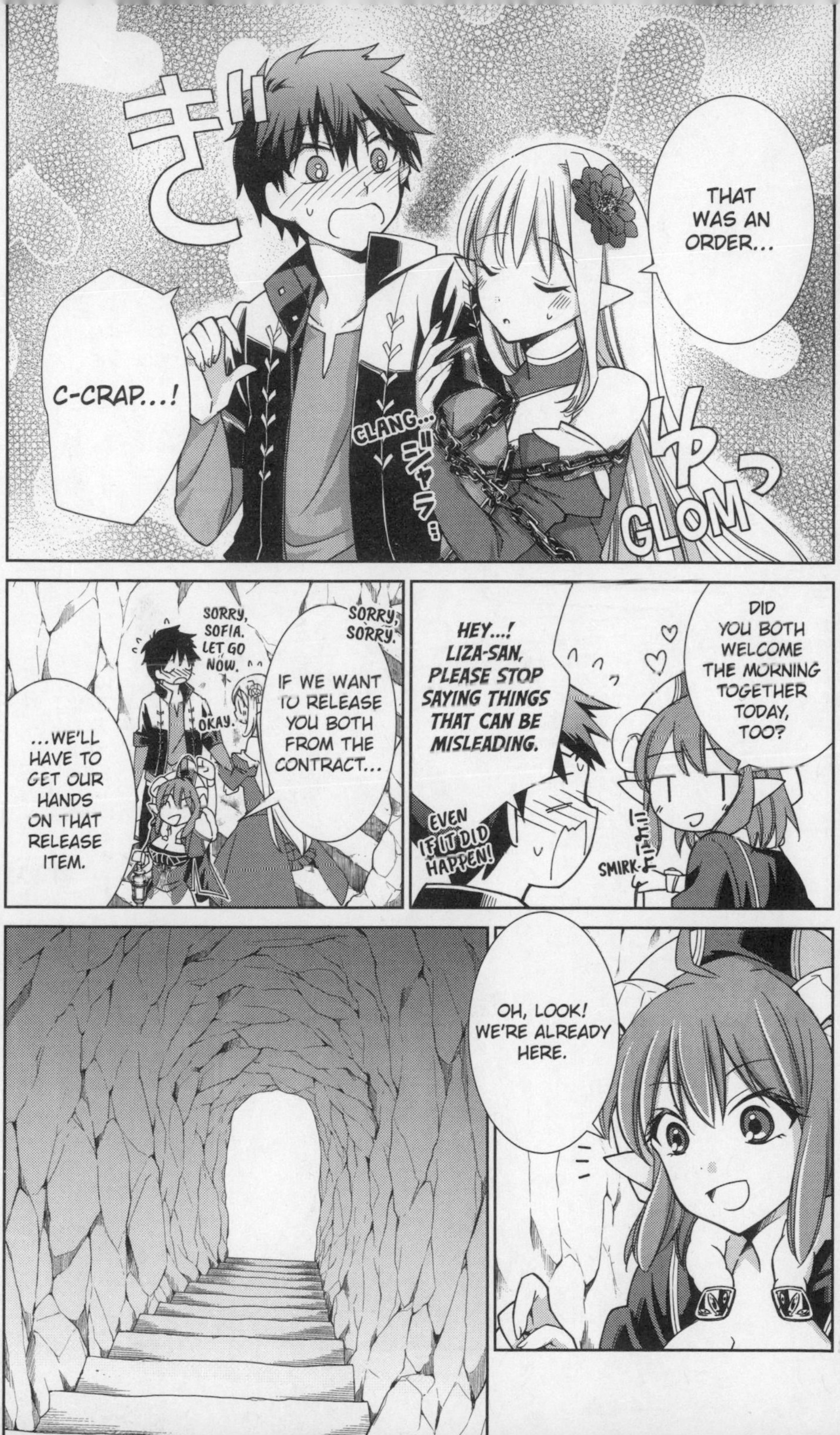
THAT WAS AN ORDER...
GLOM
CLANG...
C-CRAP...!
DID YOU BOTH WELCOME THE MORNING TOGETHER TODAY, TOO?
SMIRK
HEY...! LIZA-SAN, PLEASE STOP SAYING THINGS THAT CAN BE MISLEADING.
EVEN IF IT DID HAPPEN!
SORRY, SORRY.
SORRY, SOFIA. LET GO NOW.
OKAY.
IF WE WANT TO RELEASE YOU BOTH FROM THE CONTRACT...
...WE'LL HAVE TO GET OUR HANDS ON THAT RELEASE ITEM.
OH, LOOK! WE'RE ALREADY HERE.

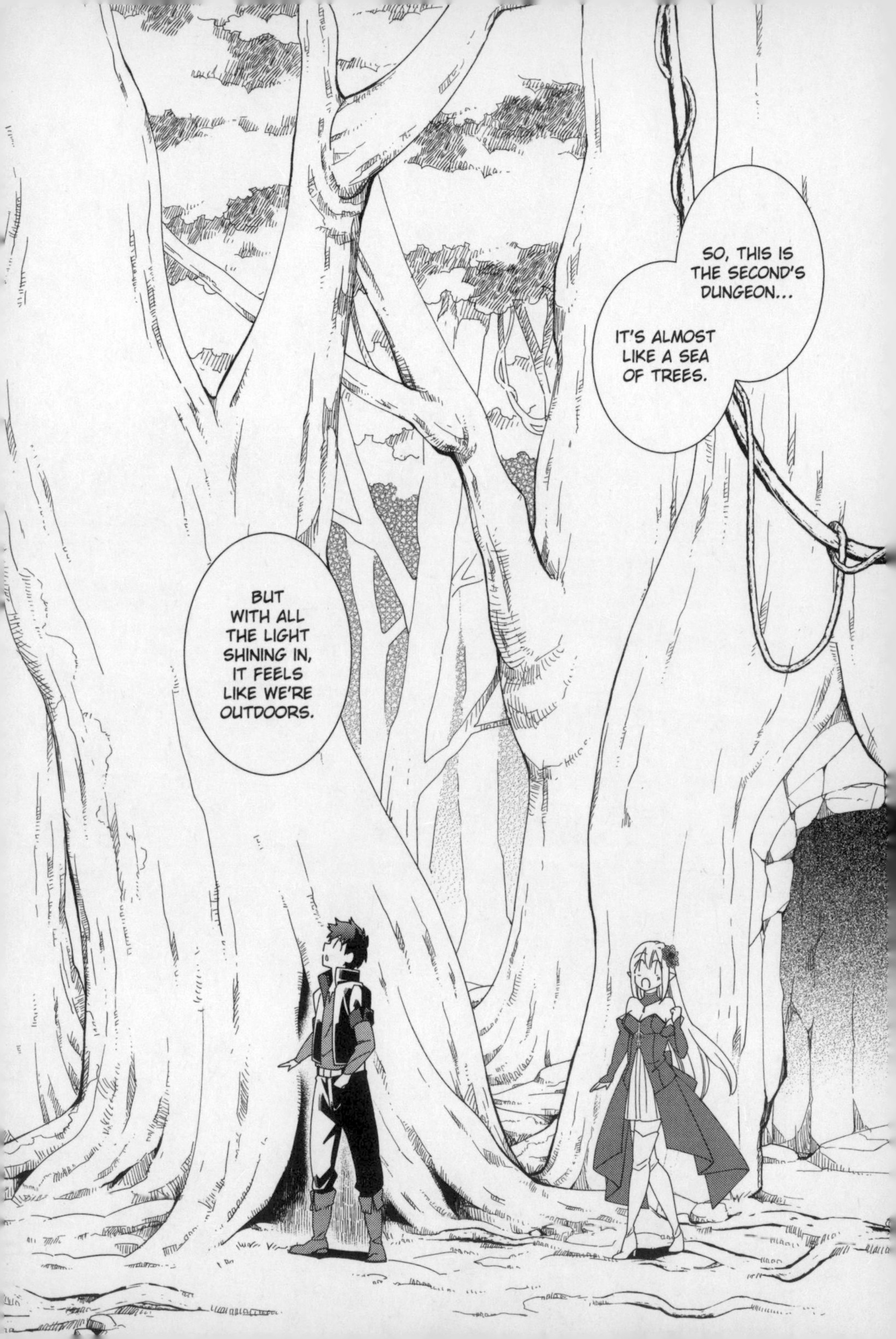
SO, THIS IS THE SECOND'S DUNGEON...
IT'S ALMOST LIKE A SEA OF TREES.
BUT WITH ALL THE LIGHT SHINING IN, IT FEELS LIKE WE'RE OUTDOORS.

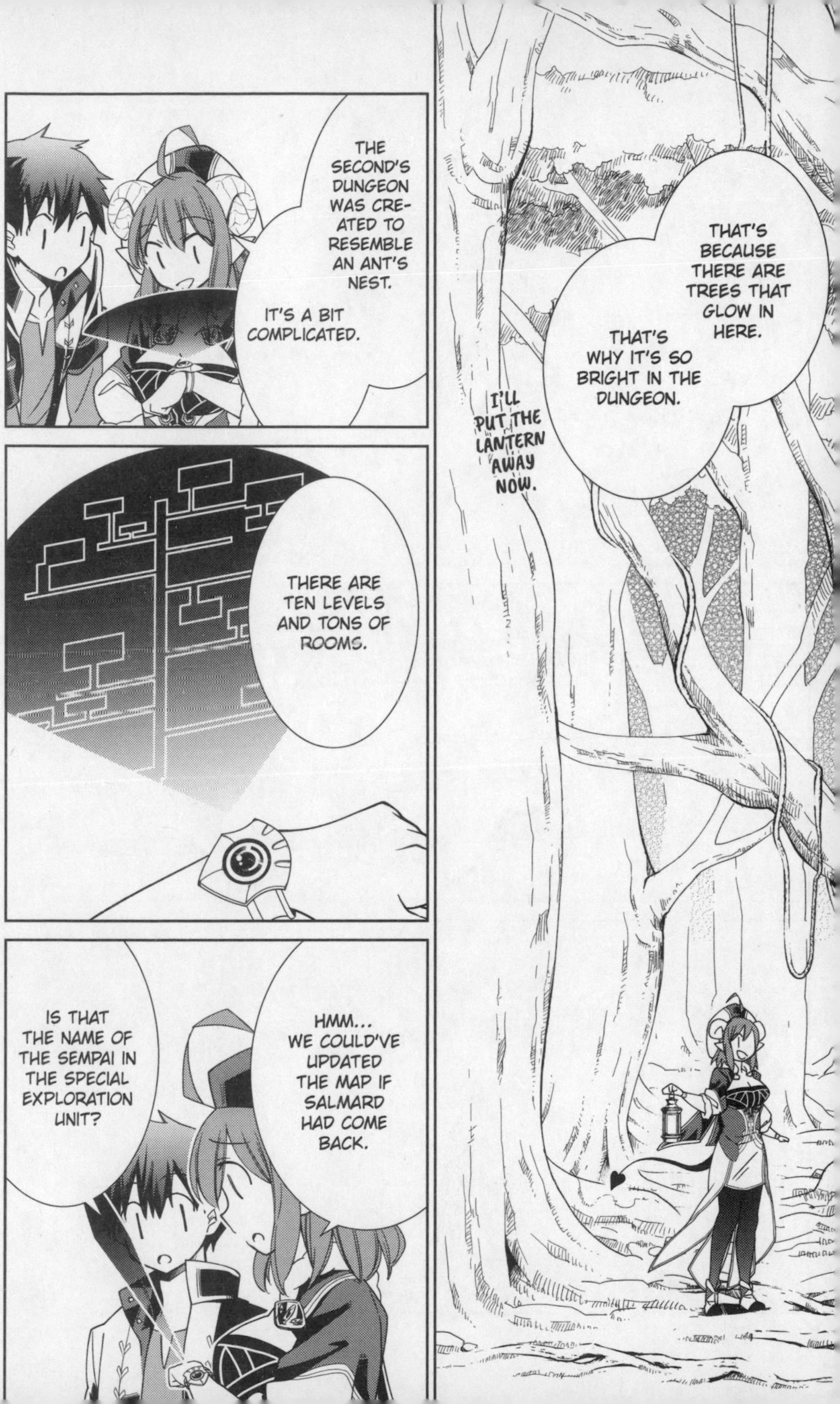
THAT'S BECAUSE THERE ARE TREES THAT GLOW IN HERE.
THAT'S WHY IT'S SO BRIGHT IN THE DUNGEON.
I'LL PUT THE LANTERN AWAY NOW.
THE SECOND'S DUNGEON WAS CRE-ATED TO RESEMBLE AN ANT'S NEST.
IT'S A BIT COMPLICATED.
THERE ARE TEN LEVELS AND TONS OF ROOMS.
HMM... WE COULD'VE UPDATED THE MAP IF SALMARD HAD COME BACK.
IS THAT THE NAME OF THE SEMPAI IN THE SPECIAL EXPLORATION UNIT?

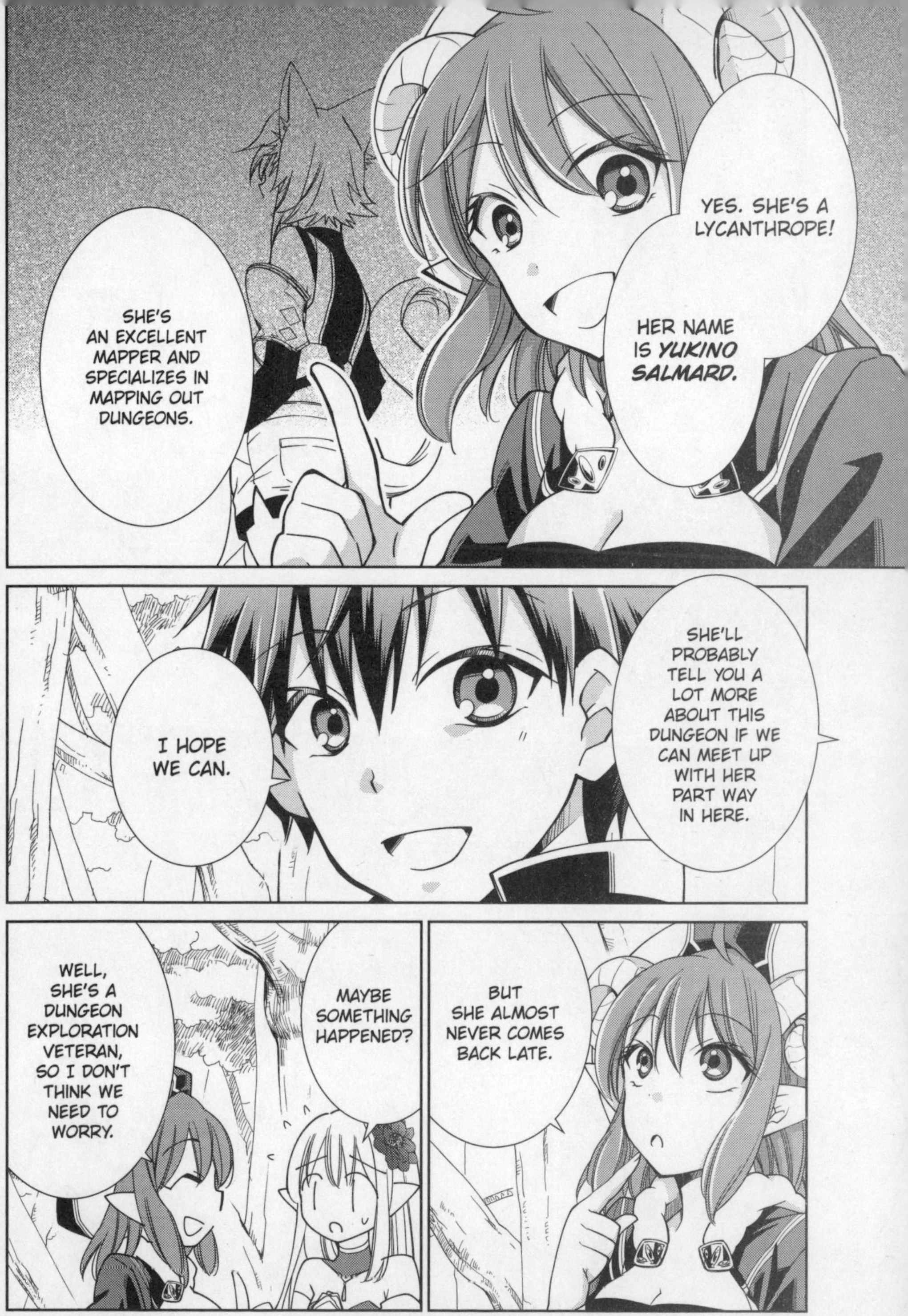
YES. SHE'S A LYCANTHROPE!
HER NAME IS *YUKINO SALMARD.*
SHE'S AN EXCELLENT MAPPER AND SPECIALIZES IN MAPPING OUT DUNGEONS.
SHE'LL PROBABLY TELL YOU A LOT MORE ABOUT THIS DUNGEON IF WE CAN MEET UP WITH HER PART WAY IN HERE.
I HOPE WE CAN.
BUT SHE ALMOST NEVER COMES BACK LATE.
MAYBE SOMETHING HAPPENED?
WELL, SHE'S A DUNGEON EXPLORATION VETERAN, SO I DON'T THINK WE NEED TO WORRY.

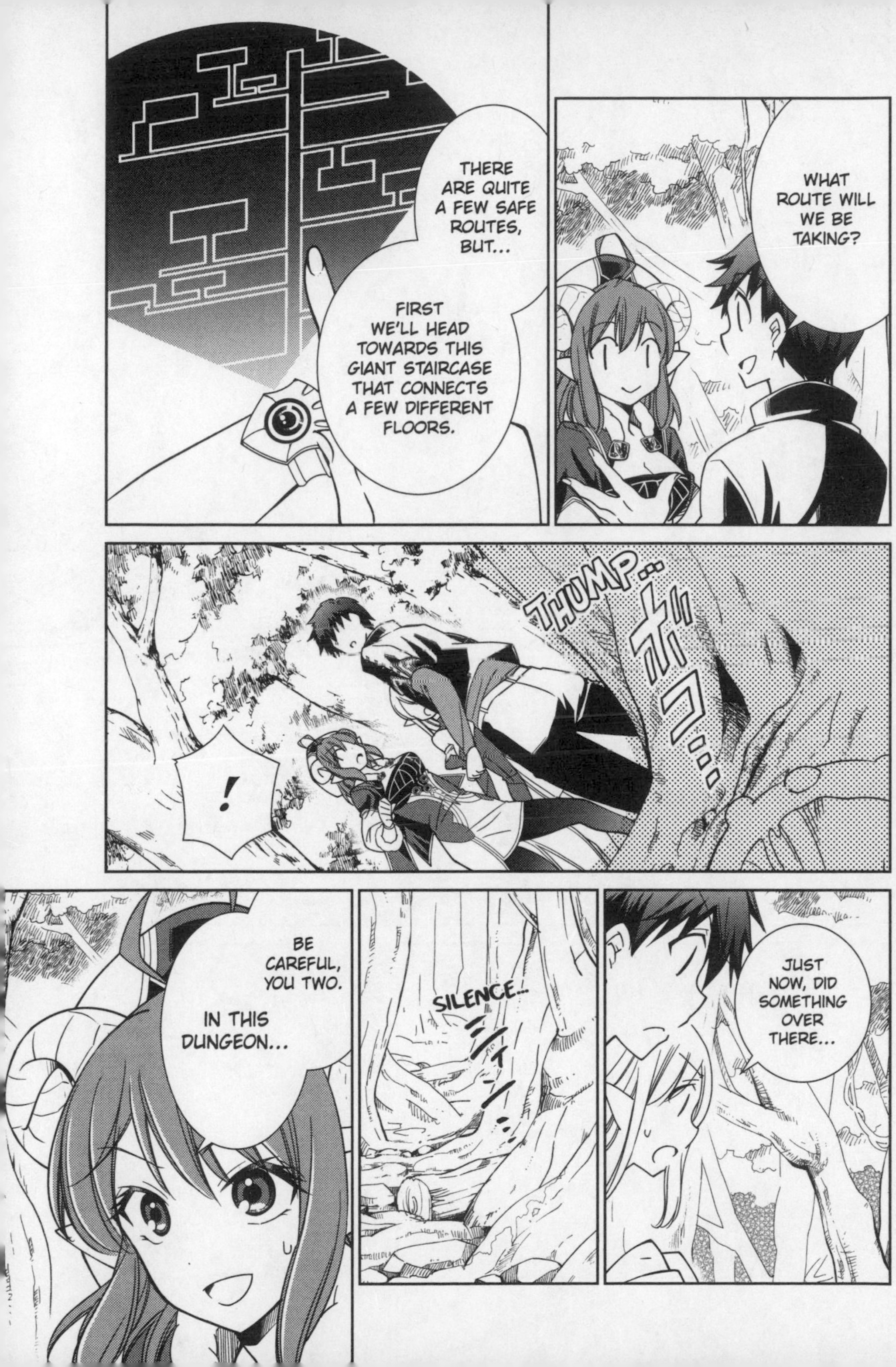
WHAT ROUTE WILL WE BE TAKING?
THERE ARE QUITE A FEW SAFE ROUTES, BUT...
FIRST WE'LL HEAD TOWARDS THIS GIANT STAIRCASE THAT CONNECTS A FEW DIFFERENT FLOORS.
THUMP...
!
JUST NOW, DID SOMETHING OVER THERE...
SILENCE...
BE CAREFUL, YOU TWO.
IN THIS DUNGEON...

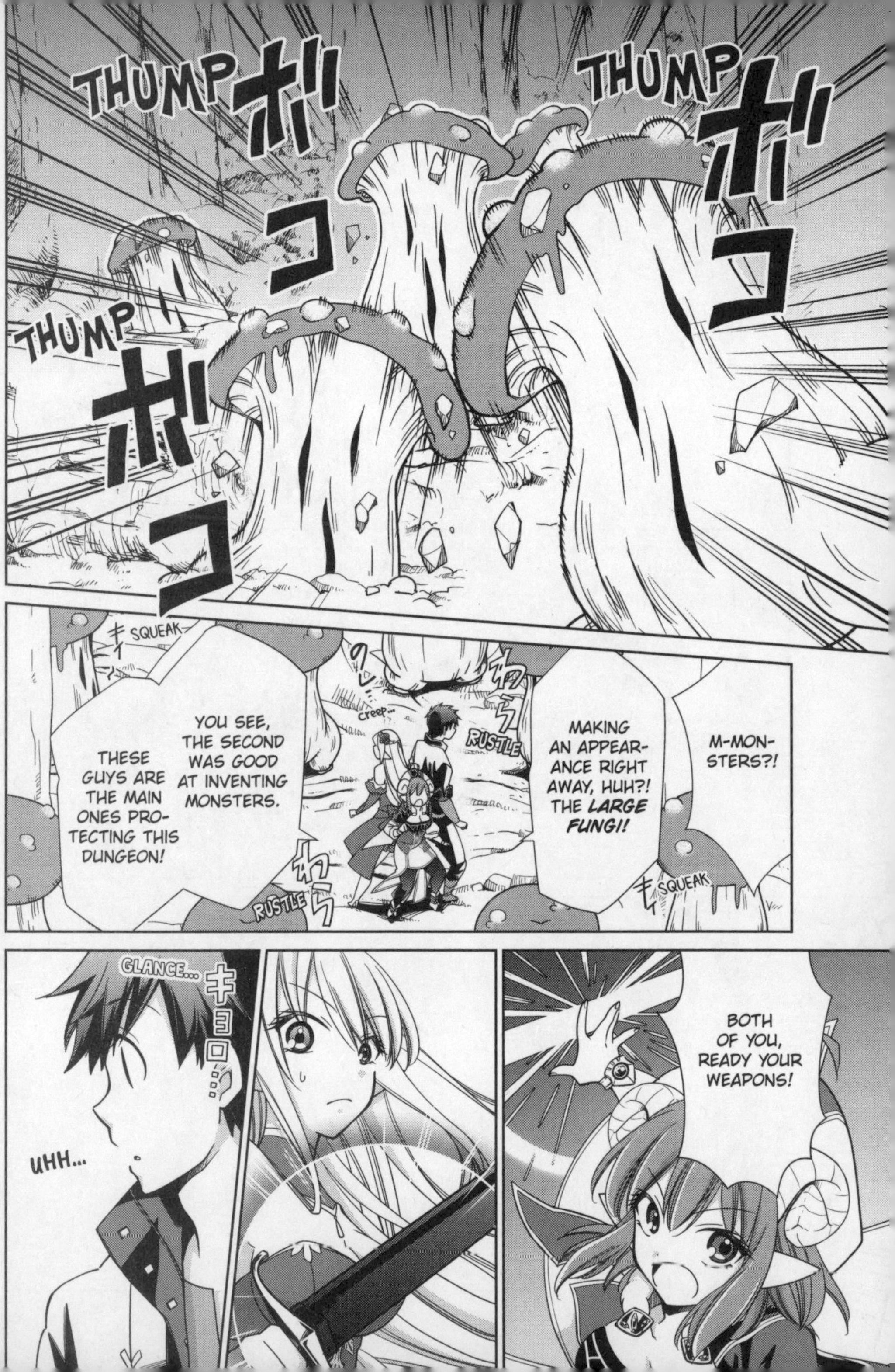
THUMP
ボコ
THUMP
ボコ
THUMP
ボコ
M-MON-STERS?!
MAKING AN APPEAR-ANCE RIGHT AWAY, HUH?! THE *LARGE FUNGI!*
RUSTLE
SQUEAK
creep...
YOU SEE, THE SECOND WAS GOOD AT INVENTING MONSTERS.
THESE GUYS ARE THE MAIN ONES PRO-TECTING THIS DUNGEON!
SQUEAK
RUSTLE
BOTH OF YOU, READY YOUR WEAPONS!
GLANCE...
キョロ...
UHH...

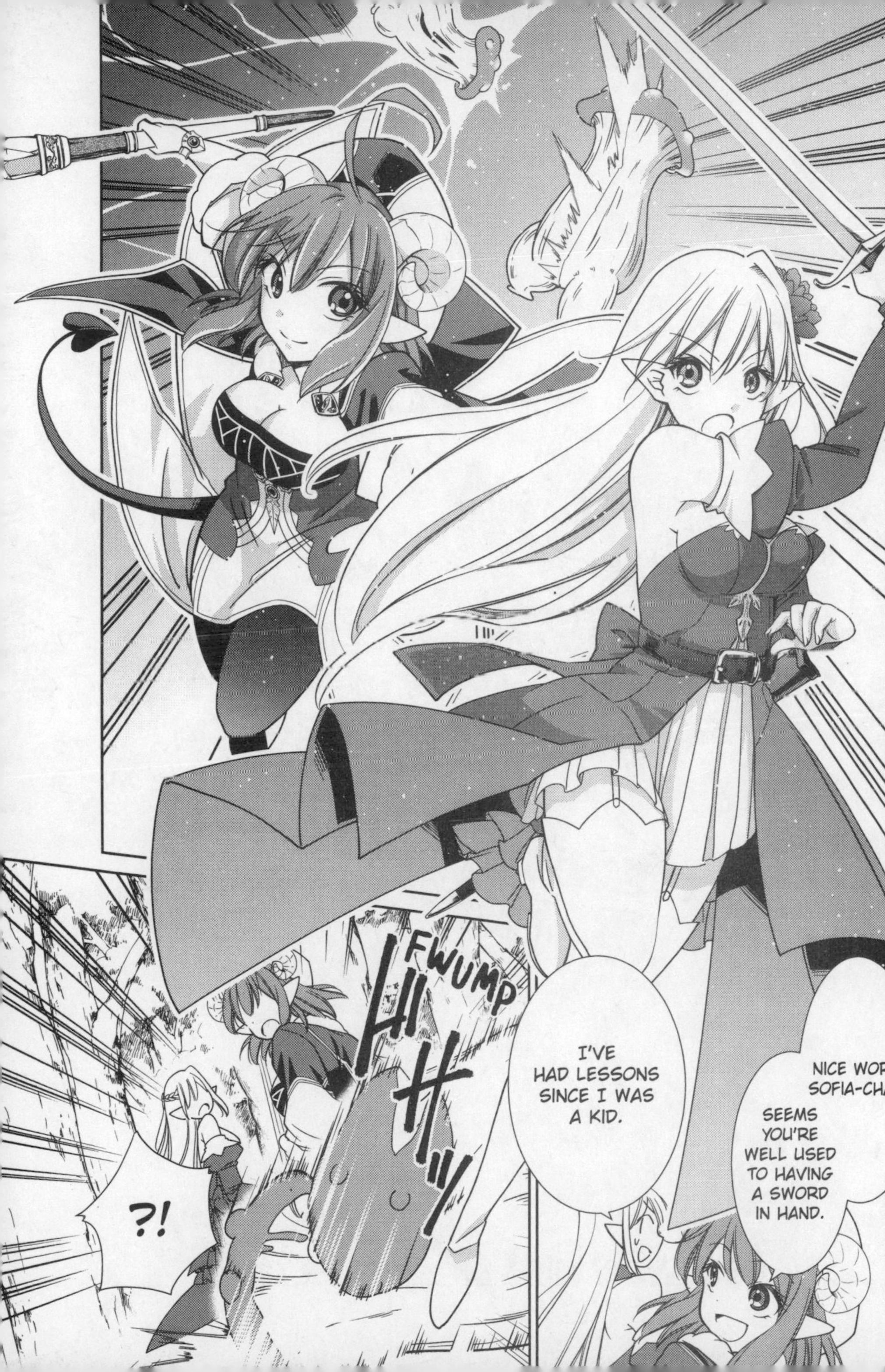
NICE WORK, SOFIA-CHAN! SEEMS YOU'RE WELL USED TO HAVING A SWORD IN HAND.
I'VE HAD LESSONS SINCE I WAS A KID.
FWUMP
?!

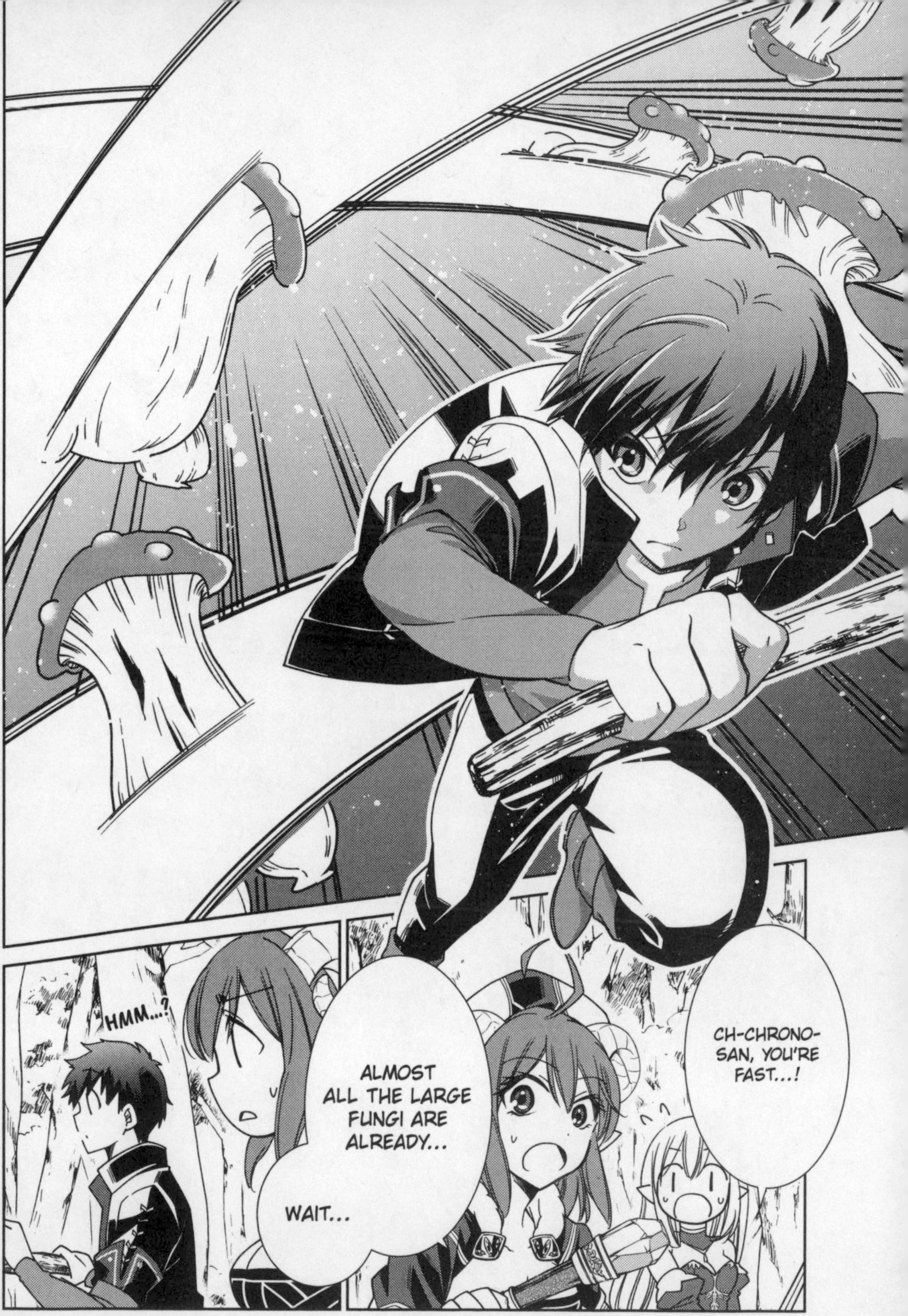
CH-CHRONO-SAN, YOU'RE FAST...!
ALMOST ALL THE LARGE FUNGI ARE ALREADY...
WAIT...
HMM...?

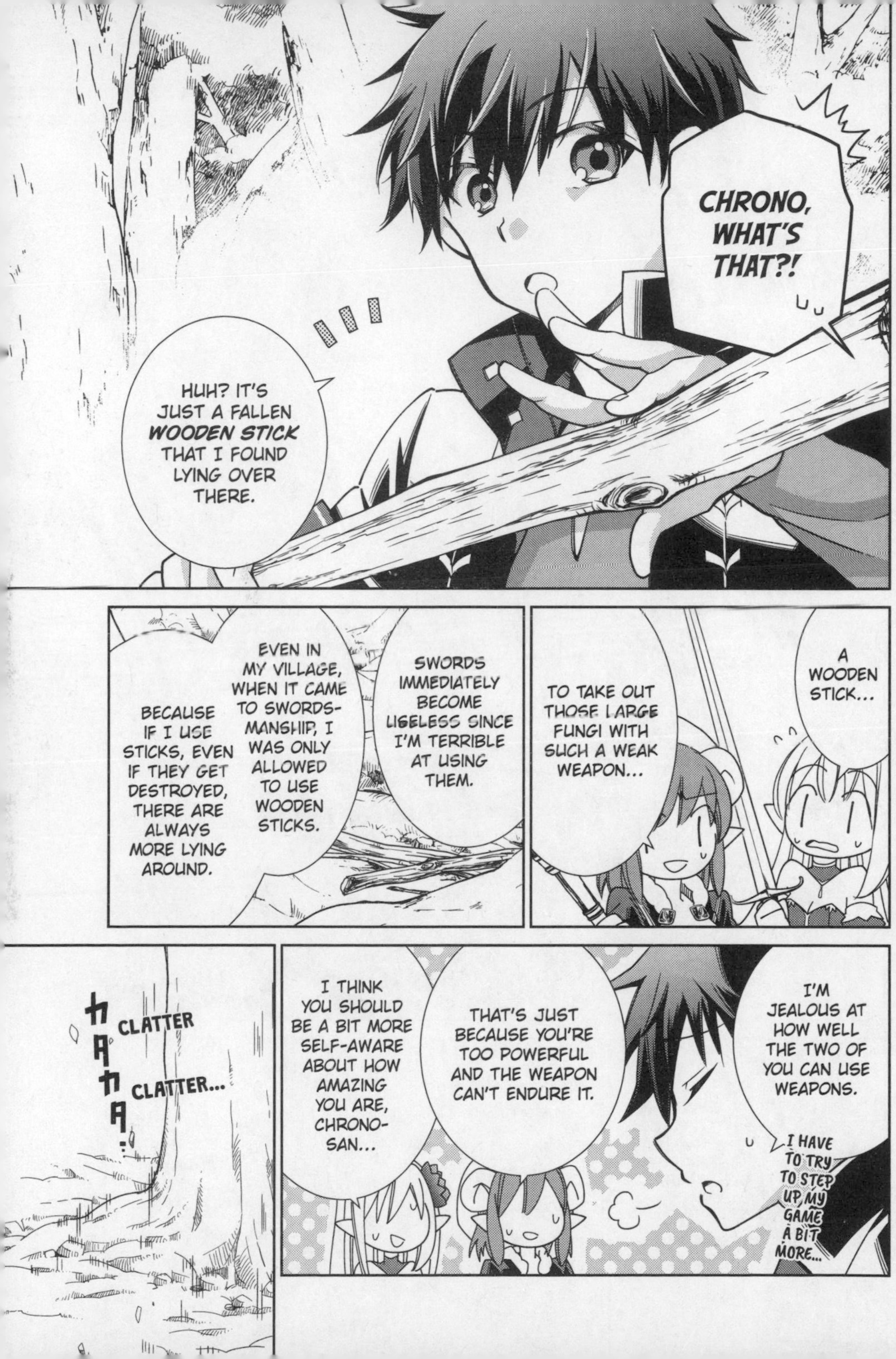
CHRONO, WHAT'S THAT?!
HUH? IT'S JUST A FALLEN WOODEN STICK THAT I FOUND LYING OVER THERE.
A WOODEN STICK...
TO TAKE OUT THOSE LARGE FUNGI WITH SUCH A WEAK WEAPON...
SWORDS IMMEDIATELY BECOME USELESS SINCE I'M TERRIBLE AT USING THEM.
EVEN IN MY VILLAGE, WHEN IT CAME TO SWORDS-MANSHIP, I WAS ONLY ALLOWED TO USE WOODEN STICKS.
BECAUSE IF I USE STICKS, EVEN IF THEY GET DESTROYED, THERE ARE ALWAYS MORE LYING AROUND.
I'M JEALOUS AT HOW WELL THE TWO OF YOU CAN USE WEAPONS.
I HAVE TO TRY TO STEP UP MY GAME A BIT MORE...
THAT'S JUST BECAUSE YOU'RE TOO POWERFUL AND THE WEAPON CAN'T ENDURE IT.
I THINK YOU SHOULD BE A BIT MORE SELF-AWARE ABOUT HOW AMAZING YOU ARE, CHRONO-SAN...
カタカタ
CLATTER
CLATTER...

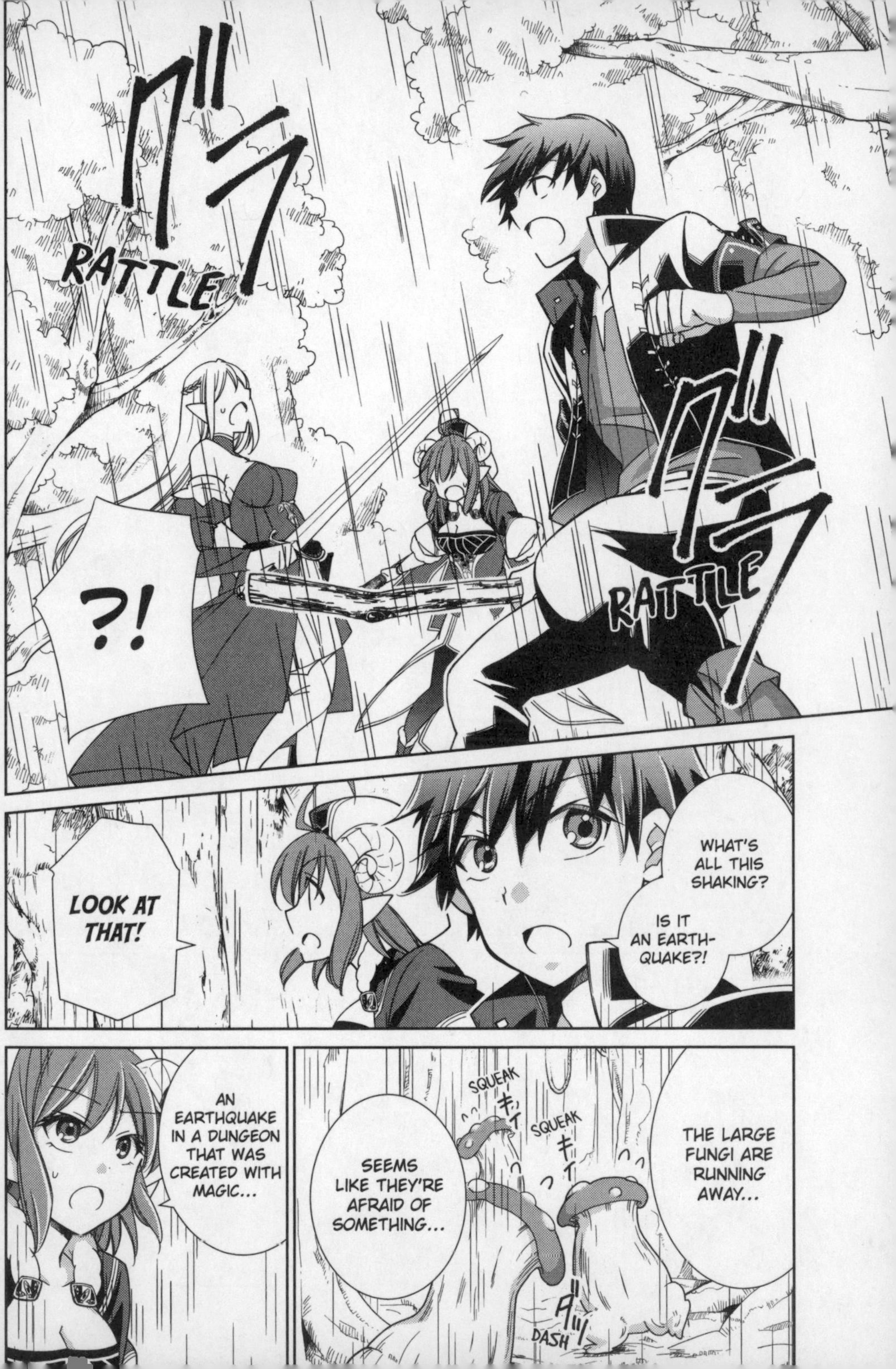
RATTLE
RATTLE
?!
WHAT'S ALL THIS SHAKING?
IS IT AN EARTH-QUAKE?!
LOOK AT THAT!
THE LARGE FUNGI ARE RUNNING AWAY...
SQUEAK
SQUEAK
SEEMS LIKE THEY'RE AFRAID OF SOMETHING...
DASH
AN EARTHQUAKE IN A DUNGEON THAT WAS CREATED WITH MAGIC...

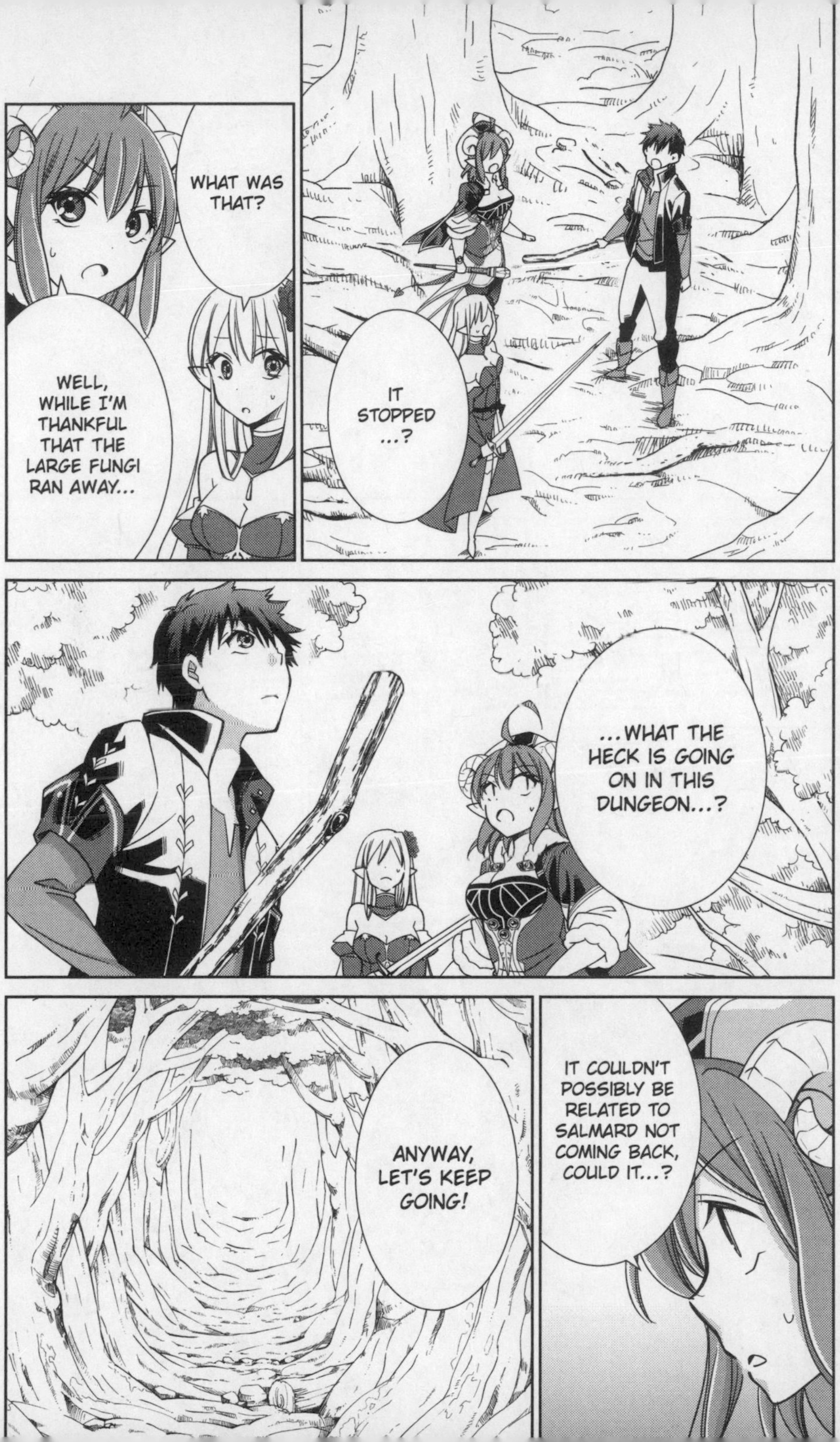
IT STOPPED ...?
WHAT WAS THAT?
WELL, WHILE I'M THANKFUL THAT THE LARGE FUNGI RAN AWAY...
...WHAT THE HECK IS GOING ON IN THIS DUNGEON...?
IT COULDN'T POSSIBLY BE RELATED TO SALMARD NOT COMING BACK, COULD IT...?
ANYWAY, LET'S KEEP GOING!

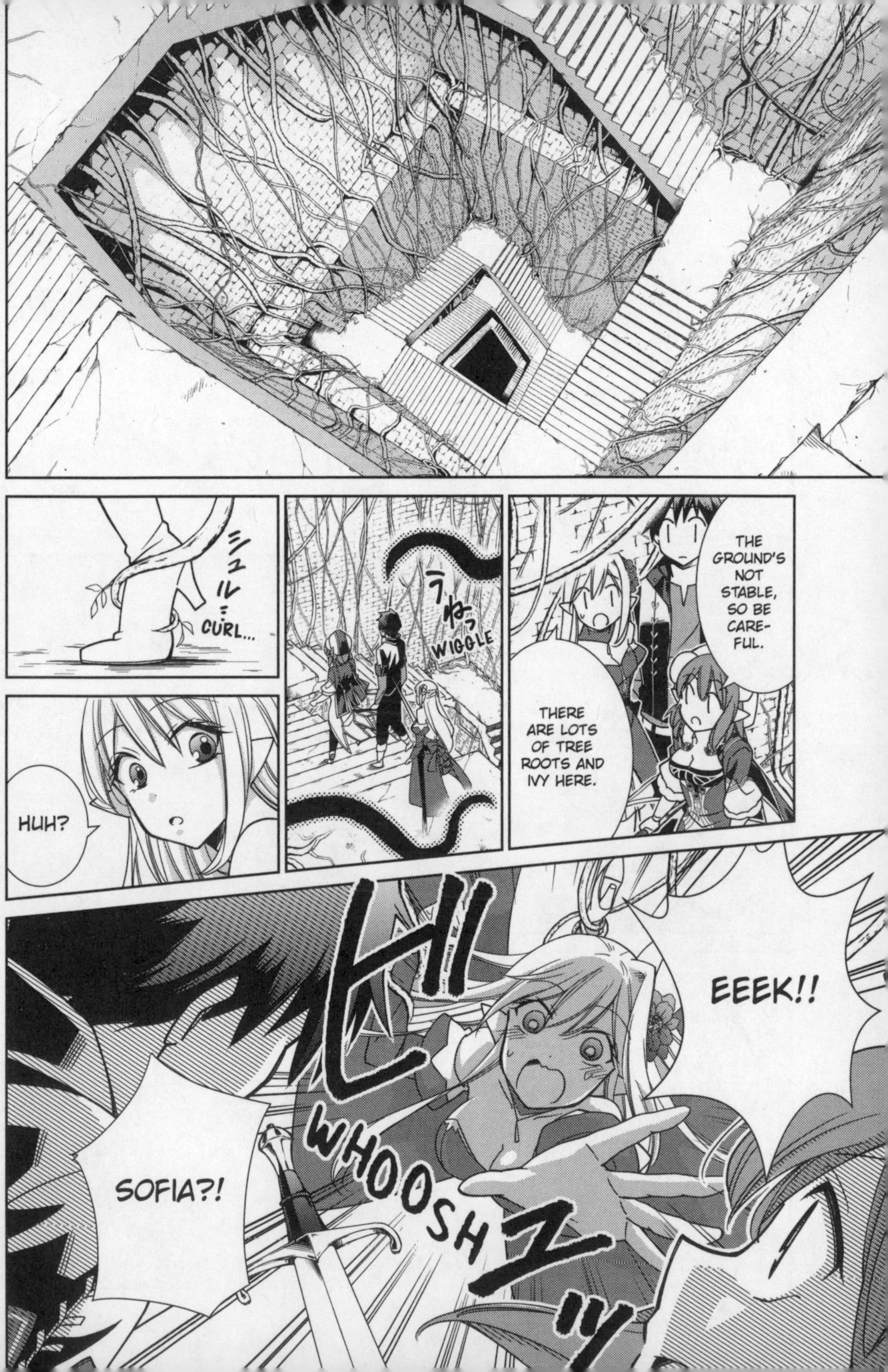
THE GROUND'S NOT STABLE, SO BE CARE-FUL.
THERE ARE LOTS OF TREE ROOTS AND IVY HERE.
うねっ
WIGGLE
シュル
CURL...
HUH?
EEEK!!
WHOOSH
SOFIA?!

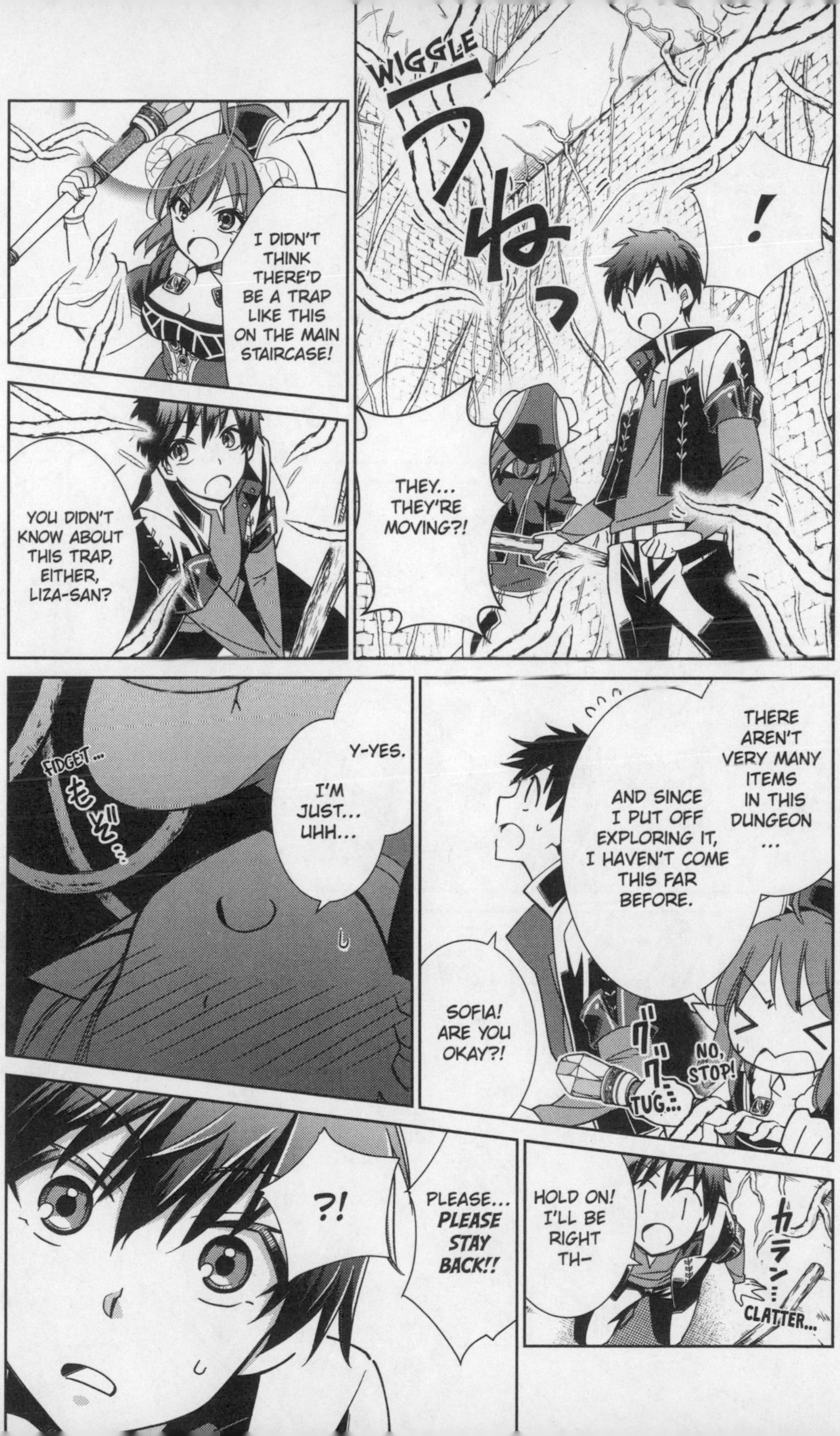
WIGGLE
うねっ
!
THEY... THEY'RE MOVING?!
I DIDN'T THINK THERE'D BE A TRAP LIKE THIS ON THE MAIN STAIRCASE!
YOU DIDN'T KNOW ABOUT THIS TRAP, EITHER, LIZA-SAN?
THERE AREN'T VERY MANY ITEMS IN THIS DUNGEON ...
AND SINCE I PUT OFF EXPLORING IT, I HAVEN'T COME THIS FAR BEFORE.
SOFIA! ARE YOU OKAY?!
NO, STOP!
TUG...
Y-YES.
I'M JUST... UHH...
FIDGET...
もぞ…
HOLD ON! I'LL BE RIGHT TH-
ガラン…
CLATTER...
PLEASE... **PLEASE STAY BACK!!**
?!

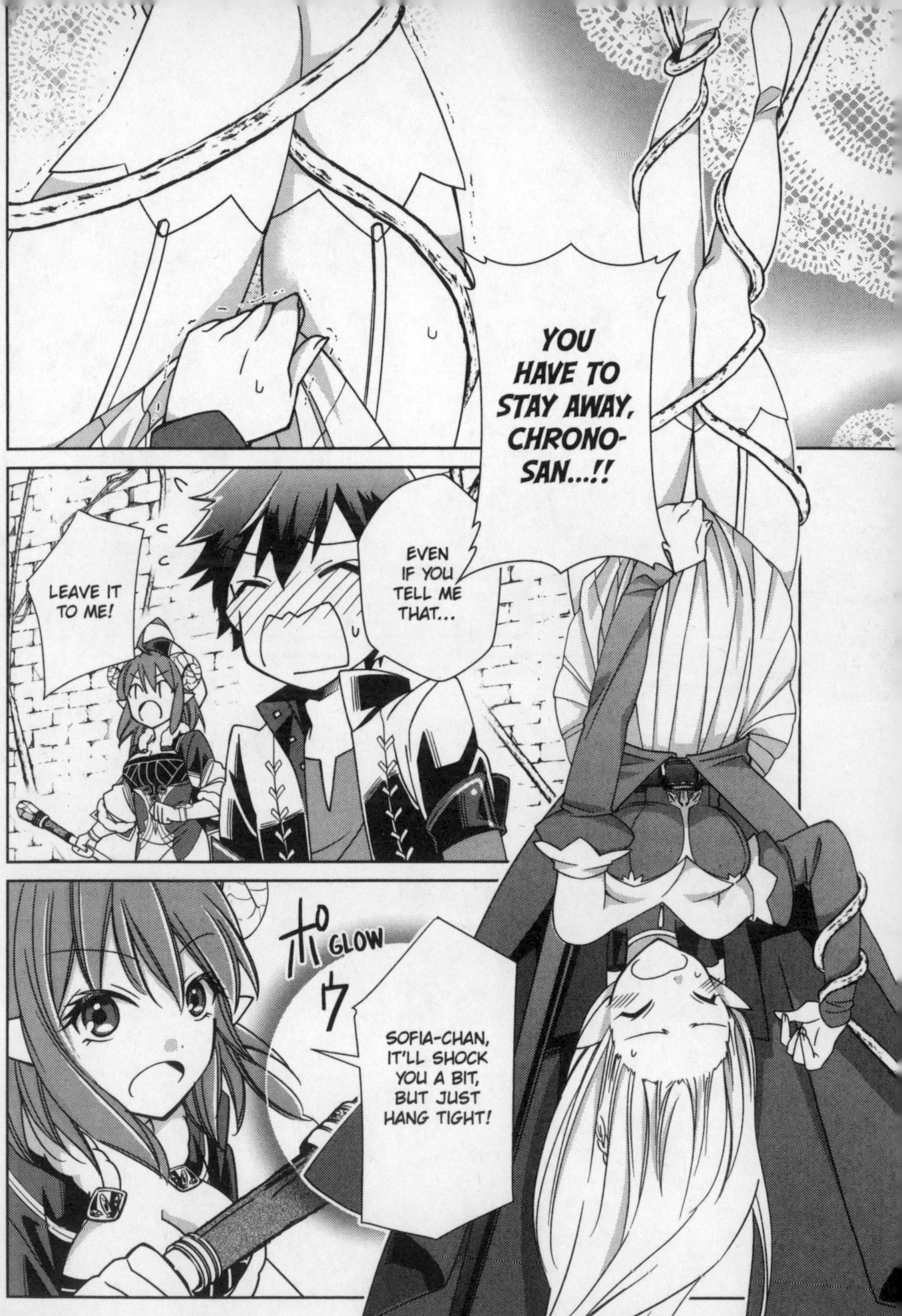
YOU HAVE TO STAY AWAY, CHRONO-SAN...!!
EVEN IF YOU TELL ME THAT...
LEAVE IT TO ME!
ポウ
GLOW
SOFIA-CHAN, IT'LL SHOCK YOU A BIT, BUT JUST HANG TIGHT!

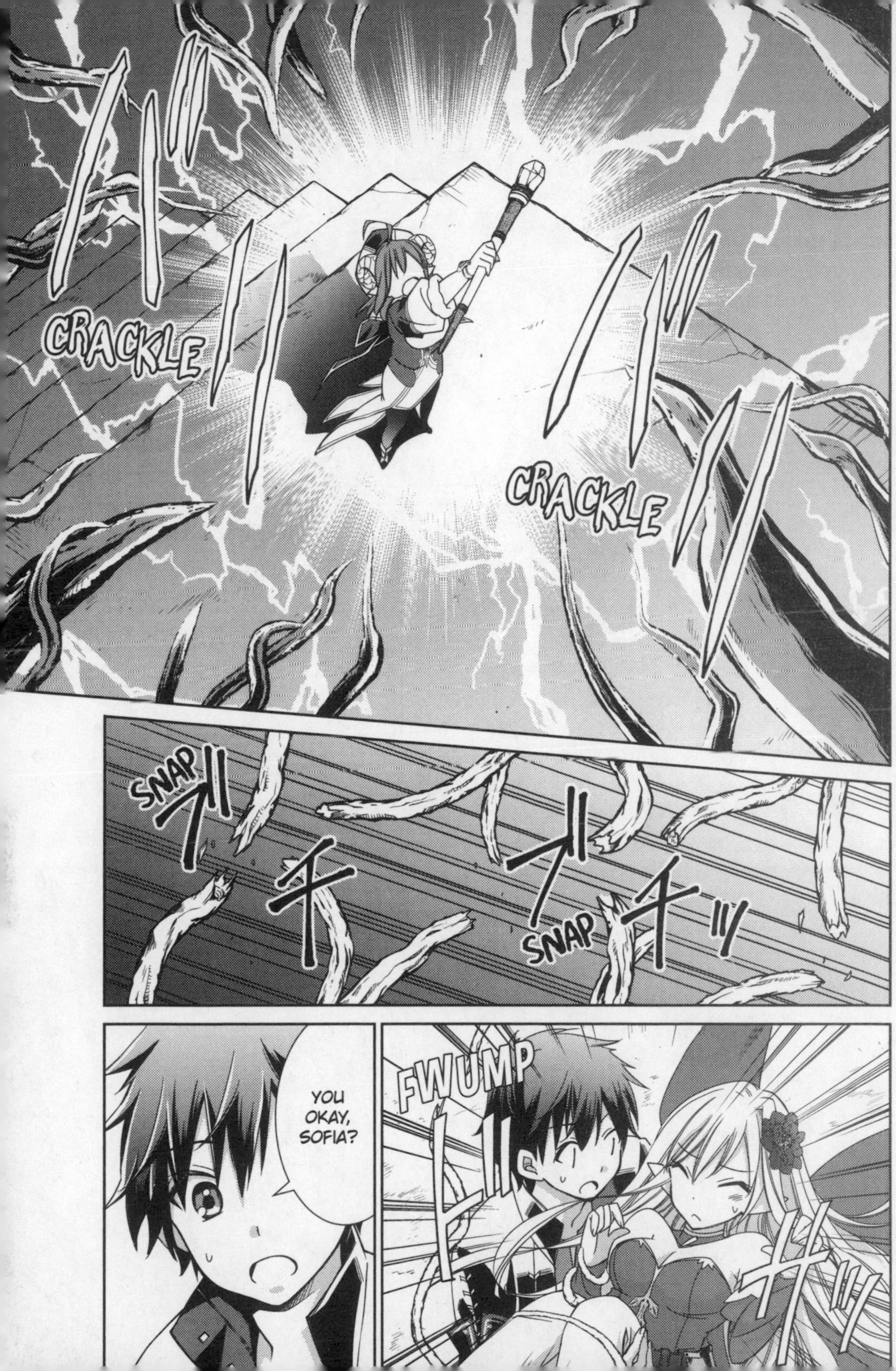
CRACKLE
CRACKLE
SNAP
SNAP
FWUMP
YOU OKAY, SOFIA?

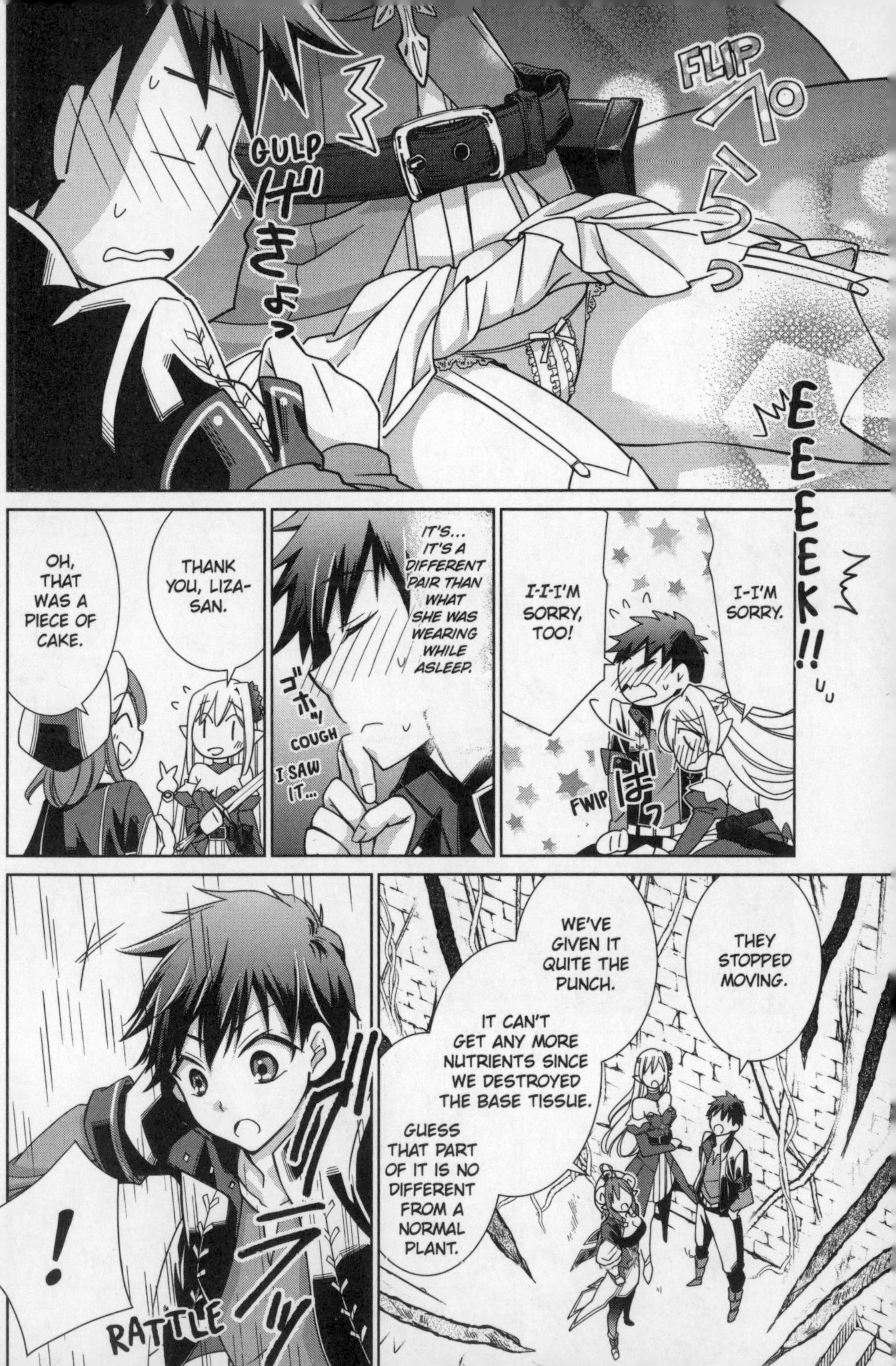

FLIP
ぺらっ
EEEEK!!
GULP
げきょっ
I-I'M SORRY.
I-I-I'M SORRY, TOO!
FWIP
ぼっ
IT'S... IT'S A DIFFERENT PAIR THAN WHAT SHE WAS WEARING WHILE ASLEEP.
ゴホッ
COUGH
I SAW IT...
THANK YOU, LIZA-SAN.
OH, THAT WAS A PIECE OF CAKE.
THEY STOPPED MOVING.
WE'VE GIVEN IT QUITE THE PUNCH.
IT CAN'T GET ANY MORE NUTRIENTS SINCE WE DESTROYED THE BASE TISSUE.
GUESS THAT PART OF IT IS NO DIFFERENT FROM A NORMAL PLANT.
!
RATTLE

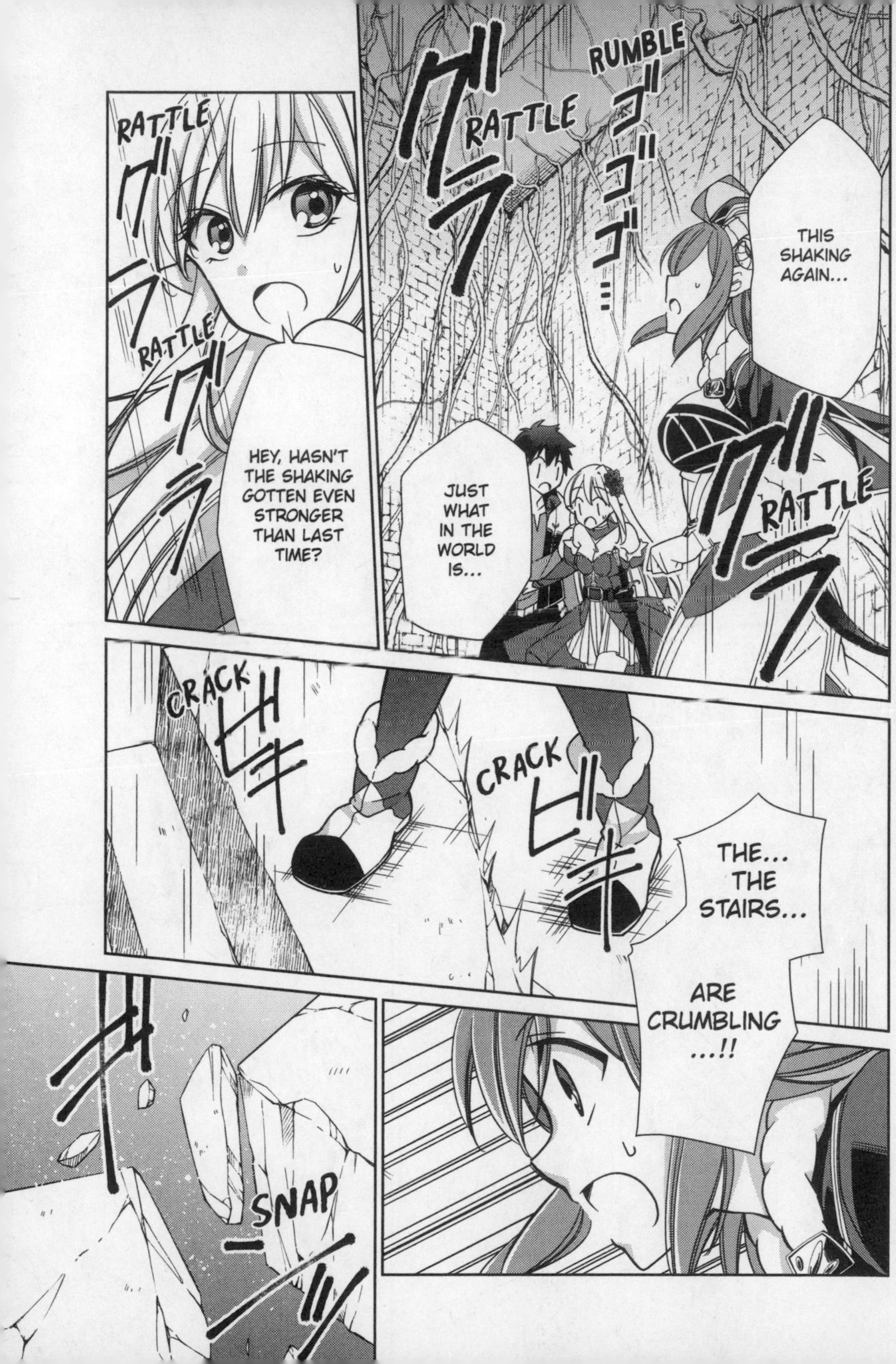
RUMBLE
RATTLE
THIS SHAKING AGAIN...
JUST WHAT IN THE WORLD IS...
RATTLE
RATTLE
RATTLE
HEY, HASN'T THE SHAKING GOTTEN EVEN STRONGER THAN LAST TIME?
THE... THE STAIRS...
CRACK
CRACK
ARE CRUMBLING ...!!
SNAP

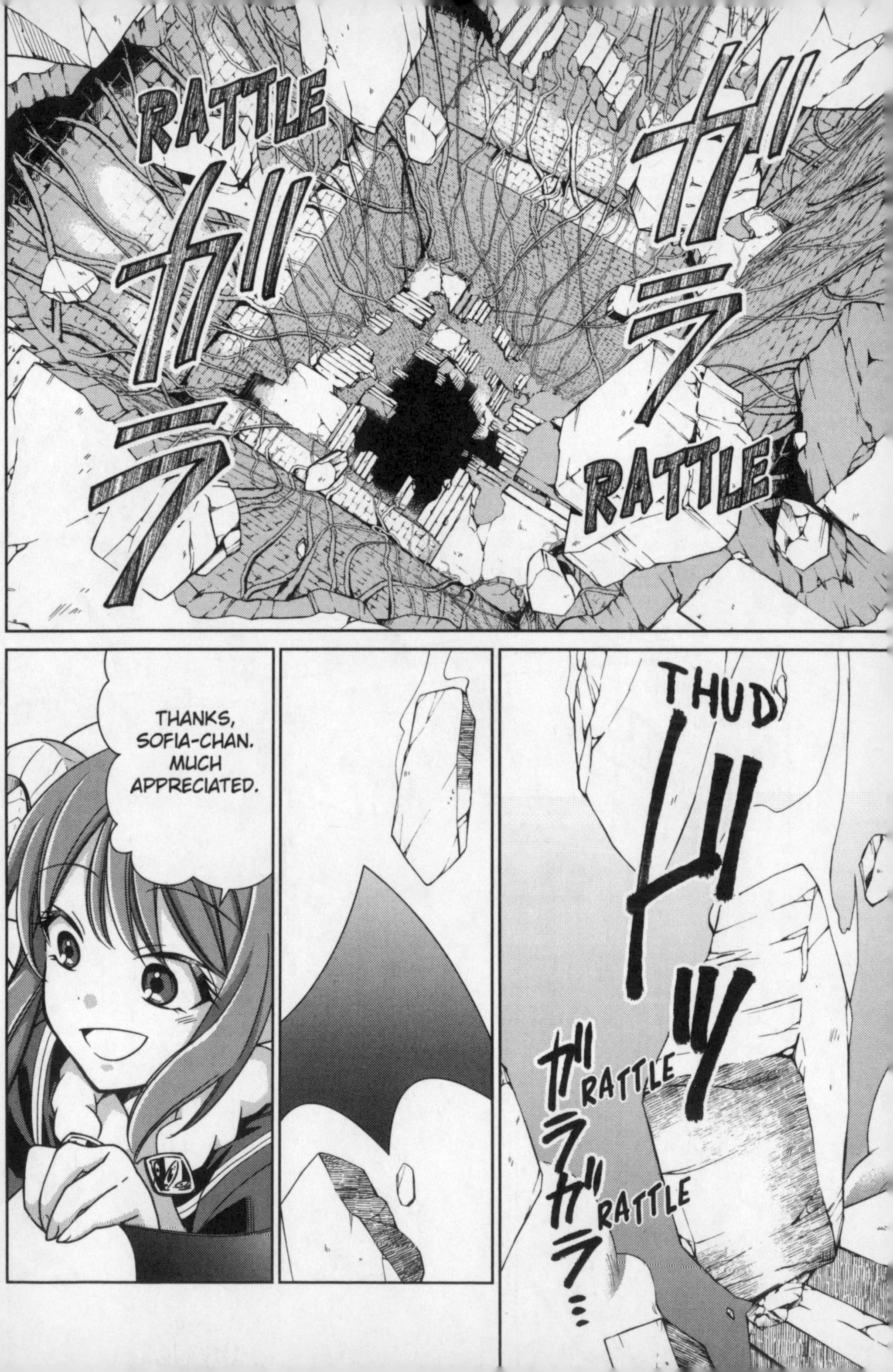
RATTLE
RATTLE
THUD
RATTLE
RATTLE
THANKS, SOFIA-CHAN. MUCH APPRECIATED.

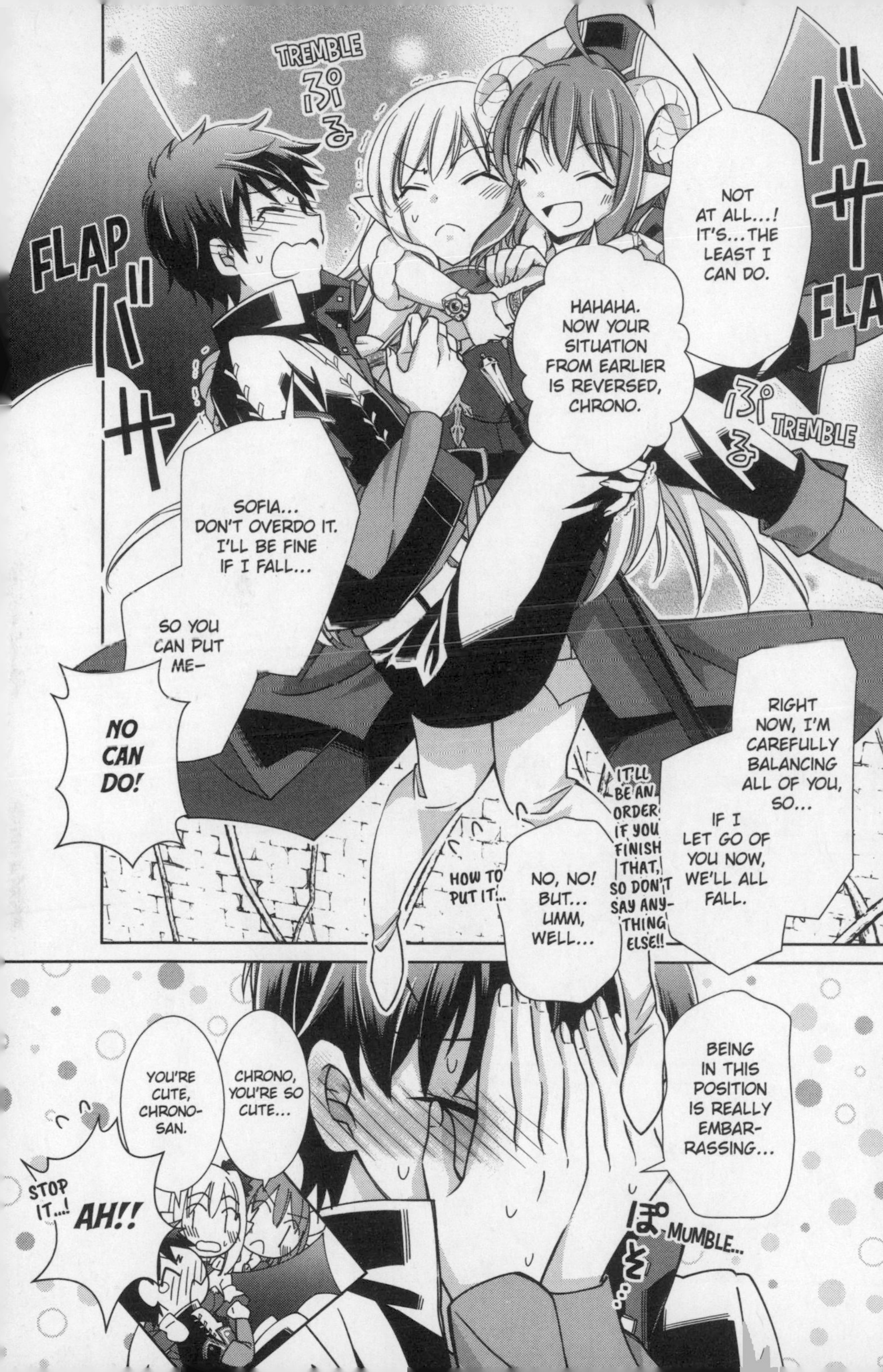

バサ FLAP
NOT AT ALL...! IT'S...THE LEAST I CAN DO.
HAHAHA. NOW YOUR SITUATION FROM EARLIER IS REVERSED, CHRONO.
ぷる TREMBLE
TREMBLE ぷる
FLAP バサ
SOFIA... DON'T OVERDO IT. I'LL BE FINE IF I FALL...
SO YOU CAN PUT ME-
NO CAN DO!
RIGHT NOW, I'M CAREFULLY BALANCING ALL OF YOU, SO...
IF I LET GO OF YOU NOW, WE'LL ALL FALL.
IT'LL BE AN ORDER IF YOU FINISH THAT, SO DON'T SAY ANYTHING ELSE!!
NO, NO! BUT... UMM, WELL...
HOW TO PUT IT...
BEING IN THIS POSITION IS REALLY EMBARRASSING...
ぽそ... MUMBLE...
CHRONO, YOU'RE SO CUTE...
YOU'RE CUTE, CHRONO-SAN.
AH!!
STOP IT...!

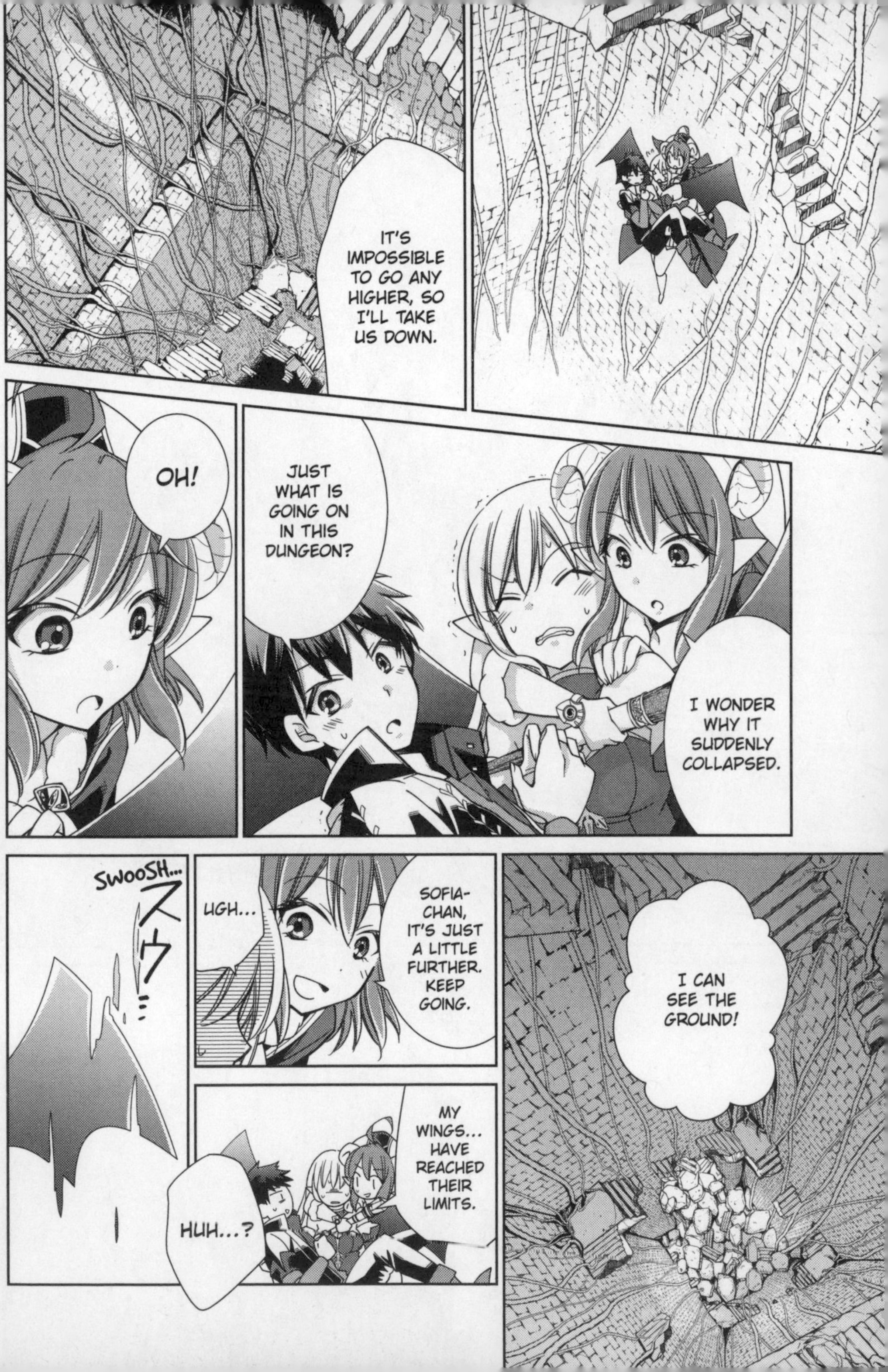
IT'S IMPOSSIBLE TO GO ANY HIGHER, SO I'LL TAKE US DOWN.
I WONDER WHY IT SUDDENLY COLLAPSED.
JUST WHAT IS GOING ON IN THIS DUNGEON?
OH!
I CAN SEE THE GROUND!
SOFIA-CHAN, IT'S JUST A LITTLE FURTHER. KEEP GOING.
UGH...
MY WINGS... HAVE REACHED THEIR LIMITS.
HUH...?
SWOOSH... スウ

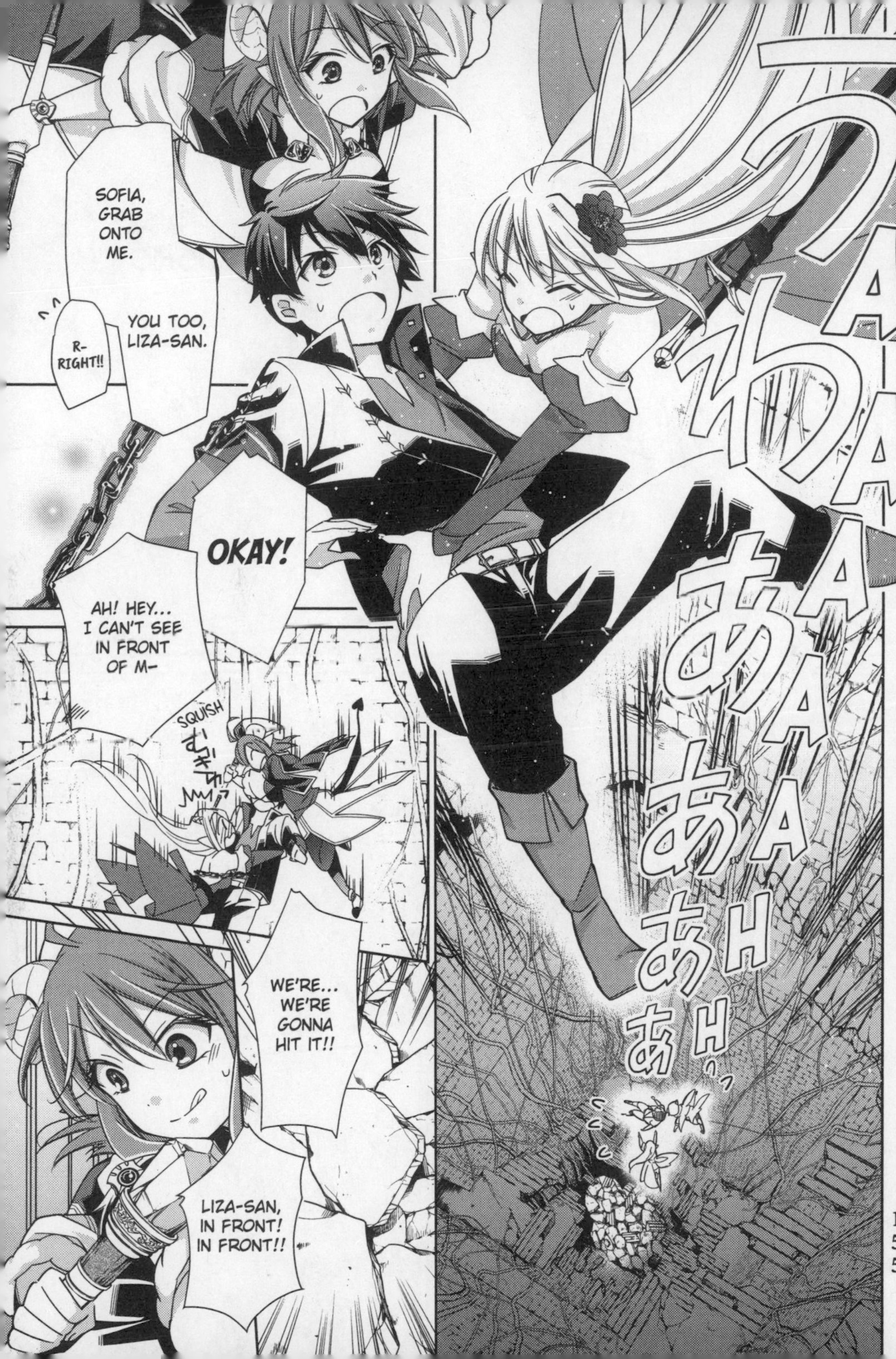

AAAAAHH
SOFIA, GRAB ONTO ME.
YOU TOO, LIZA-SAN.
R-RIGHT!!
OKAY!
AH! HEY... I CAN'T SEE IN FRONT OF M-
SQUISH
WE'RE... WE'RE GONNA HIT IT!!
LIZA-SAN, IN FRONT! IN FRONT!!

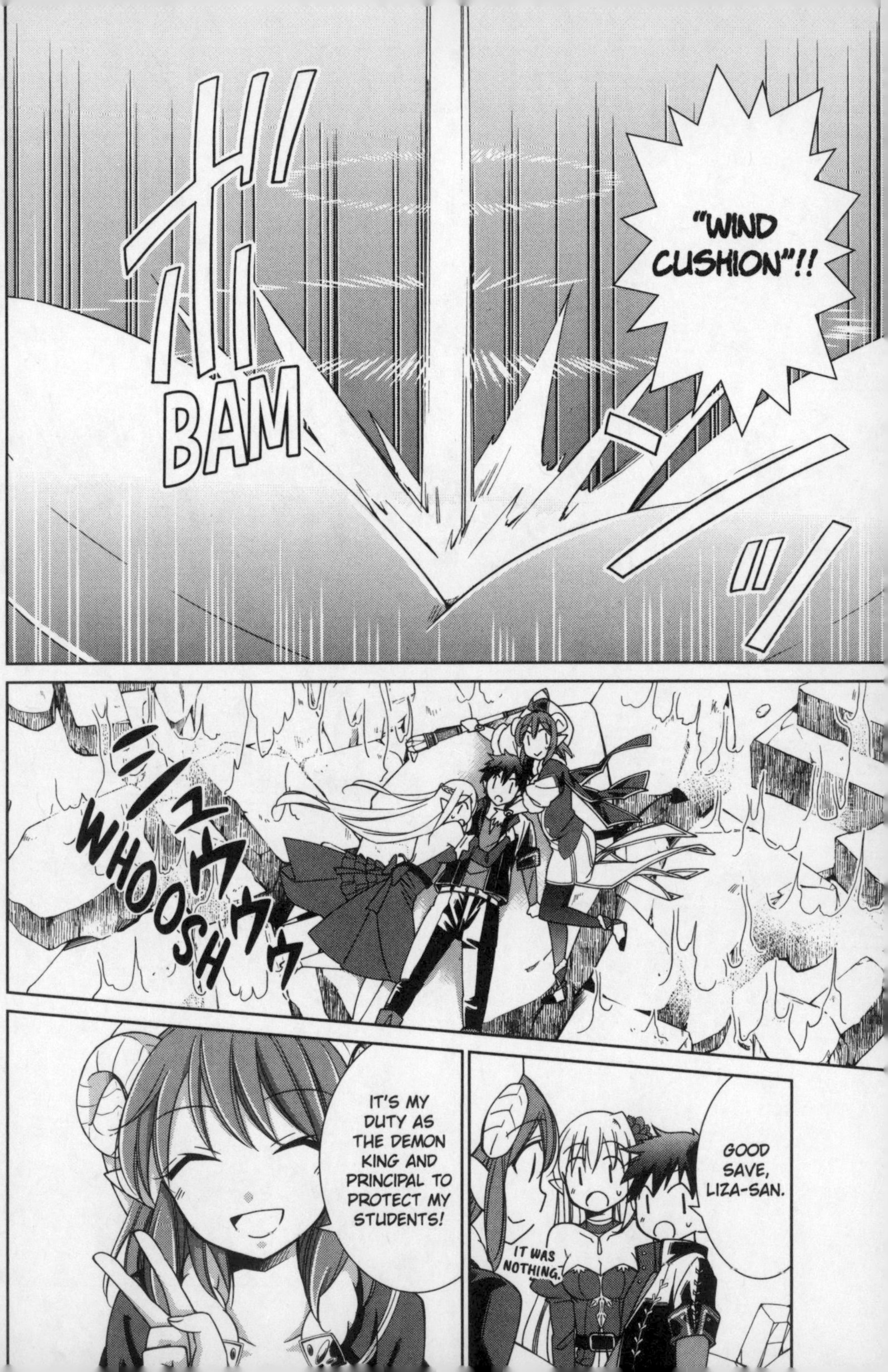

"WIND CUSHION"!!
BAM
WHOOSH
GOOD SAVE, LIZA-SAN.
IT WAS NOTHING.
IT'S MY DUTY AS THE DEMON KING AND PRINCIPAL TO PROTECT MY STUDENTS!

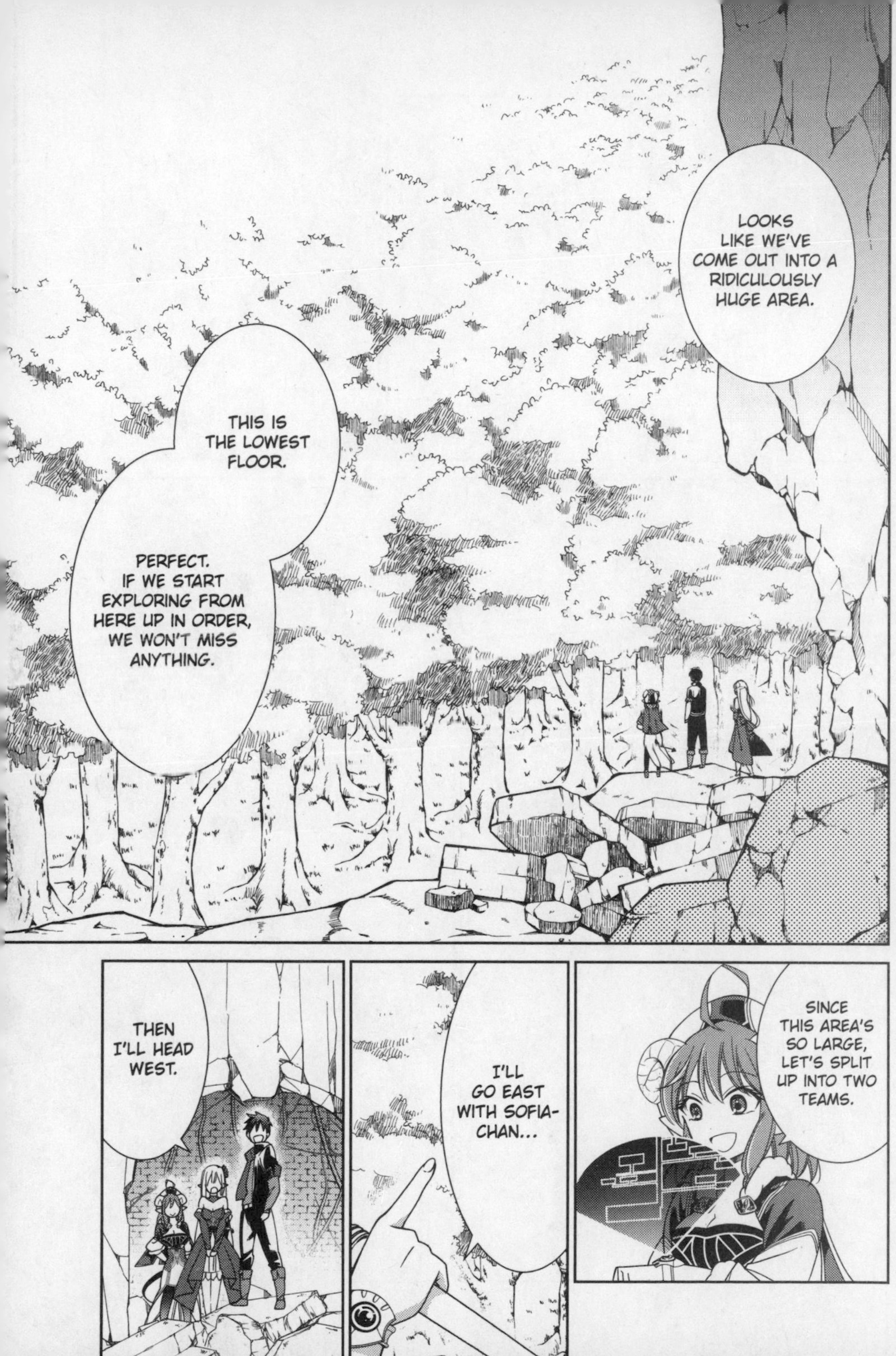
LOOKS LIKE WE'VE COME OUT INTO A RIDICULOUSLY HUGE AREA.
THIS IS THE LOWEST FLOOR.
PERFECT. IF WE START EXPLORING FROM HERE UP IN ORDER, WE WON'T MISS ANYTHING.
SINCE THIS AREA'S SO LARGE, LET'S SPLIT UP INTO TWO TEAMS.
I'LL GO EAST WITH SOFIA-CHAN...
THEN I'LL HEAD WEST.

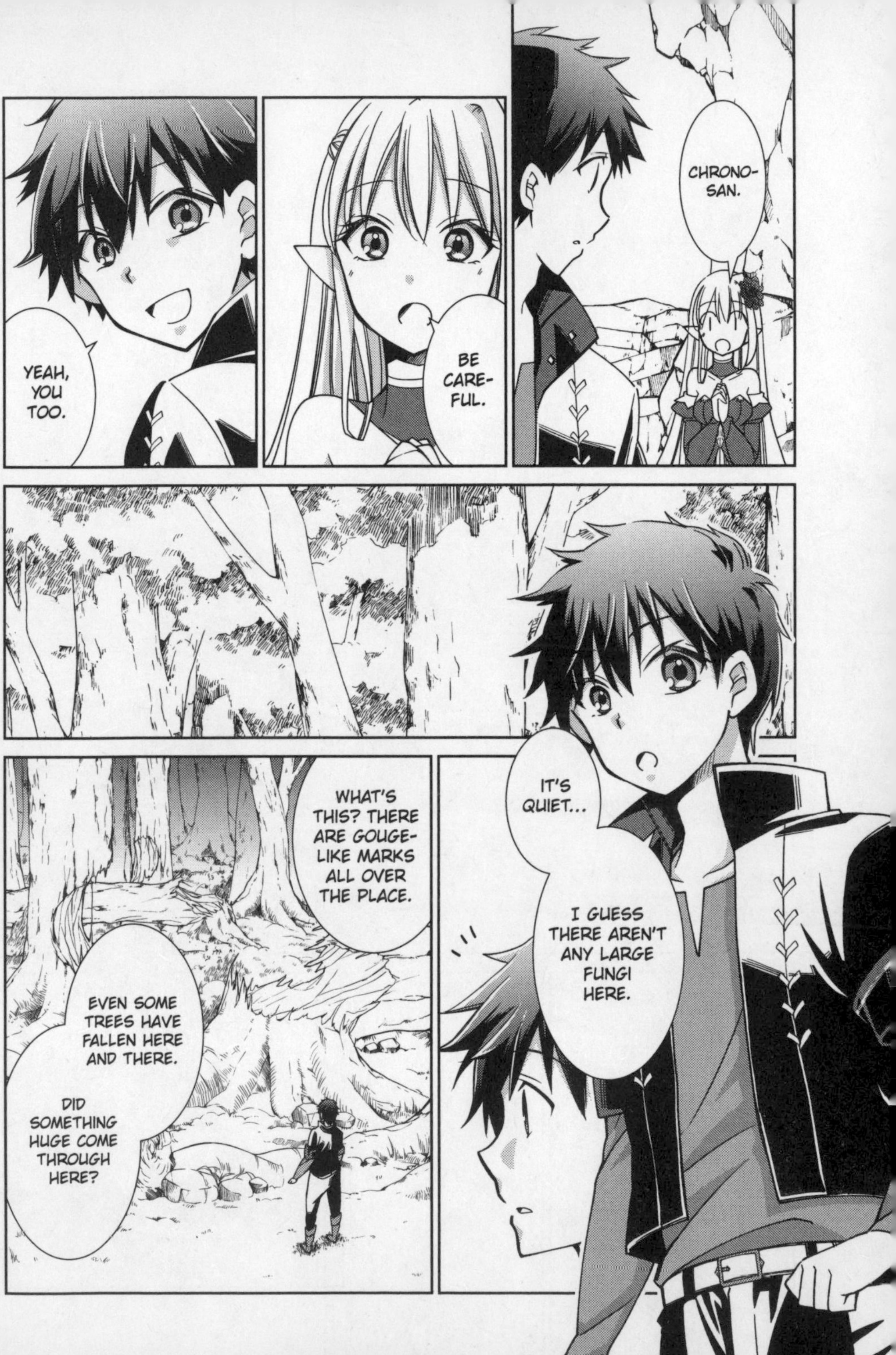
CHRONO-SAN.
BE CAREFUL.
YEAH, YOU TOO.
IT'S QUIET...
I GUESS THERE AREN'T ANY LARGE FUNGI HERE.
WHAT'S THIS? THERE ARE GOUGE-LIKE MARKS ALL OVER THE PLACE.
EVEN SOME TREES HAVE FALLEN HERE AND THERE.
DID SOMETHING HUGE COME THROUGH HERE?

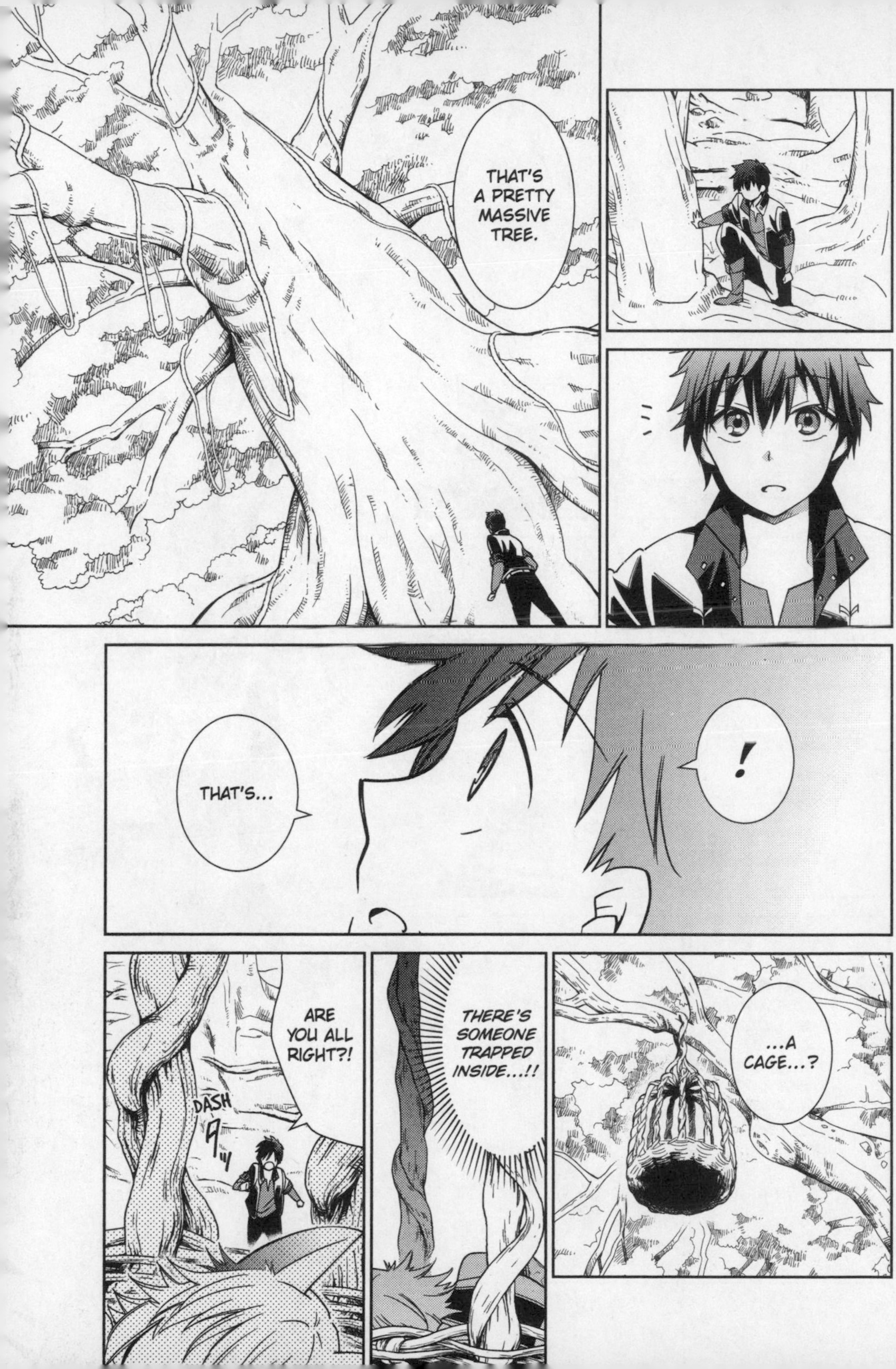
THAT'S A PRETTY MASSIVE TREE.
!
THAT'S...
...A CAGE...?
THERE'S SOMEONE TRAPPED INSIDE...!!
ARE YOU ALL RIGHT?!
DASH

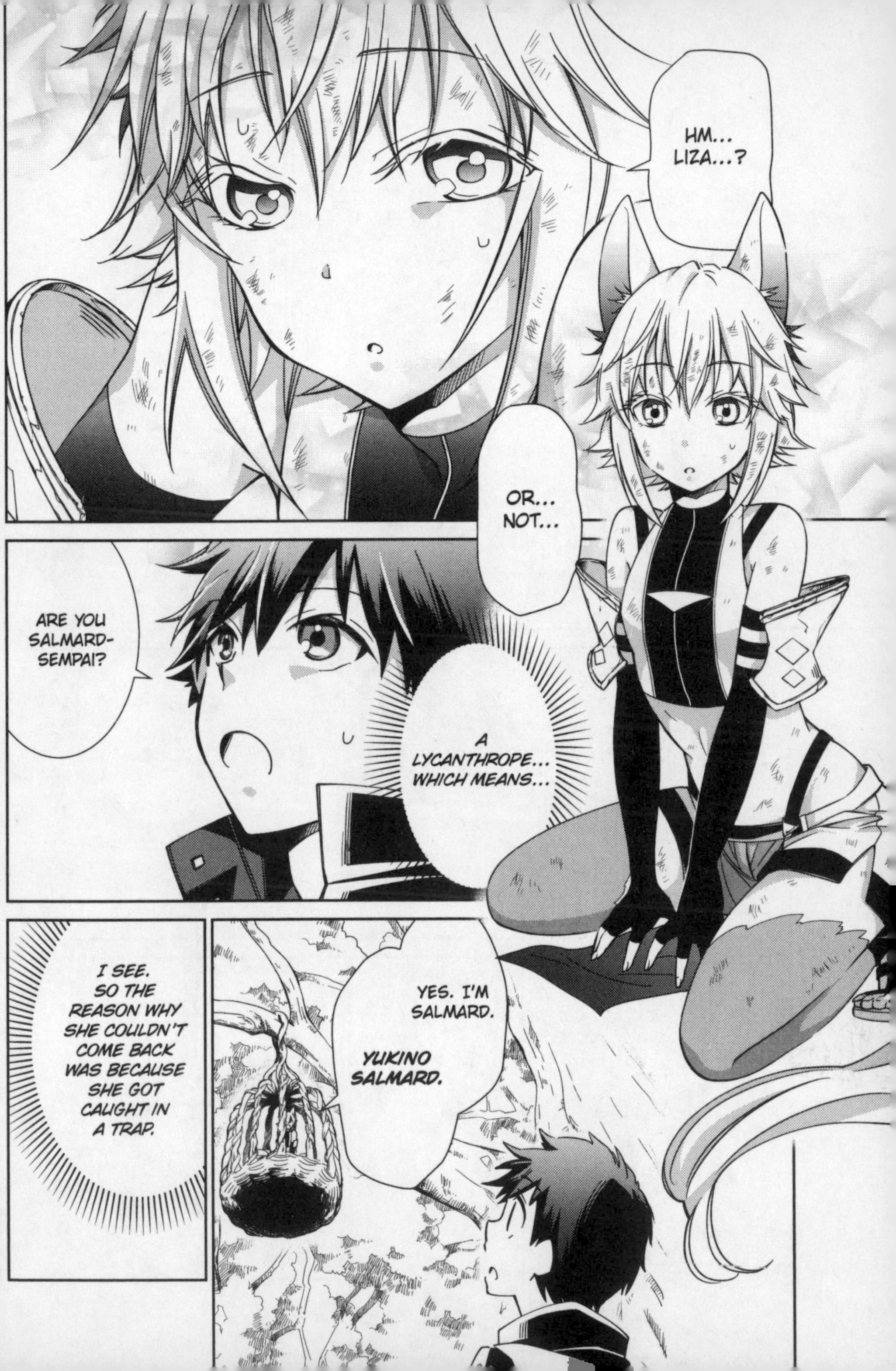
HM... LIZA...?
OR... NOT...
A LYCANTHROPE... WHICH MEANS...
ARE YOU SALMARD-SEMPAI?
YES. I'M SALMARD.
YUKINO SALMARD.
I SEE. SO THE REASON WHY SHE COULDN'T COME BACK WAS BECAUSE SHE GOT CAUGHT IN A TRAP.

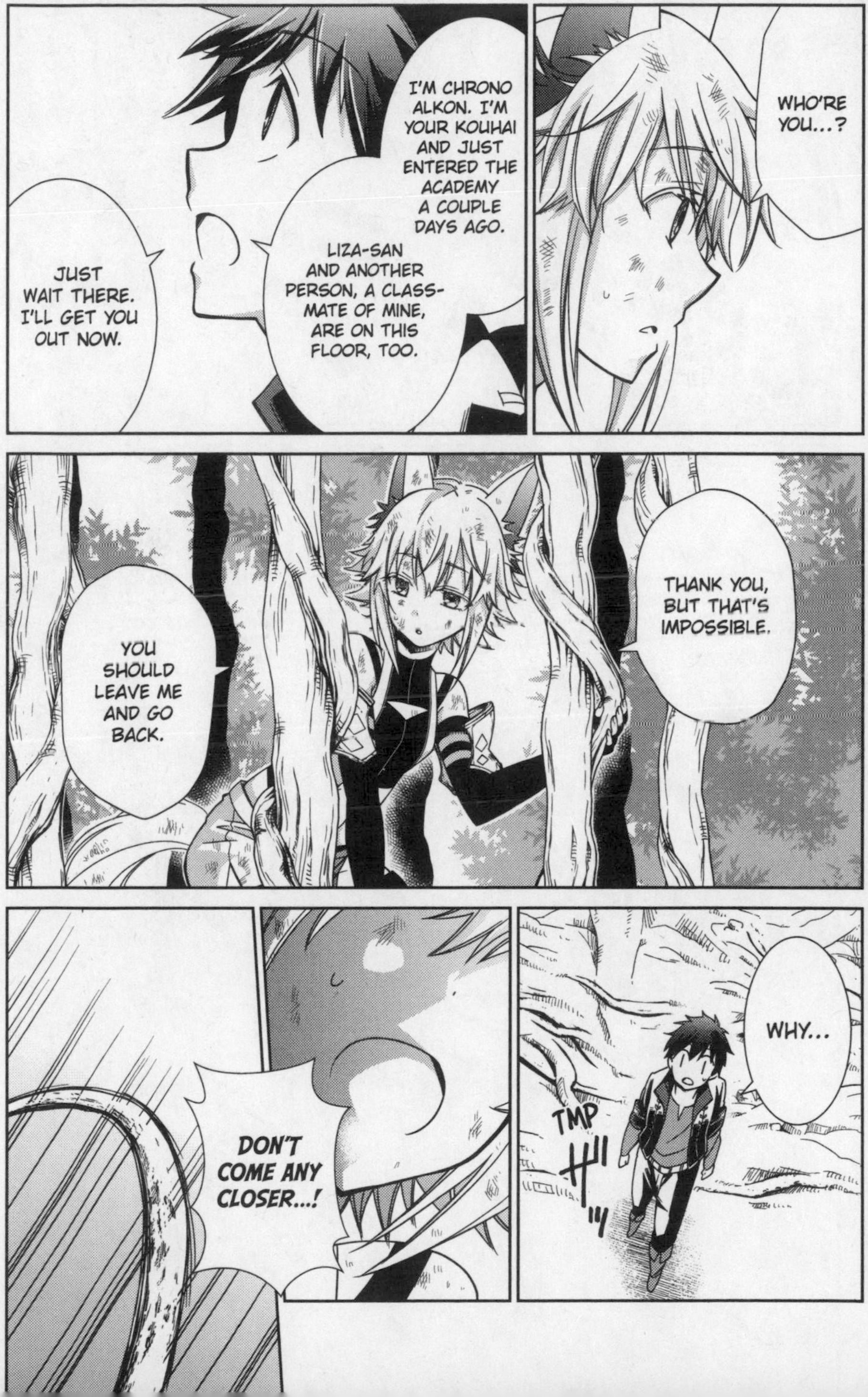
WHO'RE YOU...?
I'M CHRONO ALKON. I'M YOUR KOUHAI AND JUST ENTERED THE ACADEMY A COUPLE DAYS AGO.
LIZA-SAN AND ANOTHER PERSON, A CLASS-MATE OF MINE, ARE ON THIS FLOOR, TOO.
JUST WAIT THERE. I'LL GET YOU OUT NOW.
THANK YOU, BUT THAT'S IMPOSSIBLE.
YOU SHOULD LEAVE ME AND GO BACK.
WHY...
TMP
DON'T COME ANY CLOSER...!

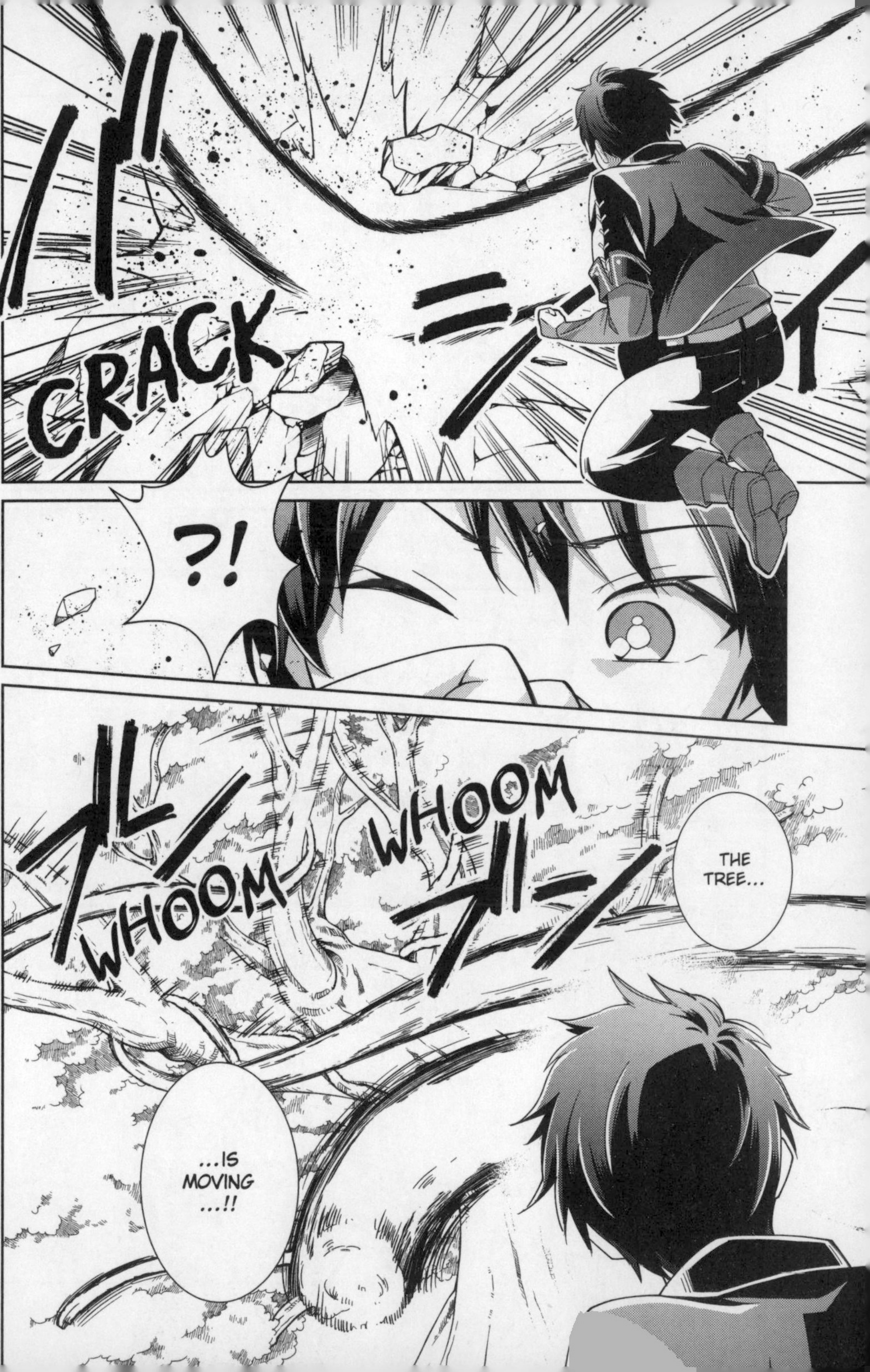
CRACK
?!
WHOOM
WHOOM
THE TREE...
...IS MOVING ...!!

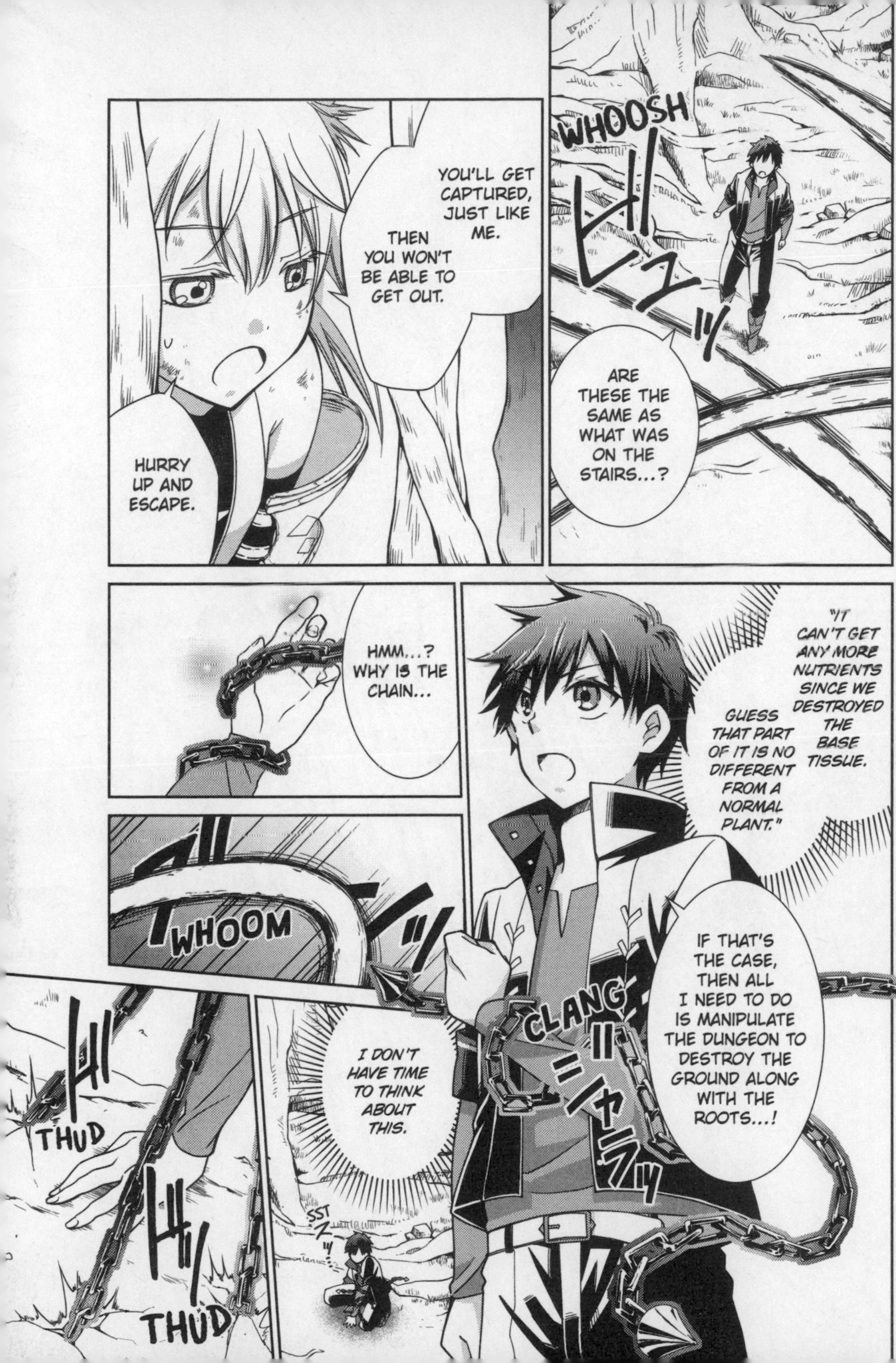
WHOOSH
ARE THESE THE SAME AS WHAT WAS ON THE STAIRS...?
YOU'LL GET CAPTURED, JUST LIKE ME.
THEN YOU WON'T BE ABLE TO GET OUT.
HURRY UP AND ESCAPE.
"IT CAN'T GET ANY MORE NUTRIENTS SINCE WE DESTROYED THE BASE TISSUE.
GUESS THAT PART OF IT IS NO DIFFERENT FROM A NORMAL PLANT."
IF THAT'S THE CASE, THEN ALL I NEED TO DO IS MANIPULATE THE DUNGEON TO DESTROY THE GROUND ALONG WITH THE ROOTS...!
HMM...? WHY IS THE CHAIN...
WHOOM
CLANG
I DON'T HAVE TIME TO THINK ABOUT THIS.
SST
THUD
THUD

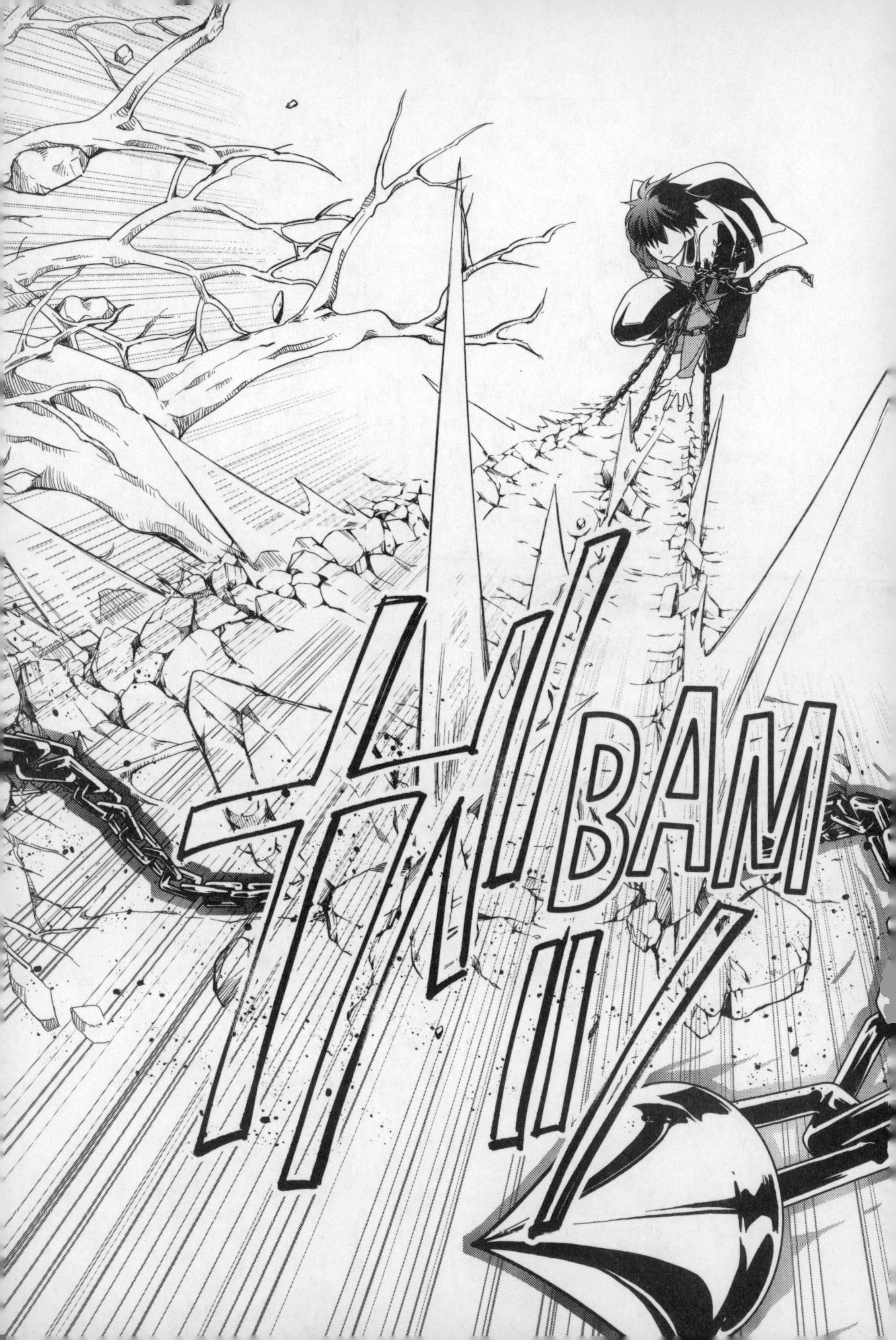
BAM

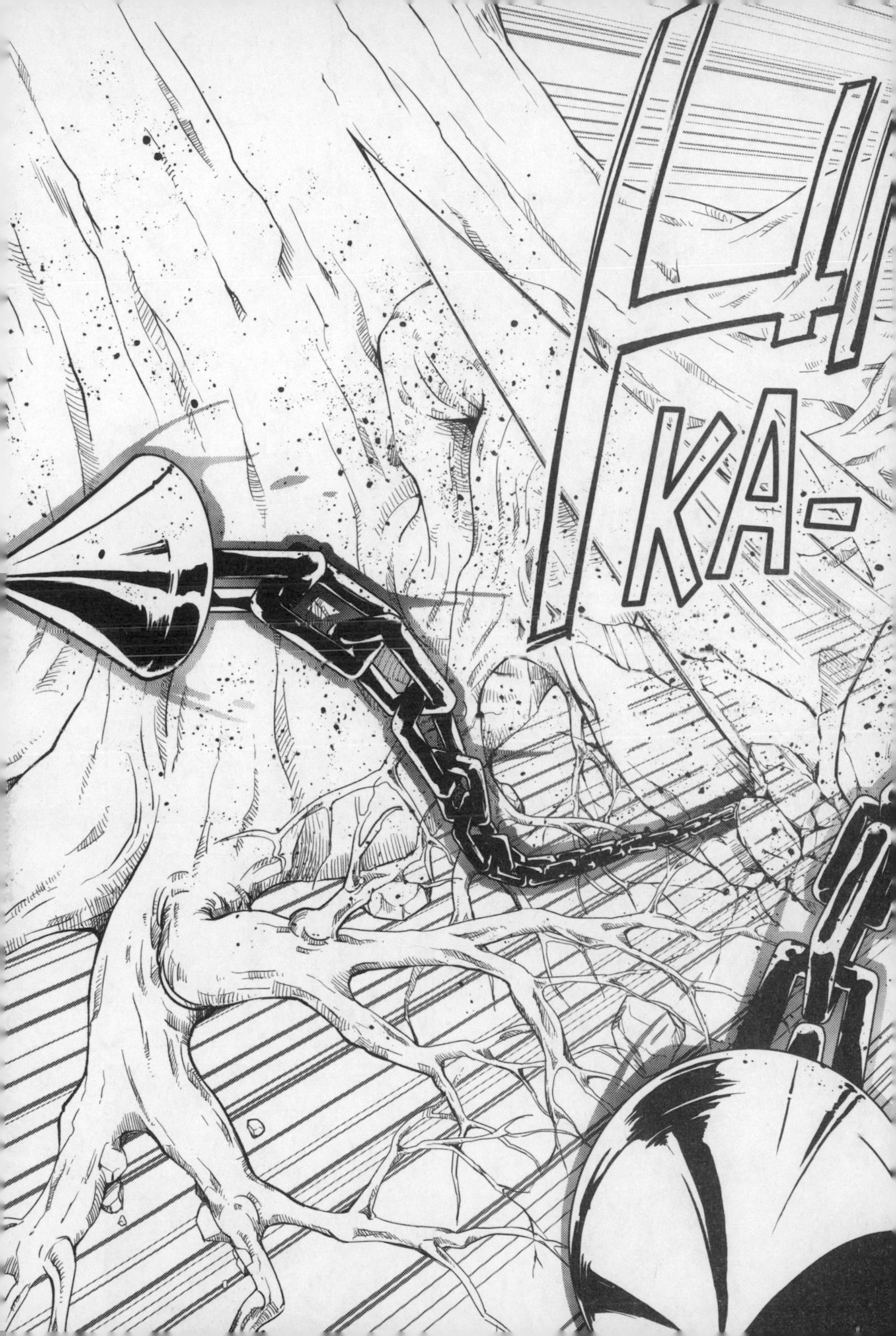
KA-

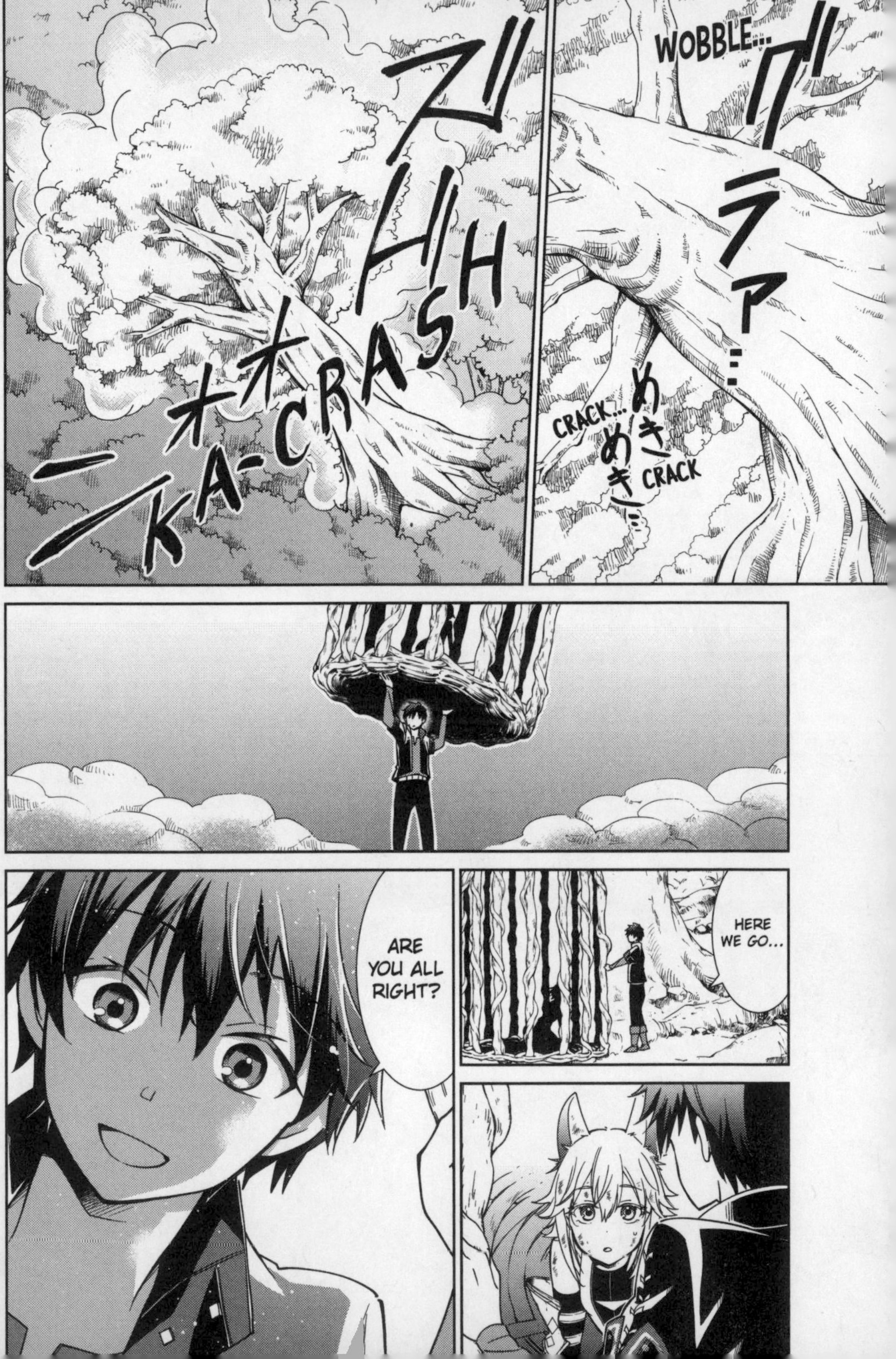
WOBBLE...
CRACK...
CRACK
KA-CRASH
HERE WE GO...
ARE YOU ALL RIGHT?

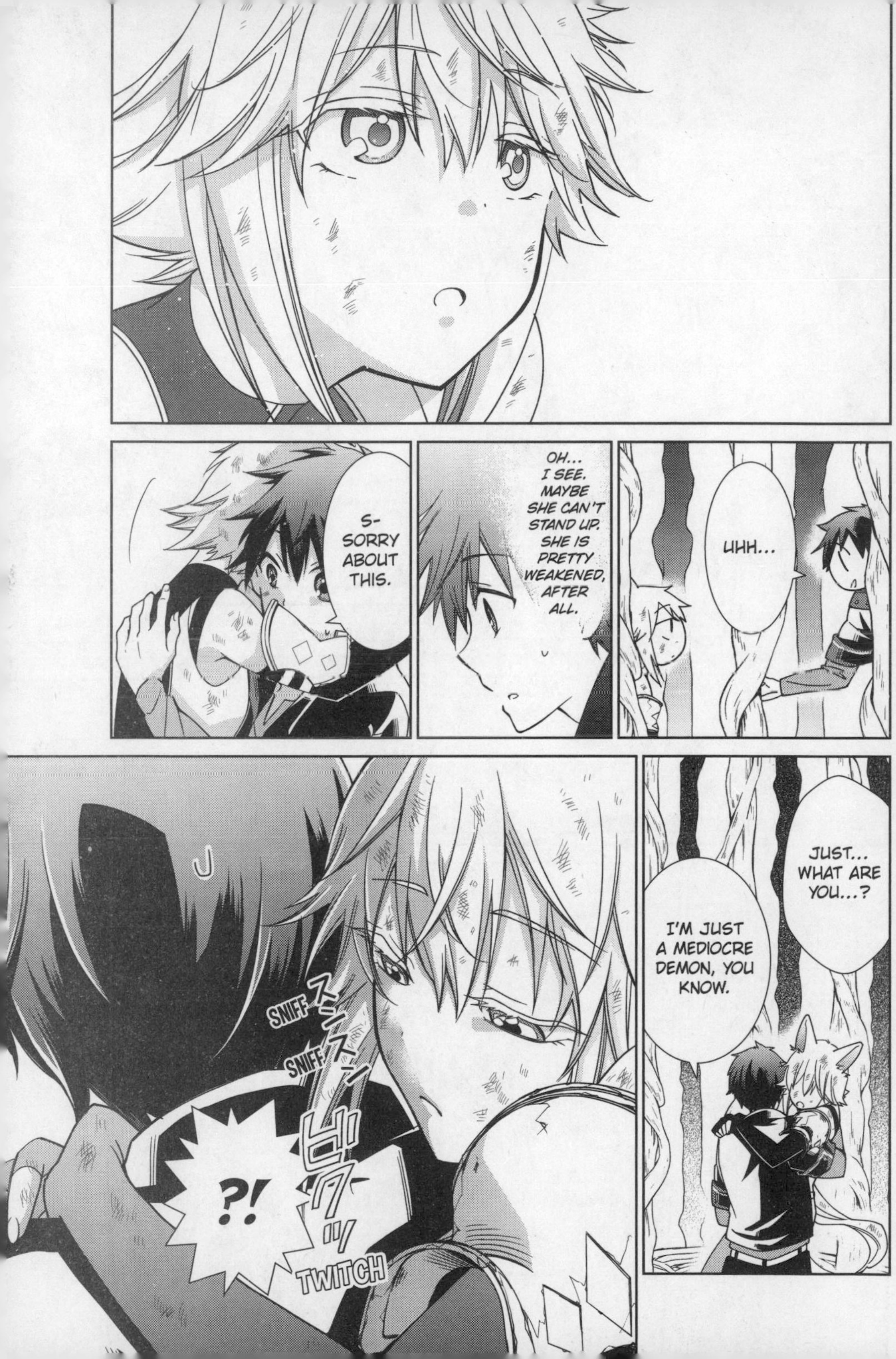
UHH...
OH... I SEE. MAYBE SHE CAN'T STAND UP. SHE IS PRETTY WEAKENED, AFTER ALL.
S-SORRY ABOUT THIS.
JUST... WHAT ARE YOU...?
I'M JUST A MEDIOCRE DEMON, YOU KNOW.
SNIFF
SNIFF
?!
TWITCH

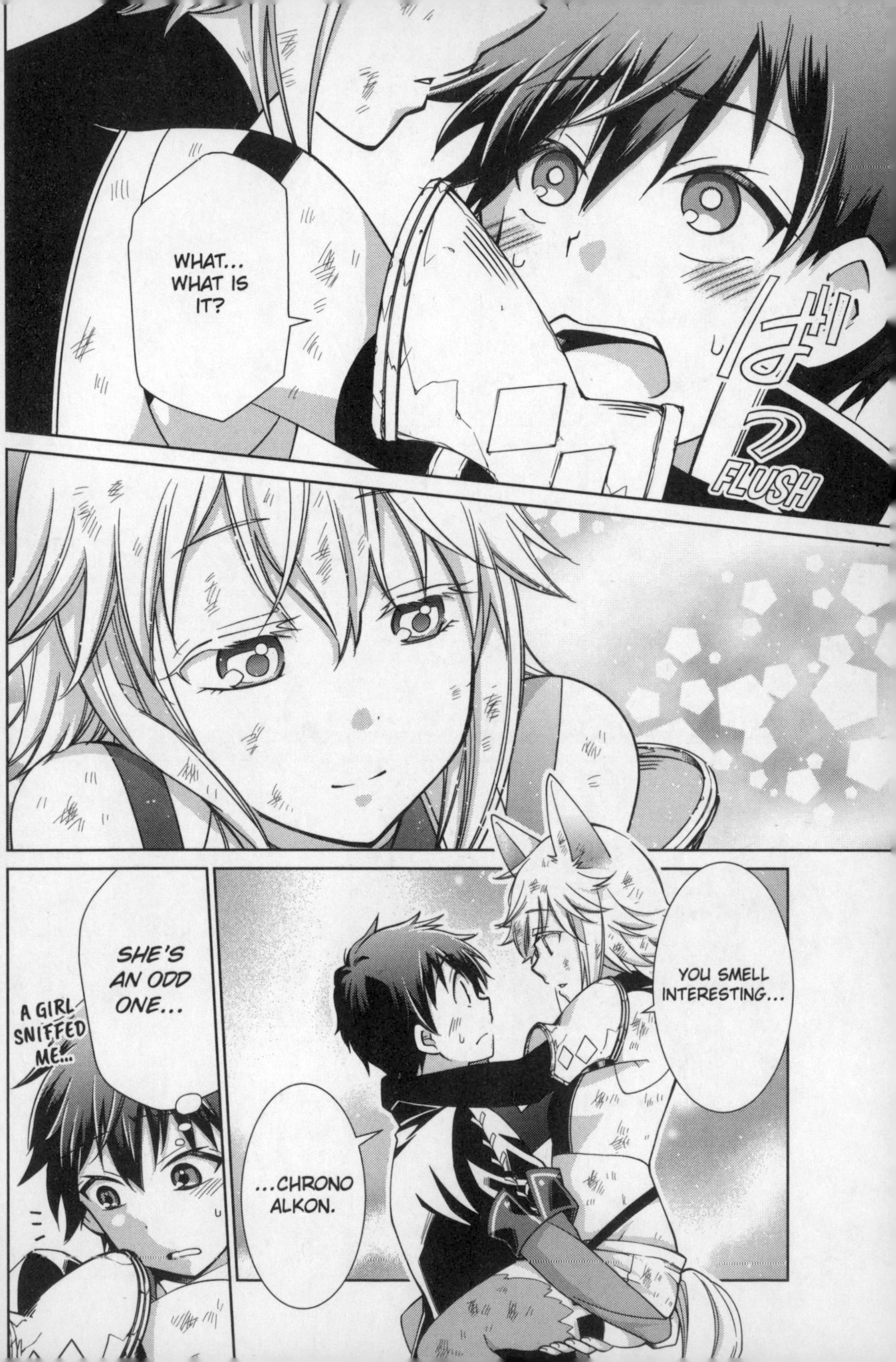
WHAT... WHAT IS IT?
ぱっ
FLUSH
YOU SMELL INTERESTING...
...CHRONO ALKON.
SHE'S AN ODD ONE...
A GIRL SNIFFED ME...

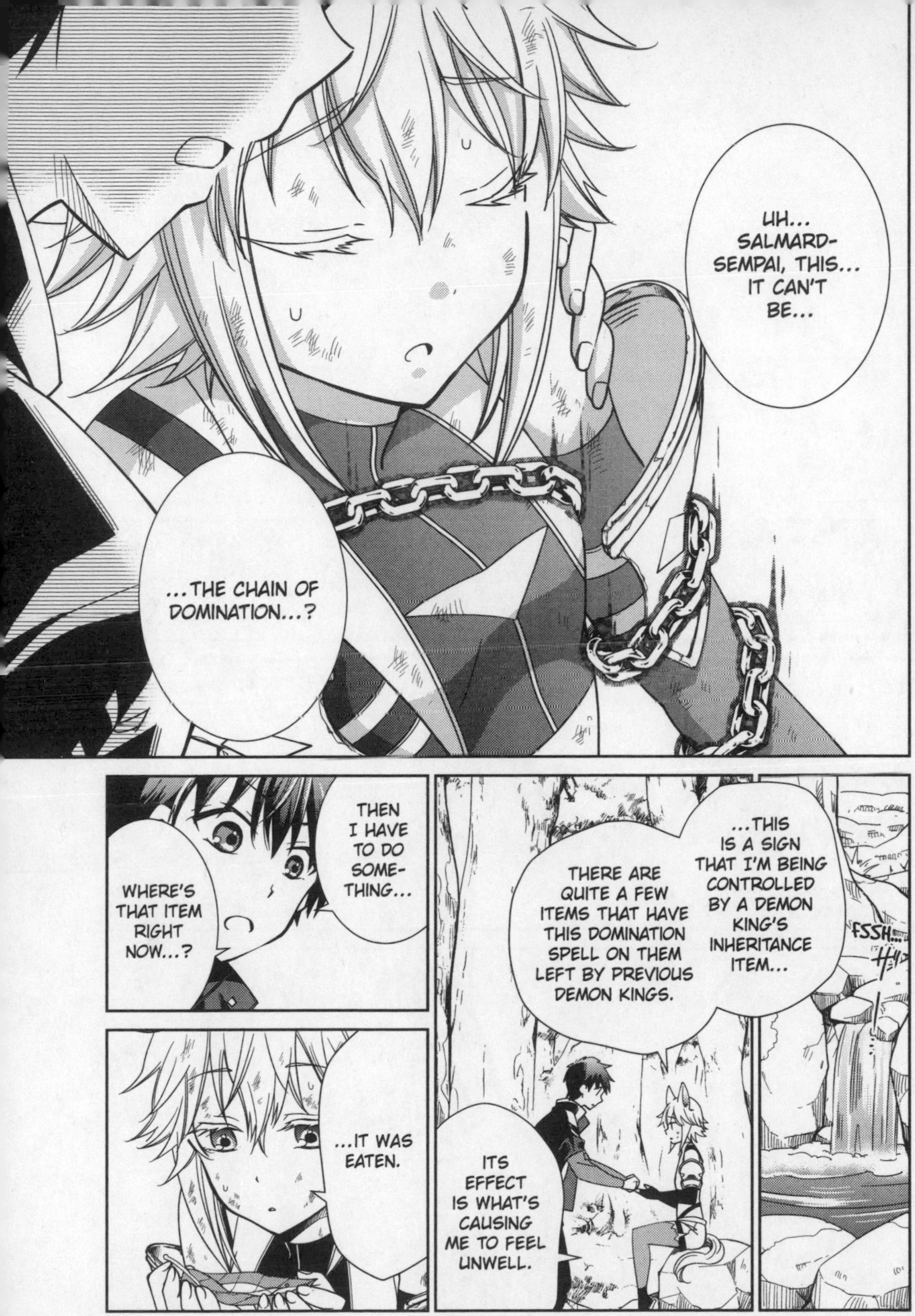
UH... SALMARD-SEMPAI, THIS... IT CAN'T BE...
...THE CHAIN OF DOMINATION...?
FSSH...
...THIS IS A SIGN THAT I'M BEING CONTROLLED BY A DEMON KING'S INHERITANCE ITEM...
THERE ARE QUITE A FEW ITEMS THAT HAVE THIS DOMINATION SPELL ON THEM LEFT BY PREVIOUS DEMON KINGS.
ITS EFFECT IS WHAT'S CAUSING ME TO FEEL UNWELL.
THEN I HAVE TO DO SOME-THING...
WHERE'S THAT ITEM RIGHT NOW...?
...IT WAS EATEN.

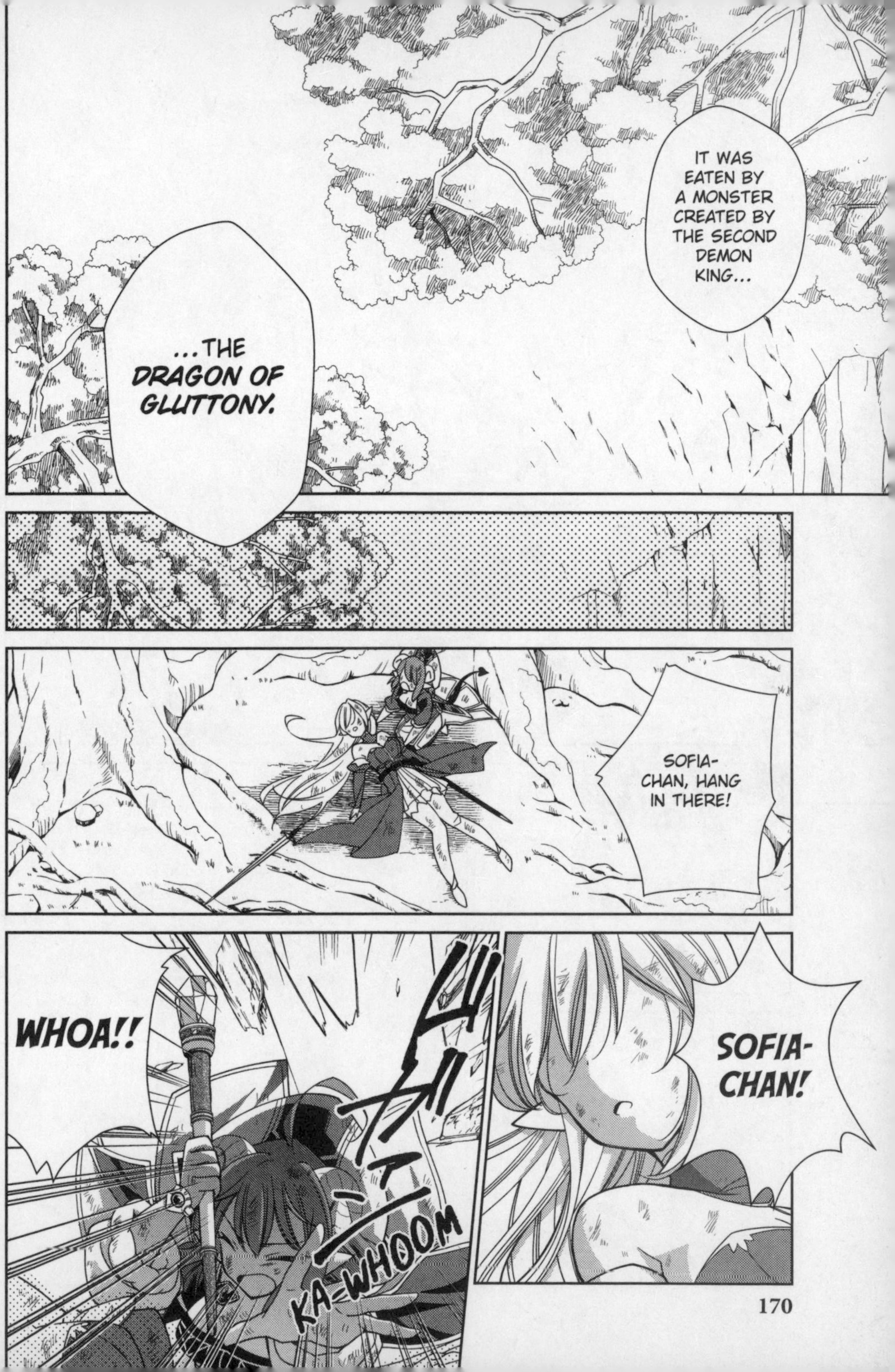
IT WAS EATEN BY A MONSTER CREATED BY THE SECOND DEMON KING...
...THE DRAGON OF GLUTTONY.
SOFIA-CHAN, HANG IN THERE!
SOFIA-CHAN!
WHOA!!
KA-WHOOM

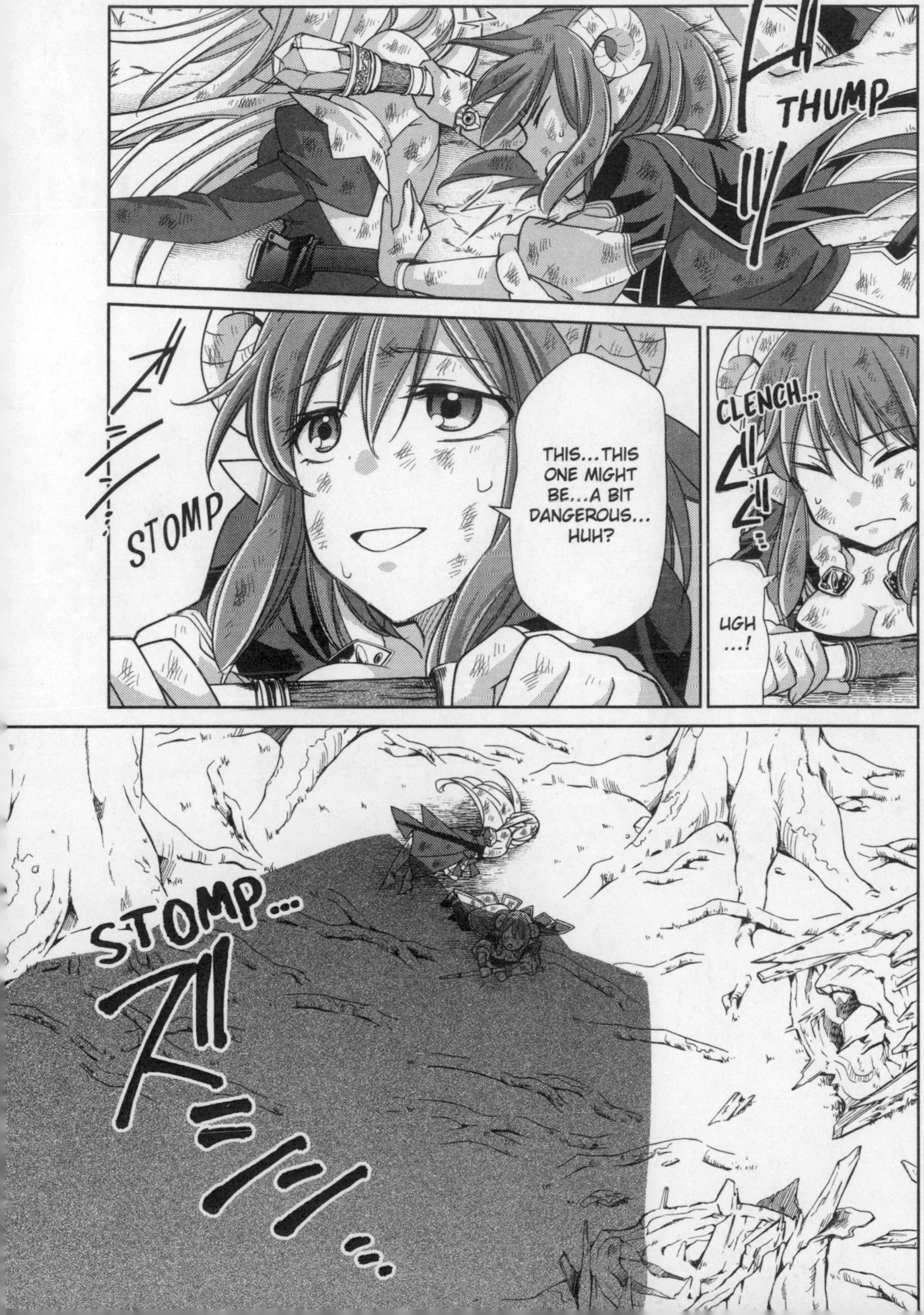
THUMP
CLENCH...
UGH ...!
STOMP
THIS...THIS ONE MIGHT BE...A BIT DANGEROUS... HUH?
STOMP...

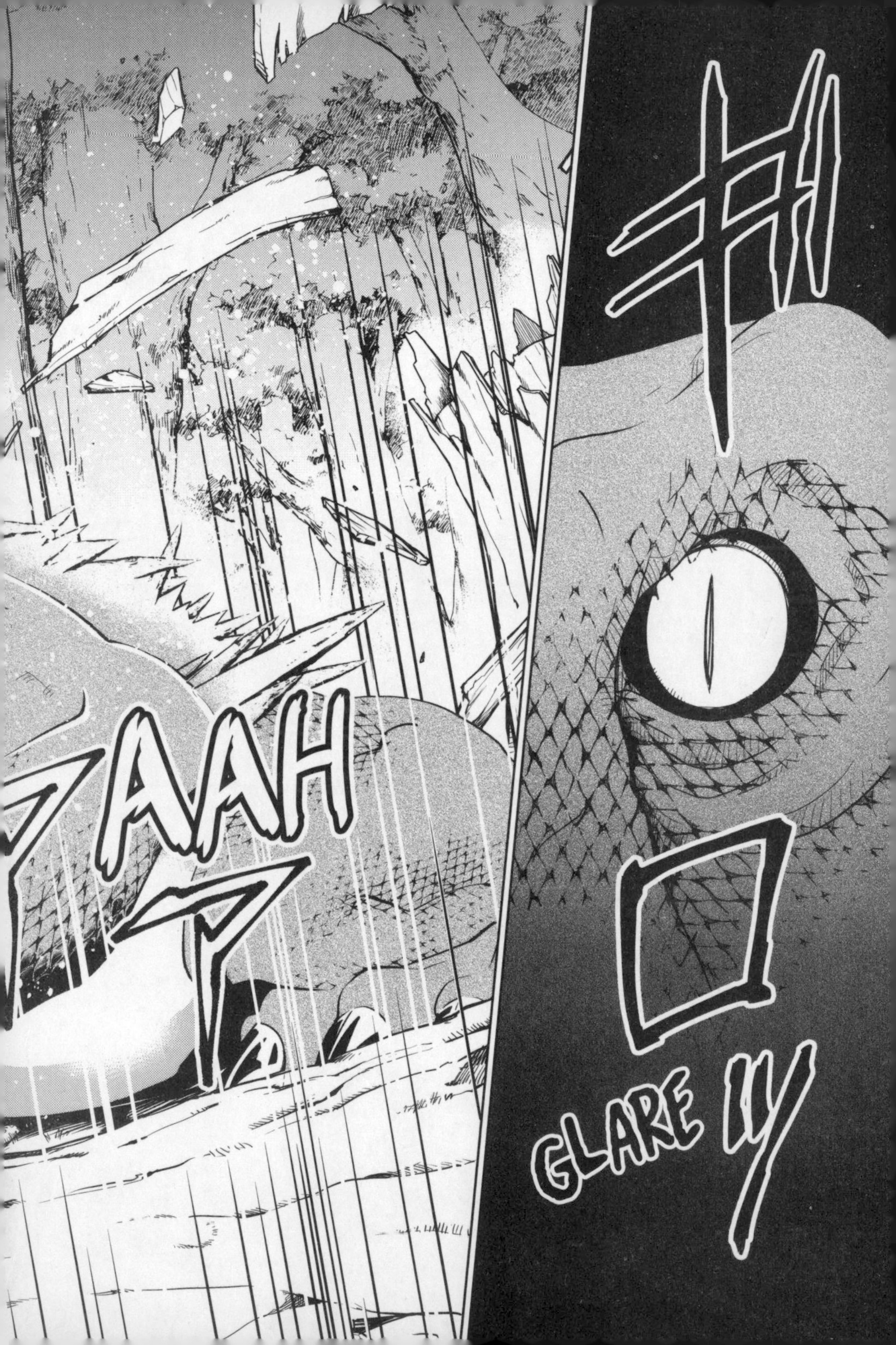
ギロ
GLARE !!
AAH

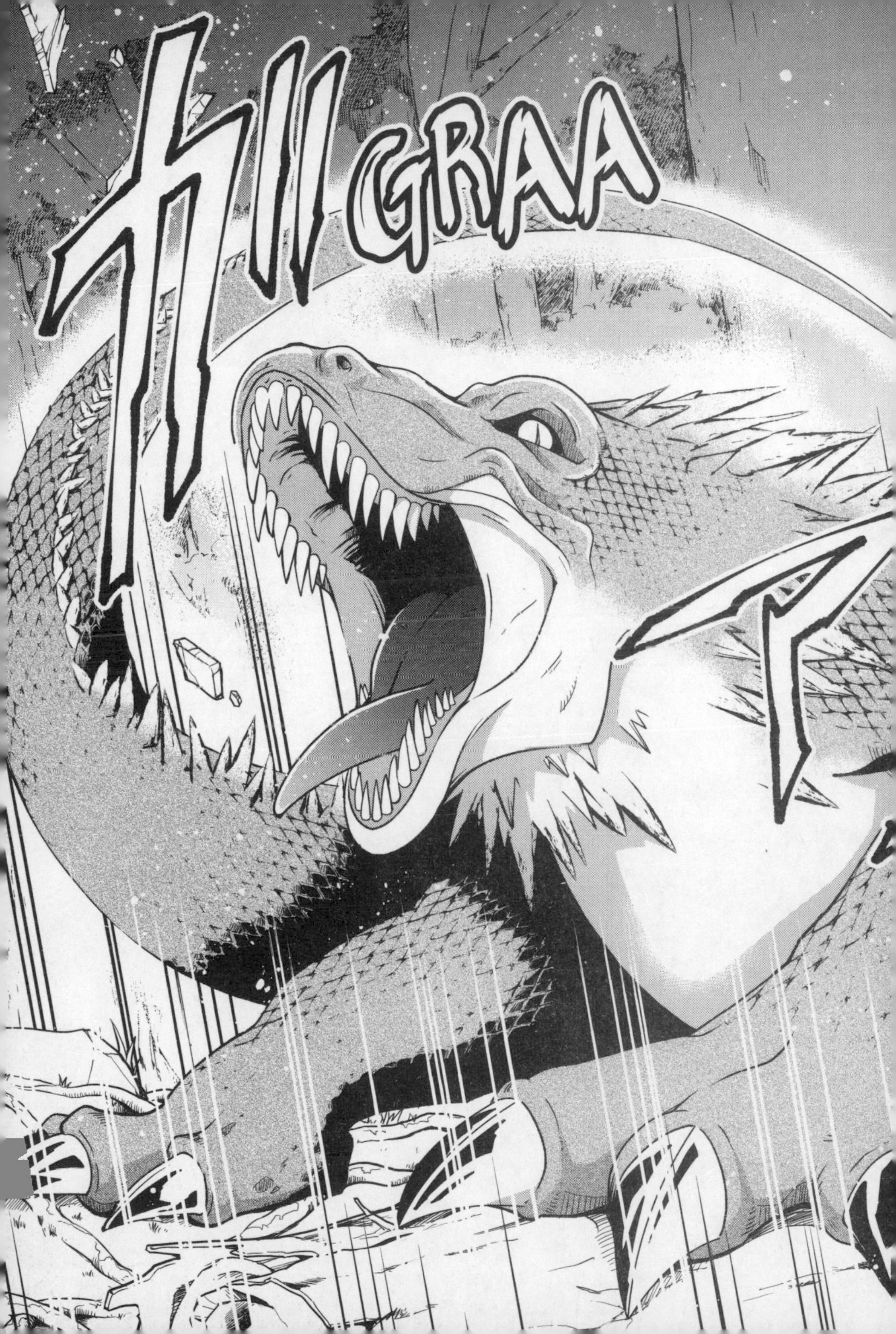
GRAA

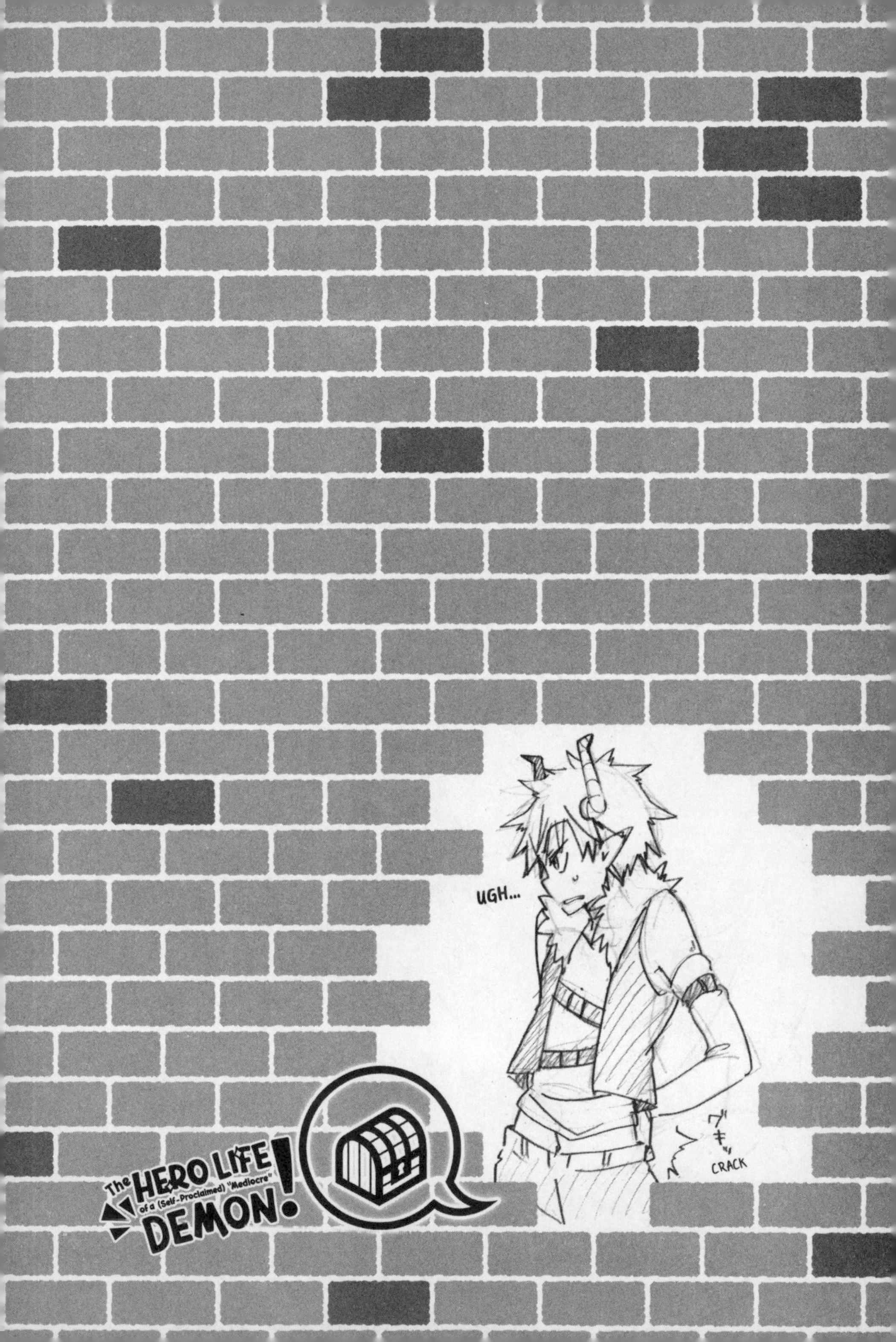
UGH...
グキッ
CRACK
The HERO LIFE of a (Self-Proclaimed) "Mediocre" DEMON!

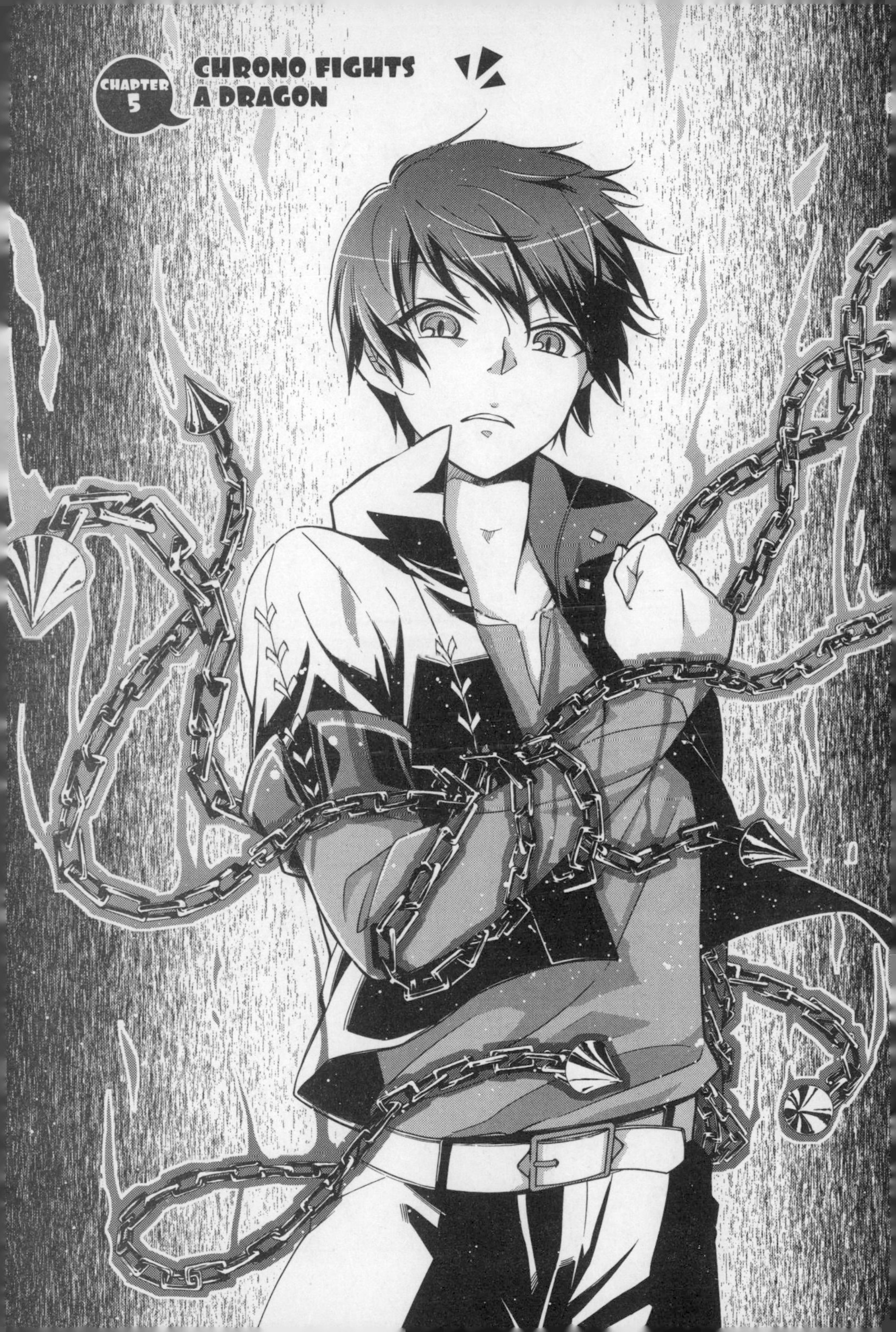
CHAPTER 5
CHRONO FIGHTS A DRAGON

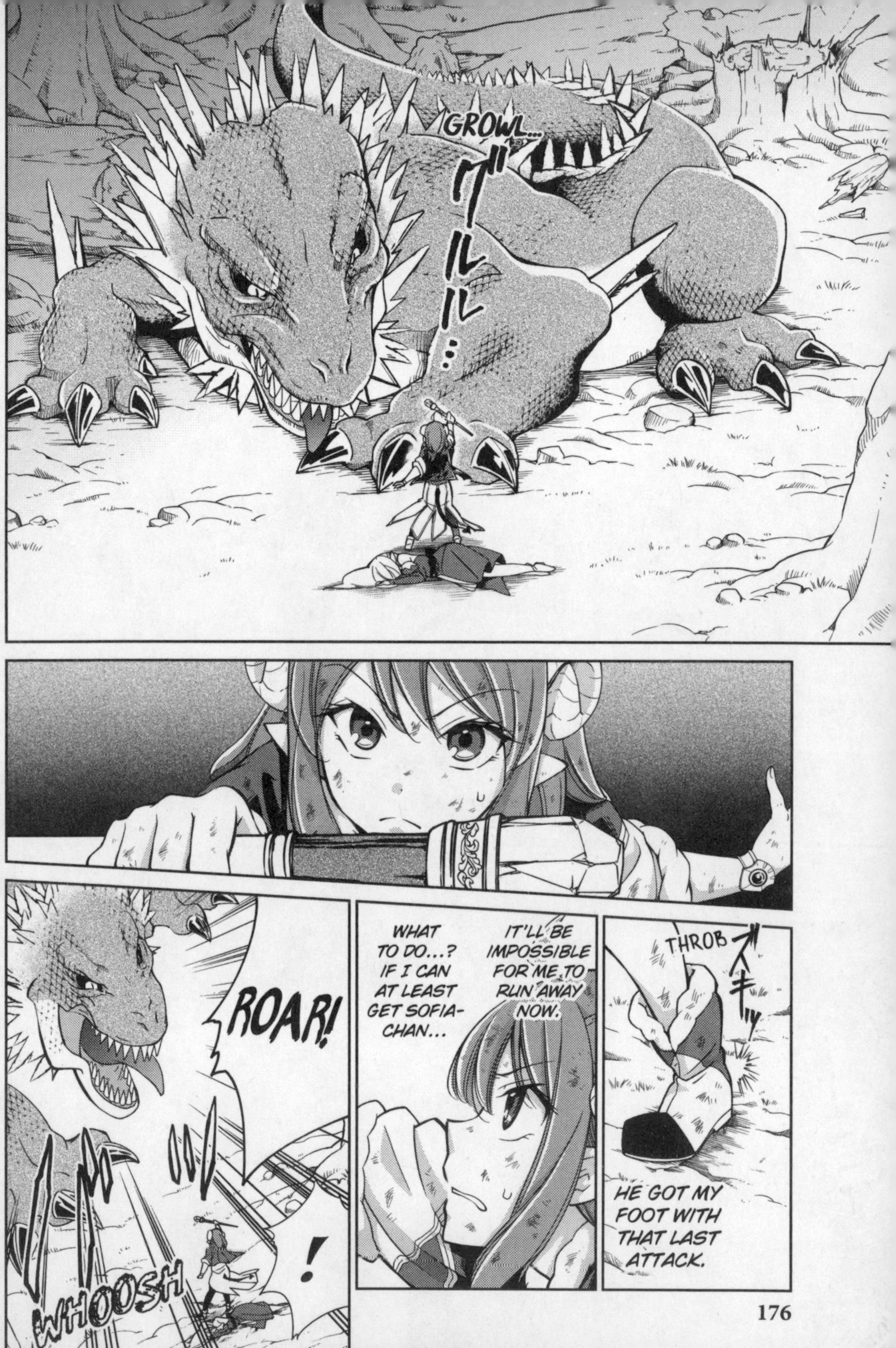
GROWL...
グルル…
THROB
ズキッ
HE GOT MY FOOT WITH THAT LAST ATTACK.
IT'LL BE IMPOSSIBLE FOR ME TO RUN AWAY NOW.
WHAT TO DO...? IF I CAN AT LEAST GET SOFIA-CHAN...
ROAR!
WHOOSH

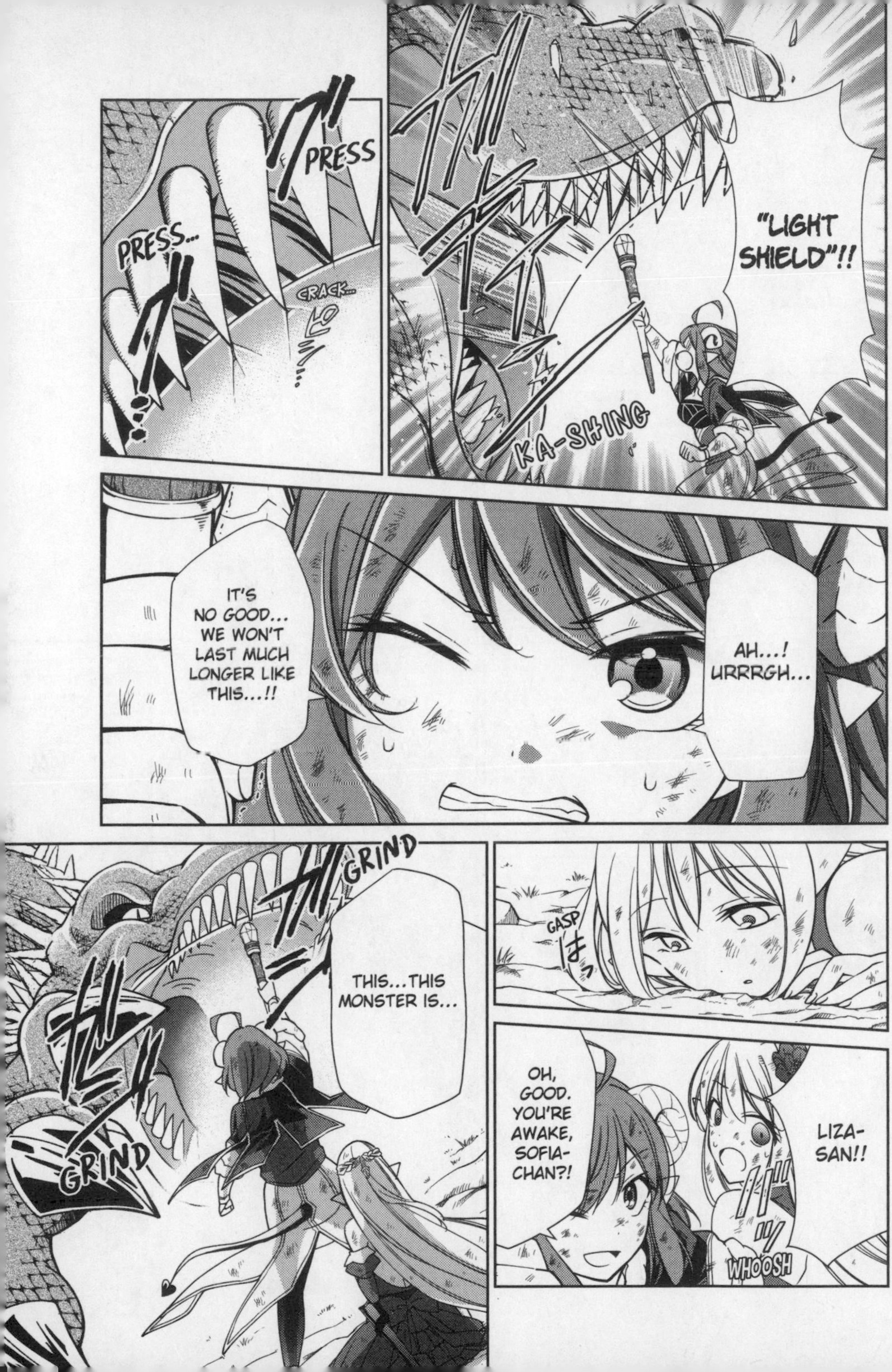
"LIGHT SHIELD"!!
KA-SHING
PRESS
PRESS...
CRACK...
AH...! URRRGH...
IT'S NO GOOD... WE WON'T LAST MUCH LONGER LIKE THIS...!!
GASP
LIZA-SAN!!
OH, GOOD. YOU'RE AWAKE, SOFIA-CHAN?!
WHOOSH
GRIND
THIS...THIS MONSTER IS...
GRIND

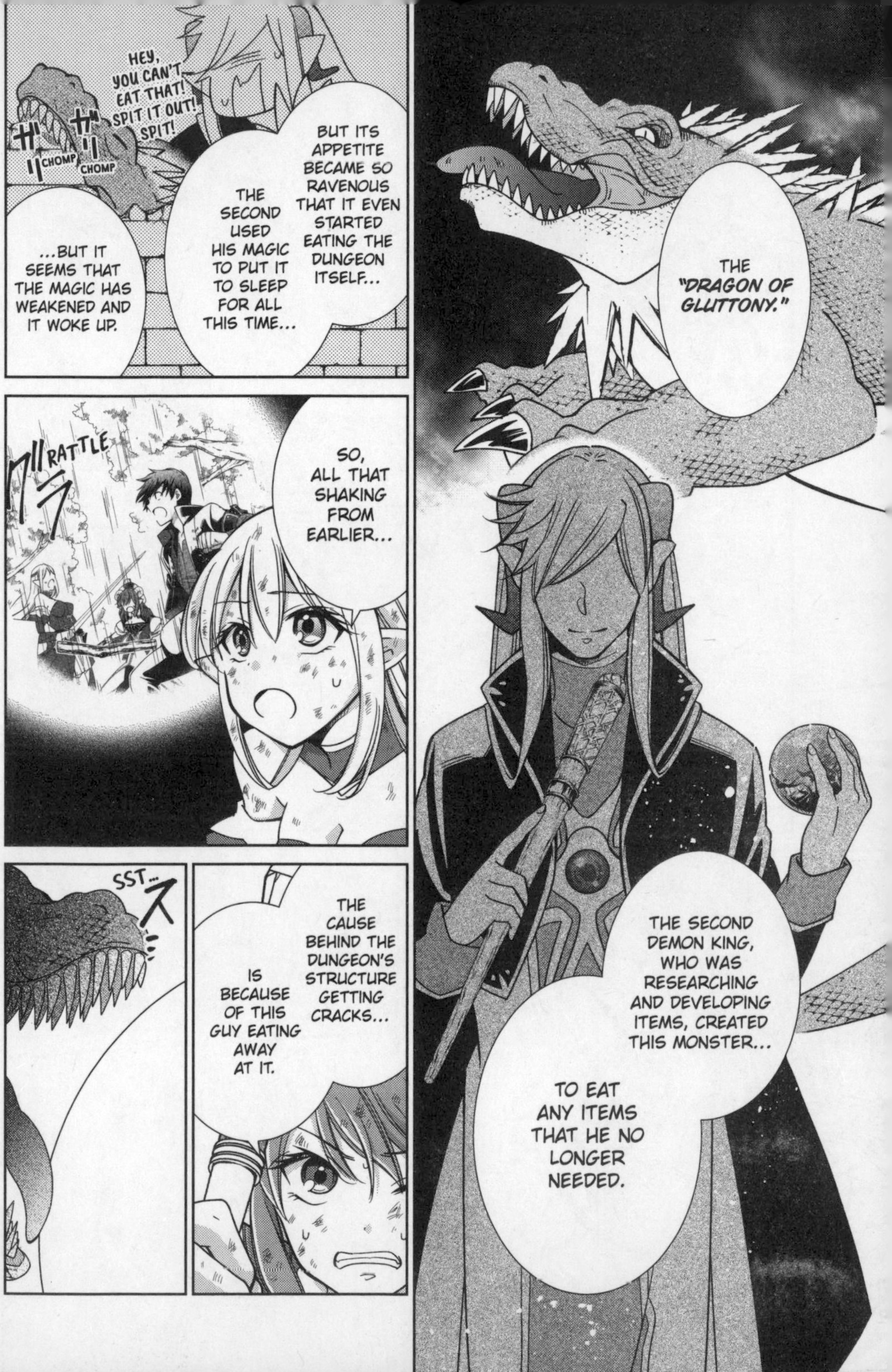
THE "DRAGON OF GLUTTONY."
THE SECOND DEMON KING, WHO WAS RESEARCHING AND DEVELOPING ITEMS, CREATED THIS MONSTER...
TO EAT ANY ITEMS THAT HE NO LONGER NEEDED.
BUT ITS APPETITE BECAME SO RAVENOUS THAT IT EVEN STARTED EATING THE DUNGEON ITSELF...
THE SECOND USED HIS MAGIC TO PUT IT TO SLEEP FOR ALL THIS TIME...
...BUT IT SEEMS THAT THE MAGIC HAS WEAKENED AND IT WOKE UP.
HEY, YOU CAN'T EAT THAT! SPIT IT OUT! SPIT!
ガリ CHOMP
ガリ CHOMP
SO, ALL THAT SHAKING FROM EARLIER...
ガラ RATTLE
THE CAUSE BEHIND THE DUNGEON'S STRUCTURE GETTING CRACKS...
IS BECAUSE OF THIS GUY EATING AWAY AT IT.
ス SST...

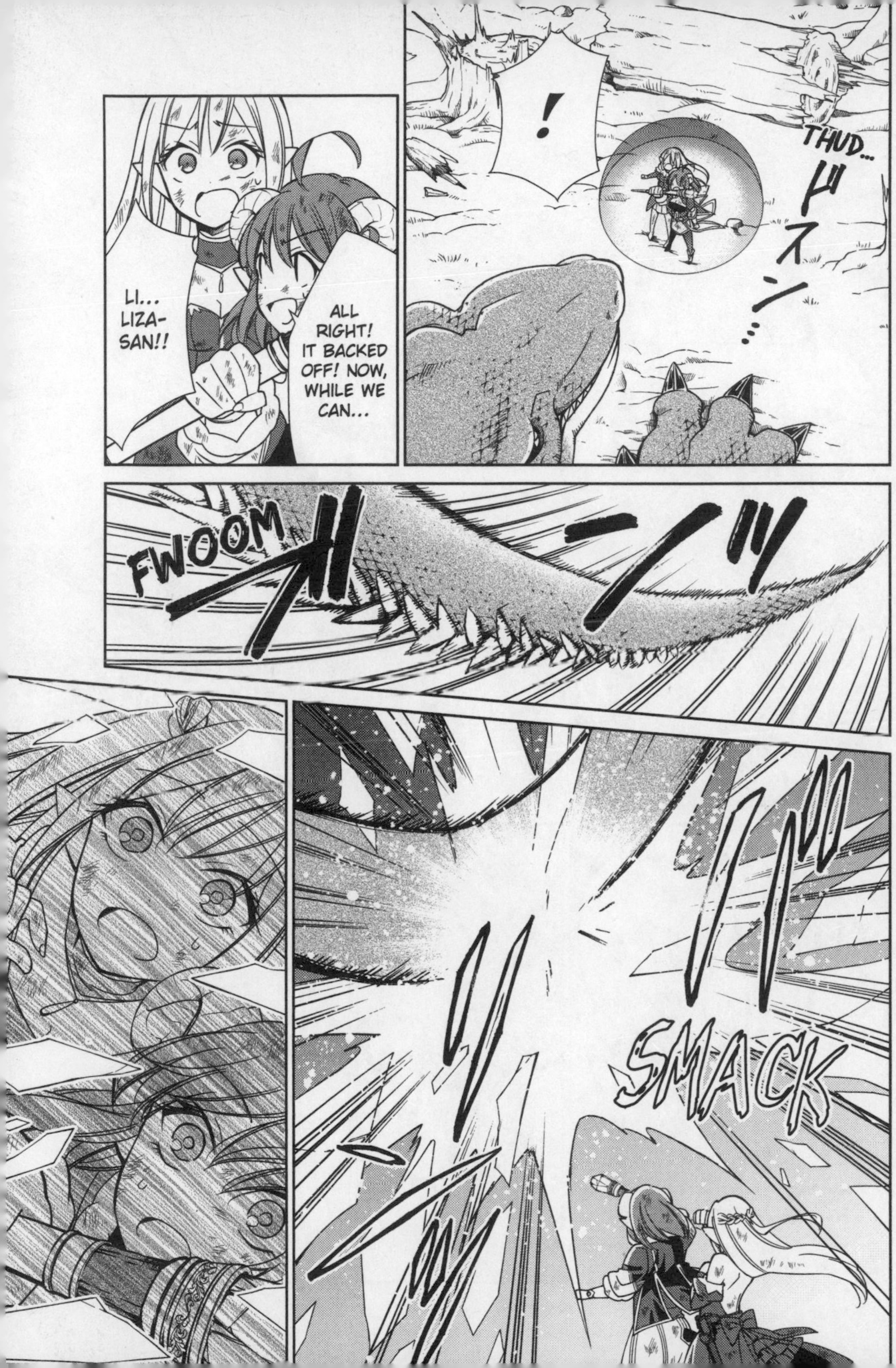
!
THUD...
ドスン…
ALL RIGHT! IT BACKED OFF! NOW, WHILE WE CAN...
LI... LIZA-SAN!!
FWOOM
SMACK

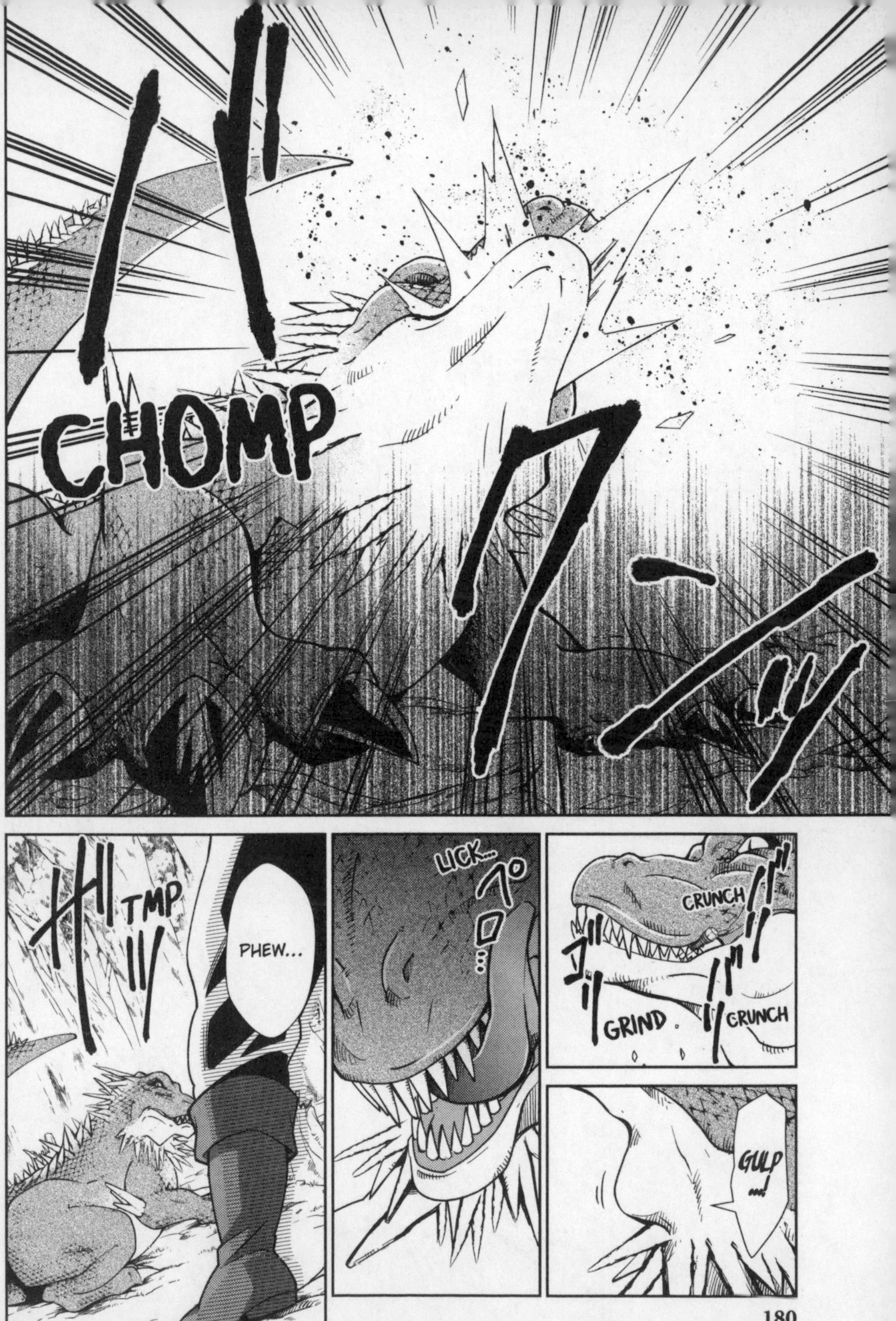
CHOMP
CRUNCH
GRIND
CRUNCH
GULP ...!
LICK...
TMP
PHEW...

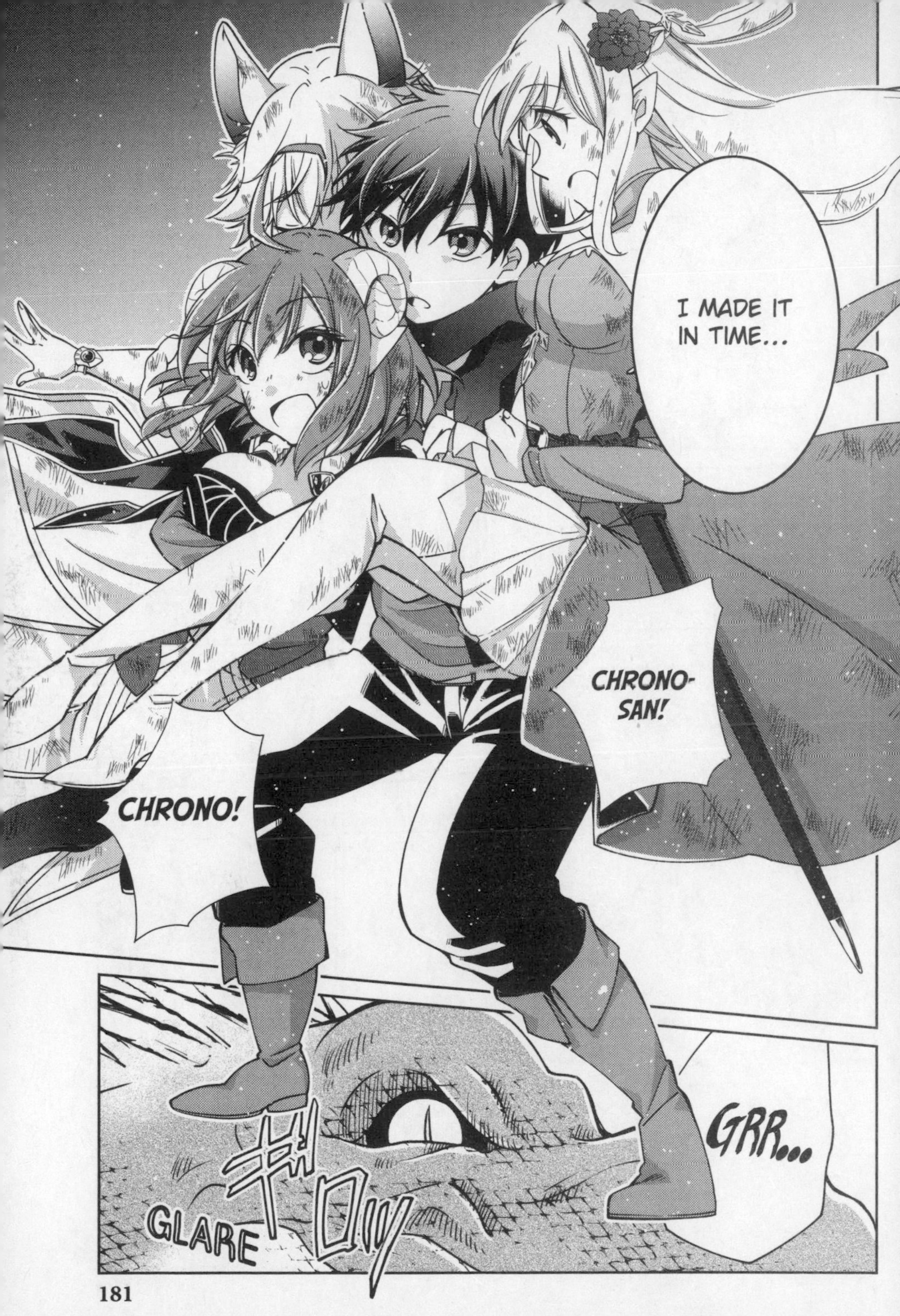

I MADE IT IN TIME...
CHRONO-SAN!
CHRONO!
GRR...
GLARE

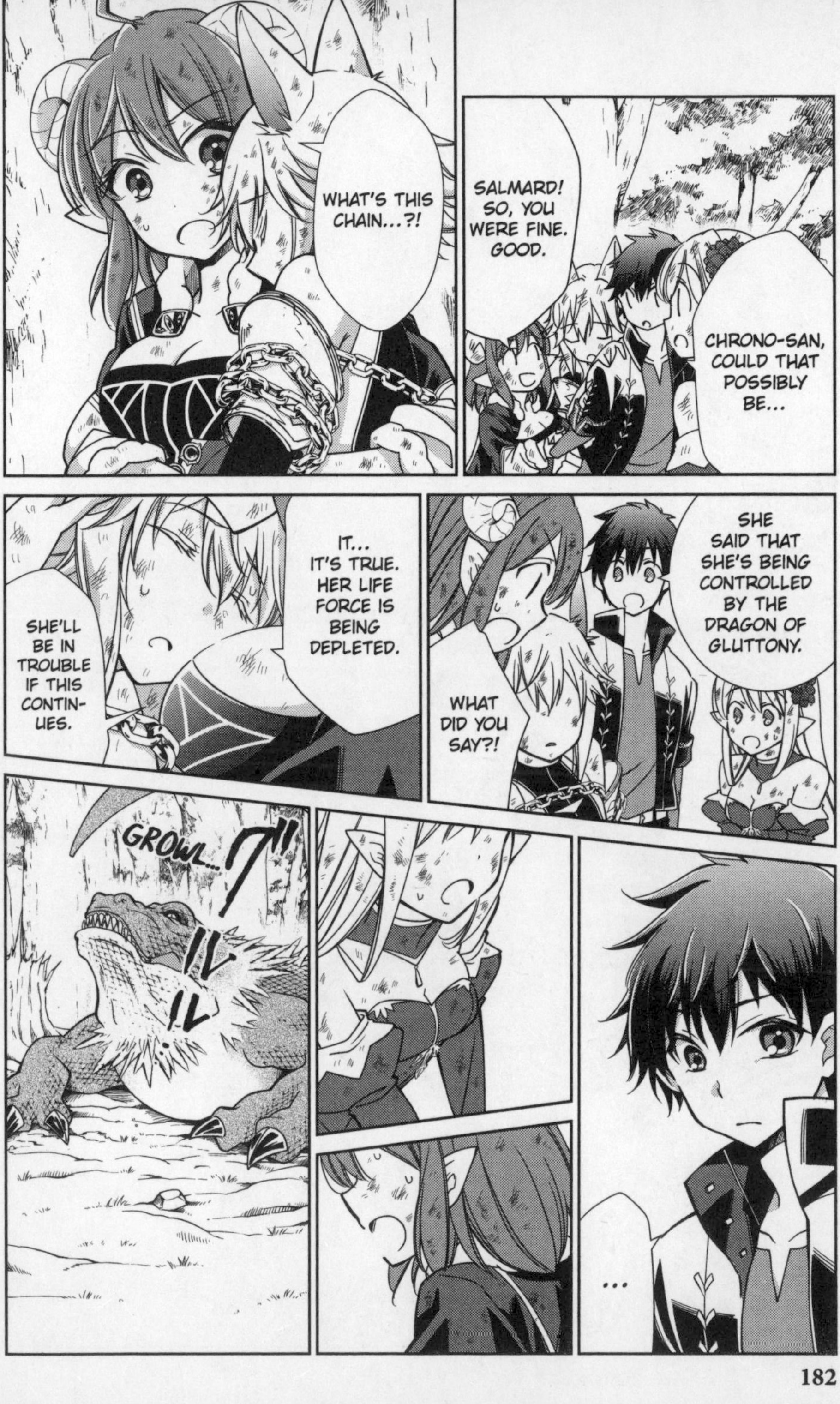
SALMARD! SO, YOU WERE FINE. GOOD.
CHRONO-SAN, COULD THAT POSSIBLY BE...
WHAT'S THIS CHAIN...?!
SHE SAID THAT SHE'S BEING CONTROLLED BY THE DRAGON OF GLUTTONY.
WHAT DID YOU SAY?!
IT... IT'S TRUE. HER LIFE FORCE IS BEING DEPLETED.
SHE'LL BE IN TROUBLE IF THIS CONTIN-UES.
...
GROWL...

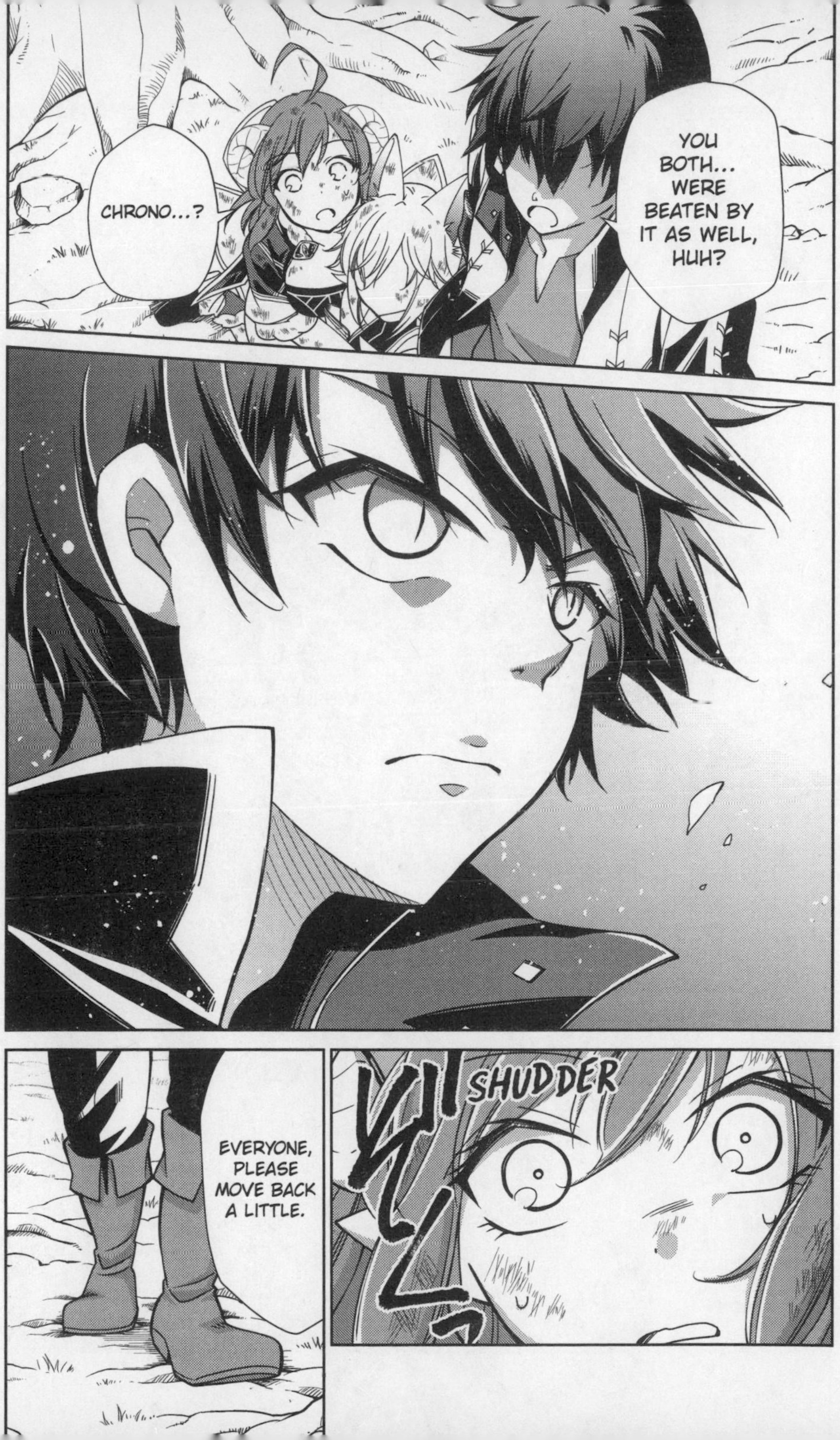
YOU BOTH... WERE BEATEN BY IT AS WELL, HUH?
CHRONO...?
SHUDDER
EVERYONE, PLEASE MOVE BACK A LITTLE.

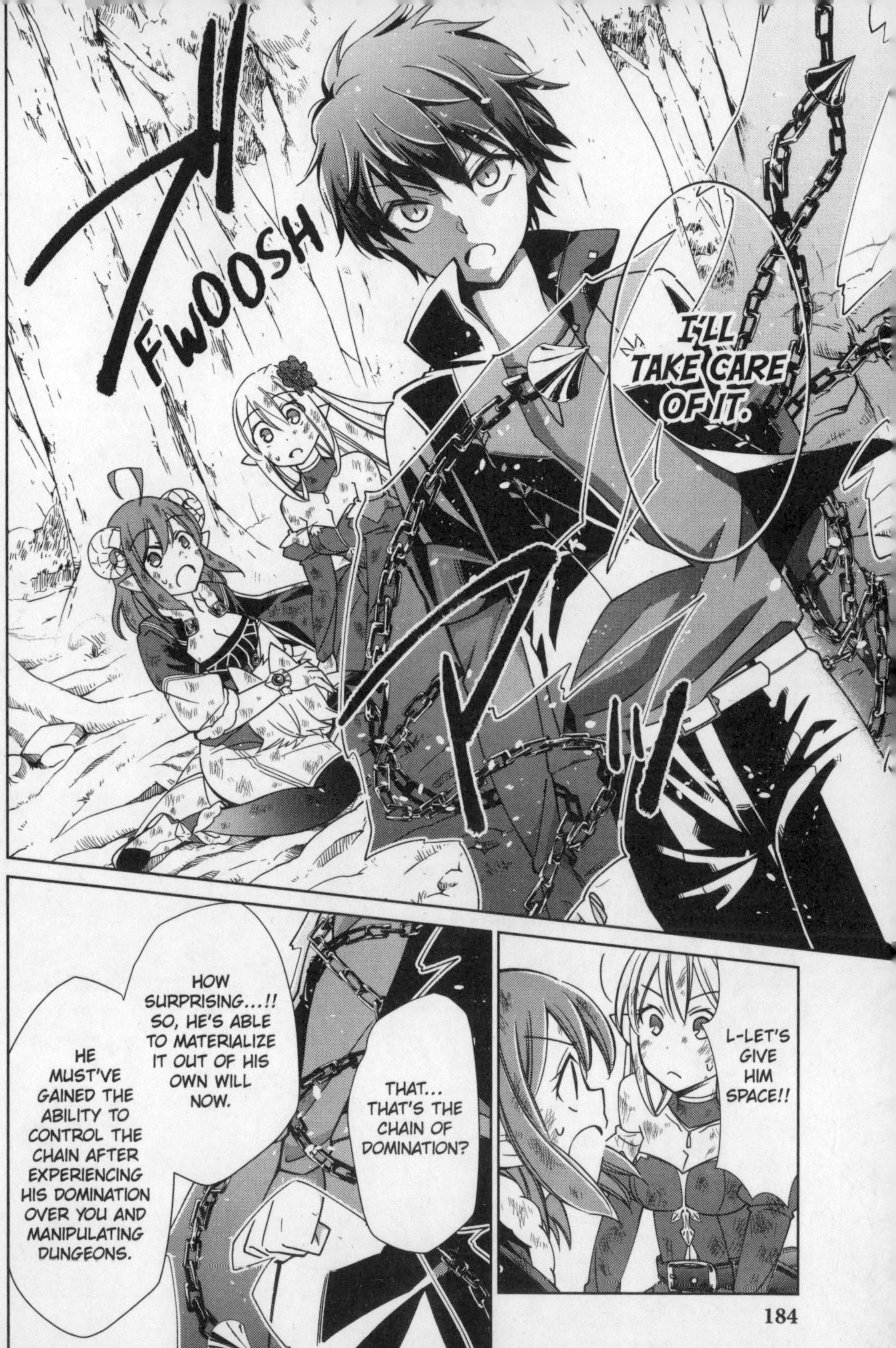
FWOOSH
I'LL TAKE CARE OF IT.
L-LET'S GIVE HIM SPACE!!
THAT... THAT'S THE CHAIN OF DOMINATION?
HOW SURPRISING...!! SO, HE'S ABLE TO MATERIALIZE IT OUT OF HIS OWN WILL NOW.
HE MUST'VE GAINED THE ABILITY TO CONTROL THE CHAIN AFTER EXPERIENCING HIS DOMINATION OVER YOU AND MANIPULATING DUNGEONS.

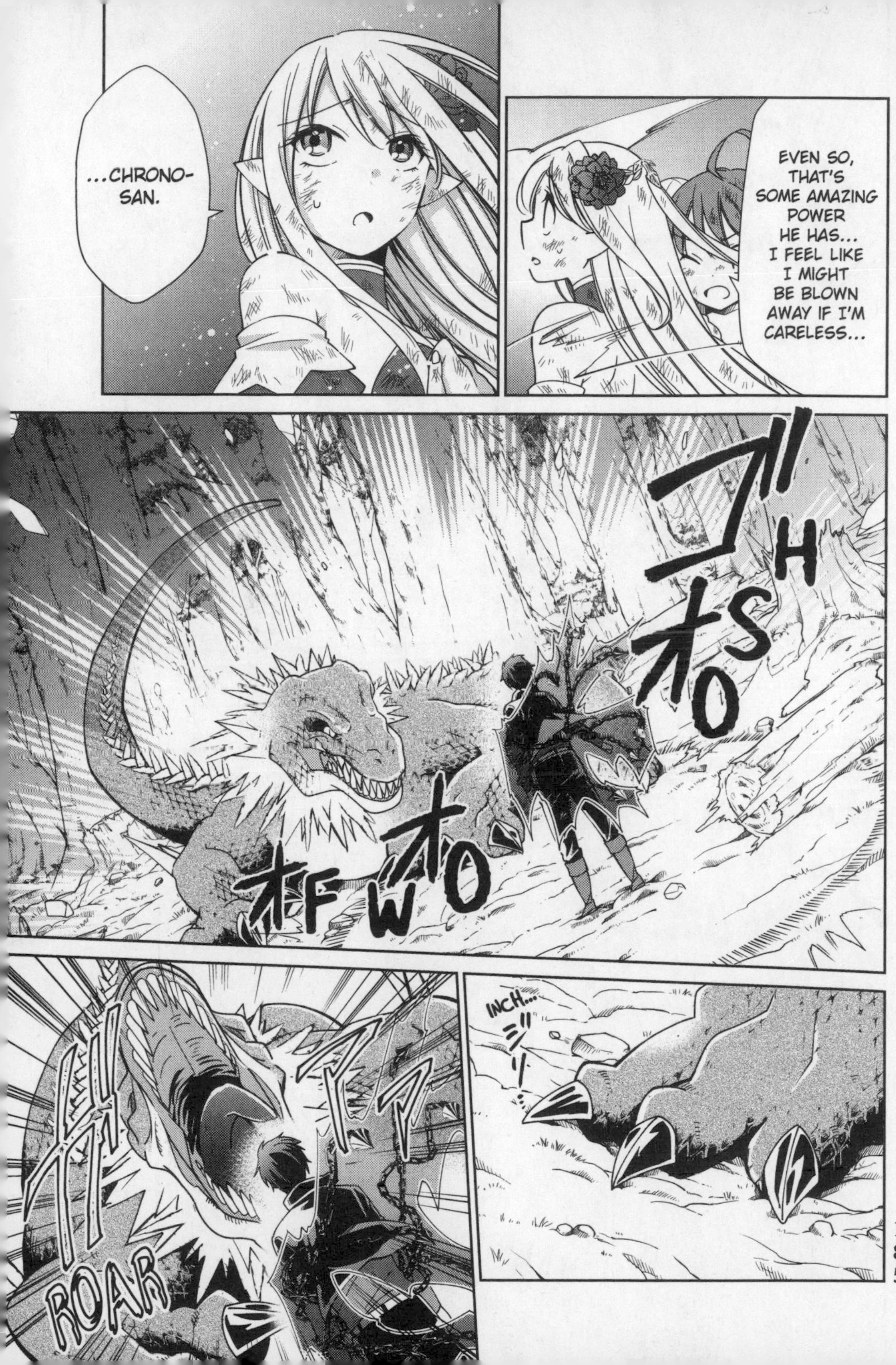
EVEN SO, THAT'S SOME AMAZING POWER HE HAS... I FEEL LIKE I MIGHT BE BLOWN AWAY IF I'M CARELESS...
...CHRONO-SAN.
INCH...
ROAR

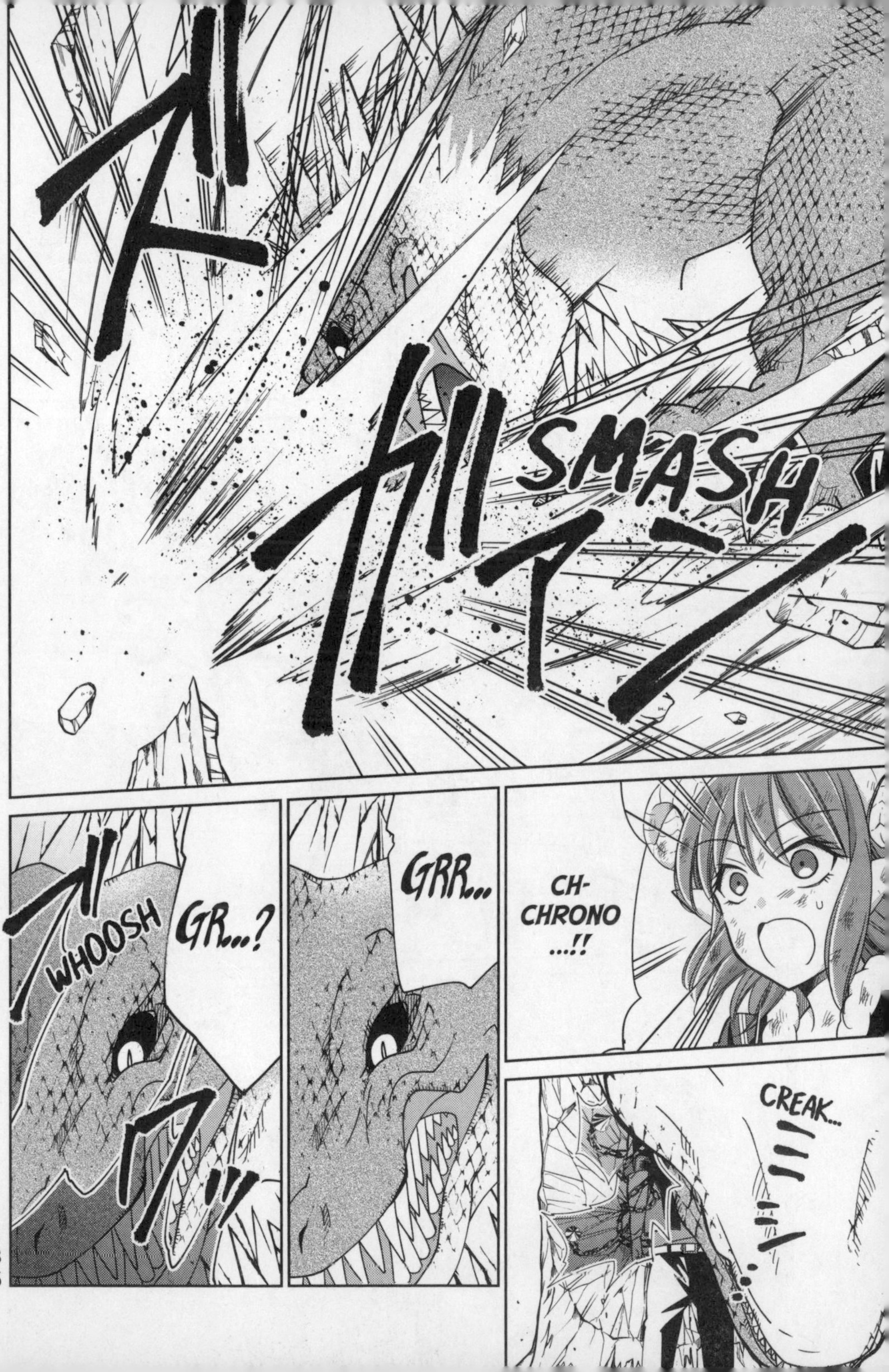
SMASH
CH-
CHRONO
...!!
GRR...
GR...?
WHOOSH
CREAK...

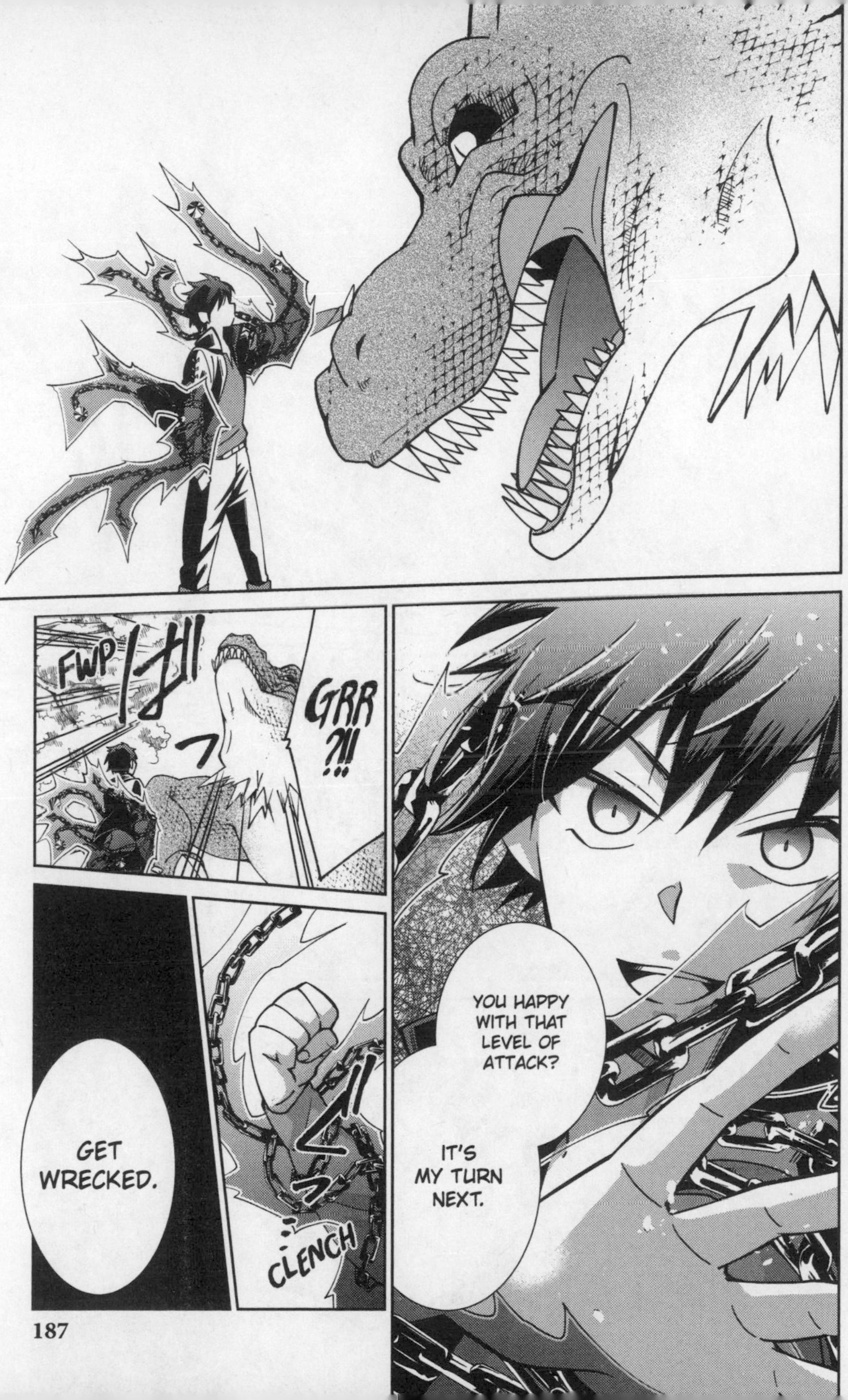
YOU HAPPY WITH THAT LEVEL OF ATTACK?
IT'S MY TURN NEXT.
FWP
GRR ?!!
CLENCH
GET WRECKED.

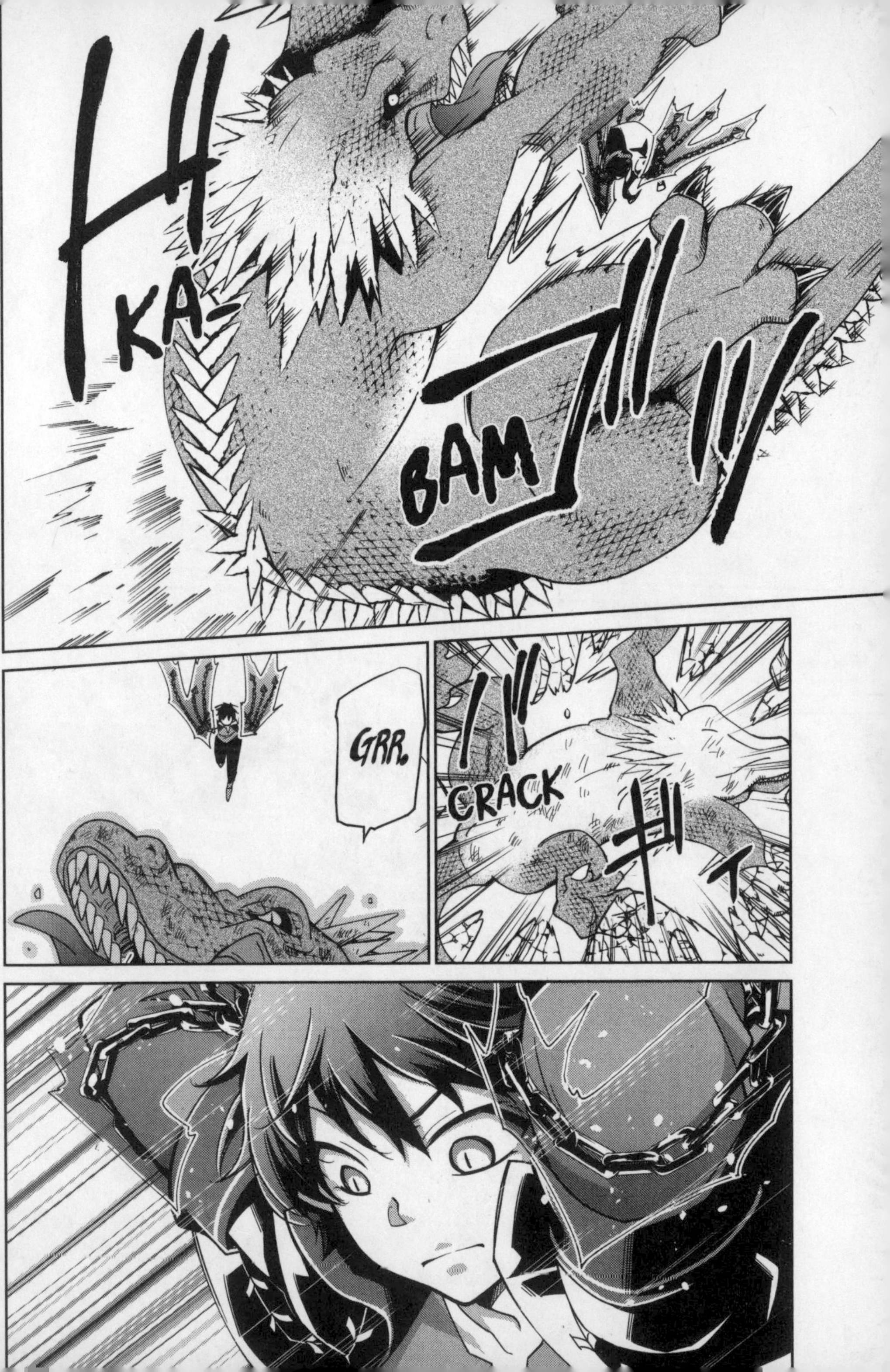
KA-
BAM
CRACK
GRR.

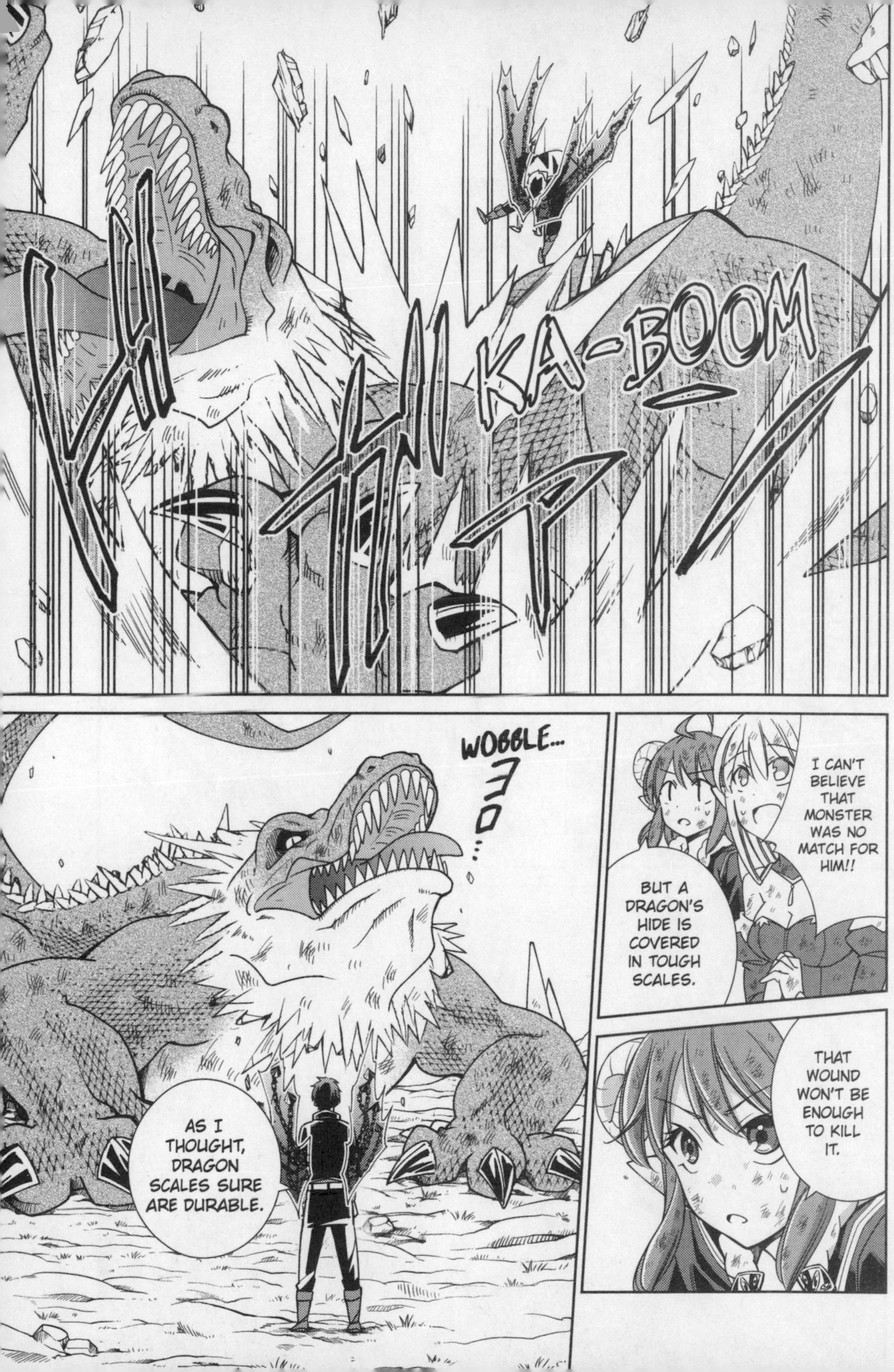
KA-BOOM
I CAN'T BELIEVE THAT MONSTER WAS NO MATCH FOR HIM!!
BUT A DRAGON'S HIDE IS COVERED IN TOUGH SCALES.
THAT WOUND WON'T BE ENOUGH TO KILL IT.
WOBBLE...
AS I THOUGHT, DRAGON SCALES SURE ARE DURABLE.

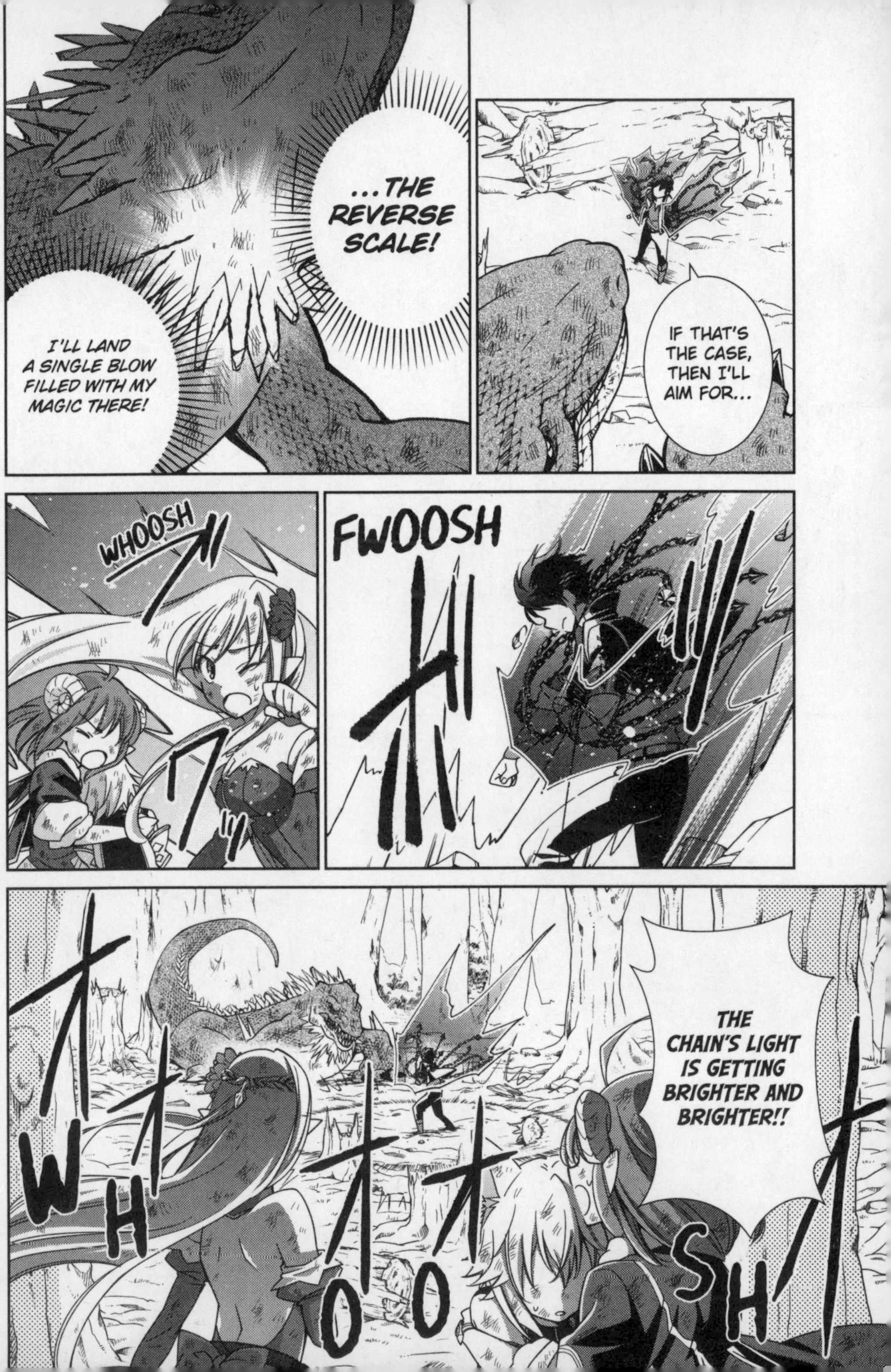
IF THAT'S THE CASE, THEN I'LL AIM FOR...
...THE REVERSE SCALE!
I'LL LAND A SINGLE BLOW FILLED WITH MY MAGIC THERE!
FWOOSH
WHOOSH
THE CHAIN'S LIGHT IS GETTING BRIGHTER AND BRIGHTER!!
WHOOSH

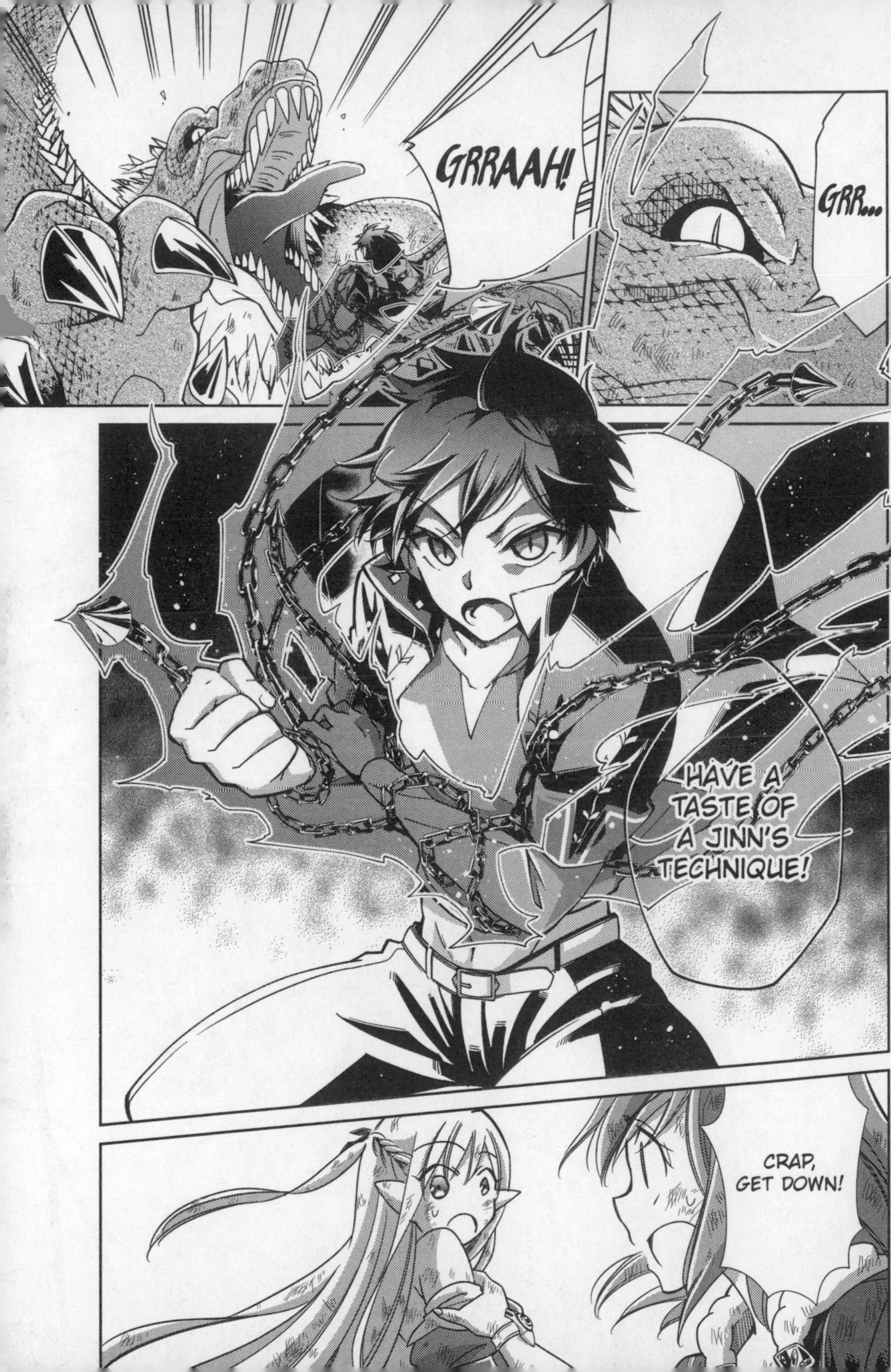
GRR...
GRRAAH!
HAVE A TASTE OF A JINN'S TECHNIQUE!
CRAP, GET DOWN!

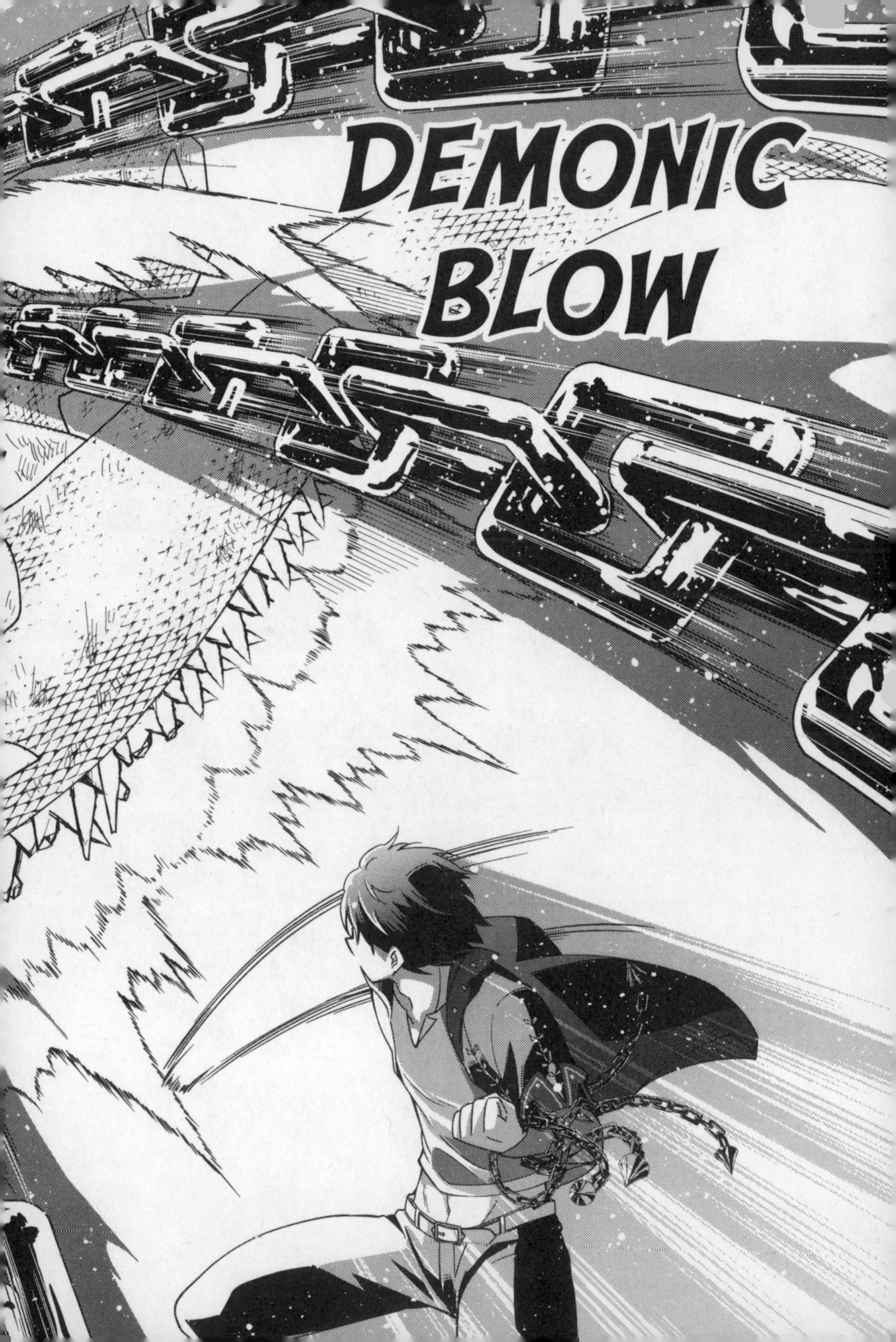
DEMONIC BLOW

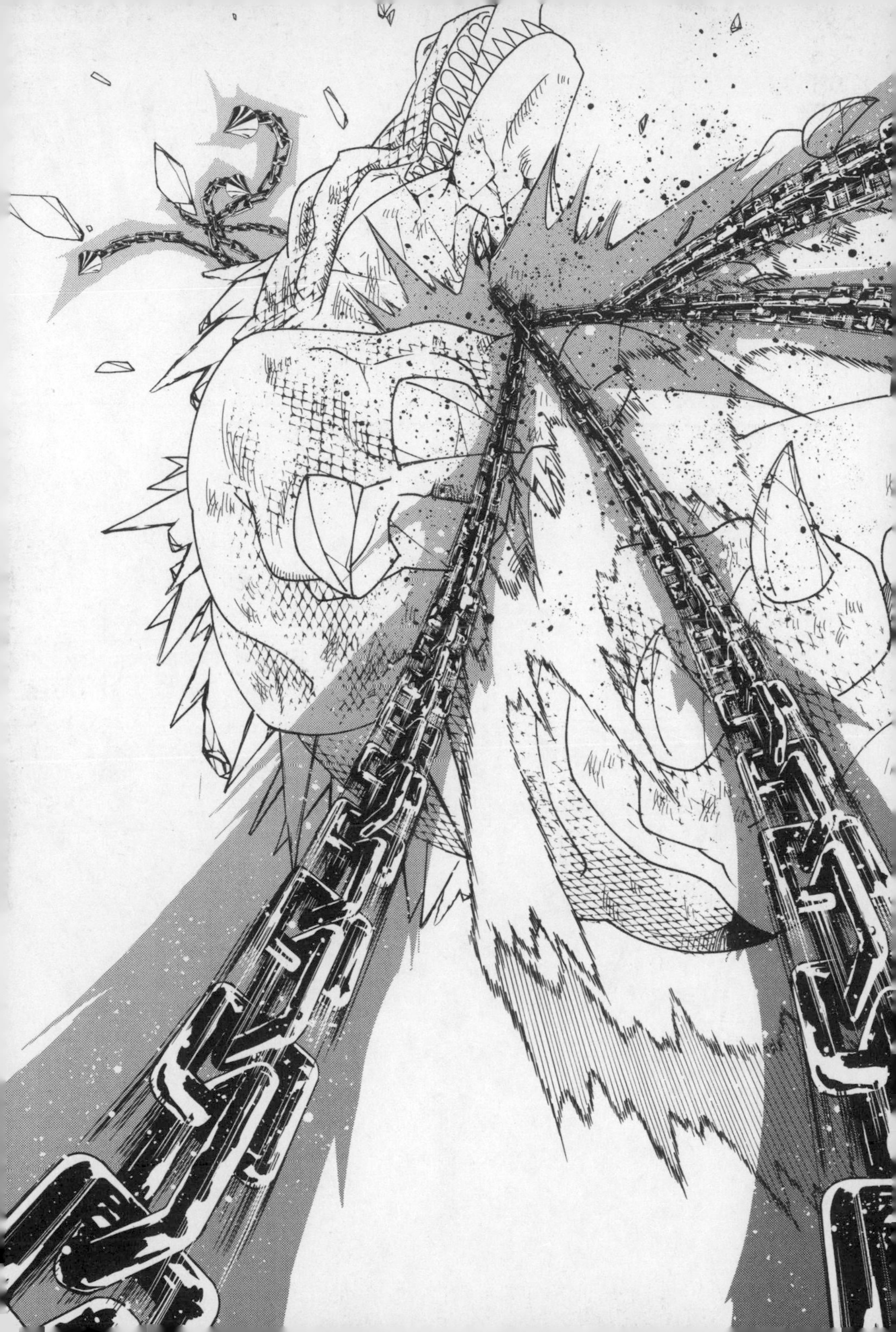

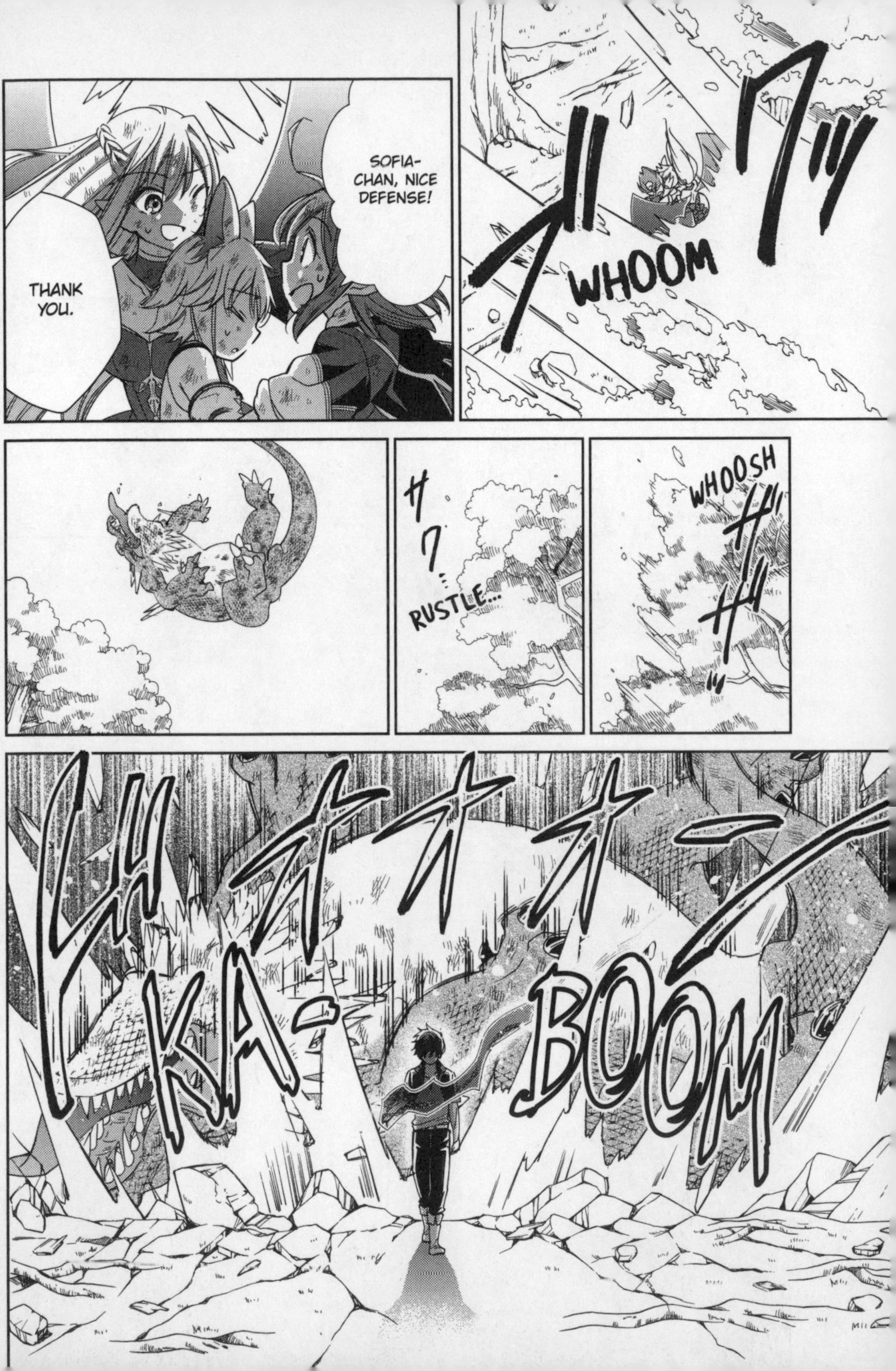
WHOOM
SOFIA-CHAN, NICE DEFENSE!
THANK YOU.
WHOOSH
RUSTLE...
KA-BOOM

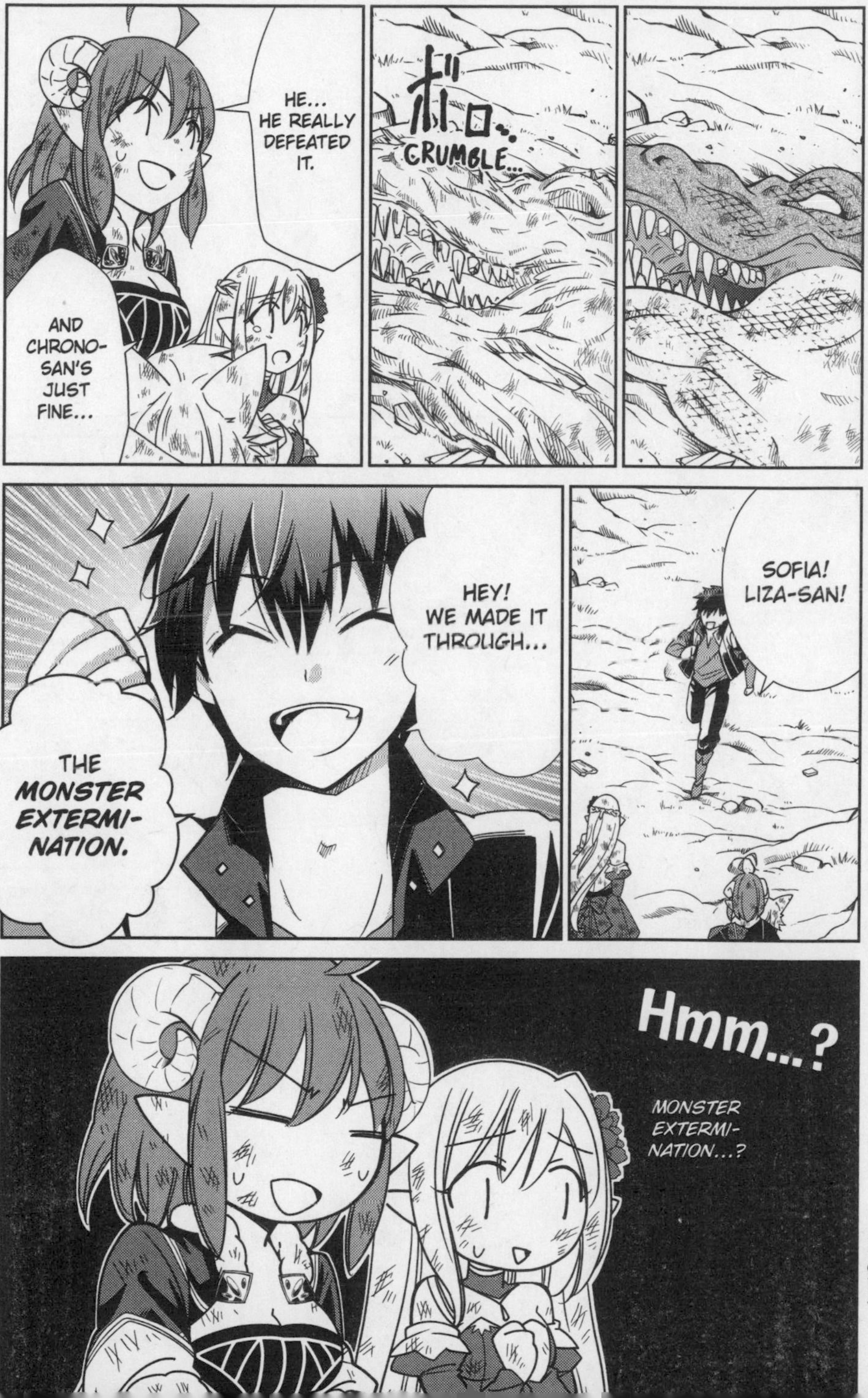
ボロ…
CRUMBLE…
HE… HE REALLY DEFEATED IT.
AND CHRONO-SAN'S JUST FINE…
SOFIA! LIZA-SAN!
HEY! WE MADE IT THROUGH…
THE *MONSTER EXTERMINATION.*
Hmm…?
MONSTER EXTERMINATION…?

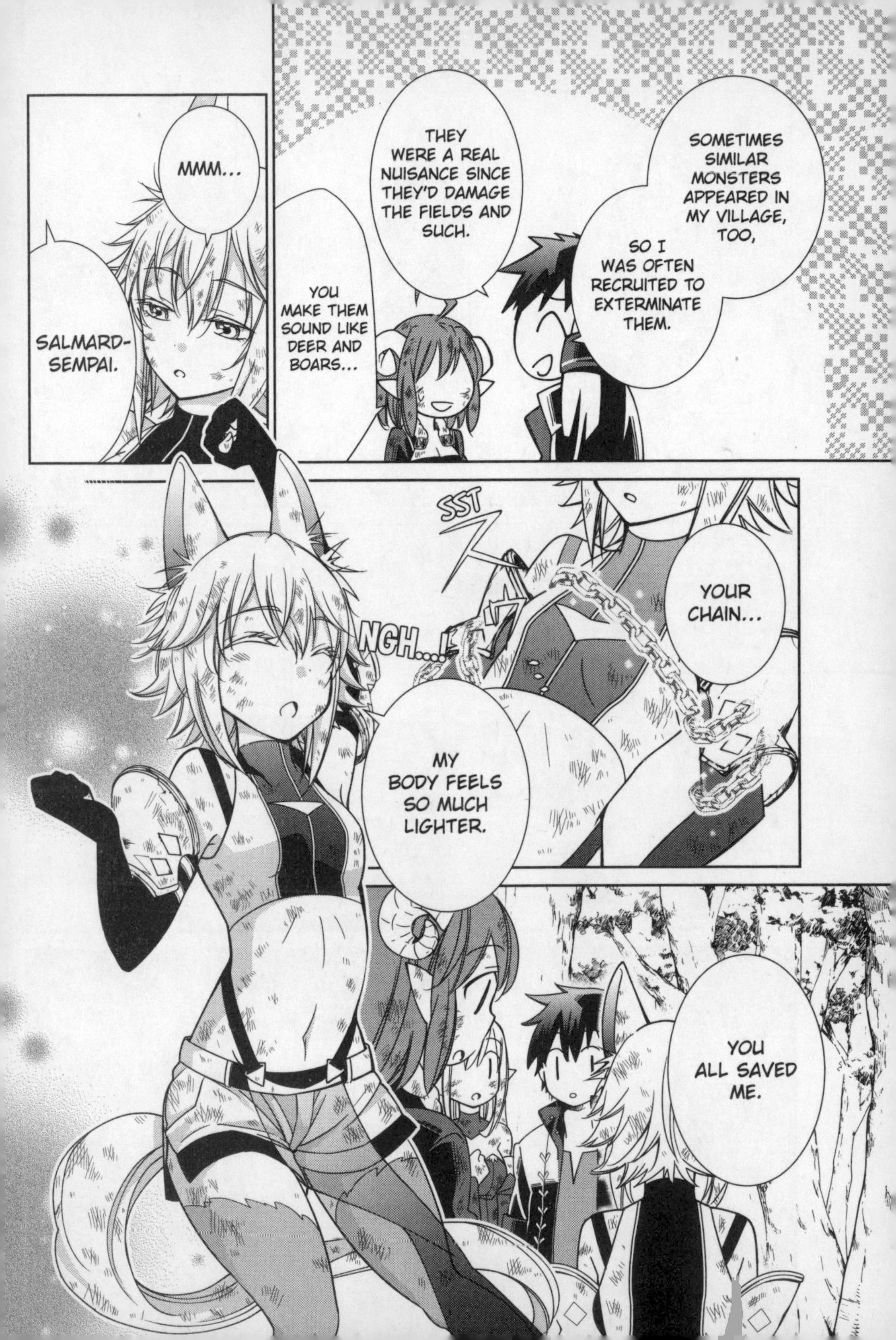
SOMETIMES SIMILAR MONSTERS APPEARED IN MY VILLAGE, TOO,
SO I WAS OFTEN RECRUITED TO EXTERMINATE THEM.
THEY WERE A REAL NUISANCE SINCE THEY'D DAMAGE THE FIELDS AND SUCH.
YOU MAKE THEM SOUND LIKE DEER AND BOARS...
MMM...
SALMARD-SEMPAI.
SST
YOUR CHAIN...
NGH...!
MY BODY FEELS SO MUCH LIGHTER.
YOU ALL SAVED ME.

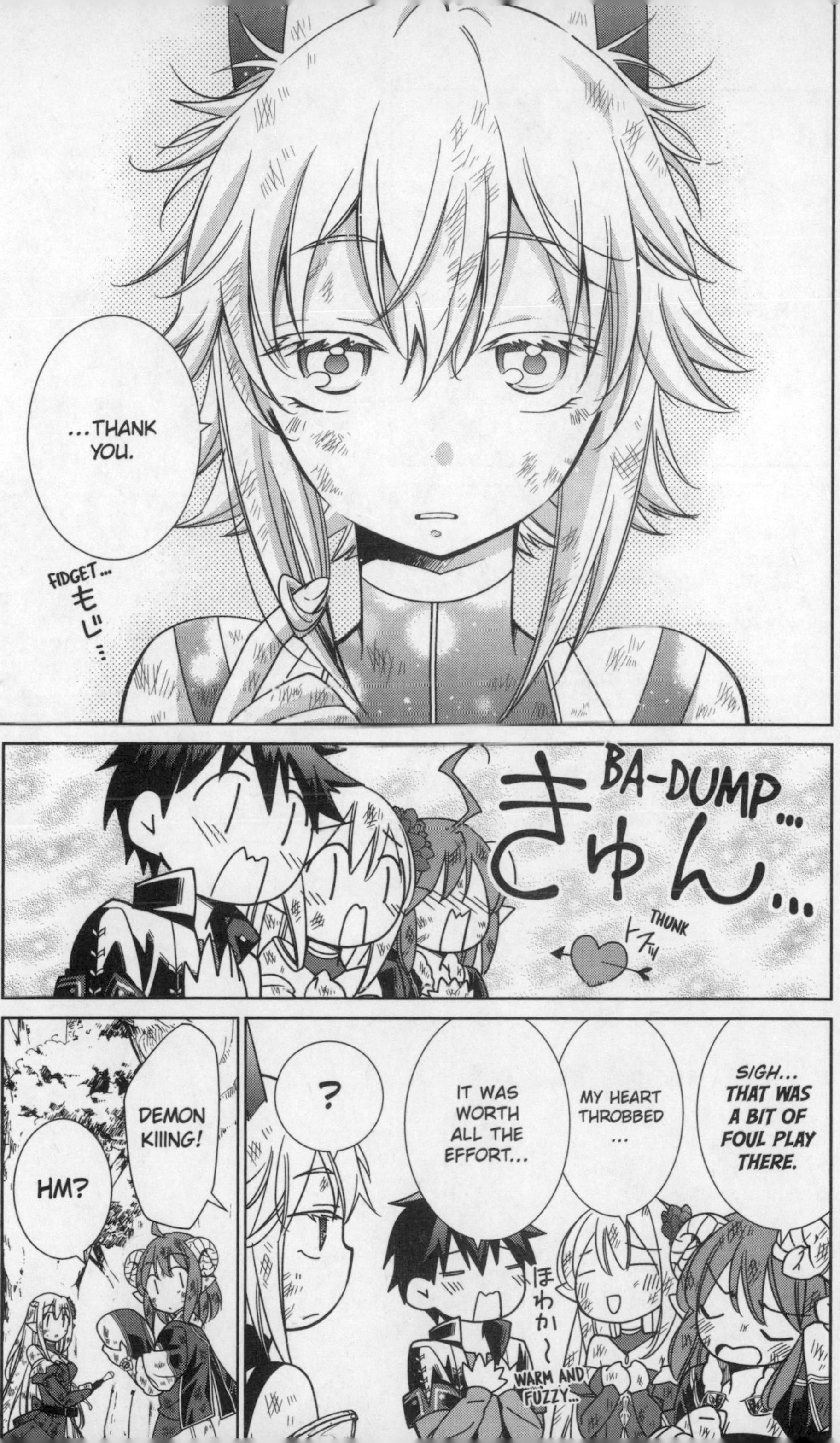
...THANK YOU.
FIDGET...
もじ...
BA-DUMP...
きゅん...
THUNK
トスッ
SIGH... THAT WAS A BIT OF FOUL PLAY THERE.
MY HEART THROBBED ...
IT WAS WORTH ALL THE EFFORT...
?
ほわか~
WARM AND FUZZY...
DEMON KIIING!
HM?

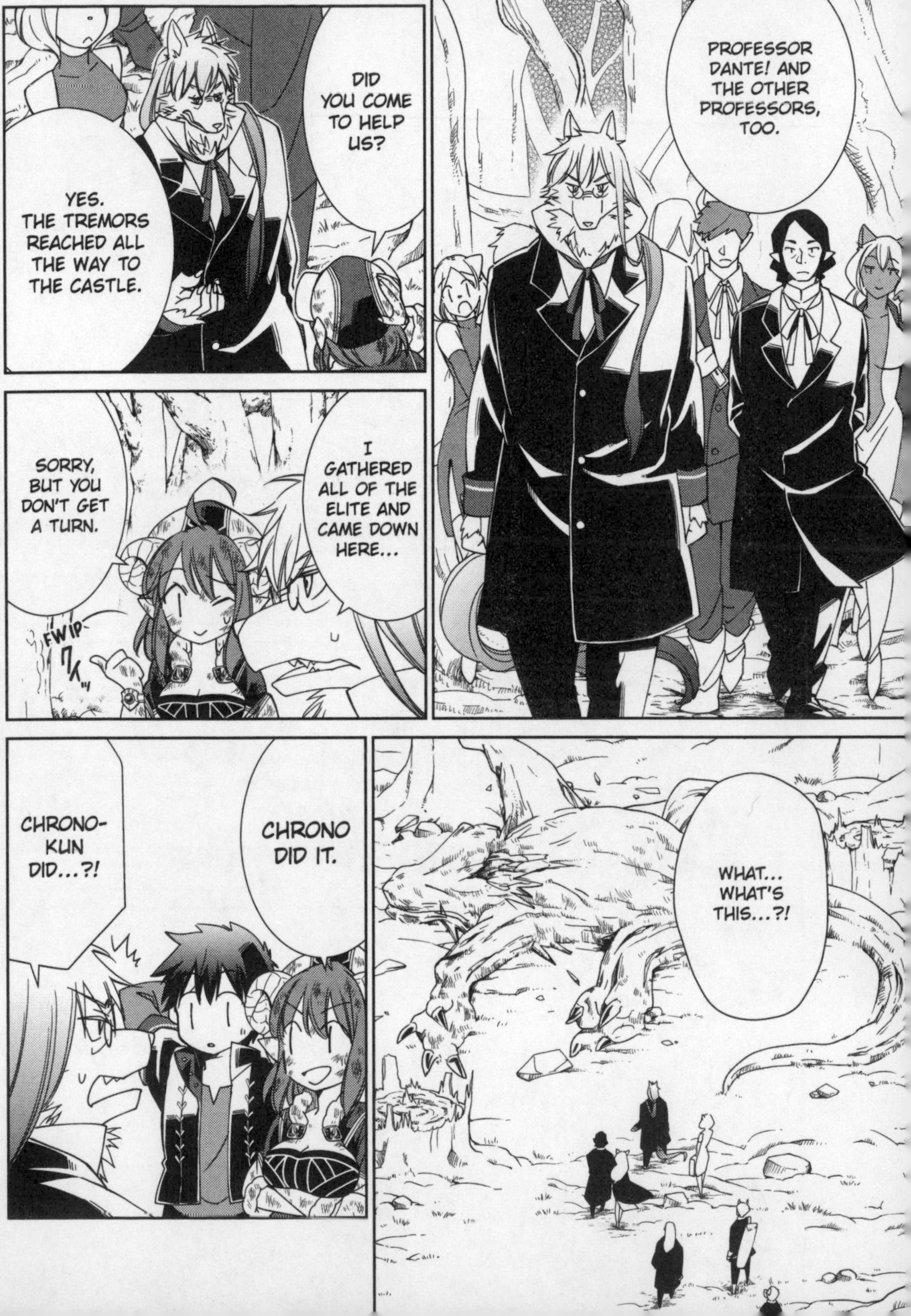
PROFESSOR DANTE! AND THE OTHER PROFESSORS, TOO.
DID YOU COME TO HELP US?
YES. THE TREMORS REACHED ALL THE WAY TO THE CASTLE.
I GATHERED ALL OF THE ELITE AND CAME DOWN HERE...
SORRY, BUT YOU DON'T GET A TURN.
FWIP
WHAT... WHAT'S THIS...?!
CHRONO DID IT.
CHRONO-KUN DID...?!

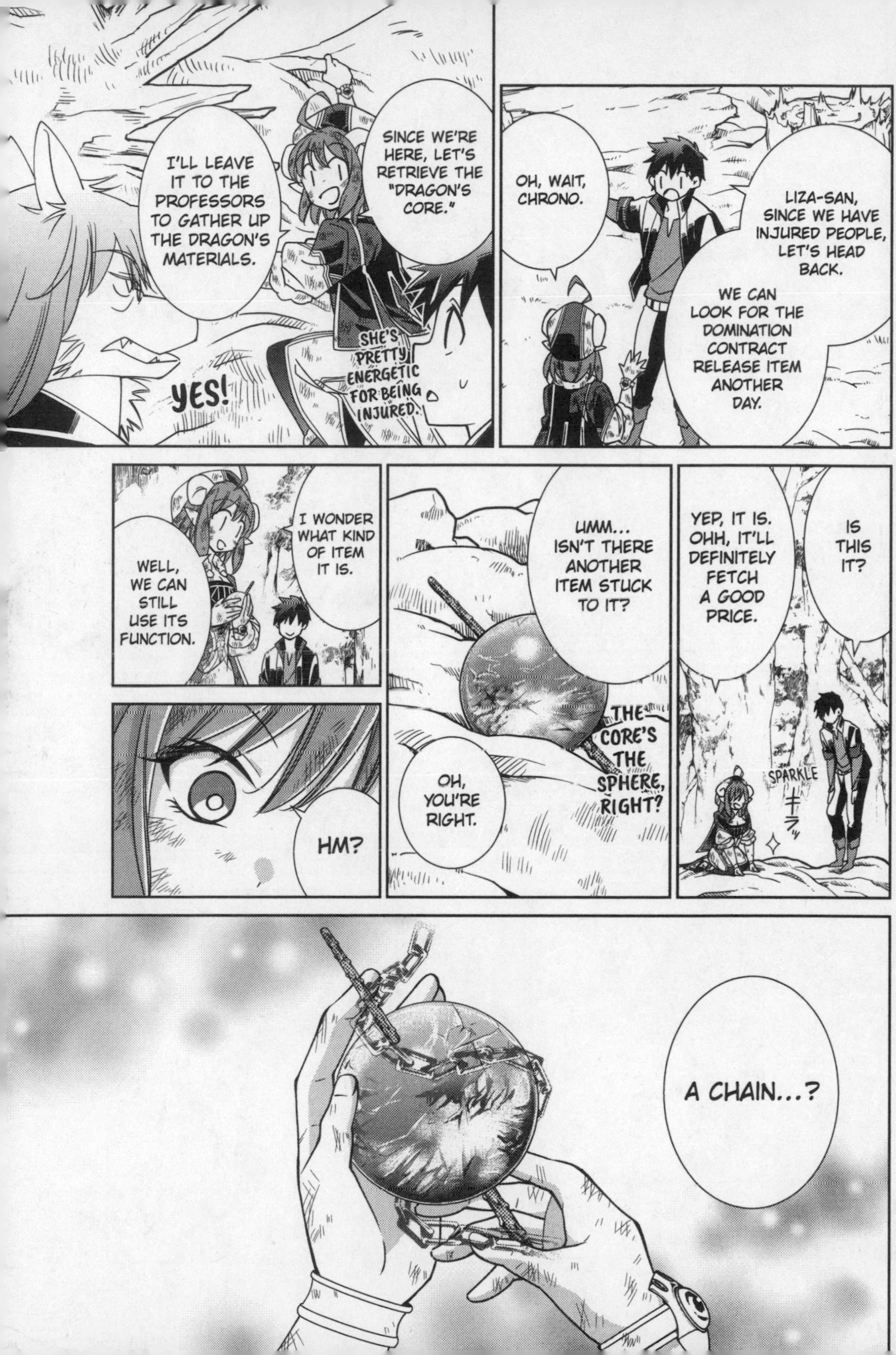
LIZA-SAN, SINCE WE HAVE INJURED PEOPLE, LET'S HEAD BACK.
WE CAN LOOK FOR THE DOMINATION CONTRACT RELEASE ITEM ANOTHER DAY.
OH, WAIT, CHRONO.
SINCE WE'RE HERE, LET'S RETRIEVE THE "DRAGON'S CORE."
I'LL LEAVE IT TO THE PROFESSORS TO GATHER UP THE DRAGON'S MATERIALS.
SHE'S PRETTY ENERGETIC FOR BEING INJURED.
YES!
IS THIS IT?
YEP, IT IS. OHH, IT'LL DEFINITELY FETCH A GOOD PRICE.
SPARKLE
UMM... ISN'T THERE ANOTHER ITEM STUCK TO IT?
THE CORE'S THE SPHERE, RIGHT?
OH, YOU'RE RIGHT.
I WONDER WHAT KIND OF ITEM IT IS.
WELL, WE CAN STILL USE ITS FUNCTION.
HM?
A CHAIN...?

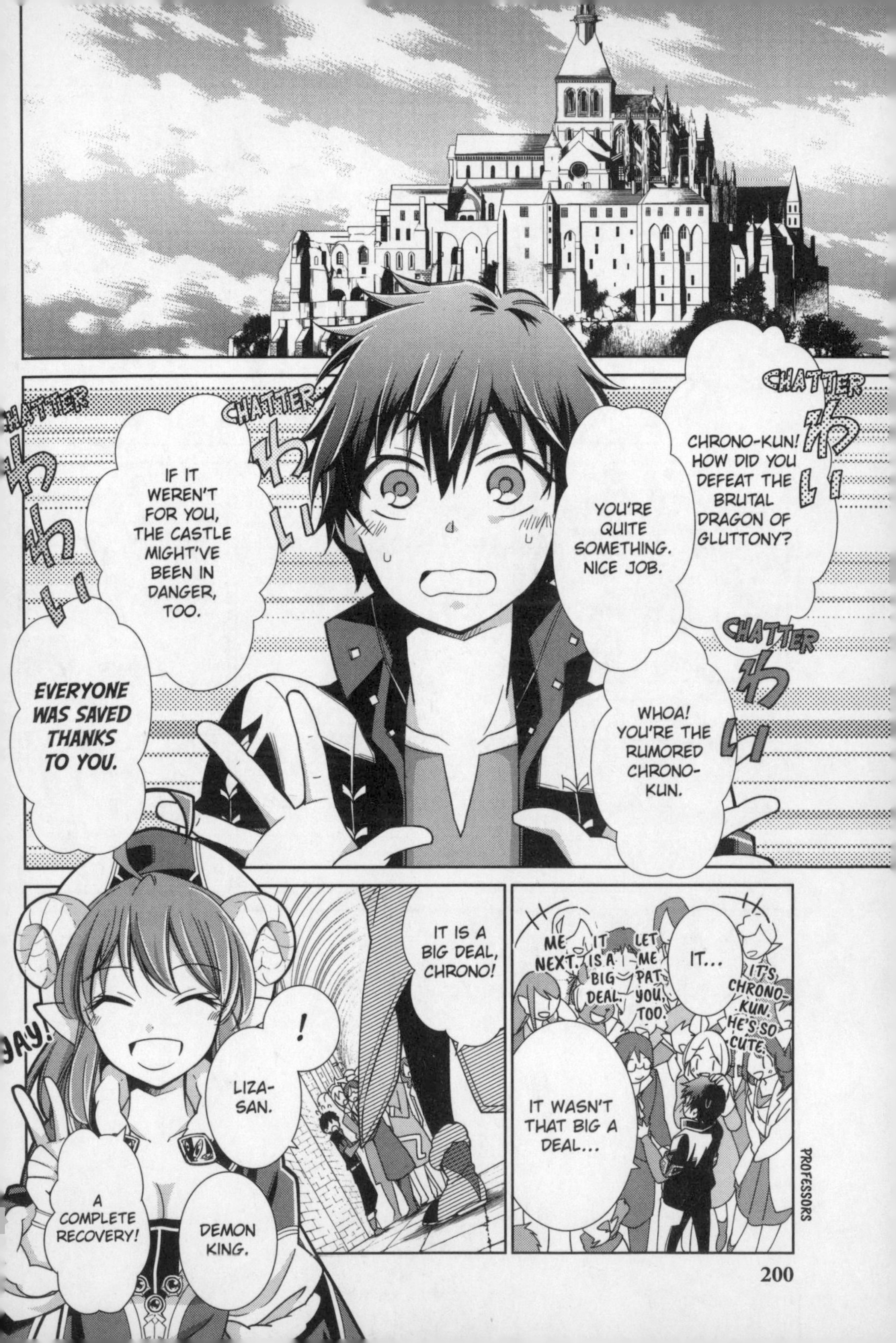

CHATTER
CHRONO-KUN! HOW DID YOU DEFEAT THE BRUTAL DRAGON OF GLUTTONY?
YOU'RE QUITE SOMETHING. NICE JOB.
CHATTER
WHOA! YOU'RE THE RUMORED CHRONO-KUN.
CHATTER
IF IT WEREN'T FOR YOU, THE CASTLE MIGHT'VE BEEN IN DANGER, TOO.
CHATTER
EVERYONE WAS SAVED THANKS TO YOU.
IT'S CHRONO-KUN. HE'S SO CUTE.
IT...
LET ME PAT YOU, TOO.
IT IS A BIG DEAL.
ME NEXT.
IT WASN'T THAT BIG A DEAL...
PROFESSORS
IT IS A BIG DEAL, CHRONO!
!
LIZA-SAN.
YAY!
DEMON KING.
A COMPLETE RECOVERY!

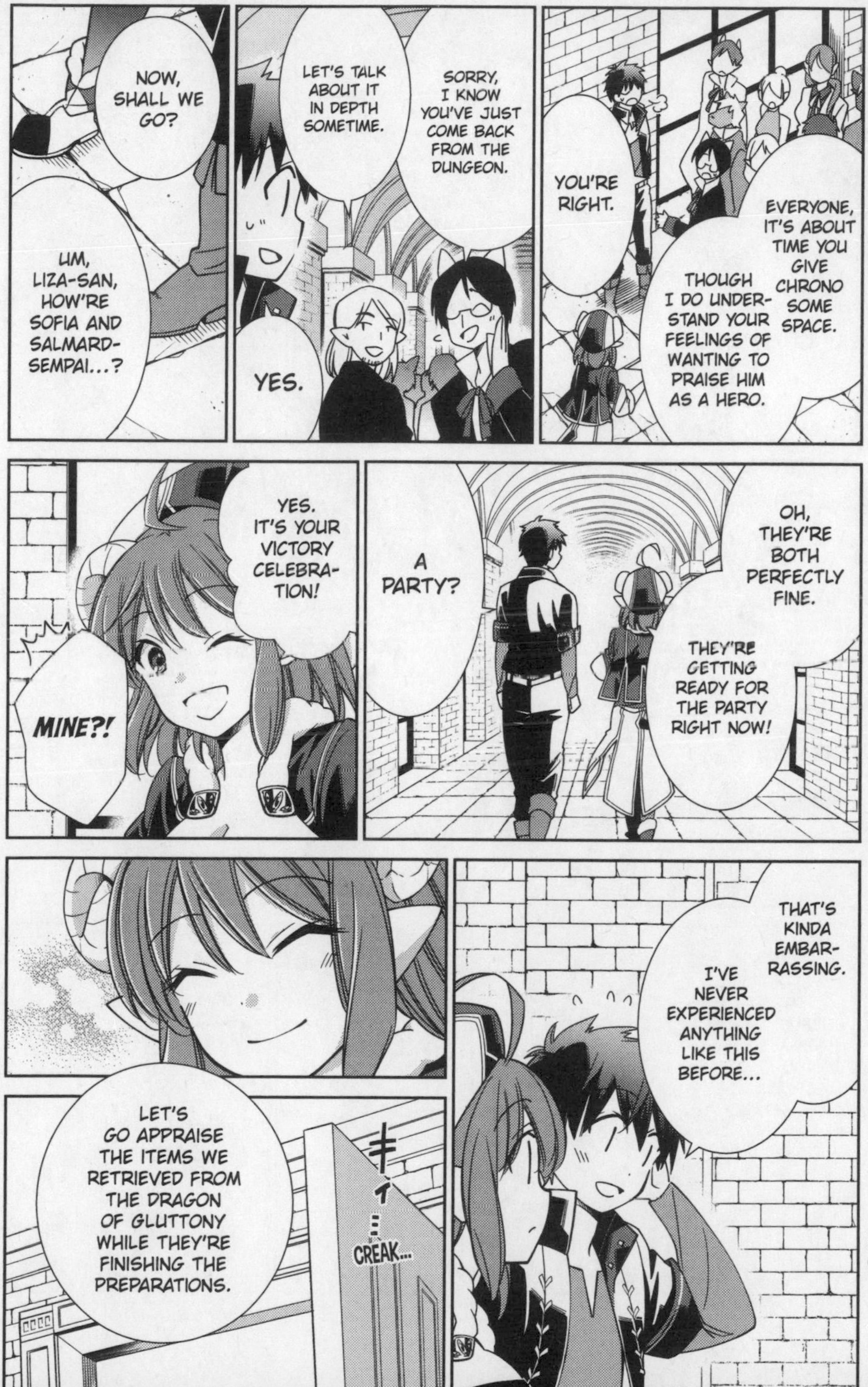

EVERYONE, IT'S ABOUT TIME YOU GIVE CHRONO SOME SPACE.
THOUGH I DO UNDER-STAND YOUR FEELINGS OF WANTING TO PRAISE HIM AS A HERO.
YOU'RE RIGHT.
SORRY, I KNOW YOU'VE JUST COME BACK FROM THE DUNGEON.
LET'S TALK ABOUT IT IN DEPTH SOMETIME.
YES.
NOW, SHALL WE GO?
UM, LIZA-SAN, HOW'RE SOFIA AND SALMARD-SEMPAI...?
OH, THEY'RE BOTH PERFECTLY FINE.
THEY'RE GETTING READY FOR THE PARTY RIGHT NOW!
A PARTY?
YES. IT'S YOUR VICTORY CELEBRA-TION!
MINE?!
THAT'S KINDA EMBAR-RASSING.
I'VE NEVER EXPERIENCED ANYTHING LIKE THIS BEFORE...
LET'S GO APPRAISE THE ITEMS WE RETRIEVED FROM THE DRAGON OF GLUTTONY WHILE THEY'RE FINISHING THE PREPARATIONS.
CREAK...

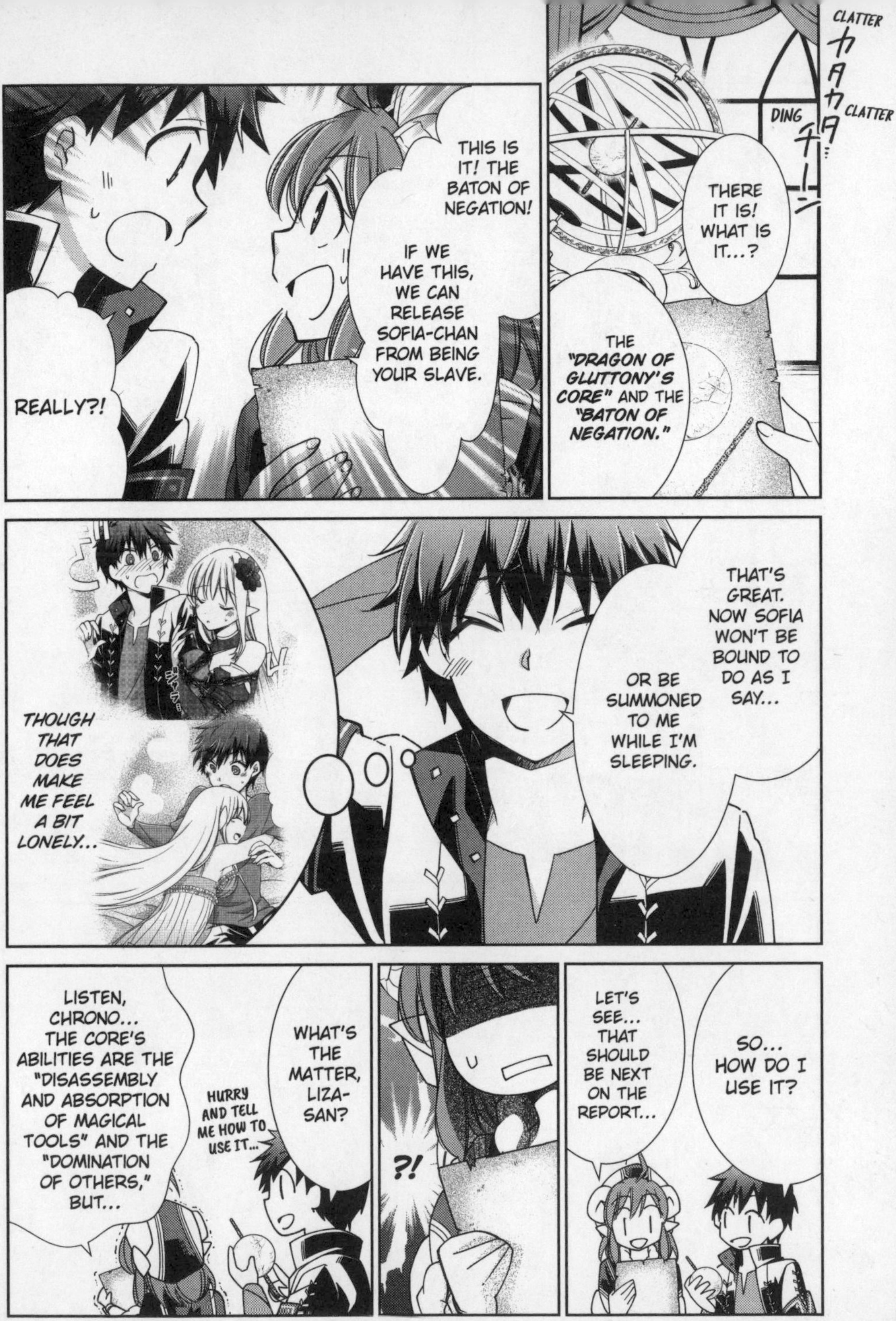
CLATTER
カタカタ
CLATTER
DING
チーン
THERE IT IS! WHAT IS IT...?
THE *"DRAGON OF GLUTTONY'S CORE"* AND THE *"BATON OF NEGATION."*
THIS IS IT! THE BATON OF NEGATION!
IF WE HAVE THIS, WE CAN RELEASE SOFIA-CHAN FROM BEING YOUR SLAVE.
REALLY?!
THAT'S GREAT. NOW SOFIA WON'T BE BOUND TO DO AS I SAY...
OR BE SUMMONED TO ME WHILE I'M SLEEPING.
THOUGH THAT DOES MAKE ME FEEL A BIT LONELY...
SO... HOW DO I USE IT?
LET'S SEE... THAT SHOULD BE NEXT ON THE REPORT...
?!
WHAT'S THE MATTER, LIZA-SAN?
HURRY AND TELL ME HOW TO USE IT...
LISTEN, CHRONO... THE CORE'S ABILITIES ARE THE "DISASSEMBLY AND ABSORPTION OF MAGICAL TOOLS" AND THE "DOMINATION OF OTHERS," BUT...

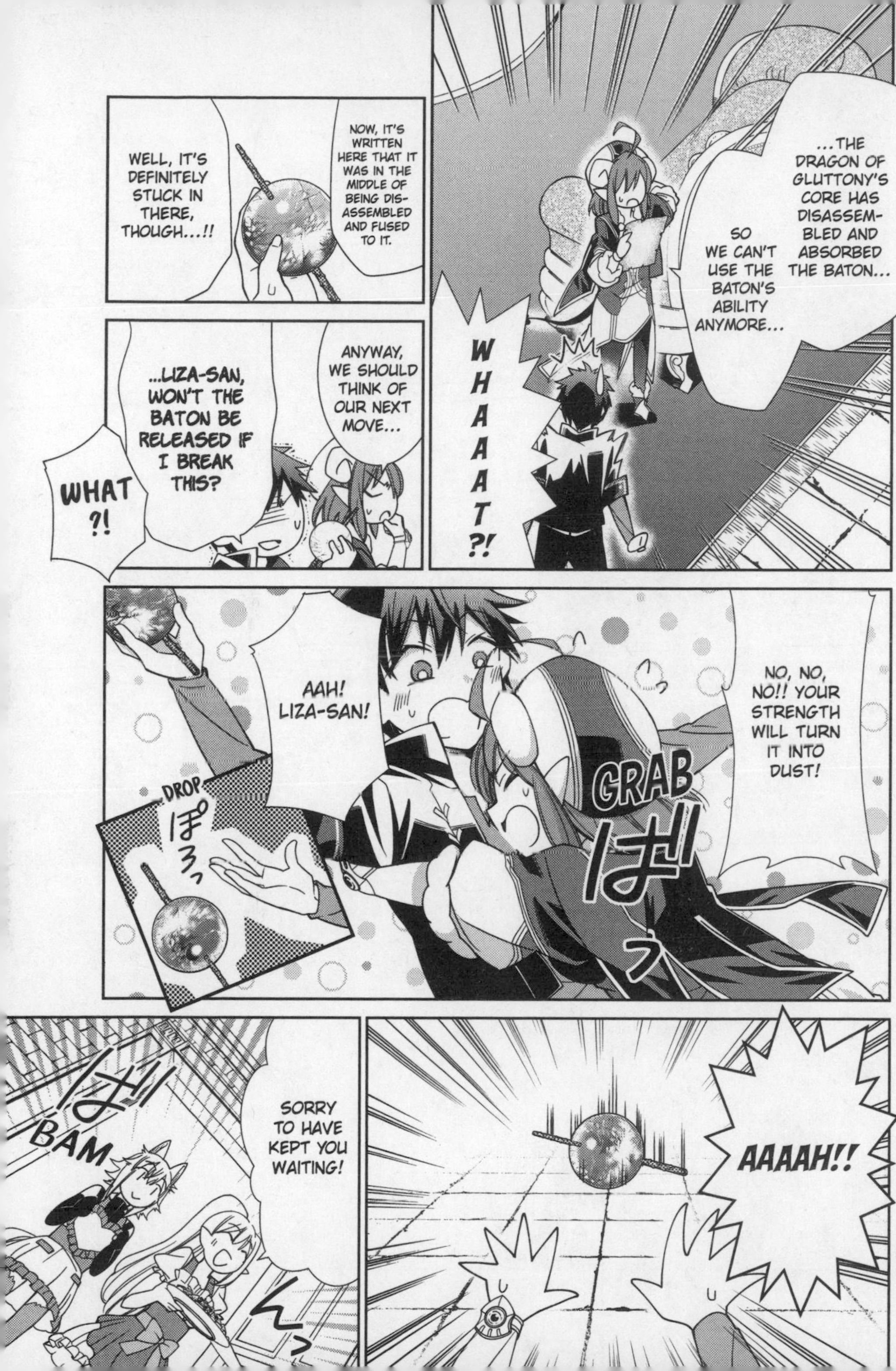
...THE DRAGON OF GLUTTONY'S CORE HAS DISASSEMBLED AND ABSORBED THE BATON...
SO WE CAN'T USE THE BATON'S ABILITY ANYMORE...
WHAAAAT?!
NOW, IT'S WRITTEN HERE THAT IT WAS IN THE MIDDLE OF BEING DISASSEMBLED AND FUSED TO IT.
WELL, IT'S DEFINITELY STUCK IN THERE, THOUGH...!!
ANYWAY, WE SHOULD THINK OF OUR NEXT MOVE...
...LIZA-SAN, WON'T THE BATON BE RELEASED IF I BREAK THIS?
WHAT ?!
NO, NO, NO!! YOUR STRENGTH WILL TURN IT INTO DUST!
GRAB
AAH! LIZA-SAN!
DROP
ぽろっ
AAAAH!!
SORRY TO HAVE KEPT YOU WAITING!
BAM

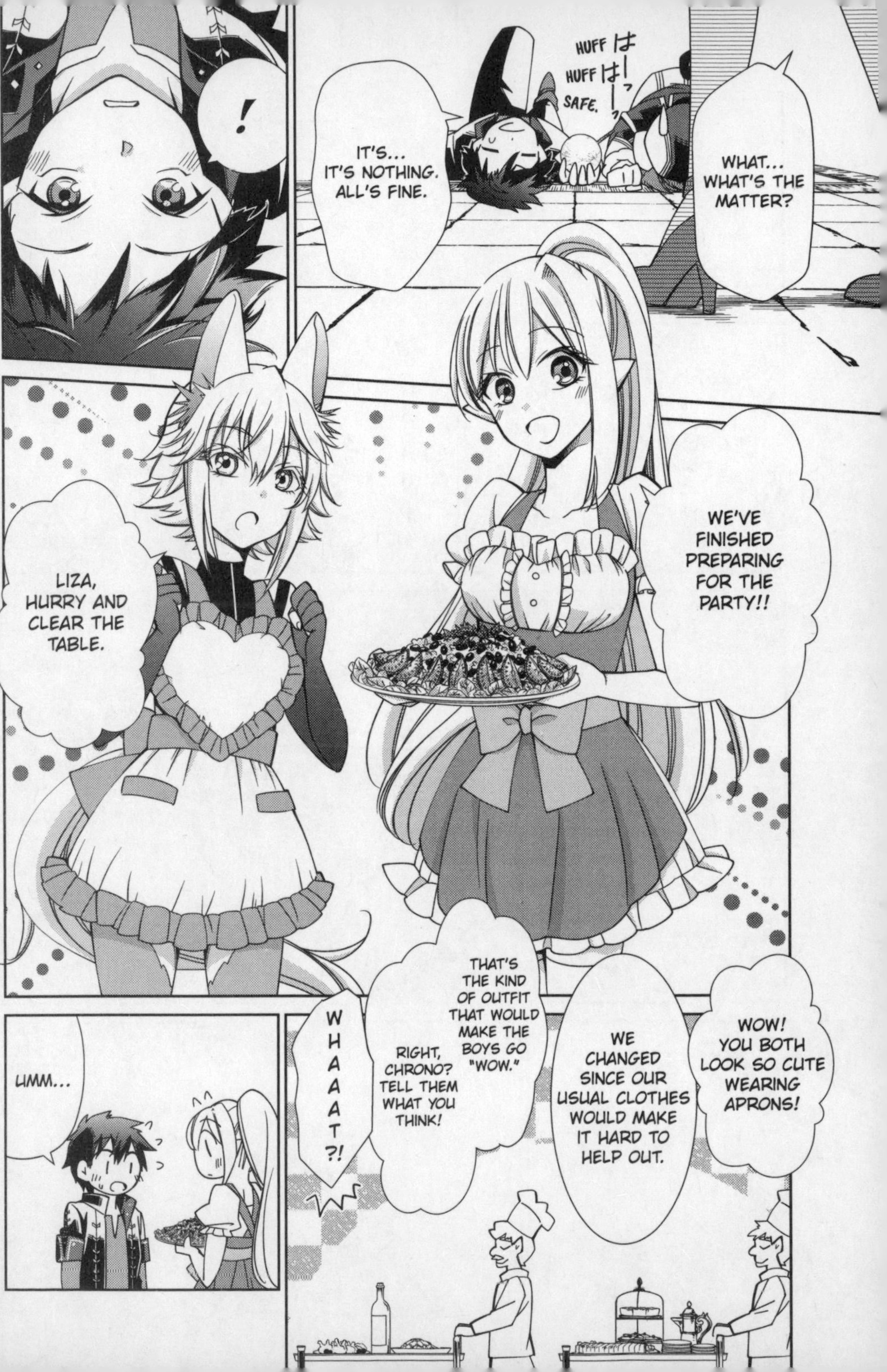
WHAT... WHAT'S THE MATTER?
HUFF
HUFF
SAFE.
IT'S... IT'S NOTHING. ALL'S FINE.
!
WE'VE FINISHED PREPARING FOR THE PARTY!!
LIZA, HURRY AND CLEAR THE TABLE.
WOW! YOU BOTH LOOK SO CUTE WEARING APRONS!
WE CHANGED SINCE OUR USUAL CLOTHES WOULD MAKE IT HARD TO HELP OUT.
THAT'S THE KIND OF OUTFIT THAT WOULD MAKE THE BOYS GO "WOW."
RIGHT, CHRONO? TELL THEM WHAT YOU THINK!
WHAAAT?!
UMM...

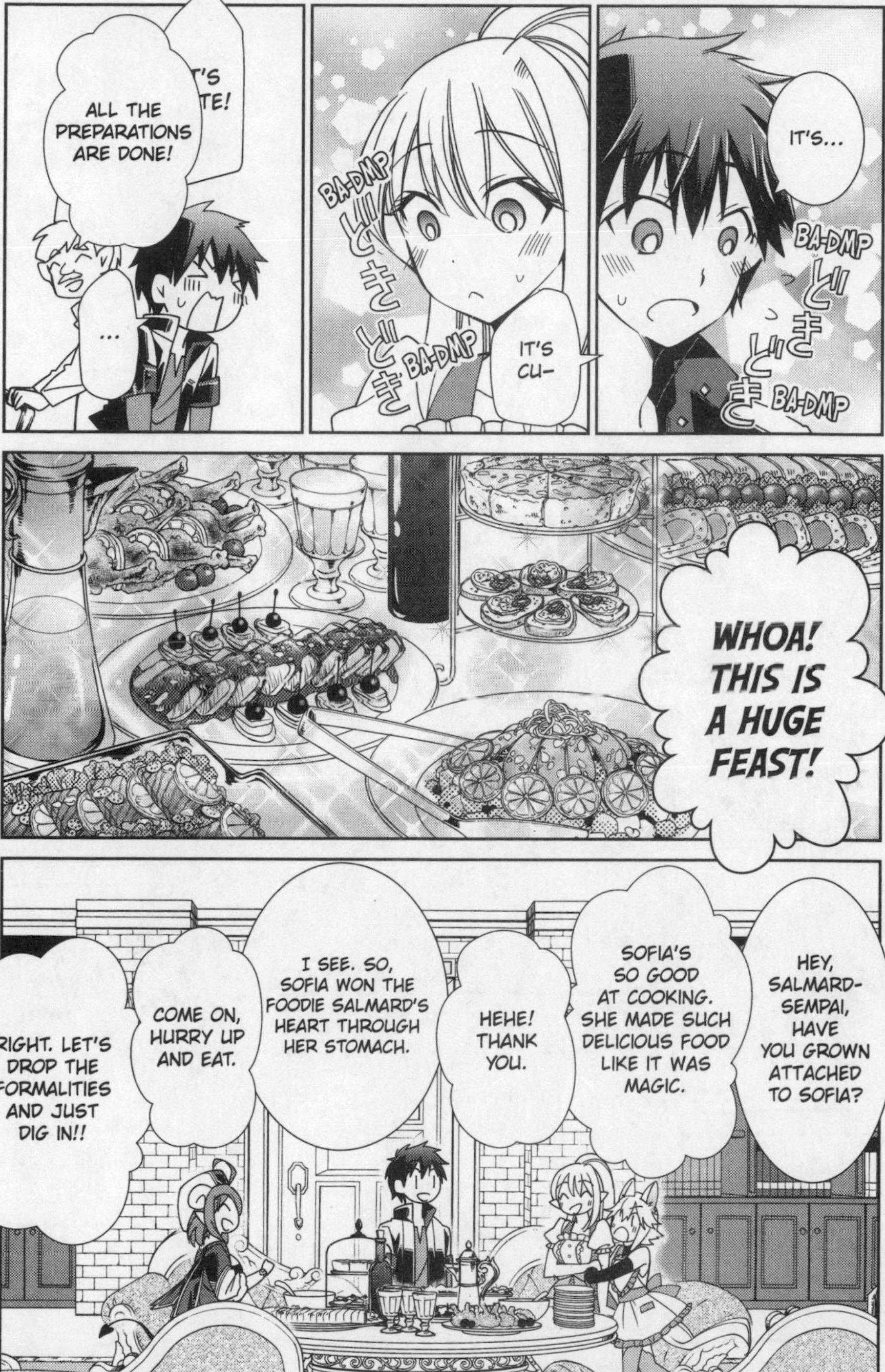
IT'S...
BA-DMP どきどき BA-DMP
BA-DMP どきどき BA-DMP
IT'S CU–
ALL THE PREPARATIONS ARE DONE!
...
WHOA! THIS IS A HUGE FEAST!
HEY, SALMARD-SEMPAI, HAVE YOU GROWN ATTACHED TO SOFIA?
SOFIA'S SO GOOD AT COOKING. SHE MADE SUCH DELICIOUS FOOD LIKE IT WAS MAGIC.
HEHE! THANK YOU.
I SEE. SO, SOFIA WON THE FOODIE SALMARD'S HEART THROUGH HER STOMACH.
COME ON, HURRY UP AND EAT.
RIGHT. LET'S DROP THE FORMALITIES AND JUST DIG IN!!

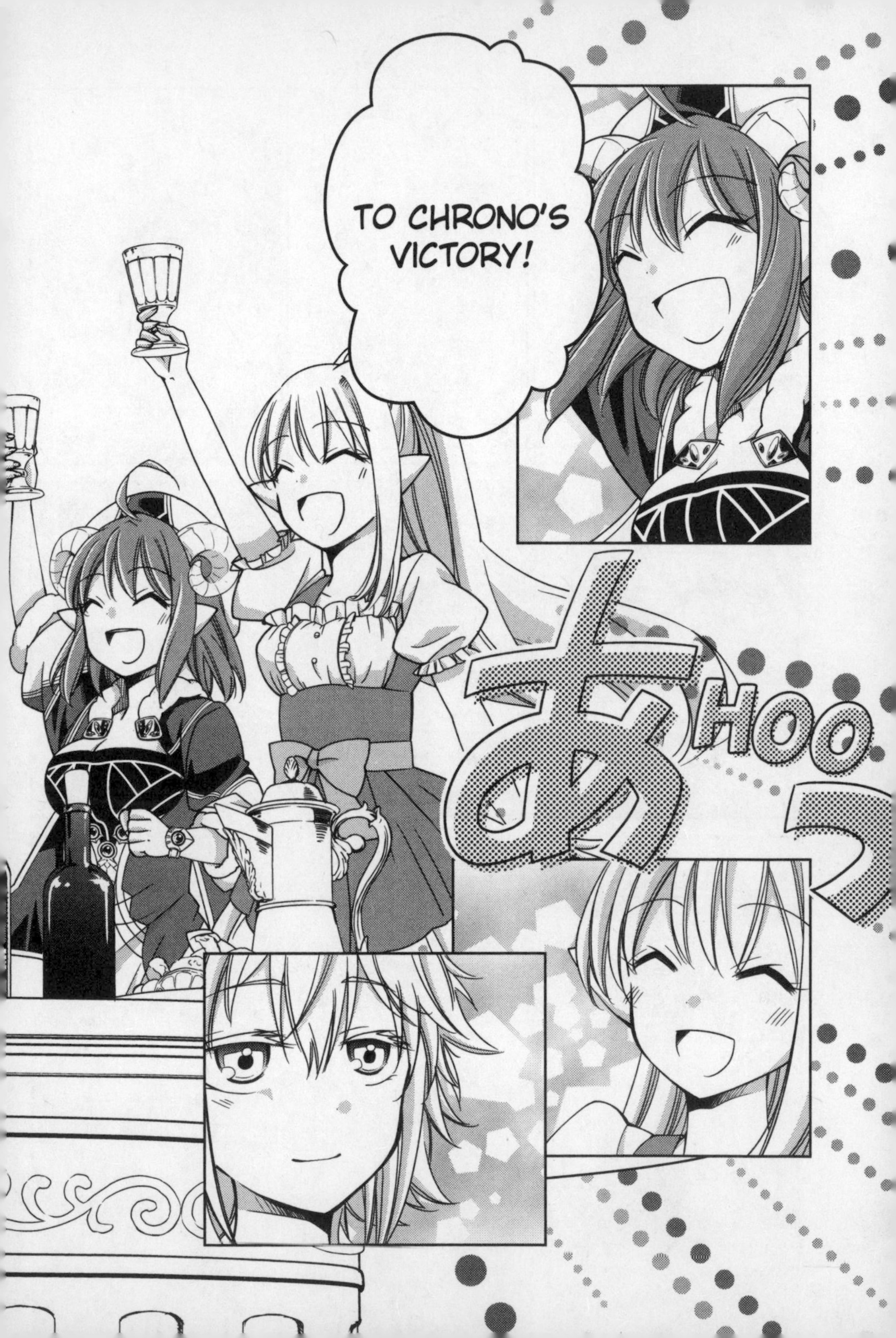
TO CHRONO'S VICTORY!
HOO

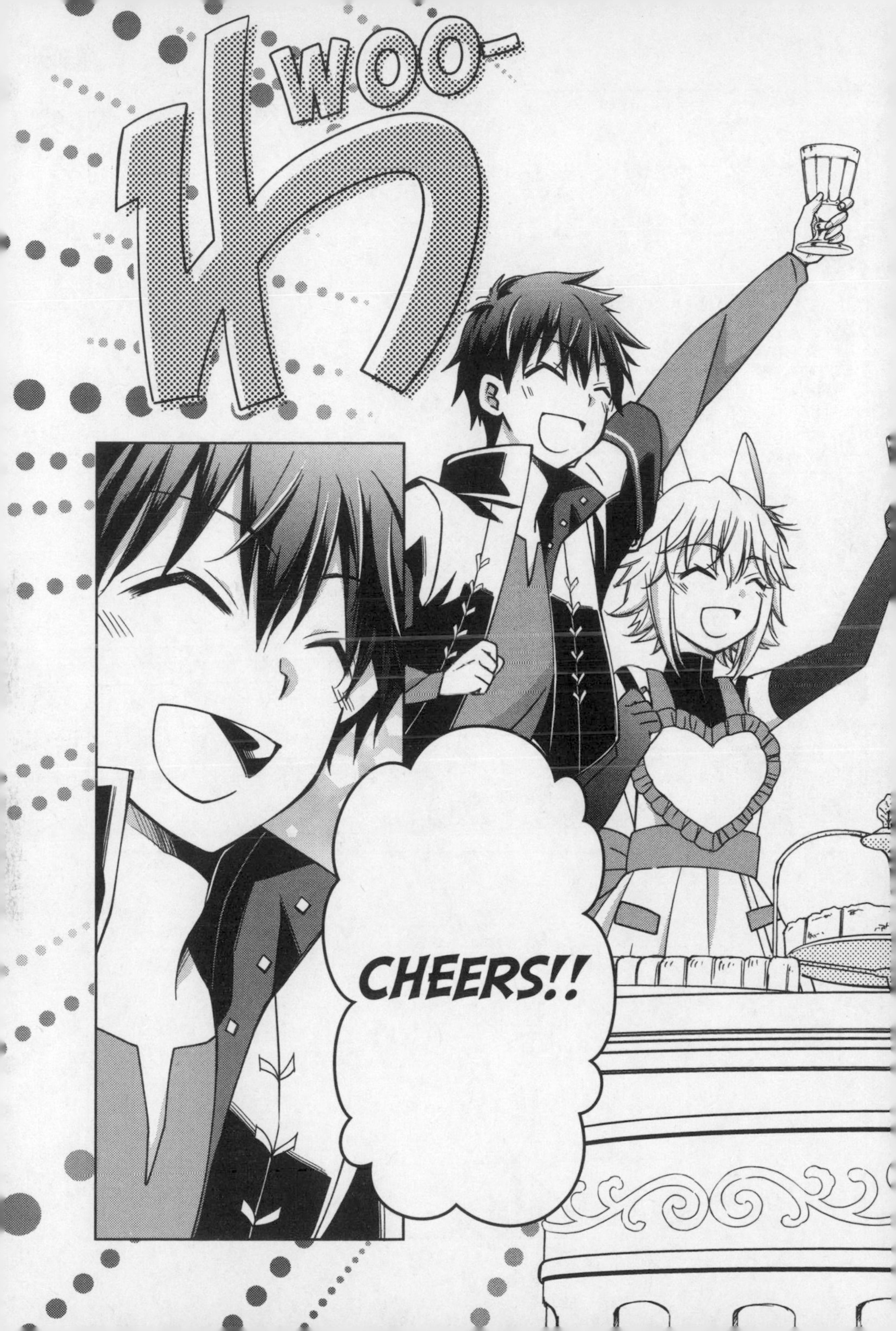
WOO-HOO
CHEERS!!

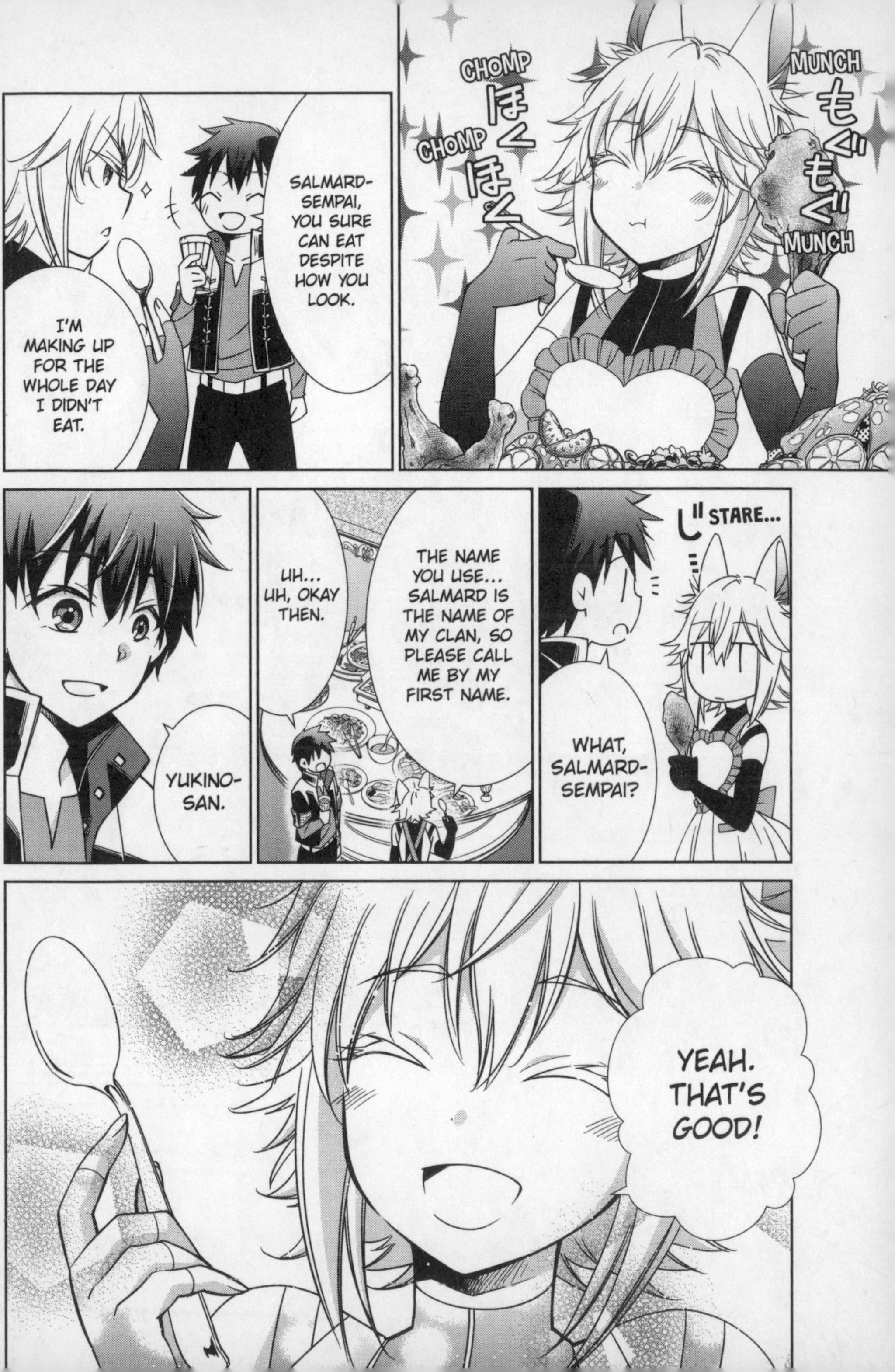
MUNCH
もぐもぐ
MUNCH
CHOMP
ほくほく
CHOMP
SALMARD-SEMPAI, YOU SURE CAN EAT DESPITE HOW YOU LOOK.
I'M MAKING UP FOR THE WHOLE DAY I DIDN'T EAT.
じー
STARE...
WHAT, SALMARD-SEMPAI?
THE NAME YOU USE... SALMARD IS THE NAME OF MY CLAN, SO PLEASE CALL ME BY MY FIRST NAME.
UH... UH, OKAY THEN.
YUKINO-SAN.
YEAH. THAT'S GOOD!

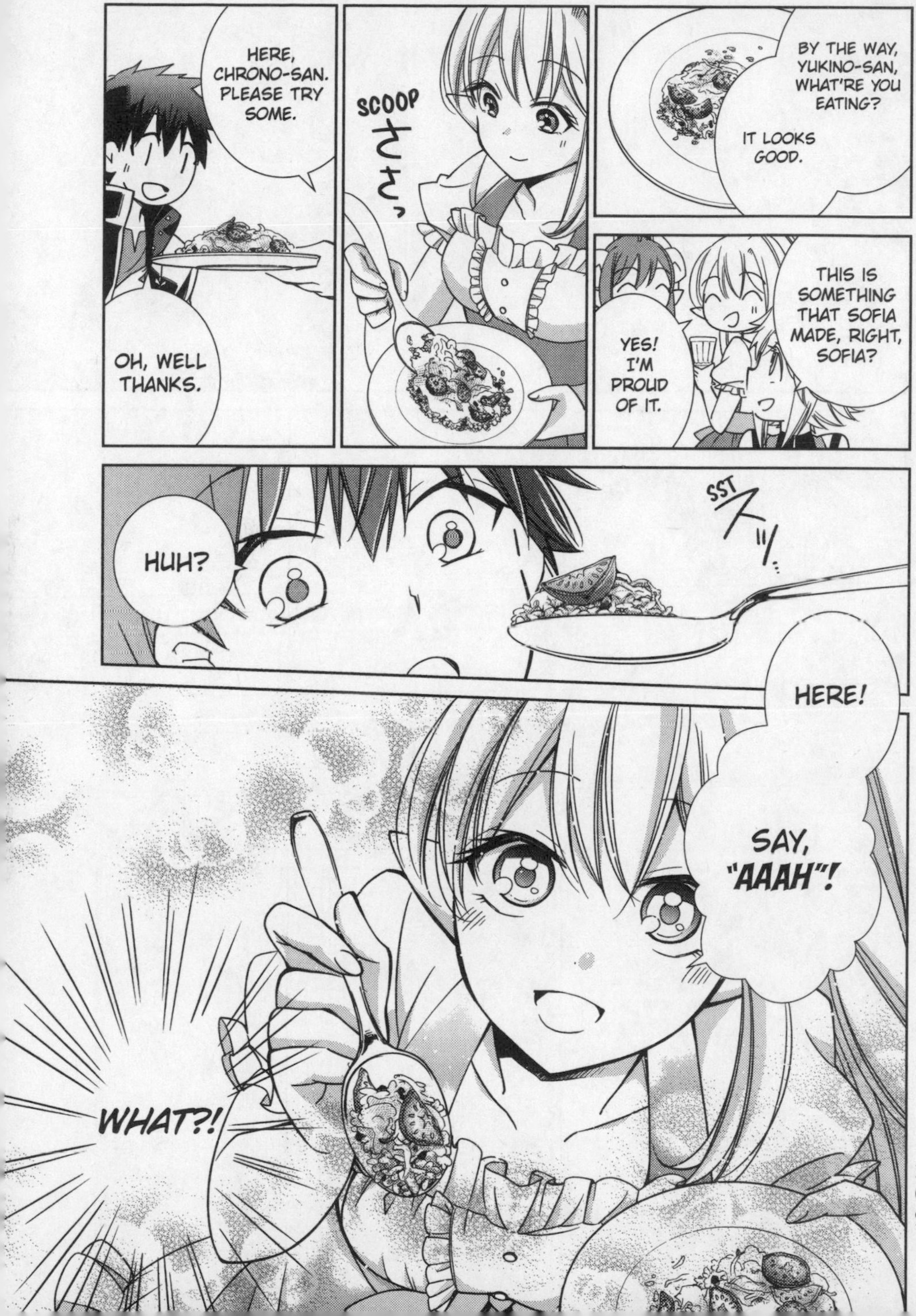
BY THE WAY, YUKINO-SAN, WHAT'RE YOU EATING?
IT LOOKS GOOD.
THIS IS SOMETHING THAT SOFIA MADE, RIGHT, SOFIA?
YES! I'M PROUD OF IT.
SCOOP
さささっ
HERE, CHRONO-SAN. PLEASE TRY SOME.
OH, WELL THANKS.
SST
スッ…
HUH?
HERE!
SAY, "AAAH"!
WHAT?!

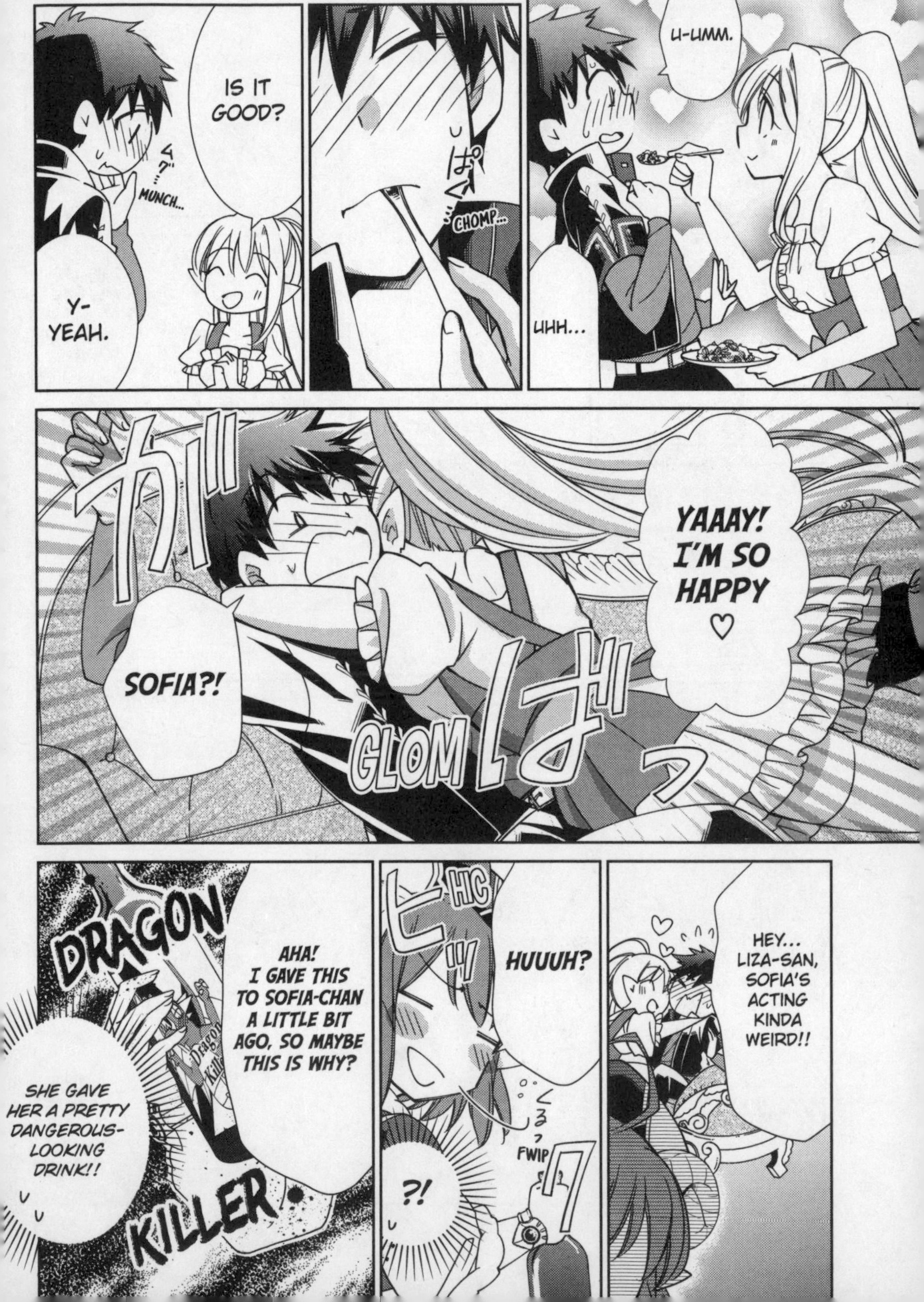
U-UMM.
UHH...
CHOMP...
IS IT GOOD?
MUNCH...
Y-YEAH.
YAAAY! I'M SO HAPPY ♡
GLOM
SOFIA?!
HEY... LIZA-SAN, SOFIA'S ACTING KINDA WEIRD!!
HC
HUUUH?
FWIP
?!
AHA! I GAVE THIS TO SOFIA-CHAN A LITTLE BIT AGO, SO MAYBE THIS IS WHY?
DRAGON KILLER
SHE GAVE HER A PRETTY DANGEROUS-LOOKING DRINK!!

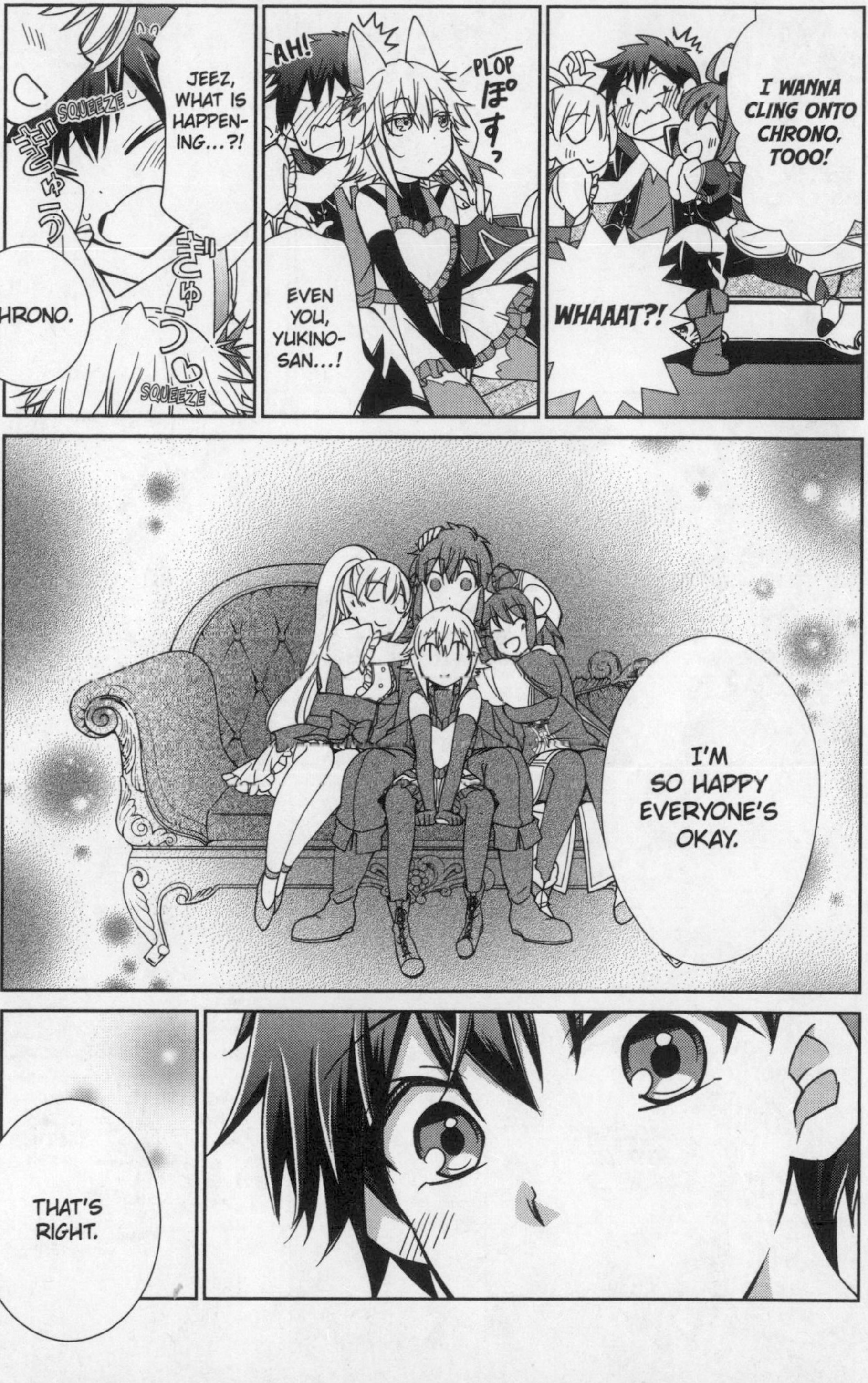
I WANNA CLING ONTO CHRONO, TOOO!
WHAAAT?!
AH!
PLOP
ぽすっ
EVEN YOU, YUKINO-SAN...!
JEEZ, WHAT IS HAPPENING...?!
SQUEEZE
ぎゅう
CHRONO.
ぎゅーっ
SQUEEZE
I'M SO HAPPY EVERYONE'S OKAY.
THAT'S RIGHT.

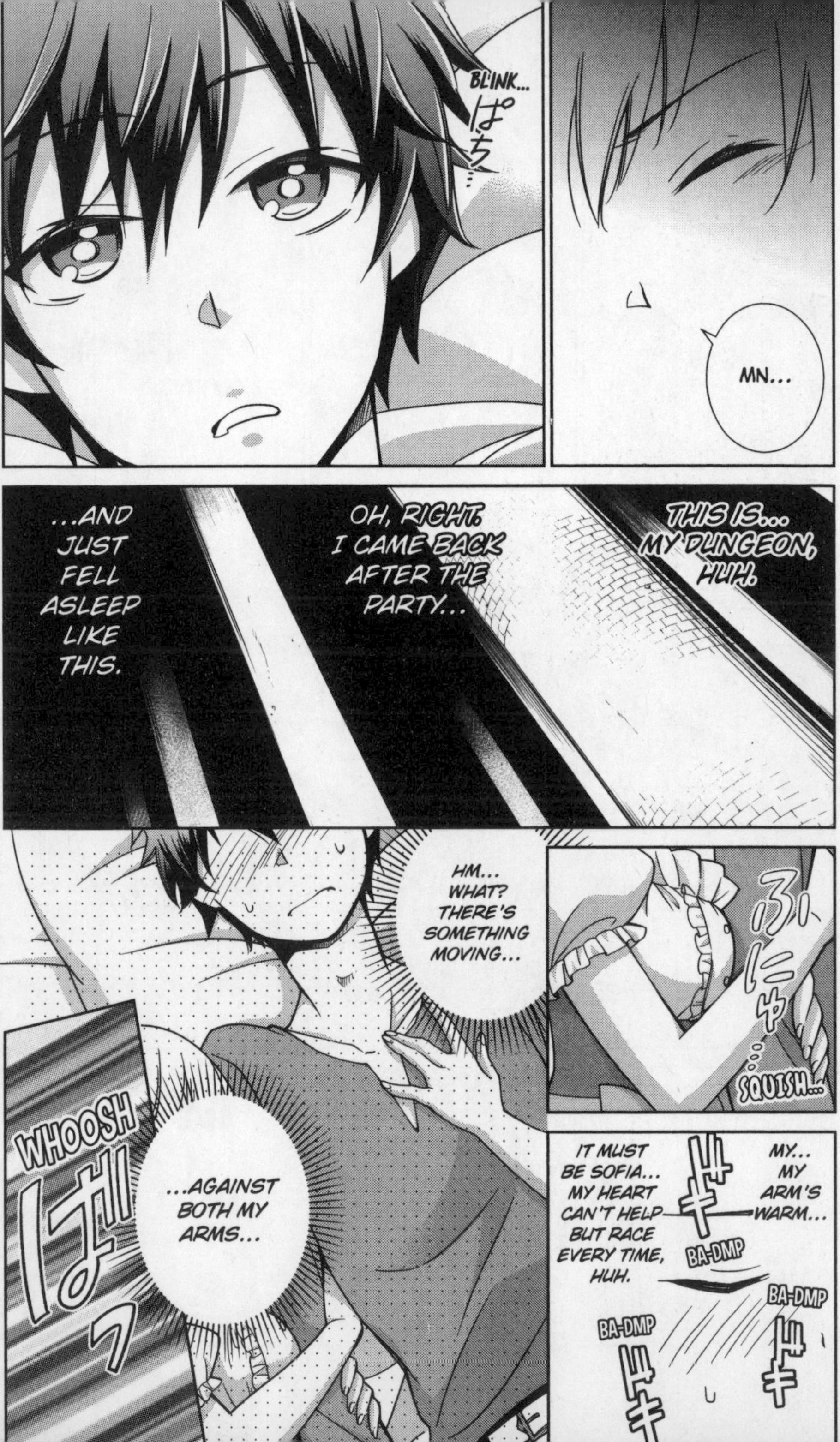
MN...
BLINK...
ぱち...
THIS IS... MY DUNGEON, HUH.
OH, RIGHT. I CAME BACK AFTER THE PARTY...
...AND JUST FELL ASLEEP LIKE THIS.
ふにゅ...
SQUISH...
MY... MY ARM'S WARM...
IT MUST BE SOFIA... MY HEART CAN'T HELP BUT RACE EVERY TIME, HUH.
ドキ
BA-DMP
ドキ
BA-DMP
ドキ
BA-DMP
HM... WHAT? THERE'S SOMETHING MOVING...
WHOOSH
ばっ
...AGAINST BOTH MY ARMS...

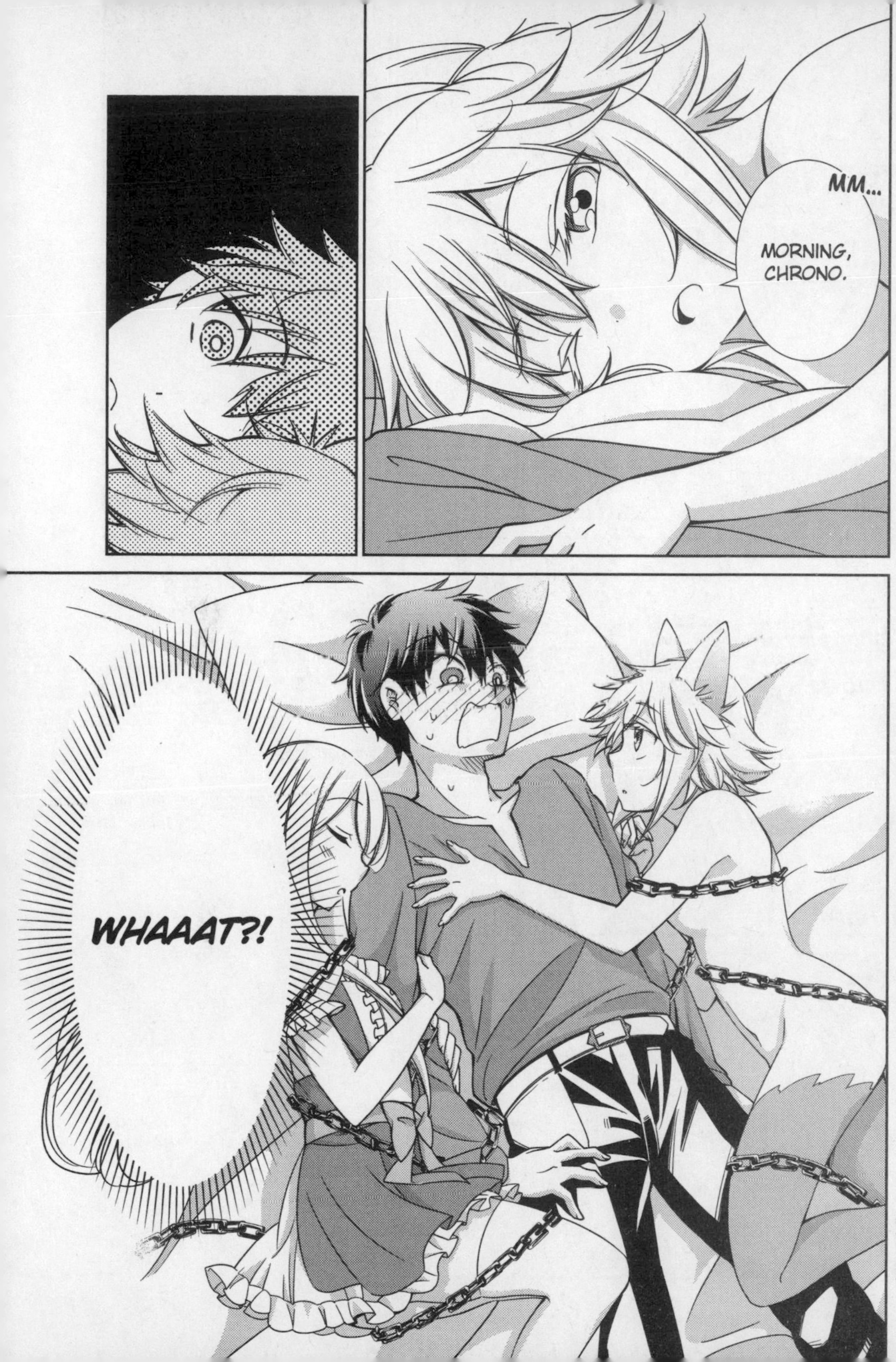
MM...
MORNING, CHRONO.
WHAAAT?!

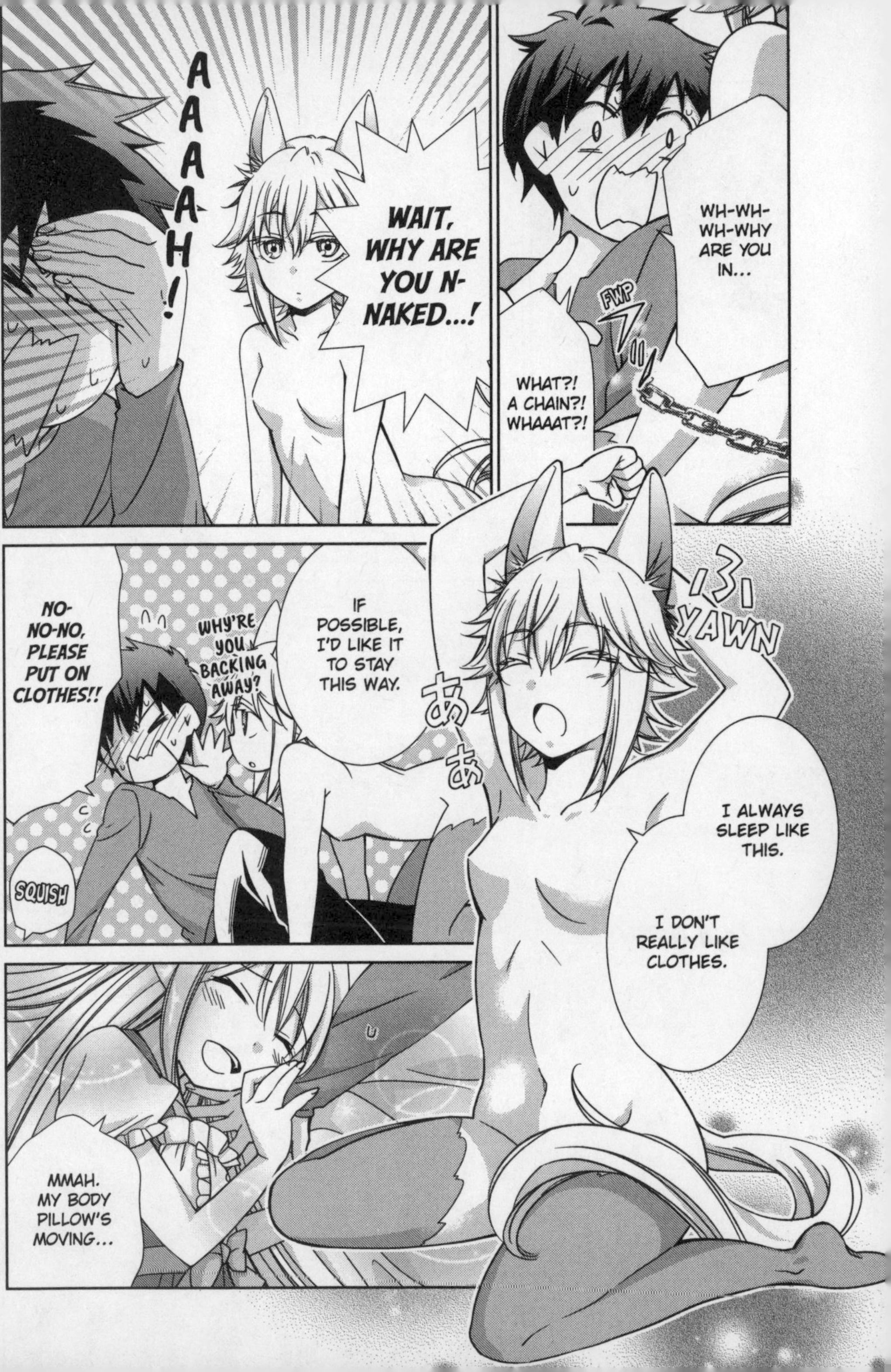
WH-WH-WH-WHY ARE YOU IN…
FWP
WHAT?! A CHAIN?! WHAAAT?!
AAAAAH!
WAIT, WHY ARE YOU N-NAKED…!
YAWN
ああ
I ALWAYS SLEEP LIKE THIS.
I DON'T REALLY LIKE CLOTHES.
IF POSSIBLE, I'D LIKE IT TO STAY THIS WAY.
WHY'RE YOU BACKING AWAY?
NO-NO-NO, PLEASE PUT ON CLOTHES!!
SQUISH
MMAH. MY BODY PILLOW'S MOVING…

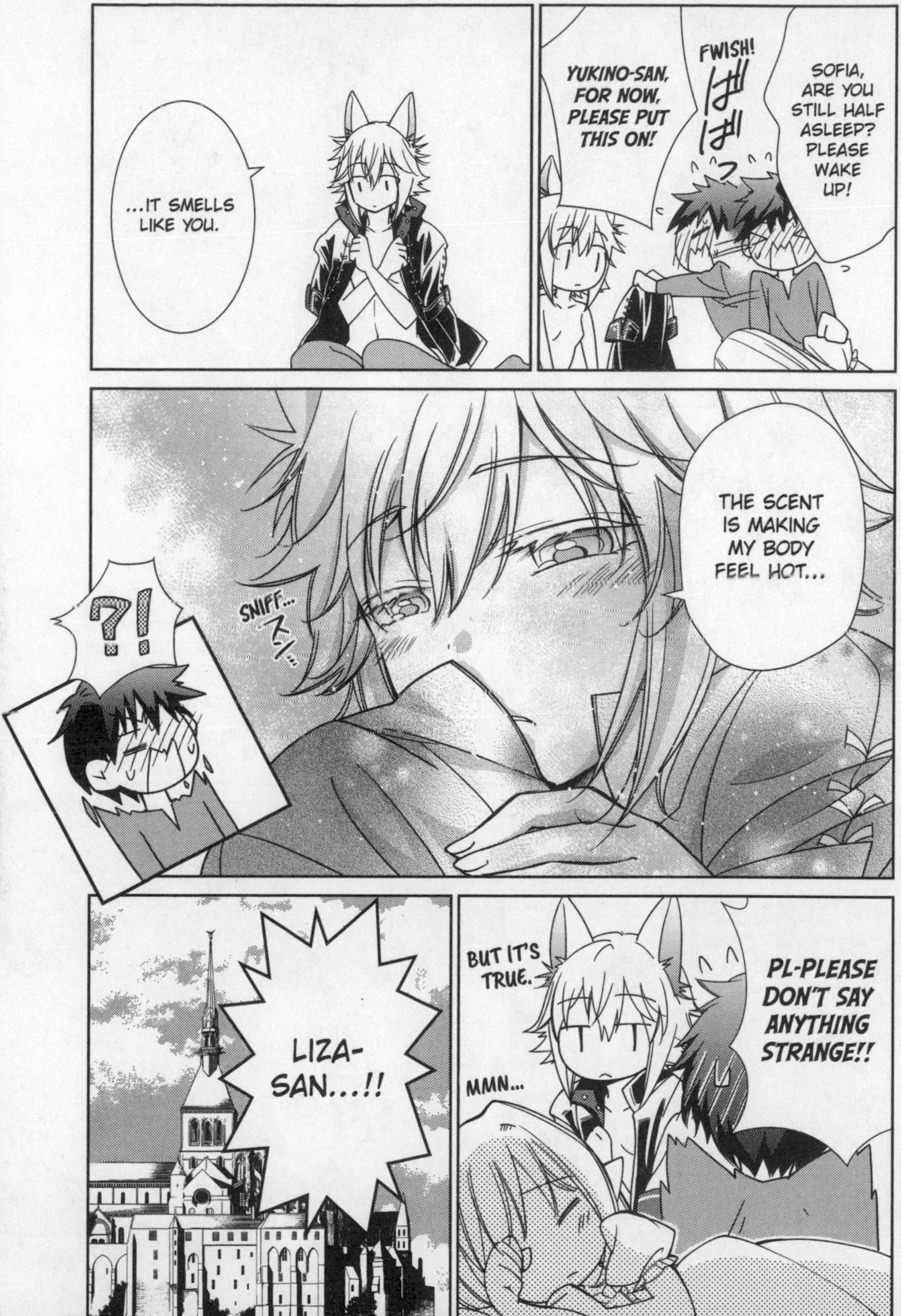
SOFIA, ARE YOU STILL HALF ASLEEP? PLEASE WAKE UP!
FWISH! ばばっ
YUKINO-SAN, FOR NOW, PLEASE PUT THIS ON!
...IT SMELLS LIKE YOU.
THE SCENT IS MAKING MY BODY FEEL HOT...
SNIFF... スン…
?!
PL-PLEASE DON'T SAY ANYTHING STRANGE!!
BUT IT'S TRUE.
MMN...
LIZA-SAN...!!

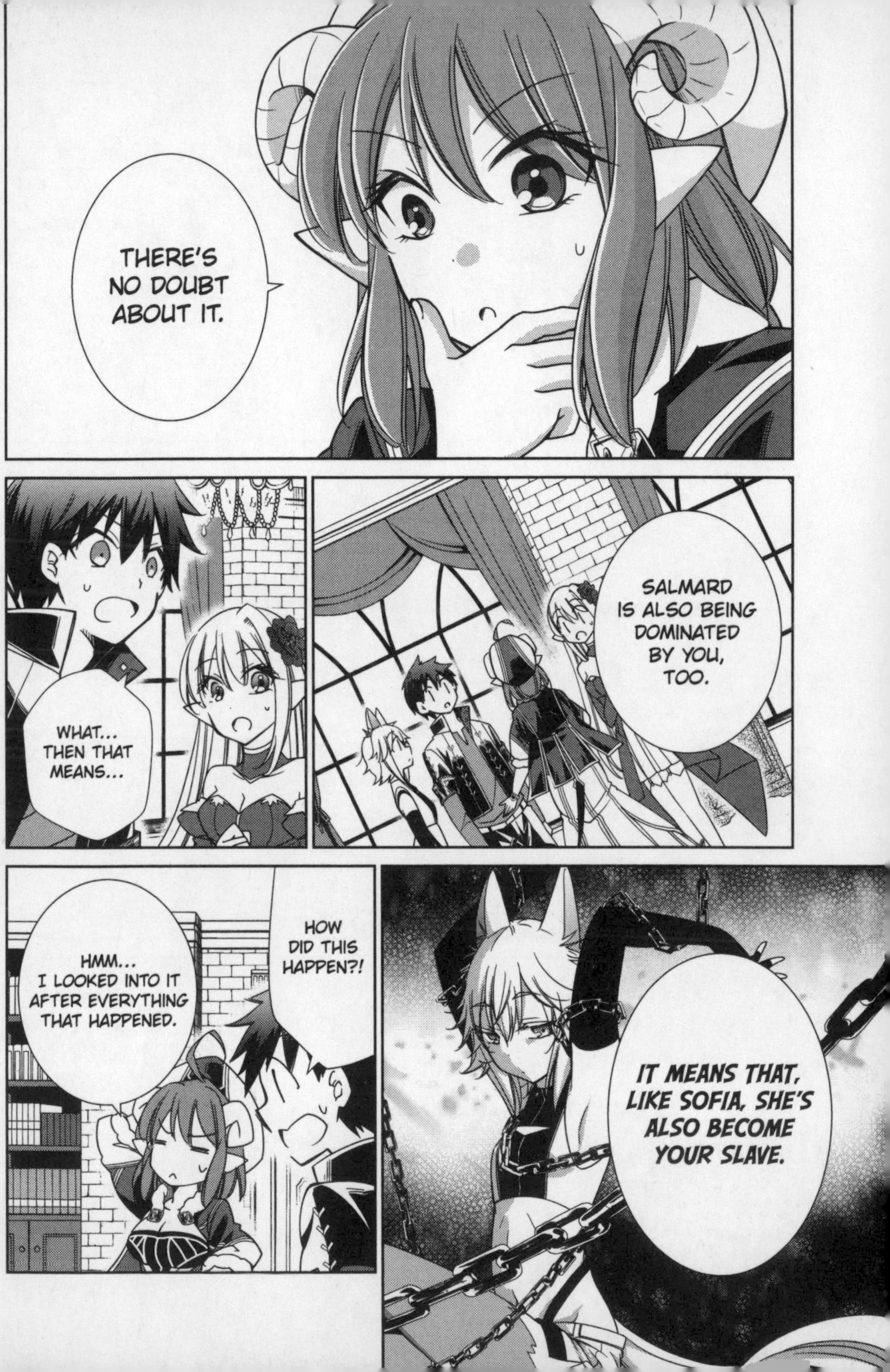
THERE'S NO DOUBT ABOUT IT.
SALMARD IS ALSO BEING DOMINATED BY YOU, TOO.
WHAT... THEN THAT MEANS...
IT MEANS THAT, LIKE SOFIA, SHE'S ALSO BECOME YOUR SLAVE.
HOW DID THIS HAPPEN?!
HMM... I LOOKED INTO IT AFTER EVERYTHING THAT HAPPENED.

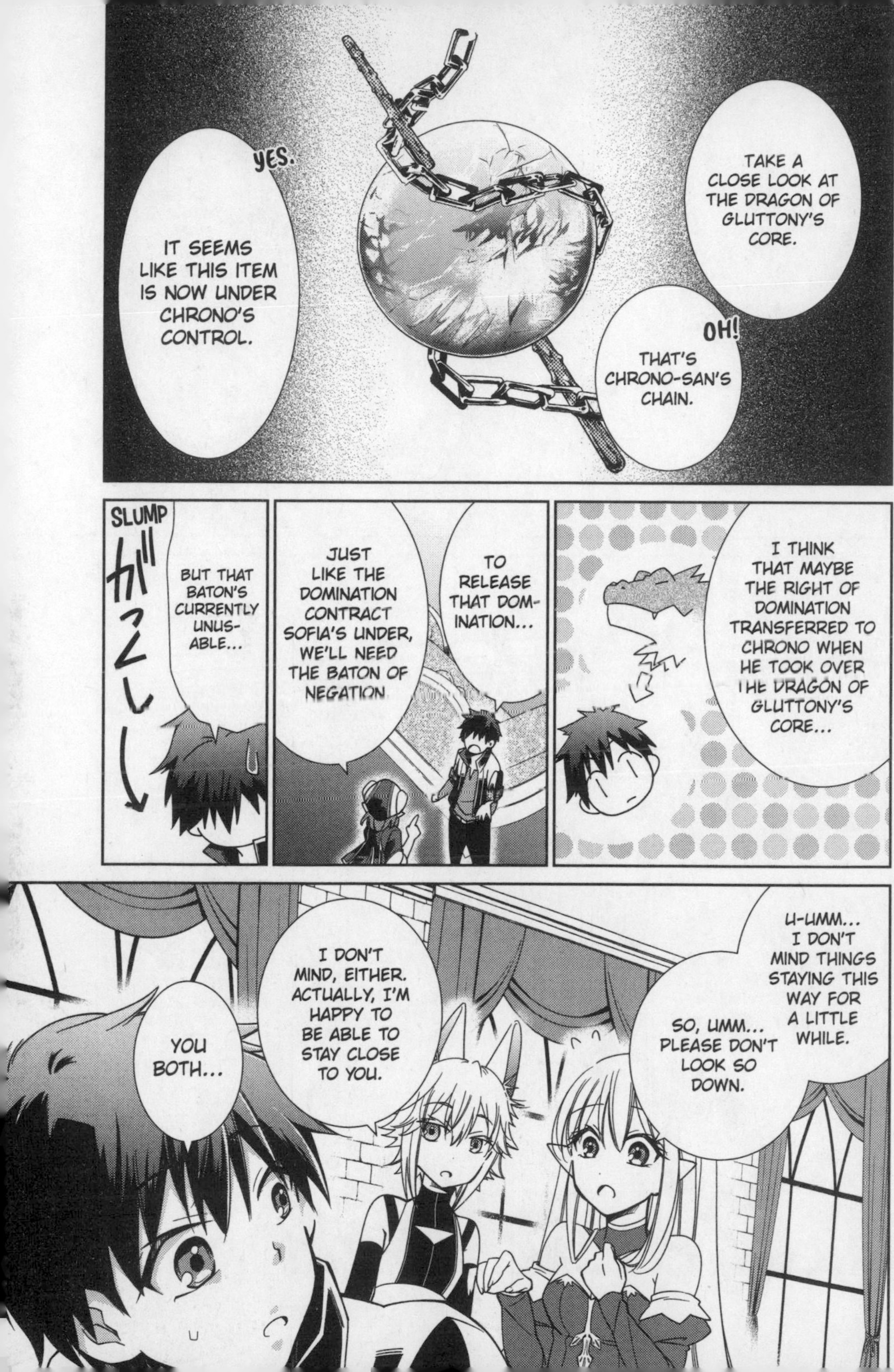
TAKE A CLOSE LOOK AT THE DRAGON OF GLUTTONY'S CORE.
OH!
THAT'S CHRONO-SAN'S CHAIN.
YES.
IT SEEMS LIKE THIS ITEM IS NOW UNDER CHRONO'S CONTROL.
I THINK THAT MAYBE THE RIGHT OF DOMINATION TRANSFERRED TO CHRONO WHEN HE TOOK OVER THE DRAGON OF GLUTTONY'S CORE...
TO RELEASE THAT DOMINATION...
JUST LIKE THE DOMINATION CONTRACT SOFIA'S UNDER, WE'LL NEED THE BATON OF NEGATION.
SLUMP
がっくし
BUT THAT BATON'S CURRENTLY UNUSABLE...
U-UMM... I DON'T MIND THINGS STAYING THIS WAY FOR A LITTLE WHILE.
SO, UMM... PLEASE DON'T LOOK SO DOWN.
I DON'T MIND, EITHER. ACTUALLY, I'M HAPPY TO BE ABLE TO STAY CLOSE TO YOU.
YOU BOTH...

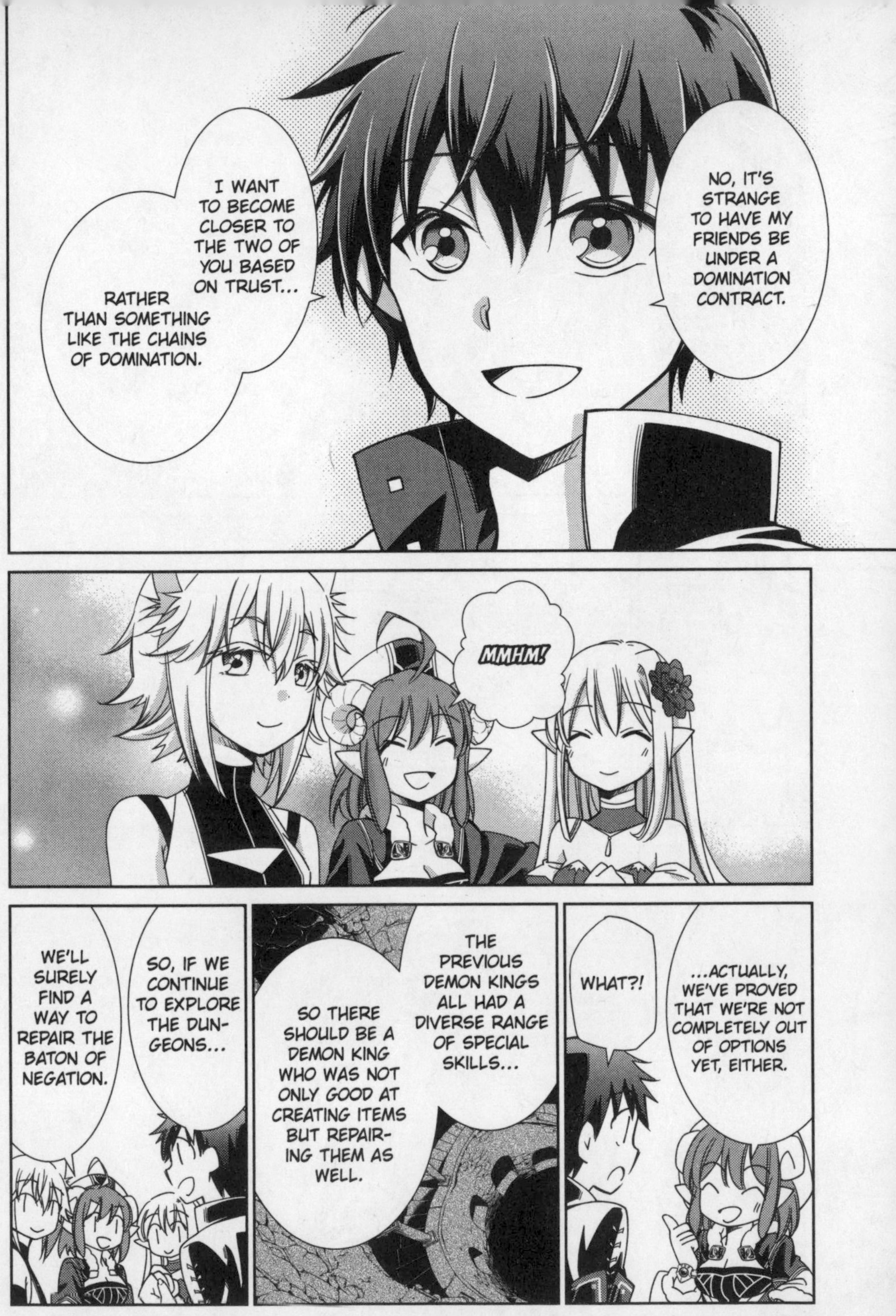
NO, IT'S STRANGE TO HAVE MY FRIENDS BE UNDER A DOMINATION CONTRACT.
I WANT TO BECOME CLOSER TO THE TWO OF YOU BASED ON TRUST...
RATHER THAN SOMETHING LIKE THE CHAINS OF DOMINATION.
MMHM!
...ACTUALLY, WE'VE PROVED THAT WE'RE NOT COMPLETELY OUT OF OPTIONS YET, EITHER.
WHAT?!
THE PREVIOUS DEMON KINGS ALL HAD A DIVERSE RANGE OF SPECIAL SKILLS...
SO THERE SHOULD BE A DEMON KING WHO WAS NOT ONLY GOOD AT CREATING ITEMS BUT REPAIR-ING THEM AS WELL.
SO, IF WE CONTINUE TO EXPLORE THE DUN-GEONS...
WE'LL SURELY FIND A WAY TO REPAIR THE BATON OF NEGATION.

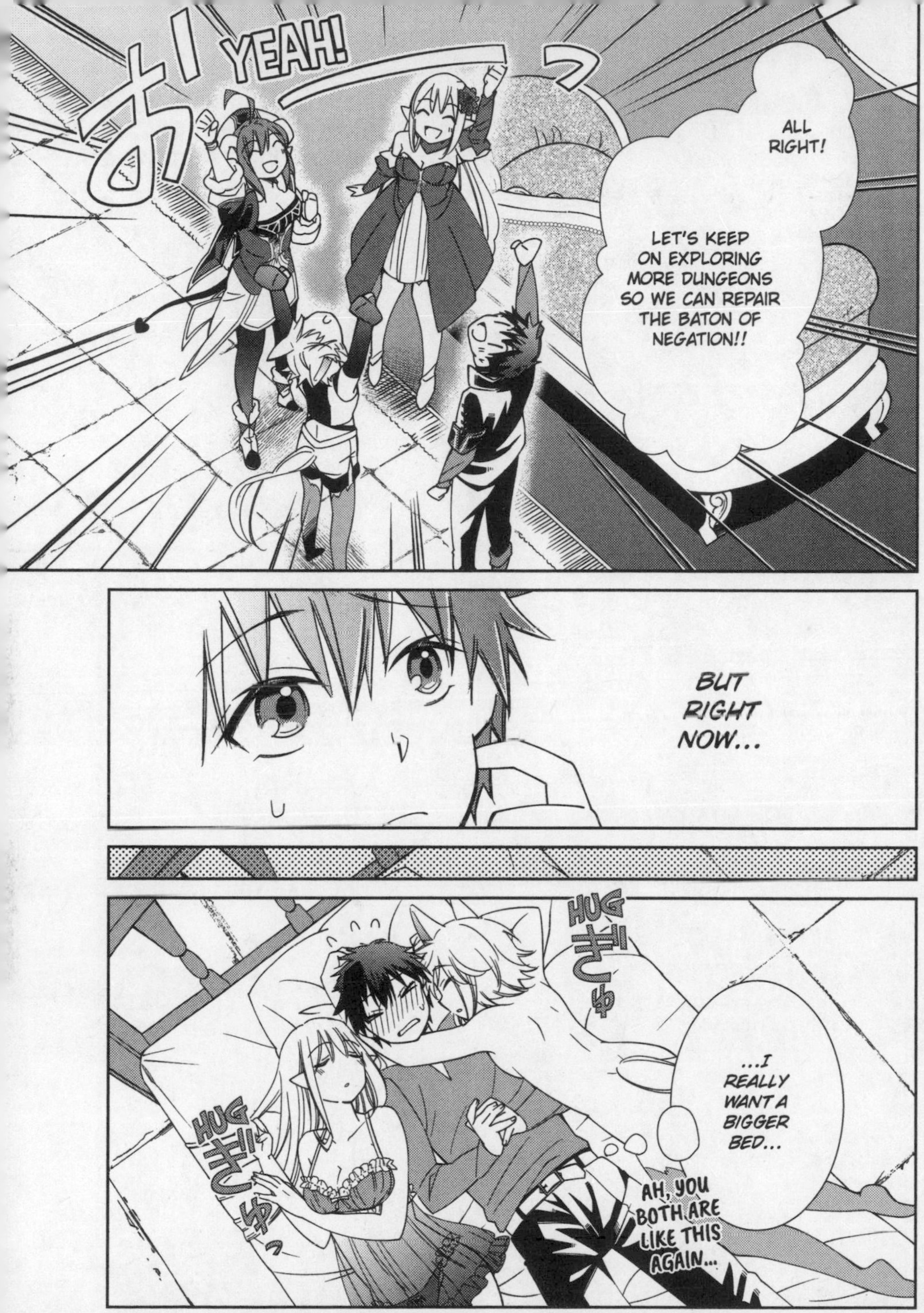
ALL RIGHT!
LET'S KEEP ON EXPLORING MORE DUNGEONS SO WE CAN REPAIR THE BATON OF NEGATION!!
あーっ YEAH!
BUT RIGHT NOW...
HUG ぎゅ
...I REALLY WANT A BIGGER BED...
HUG ぎゅっ
AH, YOU BOTH ARE LIKE THIS AGAIN...

The Hero Life of a (Self-Proclaimed) "Mediocre" Demon! 1 / End

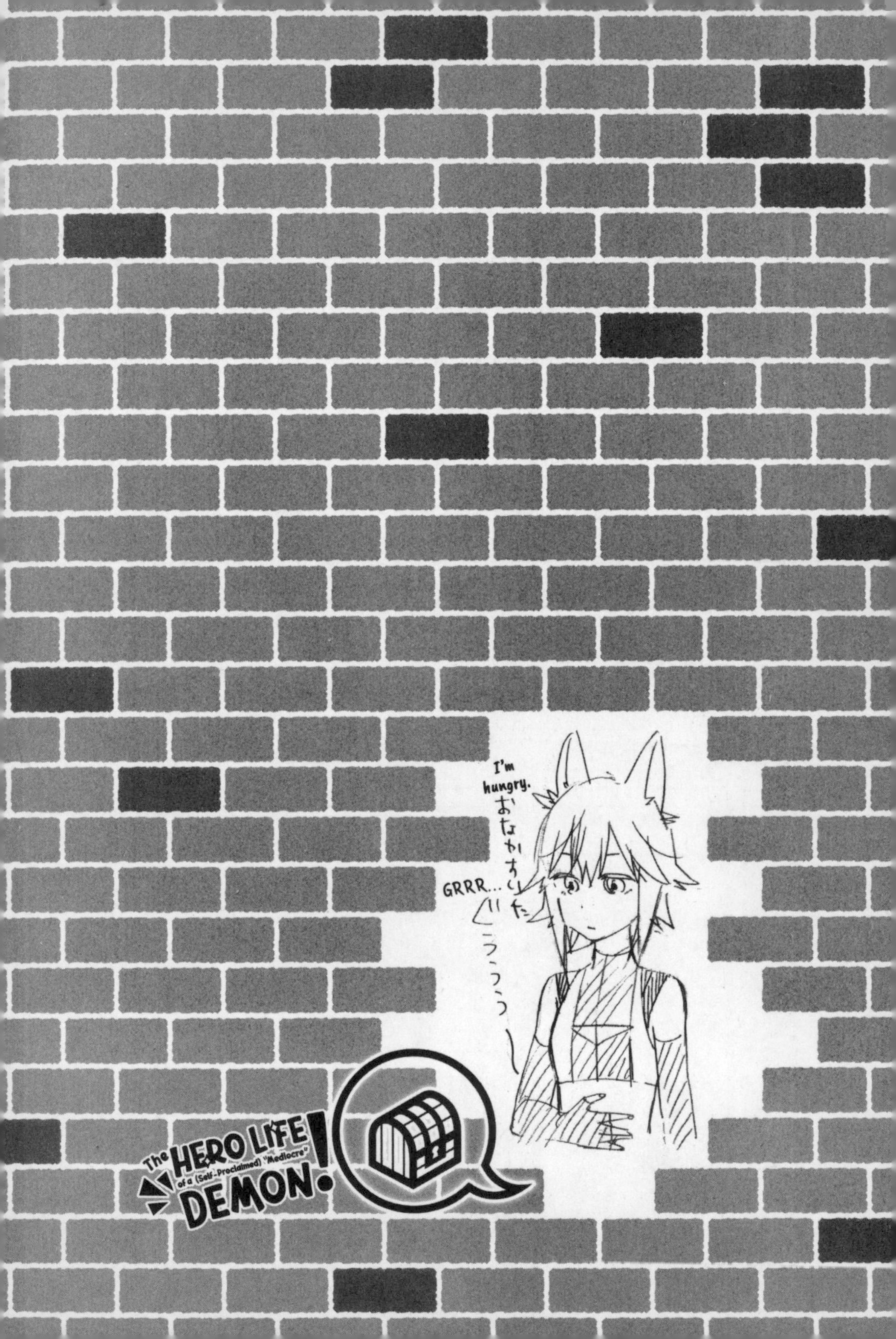
I'm hungry.
おなかすいた
GRRR...
ぐ〜うううう〜
The HERO LIFE of a (Self-Proclaimed) "Mediocre" DEMON!

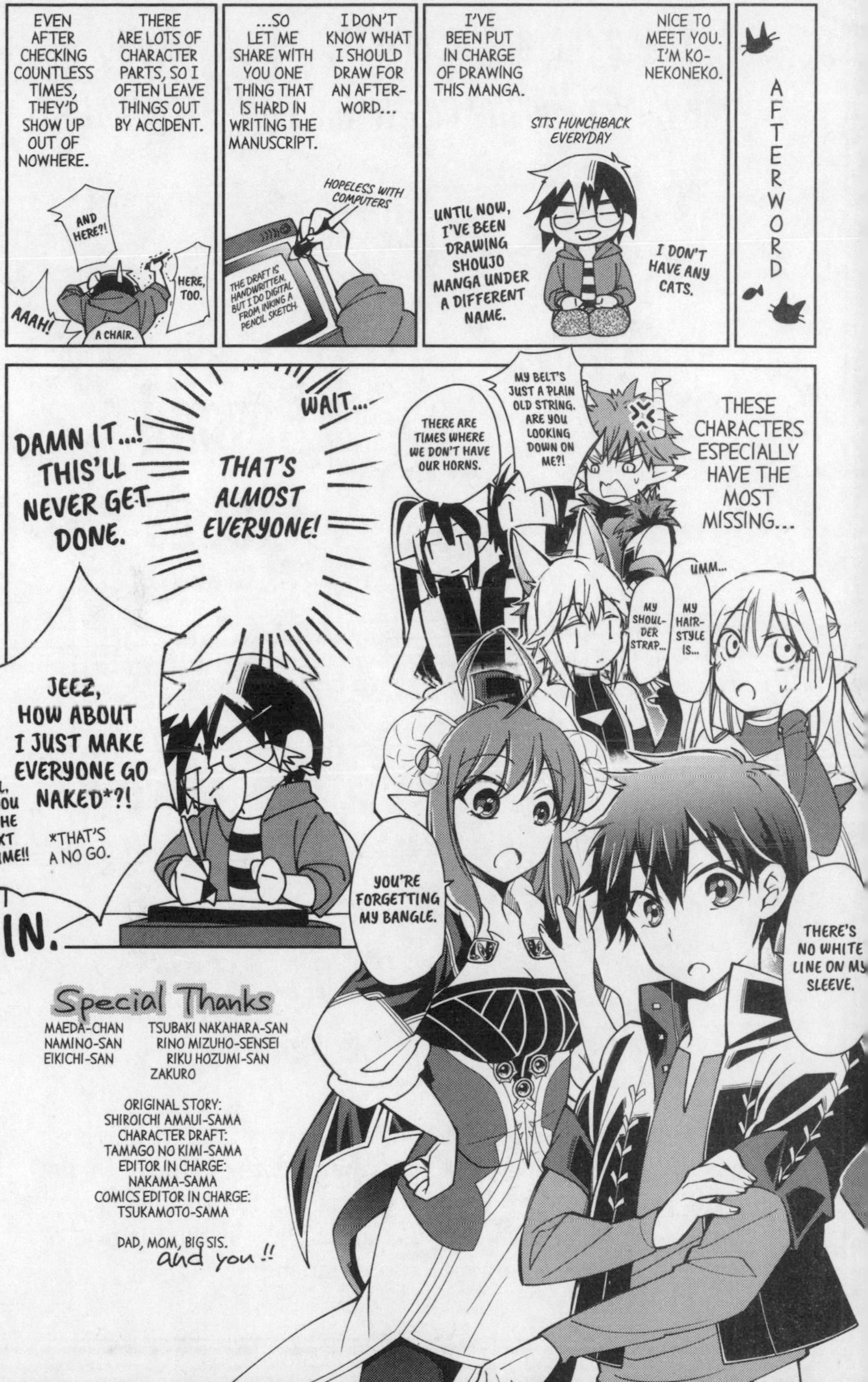
AFTERWORD
NICE TO MEET YOU. I'M KO-NEKONEKO.
I'VE BEEN PUT IN CHARGE OF DRAWING THIS MANGA.
SITS HUNCHBACK EVERYDAY
I DON'T HAVE ANY CATS.
UNTIL NOW, I'VE BEEN DRAWING SHOUJO MANGA UNDER A DIFFERENT NAME.
I DON'T KNOW WHAT I SHOULD DRAW FOR AN AFTER-WORD...
...SO LET ME SHARE WITH YOU ONE THING THAT IS HARD IN WRITING THE MANUSCRIPT.
HOPELESS WITH COMPUTERS
THE DRAFT IS HANDWRITTEN, BUT I DO DIGITAL FROM INKING A PENCIL SKETCH.
THERE ARE LOTS OF CHARACTER PARTS, SO I OFTEN LEAVE THINGS OUT BY ACCIDENT.
EVEN AFTER CHECKING COUNTLESS TIMES, THEY'D SHOW UP OUT OF NOWHERE.
AND HERE?!
HERE, TOO.
AAAH!
A CHAIR.
THESE CHARACTERS ESPECIALLY HAVE THE MOST MISSING...
MY BELT'S JUST A PLAIN OLD STRING. ARE YOU LOOKING DOWN ON ME?!
THERE ARE TIMES WHERE WE DON'T HAVE OUR HORNS.
UMM...
MY HAIR-STYLE IS...
MY SHOUL-DER STRAP...
WAIT...
THAT'S ALMOST EVERYONE!
DAMN IT...! THIS'LL NEVER GET DONE.
THERE'S NO WHITE LINE ON MY SLEEVE.
YOU'RE FORGETTING MY BANGLE.
JEEZ, HOW ABOUT I JUST MAKE EVERYONE GO NAKED*?!
*THAT'S A NO GO.
WELL, SEE YOU IN THE NEXT VOLUME!!
FIN.
Special Thanks
MAEDA-CHAN
NAMINO-SAN
EIKICHI-SAN
TSUBAKI NAKAHARA-SAN
RINO MIZUHO-SENSEI
RIKU HOZUMI-SAN
ZAKURO
ORIGINAL STORY:
SHIROICHI AMAUI-SAMA
CHARACTER DRAFT:
TAMAGO NO KIMI-SAMA
EDITOR IN CHARGE:
NAKAMA-SAMA
COMICS EDITOR IN CHARGE:
TSUKAMOTO-SAMA
DAD, MOM, BIG SIS.
and you!!

Young characters and steampunk setting, like *Howl's Moving Castle* and *Battle Angel Alita*

Beyond the Clouds © 2018 Nicke / Ki-oon

A boy with a talent for machines and a mysterious girl whose wings he's fixed will take you beyond the clouds! In the tradition of the high-flying, resonant adventure stories of Studio Ghibli comes a gorgeous tale about the longing of young hearts for adventure and friendship!

A Kodansha Trade Paperback Original

The Hero Life of a (Self-Proclaimed) Mediocre Demon! 1 copyright © 2018 Nakaba Suzuki
English translation copyright © 2021 Nakaba Suzuki

Published in the United States by
Kodansha USA Publishing, LLC, New York.

Publication rights for this English edition arranged through
Kodansha Ltd., Tokyo.

First published in Japan in 2018 by Kodansha Ltd., Tokyo as
Jishō! Heibon mazoku no eiyū raifu 1.

ISBN 978-1-64651-334-5

Printed in the United States of America.

1st Printing

Translation: Jessica Latherow / amimaru
Lettering: Chris Burgener / amimaru
Additional Lettering: Phil Christie
Editing: David Yoo
Kodansha USA Publishing edition cover design by My Truong

Publisher: Kiichiro Sugawara

Director of Publishing Services: Ben Applegate
Associate Director, Publishing Operations: Stephen Pakula
Publishing Services Managing Editors: Madison Salters, Alanna Ruse
Production Managers: Emi Lotto, Angela Zurlo

KODANSHA.US

KODANSHA

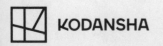